MANAGEMENT IN THE PUBLIC SECTOR

MANAGEMENT IN THE PUBLIC SECTOR

Challenge and change

Second Edition

Edited by

Kester Isaac-Henry, Chris Painter and Chris Barnes

Department of Public Policy, Faculty of Law and Social Sciences, University of Central England in Birmingham Birmingham, U.K.

INTERNATIONAL THOMSON BUSINESS PRESS
I ⓣ P An International Thomson Publishing Company

London • Bonn • Boston • Johannesburg • Madrid • Melbourne • Mexico City • New York • Paris
Singapore • Tokyo • Toronto • Albany, NY • Belmont, CA • Cincinnati, OH • Detroit, MI

Management in the Public Sector 2nd Edition

Copyright ©1997 Kester Isaac-Henry, Chris Painter, Chris Barnes

I(T)P A division of International Thomson Publishing Inc.
The ITP logo is a tracemark under licence

British Library Cataloguing-in-Publication Data
A catalogue record for this book is available from the British Library

First published by Chapman and Hall 1993

Typeset by Florencetype, Devon
Printed in the UK by the Alden Press, Oxford

ISBN 0–41273–750–7

International Thomson Business Press
Berkshire House
168–173 High Holborn
London WC1V 7AA
UK

International Thomson Business Press
20 Park Plaza
13th Floor
Boston MA 02116
USA

http://www.itbp.com

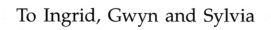

To Ingrid, Gwyn and Sylvia

CONTENTS

CONTRIBUTORS

Chris Barnes
Senior Lecturer in Public Policy,
University of Central England in Birmingham.

Author of *Successful Marketing for the Transport Operator* and *Practical Marketing for Schools* and has undertaken consultancy work in the public sector and marketing of public services.

David Cox
Professor and Assistant Dean, Faculty of Health & Community Care,
University of Central England in Birmingham

Particular interests include the sociology of organizations and the implementation of public policy.

Kester Isaac-Henry
Principal Lecturer, Department of Public Policy,
University of Central England in Birmingham.

Has researched and written widely in the field of public sector management.

Edward Johnson
Senior Lecturer in Politics,
University of Central England in Birmingham.

Particular interests are British foreign policy and the United Nations, an area in which he has published a number of articles.

Barry Loveday
Principal Lecturer in Criminal Justice,
University of Portsmouth.

Leading authority on the police and policing in Britain, an area in which he has researched and written extensively.

Chris Painter
Professor and Head of Department of Public Policy,
University of Central England in Birmingham.

Has teaching interests in public policy and management. Has researched and written widely on many aspects of the public sector, including both central and local government – most recently on relations between local authorities and non-elected agencies.

Clare Rigg
Senior Lecturer in Management Development,
University of Central England in Birmingham.

Specializes in local authority and voluntary sector urban regeneration strategy and project development.

John Rouse
Professor and Dean of the Faculty of Law and Social Science,
University of Central England in Birmingham.

Specializes in resource management in public service agencies including the non-elected state.

Francis Terry
Professor of Business Research,
Nottingham Trent University.

Specializes in regulated industries and public policy and analysis. Co-editor of *Public Money and Management*. Previously Secretary of the Public Finance Foundation and Visiting Professor in Public Management at the University of Central England in Birmingham.

Kiran Trehan
Senior Lecturer in Management Development,
University of Central England in Birmingham.

Specializes in management development in the public sector.

Keith Williams
Senior Lecturer in Public Policy,
University of Central England.

Specializes in development and change in education. Particularly interested in the implementation of recent education legislation and the management of educational change.

LIST OF FIGURES

LIST OF TABLES

PREFACE

Building on the success of the first edition, this publication has retained its essential thematic approach and reflective, critical overview of public sector development and change. Each chapter has been substantially revised and updated to accommodate new perspectives and challenges. The two additional chapters (Chapters 9 and 10), both comprising original research, incorporate some important developments in the areas of health and quangos.

Kester Isaac-Henry,
Chris Painter and Chris Barnes

DEVELOPMENT AND CHANGE IN THE PUBLIC SECTOR

1

Kester Isaac-Henry

1.1 CHAPTER PREVIEW

This book explores through a thematic approach the challenges and changes facing the public sector since the early 1980s. The objective of this chapter is to provide the background for the later chapters by briefly examining the context, content and process of change. Nearly all the themes mentioned will subsequently be developed more fully. The chapter suggests that:

- widespread change in the public sector is not new but that changes since the 1980s appear to be more transformational in character compared to those of the 1960s and 1970s;
- the context for change may have been provided by the changing economic and social conditions of the 1970s as well as the opportunities for the ideas of the public choice theorists to gain ground and influence the reforms taking place;
- the content of changes exhibit themselves in privatization and deregulation, in managerialism which fragments responsibilities into areas of accountable management, market forces, competition and the incursion of private sector practices into public sector management;
- in the process and contents of change the public sector, at least aspects of it, have been threatened in a number of ways and that accountability and probity may have become casualties in the process;
- in responding to such changes the public sector faces major problems and in order to respond may have to redefine its roles or find new ones to play.

1.2   THE CHANGING ORDER

In 1979 a Conservative administration under the premiership of Margaret Thatcher took office. Some 17 years later and after four election victories, the Conservative Party was still in (1996) power. This period has witnessed a remarkable change in the structure and culture of public administration and public sector organizations in Britain. The term 'New Public Management' has been coined to indicate the radical nature of these changes. Following what some consider to have been an (at least a theoretical) onslaught on the public sector, government or more precisely public administration, has been 'reinvented' (Osborne and Gaebler 1992), emphasizing the dramatic departure from the past. Government and its administration have become entrepreneurial, 'steerers' rather than 'rowers' (see Chapter 3). It is a period in which the government put the private sector on a pedestal as a model to which the public sector should aspire, even if that meant forcing and bullying them in to so doing.

It has been suggested that the 1970s was the 'last decade of established order for public administration' when its values, including accountability and responsibility, were clearly understood and accepted. (Taylor and Williams 1991: 174).

> But the public sector is no stranger to change. The two decades up to the 1980s were also periods when attempts were made to modify its organizations to make them more efficient and effective. So what is new or different in these more recent developments?

It could be argued that from the second half of the 1970s:

- the public sector has faced a more radically changing (transformational) environment than in the earlier periods occasioned, for example, by the rapid development in information and communication technologies (ICT), globalization and changes in the economic, social and political orders;
- the consensus surrounding the existence and practices of public sector organizations has broken down and almost no part of it is now held to be sacrosanct by those in power.
- the philosophies sustaining change differed from those of the earlier period. Whereas the concepts of unity, co-operation, co-ordination and (increased) size had informed the attempts to change the public sector in the 1960s and 1970s, the present themes are of decentralization, desegregation, competition and markets and efficiency strategies.

1.3   THE CONTEXT OF CHANGE

The context of change refers to those environmental factors influencing, restraining and driving change in organizations. They include economic, political, social and technological factors. Although each factor is important in its own right they often do not act in isolation but react to and interact with each other. They are often re-inforcive, creating, strengthening and even at times cancelling each other out. Nor, as suggested in Chapter 3, should the influence of the internal factors be played down. An organization's history, structure and culture are themselves important change inducing, changing restricting factors.

1.3.1 Ideas of the New Right and Thatcherism

Gray and Jenkins (1995) argue that it was the coming together of political ideology, economic theory and perspectives from the private sector management which 'lay behind the last decade of change in the UK public sector' (ibid: 81). Conservative governments from 1979 appeared to have been greatly influenced and sustained by the economic, political and social theories of the public choice theorists. These theo-rists (discussed in Chapter 2) were opposed to the economic ideas, practices and policies of governments between 1945 and 1979 and in particular espoused alterna-tive views to those of Keynes on managing the economy. Their prophets were Hayek and Friedman. Hayek had argued that state intervention is wrong in practice and wrong in moral principle (see Chapter 2). It is wrong in practice because it leads to the creation of monopolies, limits enterprise and encourages waste and inefficiency. It was morally wrong because it limits individual freedom of choice and leads indi-viduals into a culture of dependency (on the state). The 'market' on the other hand – the harbinger of competition – encourages freedom of choice, develops individual initiative and enterprise, increases efficiency and, through the price mechanism, ensures effectiveness (see Chapter 2). The market was the antidote to waste and to self-serving bureaucrats whose inclination is to maximize their budgets at the expense of the taxpayer. Hence public choice theorists perceived only a limited role for the state, that of enabling the laws to be enforced and economic freedom and property to be enjoyed (Harris and Seldon 1977: 1).

But these views had existed since the 1950s. Why then should they now become acceptable to the leadership of the Conservative Party and not before? Their time had come. As John Stuart Mill observed:

> ideas must conspire with circumstances if they are to be successful; such circum-stances include the availability of resources, political support among the elite and public opinion, and a widespread sense that other ideas have been tried and failed

> *(Kavanagh 1987: 63–4)*

Economic conditions appear to be one of the main conspirators in the 1980s. The post-war years had witnessed a consensus between the party elites since they shared the objectives of an expanding welfare state and full employment. It could be argued that up to 1970 these policy goals were achieved because for two decades un-employment did not rise above 3%, the inflation rate was low and the economy had grown, albeit slowly. However, the economic downturn in western democracies triggered by the (1973) Arab-Israeli War and its adverse effects on oil supply and prices, affected governments' ability to finance the public sector. The assumption of economic expansion and maintenance of full employment had to be re-examined. Yet demand for services had not slackened and indeed other factors were fanning its increase.

The 1970s also witnessed an acceleration of the decline of the British industrial base. British markets were penetrated by newly developing industrialized countries as a result of freer competition and the greater internationalization of economics, culture and politics (Cooke 1989) including the growing impact of the European Economic Community (now the European Union (EU) (refer to Chapter 11). Indeed, the development and integration of Europe provides an important backdrop against which changes and development in UK politics and public organizations have been taking place. Movement towards economic, monetary and political union in Western Europe (with Eastern Europe waiting in the wings) remains a major objective of many, although the British perspective under a Conservative administration differs from that of many of their European partners in that the latter envisage a coming together of the market and the state, while the former's (at least a substantial section of Party) interests appear to stop at economic co-operation. Certainly the integration of the market (formally acknowledged at Maastrict in 1992) has had and will continue to have enormous repercussions on the British economy (as well as on other social and political aspects of the UK). It means a massive restructuring of industry, for example, which is not necessarily to the advantage of the UK.

Some academics are now suggesting that the industrial decline and restructuring taking place is the result of a natural response to a wider economic and industrial change taking place in western economies – a 'post-Fordist' development. It is argued that these economies from the middle of the nineteenth century up to the 1970s, went through two major stages. The first, 'competitive regulation', lasted until the begin-ning of the 1930s. The second, from the 1930s to the 1970s, was characterized by mass production, mass consumption and mass labour (unions) based on collective and national bargaining and industrial action. This type of structure was epitomized by the Ford Motor Company with its conveyor belt technology and routine stan-dardized workings. The state was forced to play a major role in this Fordist period because it had to ensure that demand for mass produced goods was sustained and managed and also had to provide the infrastructure as well as playing a key role in welfare support (Stoker 1990). The post Fordist stage is characterized by

> new organizational and managerial forms ... leaner and flatter managerial struc-tures, decentralized 'cost and innovation' centres ... enlarged and more generic roles, team working, flexibility and informality, responsive back line support to the front line staff and so on
>
> (*Hoggett 1987: 225*)

De-industrialization and the consequent rise in unemployment posed major problems for many public authorities, especially in the area of the provision of social services at a time when expenditure was being squeezed. The need to relieve the problems of unemployment and to reduce the burdens on the social services forced many local authorities to forge links with private sector bodies in an attempt to attract and develop industries in their areas. At the same time the rising tide of unemployment and other demographic changes put enormous pressures on social security expenditure.

The failure to manage and control the economy was leading to the rejection of the old solutions and some of the traditional structures by both Left and Right of the political spectrum. New methods were being sought. Hence the onslaught on the traditional bureaucratic model of public administration in Britain.

1.3.2 Social and cultural changes

Other social and cultural changes were also afoot. The demographic changes have been a major cause of concern, especially the rapidly ageing population on the one hand and the dearth of young people on the other. Those over 75 years old increased by 30% between 1976 and 1984 and will increase by another 15% by 1996. Such increases have put financial and other strains on social security, pensions and health. Indeed, it was recognition of the impact that the ageing population and rising unemployment will have on these social services that informed a number of actions by the government in the 1980s, including the introduction of Family Income Credit, reductions in the numbers of those claiming Housing Benefits, the setting up of the Social Fund, and the attempt to abolish the State Earnings Related Pensions Scheme (Deakin 1987: 146–54).

The culture of the population is said to be changing too. People are becoming more sophisticated, discriminating, assertive and less subservient to official views and actions. They are demanding not only more services but also better quality provisions. (Caulfield and Schultz 1989: 3). At the same time they and interest groups representing them, are questioning the motives, values and competence of bureaucrats and professionals. They are beginning to act more like 'customers' than 'clients.'

With the changes mentioned above, the need to use existing resources to better effect became evident. Thus an ideology stressing efficiency and value for money (VFM) met with a sympathetic ear in many quarters. At the same time, given that expansion of the public services had come to an end, there was a view from both the Right and the Left that the policies based on consensus had failed. Both sides were looking for something new.

1.3.3 The end of consensus

Thus the 'New Right' and public choice theorists struck a chord with a changing society. Their views began to find favour with a number of important and influential converts. Chief amongst these was Sir Keith Joseph, himself an important player in the post-war development of the welfare state and who was now convinced that countries did better 'by using the engine of a decentralized, profit-seeking competitive economic system' (Keegan 1984: 46). As a guru of the Conservative Party his influence was enormous. But a most important factor was the singular personality, drive and conviction of one who was already a disciple of liberal economics, Mrs Thatcher, who became leader of the Conservative Party in 1975. Her strength (as discussed in Chapter two) seemed to lie in her conviction that the policies she was pursuing were the correct ones, as well as in her ability to get her message across to the public. The 'public choice theorists' position seem to have been enhanced when the voters between 1979 and 1992 seemingly repeatedly made favourable judgements on policies which appeared to be influenced by their thinking.

The ending of consensus was in no small part due to the shift of the Conservative leaders to the Right. Their aim was now to roll back the frontiers of the state. There was a conviction that the middle ground should be abandoned and the whole post-war welfare and public sector development be questioned. The mould should be broken rather than simply setting out to 'rework the elements of the prevailing philosophies (Hall 1983: 25). There is now a suggestion that the boundaries have changed over these 15 years and the consensus which appears to be re-emerging, seems to be based on a position to the right of where it was in the 1970s (see Chapter 2 for further discussion on the changing consensus).

1.4   THE CONTENT OF CHANGE

A number of commentators have suggested that the changes in the public sector have not been as extensive as we are led to believe, that the legislative agenda might have been distinctive but the outcome may not have been. However valid these arguments, the physical landscape of the public sector has nonetheless changed significantly since 1979, a change which is having its effect on the 'mental' and 'cultural' state of public organizations. The content of these changes may be summed up broadly under the headings of privatization, managerialism and enabling.

1.4.1 Privatization

Privatization refers to a number of developments relating public sector activities more closely to those of the private sector. First, in its most popularly understood form, it points to the transferring of ownership of organizations from public to private sector bodies. Thus former nationalized industries and public corporations such as water, gas, electricity and telecommunications are now in private hands. The government has thought fit however, to maintain them in some regulatory framework by creating watchdog bodies (the Office of Electricity Regulation, Office of Telecommunications etc.) to monitor 'their commercial decisions, particularly their relationships with competitors, suppliers and consumers' (Whitehead 1988: 2). Second, some public services have been deregulated in an attempt to reduce monopolistic tendencies and subject them to competition. Chief amongst these is the deregulation of all bus services outside London. Third is the contracting out of the delivery of some public services to private and voluntary organizations. Although they are forced by law to put certain services out to tender, the authorities concerned may themselves choose to bid for the tender. Where the service goes outside, the authority still holds the responsibility for seeing that it is delivered. Fourth, the government in its Education and Housing Acts of 1988, introduced the concept of 'opting out'. In the case of the NHS, hospitals have become self-governing trusts escaping the influence and regulation of the district health authorities, but the government insists that this does not imply opting out of the NHS as such. Fifth, it has been suggested that the move to inundate public sector organizations with private sector practices should also be regarded as a form of privatization.

In terms of its general acceptance by the public, and by other political parties (if with reluctance), privatization as a policy must be regarded as a government success story up to the early 1990s. Yet, as mentioned above, it was not a fully articulated policy agenda conceived by the Conservatives in opposition in the 1970s. As part of Conservative government policy after 1979 it developed slowly. Indeed, as Kingdom observed, a policy only emerged after a great deal of trial and error, 'considerable audacity and no little surprise' (1991: 43–4). From the vantage point of the 1990s, the aims of privatization appear to encompass the reduction of the public sector and its activities, increased efficiency by introducing competition, the reduction of public sector borrowing (yet currently of massive proportions) by using the finances from privatization to fund the public sector and reduce taxes, a reduction in the role of trade unions and the professions, and the development of a property and shareowning democracy.

However, by the middle of the 1990s there were many, including Conservative MPs, who thought that moving state owned industries into the private sector had gone far enough. Water privatization had not proved as popular as the earlier ones. Railway privatization is proving to be deeply unpopular, with some suggesting that ideology is drowning common sense and logic. There was the about turn on the privatization of the Post Office in 1994 after enough Conservative MPs showed their displeasure. In addition, the antics of many of the utilities managers paying themselves over large salaries and share options and at the same time under-investing in the industries, are proving to be deeply unpopular and fuel concerns about self-aggrandisement and 'sleaze'.

1.4.2 Managerialism

Raised almost to the status of theology managerialism is recognized as the defining characteristic of the changes taking place in the public sector up to the second half of the 1990s. Advocates of managerialism argue that:

- the failure of the public sector in the years up to the 1980s owes much to the lack of proper management in that sector;
- proper management should derive its existence from the practice, experience and ethos of the private sector;
- hands on professional management comes from measuring performance, laying greater emphasis on output, shifting to desegregated units and devolving management, introducing competition and emphasizing the role of the consumer so leading to improved quality and lower cost;
- there should be separation of policy and administration, with public sector bodies responsible for policy and for strategic planning, while the delivery could and should be carried out by different bodies under the mantle of competition.

The Thatcher premiership brought with it no coherent philosophy on managerialism and management in government. What seems to have taken place early on, was a series of activities designed to reduce public expenditure. Mrs Thatcher had come to power declaring a war on waste and inefficiency. The Efficiency Unit set up under Derek Rayner in 1980 was, in the main, designed to secure savings rather than to introduce a full blown managerialist culture to Whitehall (Metcalfe and Richards 1990). Although concepts such as effectiveness and efficiency are now in vogue, economy was then the ruling passion. It was seen as important to inject a cost-conscious value for money approach if savings were to be made. But if this in the end was not just to be dawn raids on departmental spending, something more was needed. Rayner himself recognized that real and lasting efficiency was bound up with a better management culture, especially when it is considered that in the public sector efficiency was more dependent on organizational and managerial factors than on market forces (Metcalfe and Richards 1990). Practices as well as beliefs and values would have to change.

In an attempt to inculcate the management culture, the importance of management was emphasized to ministers and top civil servants. The two groups, it was suggested, should be much more concerned about, and be involved in, management of their departments. Involvement with politics and policy was not enough. In the 1980s two closely allied initiatives were introduced – a Management Information System for ministers (MINIS) (1981) and a Financial Management Initiative (FMI) (1982) both designed to get ministers interested in properly managing their departments. The objective of MINIS was to give ministers and managers more information about activities in their departments as well as to promote decentralized and accountable management. Stoutly resisted at first, such management information systems are now part of the Whitehall process.

The Financial Management Initiative (FMI) followed as a consequence of MINIS. Here the foundation of accountable management was being laid. FMI was designed to provide managers in departments with clearly defined objectives; allocate clear responsibilities for resources and operations and provide the necessary support for carrying out these responsibilities. In short, it was to help managers to manage. By the latter part of the 1980s this experiment had deemed to have failed mainly because:

- the majority of ministers (and top civil servants) exhibited no great interest in the detailed management of their departments, still preferring to be involved in politics and policies;

- even when the information was available and options worked out, proper management decisions were said to founder on the rock of political expediency and short-termism;
- ministers have a multitude of roles and functions to perform (including those relating to the Cabinet, Parliament, constituencies, parties and departments) which leaves them little time to face the rigours of management (Zifcak 1994: 24–38).

In the NHS a similar initiative took place. In 1986 the Resource Management Initiative was launched with a view to involving doctors in management of the health service and at the same time to develop proper accounting and management information systems which would help 'with closer cost control'. (RMI was introduced using 6 hospitals as pilot. The initiative was expanded by Minsters before the results of the pilot studies were available.) There is a view that the initiative failed because 'the motive of RMI has changed from developing the organization towards a managerial culture to implementing the political agenda set out in the changes required by *Working for Patients*' (Willcocks and Harrow 1992) and that in any case the cost of implementing RMI was underestimated (Ham 1992: 179–80).

(a) Proper management

There was also a concern that the public services should adopt a 'business-like' approach to management based on private sector practices instead of the traditionally based professional values and ethos. The mistrust of management by professionals ran deep for three reasons. First, it was suggested that many of the decisions made in the public sector served professional rather than the public interest and in the process bid up the cost of services (Painter 1989). Second, management in the public sector was generally based on consensus and bargaining – the quintessence of incrementalism. Radical changes would be impossible to accomplish given that type of management ethos and style. Third, public sector management was thought to lack the toughness and the skills to implement the necessary changes. The government encouraged the giving of responsibility to individual general managers who possessed the skills, the status and the power to manage and make decisions for the whole organization. This is the position to which a number of local authorities have moved (Isaac-Henry and Painter 1991).

(b) Accountable management

Devolved budgets, cost centres and decentralization are now very much part of the vocabulary of the public sector. These terms are usually discussed under the title of 'accountable management' which essentially is the breaking down of large and often bureaucratic organizations into smaller more manageable units with delegated powers to individual or groups. Some commentators consider the move towards such units as merely an attempt to control costs more tightly. However, a number of advantages are said to accrue from such management including:

- A lessening of bureaucracy by allowing organizations to be more responsive to environmental factors.
- Increased efficiency, effectiveness and economy resulting from the setting in place of objectives, responsibilities and expectations, thus giving a sense of direction to both the centre and the periphery.
- The separation of operational matters from strategic ones, leaving the centre to concentrate on the latter.

The movement towards accountable management is not the prerogative of the government or the Right. A prominent form of accountable management pioneered by the Left is the decentralization of services in local government. Taking different forms, it is seen as a solution to many different problems including 'bureaucracy, big government, insensitivity to public needs, remoteness, public inaccessibility, lack of accountability' (Collingridge 1986: 9). The drive towards accountable management has been influenced by compulsory competitive tendering (discussed in Chapter 5). The public authority has, of necessity, to separate operational matters from more strategic ones in order to set objectives and targets for the contractors, the latter being judged by performance criteria set out in the contract.

In central government the most ambitious form of this devolvement is the 1988 'Next Steps' initiative. Its importance cannot be exaggerated. Some see the initiative as 'transforming' central government (Greer 1994). Price Waterhouse views it 'as the first real success (of the government) in modernising management of its operations' (1995: 23). The essence of the initiative is that services and functions are 'hived' off from government departments to executive agencies. Agencies undertake responsibilities within the framework laid down for them by the responsible department which sets out an agency's objectives, its relations with the responsible department, with Parliament, with other departments and other agencies as well as setting out performance criteria (Greer 1992).

The initiative raises fundamental issues about managing the public sector, principles of management and political accountability. It is based on the principal/agent concept and on the assumption of a clear division between policy and administration, with the presumption that the core of the department will deal with policy while agencies deal with operational matters. However, as Greer argues, a great deal of what the Next Steps agencies do is integral to government functions (1994: 25). Price Waterhouse in its 1994 survey states that

> nearly 80% of Chief Executives (of agencies) claim to have a policy input into their parent department – despite the original 'Next Steps' emphasis on their role of delivering a service rather than policy formulation.
>
> *(1995: 7–8)*

But it is in the area of accountability that the most interesting questions are being raised. The position of the Next Steps on this issue is, to say the least, confused. There is said to be a high degree of ambiguity as to whom or what the agencies owe responsibility (Greer 1994). The confusion has been amply demonstrated over Mr Howard's (the then Home Secretary) sacking of Mr Lewis the Director General of the Prison Service in October 1995.

(c) Market forces and competition

Market forces is one of the tenets at the heart of managerialism. Its manifestations are to be observed in the government's desire to subject public services to competition and concomitantly to advance the role, status and power of the one time client of public services now symbolically renamed the 'customer'. But the reforms introducing markets and competition generally fall short of a free and competitive market.

Competition and markets have advanced on three main fronts, namely compulsory competitive tendering (CCT), market testing and internal markets.

The development of CCT and its progress from being applied to manual and peripheral functions to core activities, have been well rehearsed. Arguments about its effectiveness in bringing down cost and its effect on quality are still raging although some evidence has suggested that cost of service may be lower as a result (Walsh 1995: 37). Certainly CCT is having an important impact on organizations, structures and relationships in local government. First, whether or not a contract is won in-house, when a service is put out to competitive tendering, the relationship between the delivery of the service and the local authority changes. The need to make returns on capital, the fact that accounts are subject to monitoring by the DOE and that the 'inside' contractor has to adopt a businesslike approach, ensures a change in traditional relationships. In this changed relationship, support services have to account for the costing of their services, and are more pressured to provide quality services at lower cost to the contractor.

> This changed relationship between (internal) contractor and client body communicates itself to other parts of the service which do not to want to be treated less favourably and so exert pressure for a contract relationship. Hence the development of trading accounts and service level agreements.

One of the important impacts of CCT on public service bodies is the changing culture – values and beliefs – of how services should be managed and delivered. After all, one of the major purposes of introducing competition is to change behaviour of management and employees. A commercial culture is being developed and despite opposition by, for example, some local politicians, there are younger officers who are keen to push further in this direction (Isaac-Henry and Painter 1991). But such a culture has its drawbacks. At times the relationship between client and contractor can lack flexibility and sensitivity. It can also result in the 'replacing a bureaucracy of hierarchy by a bureaucracy of contracting' (Stewart 1995: 22).

Internal markets generally refer to the trading which takes place within an organization's boundaries. Sections or departments pay for services and goods provided by other parts of the organization (Mallabar 1991: 141). The arguments for internal markets resemble those for contracting out. In the process of developing such markets responsibilities are said to be clarified, different aspects of service management effectively developed (Walsh 1994) and pressures created for lowering costs. It is also argued that such markets lessen the dominance of, and dependency on, service professionals. Most highly developed in the health service, internal markets fall short of real markets since much direction and control and most of the finance comes from the NHS and central government.

Market testing is another factor encouraging contracting out in the civil service or more particularly in the Next Steps agencies. Launched in 1991 as an adjunct to the Citizens charter and in line with so many of the other government initiatives, the intention is to use market testing to bring even more by way of private sector practice, ethos and competition into play in public services 'by testing new areas of activity in the market, to see if alternative sources give better value for money' (*Competing for Quality*: 8). Unlike contracting out in local government, market testing is not compulsory and departments agree with governments which of their services should be so tested. Nevertheless, the Government each year sets objectives as to how much (in cost terms) government services should be tested in this way.

The Public Finance Initiative (PFI) is yet another government attempt to introduce more competition and more involvement of the private sector in public services. Launched in the November budget of 1992, PFI has been introduced to get private sector organizations to:

- invest their own money in public sector projects, thereby helping to reduce public expenditure and at the same time improve the infrastructure in the UK;
- relieve the public sector of some of the risks involved in developing such projects on the assumption that they have expertise in risk taking and management;
- take on the task of raising loans from banks;
- act as a catalyst in improving value for money by providing competition.

On any major project (such as the building of bridges, roads, hospitals and schools), the responsible public authority has to investigate the potential for PFI involvement before money is allocated. It is only where it is considered that such involvement is inappropriate that funding will be allocated without such an investigation. For example, where a new prison is needed involving PFI would mean not only that tender will go out for its design and construction but the maintenance and running of the prison would also be included in the tender. As is the case with CCT, the public authority will determine its specification and advertise for tenders. Nevertheless, organizations may submit tenders that do not comply with the specifications on the grounds that such a tender may present additional benefits and/or better value for money.

In his November 1995 budget the Chancellor of the Exchequer suggested that PFI was expected to provide a sum of about £14 billion of investment in private sector projects over the following three year period. His critics claim that given the slowness of PFI to get off the ground since 1992 such an estimate is wildly optimistic.

(d) Consumerism

Consumerism is an adjunct to the concept of the market and of competition. Both presuppose the existence of the customer/consumer. On this issue, at face value at any rate, there is a rare bout of agreement by both the Left and Right and by many academics, that the relationship between public services and their users, has in the immediate past, left much to be desired. Public services need to be more responsive to the needs of those who use them. The term customer is symbolic because it conjures up a view of individuals using services and making choices and, by so doing, influencing the quantity and quality of services given. For such a concept to be a reality in the public sector, structures, policies and attitudes would have to change. The concept also encompasses consumer access (physical and informational) to public organizations, proper grievance and redress mechanisms, representation and participation in the decision making processes (Potter 1987).

A raft of legislation has attempted to make the concept a reality. The epitome of the government's stance on consumerism is the Education Reform Act of 1988. In it, consumer choice was accorded the highest priority with parents given the power to send their children to the school of their choice. At the same time schools were obliged to provide appropriate information to parents to facilitate such choice – hence the justification in the 1990s of a league table of school examination results. Representation, participation and involvement were to be achieved through the power and status given to parent governors by the Act. They now have the right (with the head teacher) to hire and fire staff and to control the school budget. Another important aspect of choice and involvement is the opportunity given to parents 'to opt' out of the local education authority if the majority vote in favour of so doing.

However, there is a realization by some commentators that consumerism, in its raw private sector form, cannot just be superimposed on the public sector, especially when it is recognized that the customer of the public sector 'is not the same as the customer in the market' (Stewart and Clarke 1987: 172). There are services, for example, where quite often not only is there a lack of choice but there is coercion from the state – as in the case of children being taken into care. Hence consumerism has to be introduced in a modified form if it is to prove effective. Stewart and Clarke (1987) have attempted to make the concept fit the public sector by eschewing the term consumerism and inventing a new one 'public service orientation' (PSO) which stresses the need to give due weight to the political processes, including participation and representation and showing concern not only for the customer but also for the citizen (Rhodes 1987).

Public service orientation is meant to meet the management challenge by public authorities adopting the fundamental principle that they exist to provide service 'for' and not 'to' the public. Once this principle has been accepted the questions of choice, access, procedures and performance will come to the fore (Stewart 1988: 44).

The Citizen's Charter, with its objectives of raising quality, giving more choice, securing better value for money and enhancing responsibility, is part of the approach to consumerism and the continuing development of managerialism. The mechanisms set out for achieving these objectives which include assessing of performance, publicizing information and standards achieved and the setting up of complaints and redress procedures, are clearly in line with the main stream of managerialism and were, as indicated above, enshrined in the Education of Act of 1988.

But despite general agreement on the need for public service bodies to be more responsive to citizens, the Citizen's Charter is not without its critics. Criticisms centre around the emphasis placed on the individual – viewed as the lone ranger who, armed with the correct information, confidence and skills, take arms against the public sector 'bandits.' The Charter admits no conflict between the individual and collective needs and yet there must be occasions when collective needs cry above those of the individual. In any case, the role of individuals appears to be one of reacting to decisions and actions of public bodies rather than one in which they participate. The language of the consumer is inadequate, for 'while it has the merit of forcing organizations to look outward to those who use and receive their services' (Stewart and Walsh 1994), it does not convey the complexity of such relationships. Charters are therefore regarded by some, as too steeped in the language of the market while ignoring other important considerations, such as citizens as participants, contributors to public life and members of the community with collective rights and responsibilities.

(e) Performance management

Emphasizing the importance of performance in the public sector is not new and was one of the major themes informing attempted changes in the 1970s. However, given the greater emphasis on reducing waste, improving efficiency, effectiveness and quality, performance management has taken centre stage in managing change. The performance of managers is now assessed, appraised and reviewed against set targets and indicators. The argument for performance management is that it gives purpose and direction to organizations because it is about defining clear responsibilities, setting clear objectives, supplying the means to measure outcomes and developing the appropriate information and training. Many of the recent developments in public sector management intended to aid objective setting and output measurement have resulted in public sector bodies focusing more on what they want done, how it is to be done, the standard of service required and the penalties to be exacted for non-performance (see Chapter 4).

Measuring performance in the public sector is not, as some of its advocates imply, politically neutral. As discussed in Chapter 4, there are often numerous stakeholders involved with different views and interests that are affected differently both by what is measured and by the methods of measurement. Importantly too for the public sector, performance is not just about end results but also about **how** things are done.

Critics point to other problems and dangers. The managers' tasks may be reduced to that of a set of targets ('management by numbers'). Services not included in the targets might be neglected and those may be the ones involving quality judgements which are difficult to make. Public sector bodies can be diverted from their strategic purpose by performance targets, particularly when those targets are externally imposed. A preoccupation with performance and targets can also compromise efficiency and effectiveness. Through-put targets for hospitals, for example, may satisfy some stakeholders such as government ministers and hospital managers, but may not satisfy another set such as patients who may be released from hospitals 'quicker and sicker' to satisfy the achieving of targets.

1.4.3 The enabling state

Given the movement towards privatizing, the loss of functions and roles to non-elected bodies and the resulting inability to act directly to provide services for their constituents, some public service organizations are viewing their role as that of 'enabling' services to be provided, by working with, supporting and encouraging other organizations into such provision. Nowhere is this more pronounced than in local government.

> Buffeted by a plethora of legislation mainly restricting what it can do, starved of finance over a number of years and losing major services partly by the inexorable rise of non-elected agencies, local government appears to be seeking a different role from that of the traditional bureaucratic direct provider of services since that is no longer sustainable. Increasingly the role of the enabler is being explored.

The Conservative Right had long held the view that the inherent inefficiencies in the public sector were the result of lack of competitive pressures, which private organizations have to face and which forces them to be efficient. One way of introducing such pressures is to force such bodies to contract out services. In its ideal form local government was to be seen as merely one of the local agents providing those services which the market could not or would not provide. Since then the **enabling** concept has been subject to wider and more favourable interpretations. Stewart and Clarke see it opening up a window of opportunity for local government by increasing its role in the management of the community. Liberated from the pressures of service delivery and operational matters, which can be a distraction, a local authority can give its full attention to strategic matters and be responsible for the governance of the local community. Such an authority would rely not only on its statutory powers but also on its influence, its negotiating and bargaining skills, and its ability to support or oppose effectively other agencies as deemed appropriate. It would entail a positive effort to work with and involve all the stakeholders in the community, including the private sector and other public and voluntary bodies. Management would be a matter of influence and networking rather than direct action. Here participation and representation would be writ large and the individual as a citizen with rights and responsibilities would be stressed, although the individual as a consumer would still be an important factor.

1.4.4 Quality

Quality is a management buzz word of the 1990s. For the government, ostensibly much of what goes under the heading of managerialism is designed to raise standards, improve quality and value for money. Certainly the objective of improving quality has been made explicit in the emphasis on consumerism and choice, the establishment and development of the Citizen's Charter and the ever expanding programmes of CCT and internal markets. The emphasis on quality is part of that transference of ideas and practices from the private sector, designed to make public sector organizations more effective and responsible. And as with many such transferences, quality, as defined and practised in the private sector, sometimes sits uneasily with public sector values, objectives and practices. For some, the quality process may not be appropriate to the sector because

> concern for a product's suitability, perfecting the technical process of production, minimising waste, 'right first time', pursuing cost reduction, are understandable objectives in production based industries

> *(Hinton 1993: 64)*

and not in public services. Critics reject a universal paradigm and the concept of the one perfect way of introducing and achieving quality.

Nevertheless, it is generally accepted that quality in the public sector involves the paying of particular attention to the:

- technical aspects – i.e. the service should do what it is supposed to do – be fit for the purpose it was designed to accomplish;
- non-technical aspects – i.e. the service relationship will be of vital importance in obtaining quality in delivering certain services – non technical aspects involve the service setting (environment) and aspects such as formal and informal relationships;
- views of interested parties (stakeholders) including citizens, consumers, policy-makers, managers, front-line staff, trade unions and other interests (Gaster 1995: 6).

Above all, the development and setting of quality objectives and standards should reflect the values of the public sector and not merely ape those of private organizations. Thus, democracy, accountability, consideration of environmental factors, equity and equality of opportunities should be values informing the development of quality processes in addition to economy and efficiency.

One of the problems faced, is that many of the quality criteria set are external to the organization and can at times be opposed to its values and needs. Too often, it seems that the value of the quality movement to the public sector is its attractiveness of efficiency savings and increased value for money. But as Gaster suggests, quality and increased efficiency savings do not always go hand in hand:

There is no neat and tidy relationship between value for money and quality. A good quality service needs to be efficient, but an efficient service may not be meeting agreed needs, one of the tests of quality

(ibid: 51)

Quality is still a contested issue in the public sector. The question of 'whose' and 'what' quality has still to be answered. Many of the values informing changes appear to be anti-pathetic to the achievement of quality.

> The number of stakeholders involved in the provision of a public service together with public sector values such as democracy, accountability. equity and fair treatment, equality, consultation and participation tend to suggest 'collectivity', co-operation and compromise, policy coherence and integration. However, the reality is rampant individualism and fragmentation of services.

1.4.5 The Public Sector and Europe

The European Union is an important factor in the context as well as in the content of change. The development of the European market and the European Union has enormous consequences for politics, politicians and public administration in the UK. It raises issues (apart from economics) relating to social services and their provision, industrial relations and human resource management, accountability, citizenship and the relationship between the UK central government and other UK public bodies. In short, it has an important effect on management of public organizations. Perhaps this is not surprising when it is noted that by the turn of the 21st century 80% of all social legislation implemented in the UK will emanate from the EU.

Its influence on the management of public services is nowhere better manifested than in the threatened derailment of the government's policy on CCT by the European Court's judgement that public sector organizations under CCT, come within the Transfer of Undertakings (Protection of Employment) Regulations 1981 (TUPE) thus protecting jobs, pay and conditions of those transferred (see Chapter 5).

However, it is only very recently that public authorities have woken up to the possibility of exploiting the opportunities presented by the EU. Many of them have become much more proactive in obtaining funds from the EU, in fostering cross national co-operation and indeed in realigning themselves in Europe (see Chapter 11).

1.5   THE PROCESS OF CHANGE

The development of new management paradigms is itself an important part of the context influencing organizational change. A prominent theme in management thinking in the last 15 years or so is the need to manage strategic and transformational change. To do so effectively necessitates an understanding of the organization's external and internal environments, its strengths and weaknesses and its beliefs and value systems. Only then should decisions concerning missions and objectives be made and strategies to achieve them be decided. Above all the whole process has to be integrated, led and managed.

The pitfalls in the way of effecting transformational change are legion and have been well documented (e.g. Plant 1987; Carnall 1991; Wilson 1992). Among the most common reasons for resisting change are self-interest, misunderstanding, lack of trust, different assessments (perceptions) of change, and the reluctance to relinquish procedures and customs. Advice to reduce resistance to change, to make it happen and to make it stick, is not in short supply. However, most of that advice suggests that effective change emerges from changing the culture of people within the organization. Changes rely not so much on compliance as on the commitment of those involved. Imposed changes are less likely to succeed than those which are approved. This immediately poses a problem for public sector organizations because, despite much initiative on their part, many of the major changes in recent years have been imposed by legislation, with those responsible for its imposition usually at least once removed from those affected.

Thus in determining the strategies and process of managing the 'how' of change (issues dealt with in Chapter 3), public sector managers face a number of problems and dilemmas as well as opportunities. A major dilemma concerns the contestability of the public sector. A major concern is the fragmentation of services which reduces influence and power, making management more complex and effective management more difficult to achieve.

1.5.1 The contestability of the public sector

The dilemma facing public sector managers is that some of the changes they are required to make, call into question the existence of the organizations they are managing. The threat comes not only from the transferring of activities to other sectors, but also from the fact that private sector language tends to dominate public sector thinking. That is why some public sector supporters are at pains to stress the obvious, that the 'public domain is not constituted to replicate the private sector but that it has its own purpose, conditions and tasks' (Ranson and Stewart 1988), and that its distinctiveness is to be seen in its pursuit of equity, justice and fairness, accountability and the enhancement of citizenship.

The optimist sees the changes as making for a more efficient, effective, resourceful and resilient public sector. For example, tighter financial control is said to have left organizations fitter and leaner than before and much more able to respond to the needs of the customer and the environment generally. The enabling role is viewed as giving public sector organizations more meaning and direction and allowing them to be more involved with the community.

Others take issue with such views. They pose the question of how leaner the public sector must become before anorexia nervosa sets in. Is the reinventing of government in the British experience tantamount to abandoning government? Privatization and contracting out have made deep and wounding cuts into the body of the public sector. Supporting the enabling role may be no more than accepting the inevitable or fiddling while the public sector burns. Elected yet again in 1992, another Conservative administration has extended further the practice of privatization, forced CCT to the very core of local government and thrust market testing into the heart of the civil service. The 1990s have seen a consolidation of practices of the 1980s and the continued slimming down of the public sector.

But even if large parts of the public sector were to remain, important facets of it could still be lost. Accountability falls into this category. Accountability is said to be central to the process of British government in the twentieth century and is a feature which divides the public from the private sector (Elcock 1991: 8). Accountability to Parliament 'is the tool by which the British public, in theory at least, have been able to check the action of the Executive' (Greer 1994: 81). However, despite its centrality as many of the subsequent chapters demonstrate, the meaning and effects of accountability on the workings of the public sector are still debatable. Elcock suggests that accountability can be viewed along three dimensions. It goes upward, outward and downward. The upward direction is concerned with the constitutional principle of the executive being answerable to, and punishable by, the elected governors in central and local government, with ministerial responsibility being the epitome of this accountability. This represents the electoral chain of command where ministers are said to be responsible to Parliament, which is in turn responsible and responsive to the electorate (Birch 1964). In practice the concept is honoured more in the breach than in the observance. Advocates of the new managerial ethos can argue, with some conviction, that accountability in this sense does not work in practice. Responsibility going outwards concerns the role of the professions in the public sector and relationships with their members. Professions have some control over their members through the codes of conduct they lay down and the punishment they can exact for breaches of that code. Although they provide important safeguards, professional behaviour can degenerate into interest protection at the expense of those they are meant to serve. It can therefore lead to distortion of policies and priorities and, given the fact that they are so entrenched in public sector organizations (although less so in recent times), they present problems of co-ordination (Elcock 1991).

Managerialism has highlighted the tensions within the concept of accountability. The introduction of general managers threatens the power positions and status of the professionals. Responsibility now often appears to be owed to the general manager and or to the organization. Responsibility to the politicians in the 'constitutional' sense has been played down, with managerialism often being treated as if it were politically neutral. Accountable management, for example, may be regarded as the pinnacle of accountability because those who are given responsibility have to account for their stewardship at regular intervals. In addition, and perhaps more importantly, the new managerialism has given pride of place to the user. The essence of public service is to be responsive to and be accountable to the consumer – a more direct responsibility than the idea of the electoral chain of command. Political accountability seems to be giving way to consumer/customer, financial, budgetary and managerial accountability. The fact that new models of accountability are emerging, especially as a result of placing the consumer and not the professionals or politicians at the centre stage of public service organizations, is considered by some to be to the benefit of the public sector as well as to the consumer and is deemed an improvement.

(a) Quangos

One such change in line with the new model of accountability is the increasing reliance on nominated or appointed individuals and bodies to carry out public sector functions quite often at the expense of elected bodies. Indeed, the development of 'quangos' (the subject of Chapter 10) raises issues relating to accountability as well as probity and the concept of a public sector ethos. Despite providing public services using public money, many quangos are not subject to the democratic checks and balances which (at least in theory) apply to government departments and to local government.

> For the critics, quangos offend the political principle that those who exercise public power and responsibility should be accountable to those on whose behalf such responsibility and power is exercised.

Many of these criticisms were, in part, shared by the **Nolan Committee** which argued that even if things are not as bad as were being suggested, the widespread perception of a lack of accountability made them so. A factor which clearly alarmed the Committee was the lack of mechanism in place to compel the observance of accountability principles. The Committee commented that

> if decisions are not made on a personal or party basis – or even on caprice and whim – it is largely because of the good sense of those in office, rather than because the system prevents such abuses

(ibid: 71)

By the middle of the 1990s criticisms of such bodies had reached such a crescendo that the government began to take notice of them and began to set out guidelines for the appointment and encouraging of good practice. It is a process which was followed up by the Nolan Committee in setting out a code of conduct for appointments and propriety.

(b) Probity

Bureaucracy has its drawbacks but it made for honesty and neutrality (Hood 1991: 6). In January 1994 the Committee of Public Accounts (PAC) produced a report pregnant with examples of what it labelled 'serious failures in administrative and financial systems and controls within departments and other public bodies which have led to money being wasted or otherwise improperly spent'. Just over a year later (May 1995) following the cash for question scandal, when, in 1994, a number of MPs were accused of receiving payments in return for asking questions in parliament, the Nolan Committee published its report, *Standards in Public Life*. The two reports coming so close together indicated that there were major concerns in the area of probity. Breaching the rules of probity is nothing new but there is a view abroad that the 'new public management' and managerialism have exacerbated the problem. Factors said to be leading to less propriety and against traditional 'public sector values' include the:

- hands off approach to agencies;
- attempt at cultural changes so as to ensure the imbibing of private sector values and practices by public sector organizations;
- increasing practice of judging action by results (and performance management);
- development of a managerial culture which applauds risk and initiative taking as well as innovation, giving wider discretion to public servants thus posing threats to the concepts of openness, equity, fairness and impartiality.

It is argued that managerialisim provides the opportunity for public sector values to be compromised because it encourages self-aggrandizement and the cutting of corners, leading not only to breaches of financial probity but sometimes to policy disasters (Dunleavy 1995) and generally to what Hood terms 'malversation'(1990).

1.6 INFORMATION TECHNOLOGY

Information technology is a cardinal factor affecting the structure, processes, and change of organizations and is having a profound effect on both public and private sector organizations since it is now regarded by them as an essential resource. There are now a large number of services in the public sector planning and delivery of which is difficult to contemplate without the use of IT. With the emphasis on 'new management', information has become a major resource whose effective management is of the essence.

Nowhere is information more important than in the public sector where it is said that organizations are structured according to their need to manage, process and react to information. The technology appears to be the key to the effective use of such information. It has become critical to the effective management of many public sector organizations.

Information technology is in a constant state of revolution and with the integration of data, text, voice and image combined with an open system together offering virtual reality there is the potential to use the technology in ways we cannot yet imagine. This powerful technology could itself be causing a paradigm shift. Yet the pace of the technology presents problems of understanding and management. It poses threats as well as opportunities, a situation summed up by the Audit Commission (1994) whose survey of use of IT in local government was titled *High Risk/High Potential*. These issues are returned to in Chapter 6.

1.7   CONCLUSION

There is a train of thought in academic circles which believes that the extent of the changes in the public sector in the last decade and half has been exaggerated. That the outcomes of policies are often not the ones anticipated. Be that as it may, it is difficult to deny that quite fundamental changes to structures have occurred, fundamental problems are being faced and that the increased pressure of market forces are changing the way that the public sector operates. Indeed, some would argue that some of these changes amount to a change in culture – a paradigm shift. So whilst acknowledging that changes in structures and other mechanisms do not by themselves change beliefs and values, such changes are nevertheless a factor influencing changes in culture. Certainly a number of traditional assumptions about the public sector and its relationships have been challenged. These include the concepts and practice of self-sufficiency, direct control, uniformity of provision, standardized procedures (Stewart and Walsh 1992: 509–10), being replaced by the new paradigms which are having some influence on the ideas and actions of public servants, politicians and organizations.

These changed circumstances, characterized by differentiation, separation of policy from administration and a purchaser provider split are casting many public sector organizations into the strategic role, forcing them to take a longer and a wider view. Strategic management, taken up in Chapter 3, helps organizations to see more clearly where they are going and to make plans about how to get there. Here the public sector faces a number of problems. First, over the last 15 years or so governments have been hyperactive in passing legislation which impacts on the public sector, in setting goals and changing them frequently and at will and often times failing to provide the necessary resources. Public organizations therefore find it difficult at times to take a long term view when short term problems come in battalions. Nevertheless, it has been argued, that it is precisely such situations which, more than ever demand a strategic approach. Second, fragmentation and loss of power and influence make it difficult to develop missions and objectives in the area of responsibility. Indeed, given that that there is not only major differentiation between but within organizations providing public services, the position at times must seem analogous to putting 'humpty-dumpty' back together and without the resources.

The following chapters develop and analyse most of the themes mentioned here. Ted Johnson in Chapter 2 paints a broad picture of the development of the welfare state/public sector: the role both the Conservative and Labour parties played in that development, the rise and decline of consensus politics in Britain, as well the rise and consequences of Thatcherism as a force in public sector services in the last quarter of the twentieth century. He also explores, the possibilities of a new consensus developing after the departure of the main actor, Mrs Thatcher, from the stage.

In Chapter 3 Chris Painter deals with one of the major concerns of the book, that of managing change. It examines and analyses the catalyst for, constraints on, and the paradigms for implementing transformational change in public sector organizations. Based on original research material, the author uses a case study to throw light on some of the change processes involved including the varying responses and adaptation by some public authorities. Managing and evaluating performance in public services are central to the changes occurring in the public sector and have been responsible for much of the emphasis on performance management, effectiveness, efficiency and value for money.

In Chapter 4 John Rouse explains the most important of these concepts and examines the reasons for their prominence in the public services. In particular, he not only develops and explains the concept of managerial accountability, techniques and strategies for enhancing performance but he also provides a critique throughout. Chapter 5 relies mainly on original research by the two authors Clare Rigg and Kiran Trehan, who examine the impact of the new managerial paradigm on employee/human resources management in local government. More particularly it explores the extent to which the new 'culture' is bedding down in local government and how effectively the new skills, which are supposedly needed, are acquired by training and management development. The chapter also poses the question as to whether local authorities are becoming learning organizations, moving away from personnel management to human resource management and indeed, even if there is such a movement whether it carries any special significance. The importance of information technology to the public sector has already been mentioned in this chapter. With a number of case studies Kester Isaac-Henry in Chapter 6 traces the development of IT in that sector, evaluates the role of IT in local and central government and in the NHS and discusses the attempt to manage a technology in almost a constant state of revolution.

The concept of consumerism and marketing looms large in the government's rhetoric of change. However, there are conflicting views as to how easily such concepts fit in and apply to the public sector. In Chapter 7, Chris Barnes and Keith Williams examine, through a case study, these two concepts as they relate to the education reforms of the 1980s and 1990s. Chapter 8 continues the theme of the 'customer' by exploring recent developments in the NHS relating to the customer/consumer movement and the effect that movement has had on the services offered. Using a case study undertaken especially for the chapter the authors Chris Barnes and David Cox examine the role and functions of community health councils and attempt to evaluate their effectiveness in influencing services to 'customers'.

The 'new public sector management' with its increasing emphasis on performance is appearing to challenge some of the traditional concepts associated with accountability. The police service, which seemed to have had a charmed existence in escaping the changes common to public organizations in the 1980s was to bear its share of the burden in the 1990s. In Chapter 9 Barry Loveday explains the reason for this, as well as outlining and evaluating the changes. In a service which relates to some of the most sensitive areas of public life, accountability is of the essence. The chapter examines the changes taking place in the service, not only in terms of efficiency and effectiveness but also the extent to which such changes are hindering or enhancing the accountability of the police service. The development of non-elected agencies (quangos) goes to the heart of the debate concerning accountability, performance, responsibility and fragmentation in public services. In Chapter 10 Chris Painter discusses some of these issues but goes further by exploring (through original research) the issue of the developing relationship between local authorities and these agencies (categorizing such relationships) and suggests ways by which local authorities could better protect theirs and their communities' interests in their dealings with non-elected agencies.

Europe is a major concern and influence on public authorities. Concentrating mainly on local government, Francis Terry in Chapter 11 focuses on the changing attitude of public bodies to the Community – namely from one of being negative and reactive in the 1970s, to being more proactive and willing to seek out opportunities in the 1980s and 1990s. This changing attitude can be viewed as an important aspect of managing the changing environment.

The concluding chapter evaluates the extent to which the changes discussed in the rest of the book have embedded themselves in the culture of the public services. It points to some of the advantages gained by such changes and discusses the dilemmas and difficulties faced in the attempt to reconcile stated objectives such as achieving quality services through citizen empowerment and proper accountability with the new market and managerialist paradigms. Finally, it poses the question of whither public services and public sector management.

TEXT-BASED QUESTIONS

1.   Explain the concept of managerialism

2.   Which factors present in the 1970s and 1980s helped to bring the ideas of the 'public choice' theorists to the front of stage of politics in Britain?

3.   Is the concept of accountability a contested one in the new public management at the present time?

4.   Explain your understanding of consumerism as it applies to the public sector pointing out its advantages and limitations.

5.   Outline the factors which are making for the contestability of the public sector.

ASSIGNMENT

Interview three middle managers from different parts of the public sector and ask them the following questions

a)   What in your opinion distinguishes the public sector from the private?
b)   How would you define the culture of your present organization?
c)   How does the present culture differ from the one of say five years ago?
d)   What have been the five most important changes taking place in your organization in the last five years?
e)   Have these changes been the result of government direction or legislation or have they been the result of internal factors?

Evaluating and using this information obtained from the interviews, as well as information obtained from other sources, write an article of no more than 1500 words on the changing nature of the public sector in Britain.

FURTHER READING

Osborne, D. and Gaebler, T. (1992) *Reinventing Government*, Addison Wesley, Reading. Mass. Certainly one of the most talked about books in the 1990s in relation to the public sector – criticizes without condemning.

Potter, J. (1987) Consumerism and the Public Sector: How Well Does the Coat Fit, *Public Administration*, **66** (2) pp. 149–64.

Stewart, J. and Clarke, M. (1987) The Public Service Orientation: Issues and Dilemmas, *Public Administration*, **65** (2) pp. 161–77. Importantly it demonstrates that those who support the public sector are not blind to its faults.

Stewart, J. and Walsh, K. (1993) Change in the Management of Public Services, *Public Administration*, **70** (4) pp. 499–518. Very useful summary of the changes taking place in the public sector and the arguments for and against such changes.

Walsh, K. (1995) *Public Services and Market Mechanisms – Competition, Contracting and the New Public Management*, Macmillan, Basingstoke.

Willcocks, L. and Harrow, J. (1992) *Rediscovering Public Services Management*, McGraw Hill, London.

THE CHALLENGE TO THE PUBLIC SECTOR: CHANGING POLITICS AND IDEOLOGIES 2

Edward Johnson

2.1 CHAPTER PREVIEW

The broad objective of this chapter is to examine the political, social and economic factors which led to a thorough-going re-appraisal of the role of the state and the public sector in British politics after 1979.

From 1945–79 there was a broad political consensus about the appropriate role of the state in British politics. This post-war settlement, which tied the state into economic management and social provision, was subject to strain and erosion before the election of the first Thatcher government, but after 1979, the ideas of the New Right undercut the settlement and challenged the role, culture and scope of the public sector.

- The New Right took as its central idea the importance of the free market and the reduction of state responsibilities.
- Driven by these and other ideas, the Thatcher government dismantled the post-war settlement.
- The public sector was reduced in scope and commercial practices from the private sector introduced.

After Thatcher's resignation in 1990, a new settlement on the role of the state and public sector appeared possible yet failed to materialize and the chapter concludes by providing some explanations for this failure:

- That Thatcherism was never fully accepted by the electorate.
- That Thatcherism split the Conservative Party and undermined the basis of traditional One Nation Conservatism
- That Thatcherism destroyed the post-war settlement for good but in doing so unpicked much of the fabric of British politics and that a new settlement must now go beyond the mere new public management instituted under Thatcher and Major and encompasses a broader constitutional settlement.

2.2   THE INHERITANCE

The extension of the role of the state and the development of the public sector can be traced back to the beginning of the last century. Prior to then, the British state had been organized around what is called the 'caretaker role', one largely concerned with the defence of the realm and a foreign policy which sought to protect British interests overseas. There was some maintenance of law and order affording protection to powerful interests in society, but the state played only a minimal role in the organization of the economy and industry. This limited role owed much to the fears of excessive central control expressed by those vested interests who saw state intervention as inimical to the protection of individual rights and liberties.

After the Napoleonic wars however, demands for reform and for the state to play a more interventionist role developed and from that time it is possible to trace how the state took an increasingly larger part in the provision of a range of public services. By the end of the century these included, amongst others, a commitment to the improvement of public health, an organized police force, a postal service and the creation of a system of elementary education. In addition, the operation of the Poor Law after 1834 was a recognition that the state should provide some minimum social provision for those who had no other means available: in doing so it set an administrative pattern of central determination of policy, local administration and inspection that became a model for other parts of state activity. This process of reform was neither rapid, nor always coherent, and the motives were mixed. In some cases reforms were brought about by the need to provide improved social conditions for an enfranchised urban working class; in others they followed from the demands of those owners of industry who required an educated and healthier work force in order to compete with newly industrializing and competitor states.

The evidence for this growth of state involvement can be seen in the expansion of the number and range of central government departments in Britain: between 1825 and 1860, sixteen new government agencies were created (Greenleaf 1983a: 38). In turn, the state required a competent and professional bureaucracy to manage these departments and their increased responsibilities. Hence the civil service was reformed in the 1870s, in the wake of the Northcote-Trevelyan report of 1854. This transformed a bureaucratic machine based on patronage and geared to managing a minimalist, caretaker state into one based more on merit, though not exclusively so, and established to run an urbanized, industrial state with global responsibilities. Changes were also evident at local government level with the beginnings of municipal reform and some democratic local government in 1835.

The development of the public sector continued into this century, driven by a number of factors. Of major importance was the rise of the Labour Party, charged as it was to improve the social and economic conditions of the working class through state action. The progress of Labour after 1906, with its commitment to interventionism, had the effect of further stimulating other collectivist tendencies within British politics, and particularly within the Liberal Party. Thus the 'new Liberals' were successful in dominating the Party and associating it with a commitment to the implementation of social reform and state provision of old age pensions and national health insurance in the decade before the First World War.

The role of warfare was also important in that it not only changed attitudes about the appropriate role for the state in Britain, but it also highlighted deficiencies in many areas of society which required the intervention of the state into the successful management of the war effort, an intervention which it was subsequently difficult to renounce. The Second World War was especially significant in this respect. It witnessed a huge increase in the role of the state as employer, regulator and distributor in the civil economy. Food, materials, manpower and transport were all highly regulated in order to prosecute successfully the war, and the state became a massive employer of labour. In departmental terms, this extension of a state role could be seen in the wartime creation of a number of Ministries: Food (1939), Supply (1939), Fuel, Light and Power (1942), Town and Country Planning (1943), National Insurance and Civil Aviation (both 1944) (Greenleaf 1983a: 38).

Some indication of this growth over 150 years can be seen by comparing the numbers employed in the armed forces, central government and local government from the middle of the nineteenth century with the period just prior to the outbreak of the Second World War. In 1851 the percentage of the total working population employed in these sectors was 2.4% while in 1938 it was 9.9%: the figure was to reach 23% by the mid 1970s (ibid: 36).

Thus the Churchill wartime coalition government, together with its successor government under Attlee, did much to construct a post-war settlement about the appropriate role of the state and hence the extent of the public sector. Much of the foundations of this settlement were laid in accordance with the reconstruction blueprints of Keynes and Beveridge during the war and which senior figures in all the political parties could accept. The principal characteristics of this settlement, and the acceptance of them as significant parts of the management of British politics by all the major political parties, meant that the period from 1945 to the mid 1970s was one of considerable consensus in British politics.

The first element in the settlement was the extension of social provision. The seminal 1942 Beveridge Report identified five evils of British society which could be eradicated through social and economic policies of the state. These evils were: want, squalor, disease, ignorance and idleness and the political consensus that emerged after 1945 sought to remove them through a range of measures. These included a comprehensive system of national insurance and a National Health Service, recommended by Beveridge and implemented by the Labour Government; a national system of secondary education which derived from the 1944 Education Act; and finally the creation of a housing policy to rebuild the slum and derelict housing of urban Britain in which the Beveridge evils so easily festered. Thus welfare assistance was to be universally available rather than targeted specifically at some sections of society.

Its consequences were to be the adoption of increased health, education, housing and social security responsibilities by central and local government.

The successful achievement of these social goals required an economy which could not be left to market forces. Thus the second element of the settlement was the state management of the economy committing the government to the maintenance of a high and stable level of employment as one of its major responsibilities. This target had been identified in the 1944 White Paper on Employment, as well as constituting a remedy for the evil of idleness highlighted by the Beveridge report (Abel-Smith 1992). The third and related part of the post-war settlement centred on the creation of a 'mixed economy' through the adoption of a programme of public ownership of major industries by the Attlee government. In some cases this change from private to public ownership was not dramatic, the industries already having experienced a significant element of state control during the war years, and to which therefore the Conservatives gave only token opposition (Addison 1977: 273).

Finally, the organization of much of industry during the Second World War had been based on tripartite co-operation and consultation between the managers, the trades unions and the government. Commentators such as Middlemas (1979) date this corporatist relationship from an earlier period, as a way of the government buying peace and a repudiation of ideological politics by the unions in return for a role in the management of the state. There can, however, be little doubt that this process was at least continued after 1945 when the tripartite relationship became a common feature in the nationalized industries and the public sector more generally, including the health service and education.

THE BASIS OF THE POST-WAR SETTLEMENT

- Social provision through the creation of a welfare state
- The state management of the economy
- The creation of a mixed economy
- Tripartitism: government, industry and unions

This then was the bedrock on which much of British politics after 1945 was built: a universal welfare system to provide care, 'from the cradle to the grave'; a commitment by governments to Keynesian economics in which the government had a commitment to full employment brought about by 'fine tuning' the economy through the adjustment of fiscal policy to regulate demand; and finally the securing of control of many basic industries and utilities through public ownership. The acceptance of this remedy for Britain's social and economic problems was easy for the Labour Party: it was after all the Attlee government which was responsible for implementing it and it echoed much of the 1918 Labour Party constitutional goals.

The Conservative Party was in more difficulty however. The Party had accepted an increased role for the state from the time of Disraeli, but there was no desire to accept what could be seen as 'socialist' goals for Britain. On the other hand, the reforms implemented by the Attlee government had some of their origins in the wartime reconstruction plans of the Churchill government. Moreover, they had a popular appeal, as evidenced by the 1945 election result, and by the time the Conservatives regained power in 1951, the reforms were accomplished and working. In the past, the Conservative Party had remained in power through its ability to adapt to prevailing orthodoxies. In this respect, the Party had been pragmatic rather than dogmatic, and it was this tradition which was summoned in 1951 when the Party inherited the Attlee settlement. Therefore, while the Party was not prepared to outbid Labour in its drive for socialism, nor was it prepared to undo fundamentally the work of the previous six years. Thus under the long period of Conservative government from 1951–64, the essential components of the post-war settlement remained. There was some de-nationalization, but the National Health Service was retained and the economy was managed along Keynesian lines. Both the Conservatives and the later Labour governments of Harold Wilson intervened in the industrial management of the state to stimulate economic growth and efficiency. There was a fascination with planning: the Conservatives introducing the National Economic Development Council in 1962, a clear example of the tripartite relationship of government, industry and unions co-operating to improve Britain's economic performance. This was taken up vigorously by the Wilson government which introduced a National Plan and created a new government department of Economic Affairs to implement it.

2.3   EROSION

This broad consensus then infused British politics throughout the 1950s and 1960s, but was not always accepted with equanimity within the political parties. Discontent bubbled from the back benches to the front, a feature that was conspicuous in the Labour Party but was also evident within the Conservative ranks. And it was the irritation within the Conservative Party that was to be the source of Mrs Thatcher's later rejection of the canons of the post-war consensus. The reasons for this dissent lay in the competition between two different and contradictory strands of thought. There has, for long, been an interventionist tradition in Conservatism, which can be traced back at least as far as Disraeli (Greenleaf 1983b). This benevolent Tory paternalism is based on the premise of a strong state; that whilst the governed should respect the authority of the government, the latter should also meet its responsibilities which went beyond mere minimalism and included social provision. This position of One Nation Conservatism, which in effect signals the existence of two nations, one allowing the other through a deferential relationship to govern it, became dominant after 1945, as it meshed with the assumptions and orthodoxies of the post-war settlement, with its increased role for the state in the management of the economy and industry, and the provision of a range of public services.

However there is also an individualist strand in Conservatism; a type of politics associated more with classical liberalism. The central feature of this brand of Conservatism is its conviction in the superiority of the free market over state imposed mechanisms. Thus supporters from this side of the Party have emphasized the importance of individual choice and freedom while seeking to limit the role and scope of the state.

However, there is also an apparent contradiction in this variety of conservatism one which has been used to characterize the Thatcher period of office (Gamble 1988). It is that while the liberalism of this part of the Party seeks a weak and limited state in economic affairs, the conservative side of it requires a strong state in order to maintain order and authority: two traditional elements of conservative thought. Thus there is a tension, and one which can freely exist within an individual conservative and did so in Mrs Thatcher. For most of this century, this liberal strand of conservatism has been subordinate in the Conservative Party and has been managed, yet it has retained a following. Even during the halcyon days of One Nation Conservative government under Macmillan from 1957–63, there were those Conservatives who rejected Keynesianism and the dominance of government intervention over market forces. Three in particular, Nigel Birch, Enoch Powell and Peter Thorneycroft resigned from the Treasury in 1958 in opposition to what they saw as their government's inflationary policy of refusing to limit public expenditure.

It was in part this factor of reining in public expenditure and controlling inflation which led to the Conservative Party seeking to break with consensus politics, albeit temporarily, following the election of the Heath government in 1970. Prior to this the Conservatives had rethought their position on government and the state, and decided that too much was expected of both. A consequent reduction in their activities was both necessary and desirable. This 'Selsdon Man' approach (after the Selsdon Park Hotel in South London where the Conservatives finalized their new position) appeared to indicate the revival of the individualist element in the Conservative Party and between 1970–72 seemed set to change the role of government and the nature of the relationship of the state to the people. Some of the core elements of the post-war settlement were challenged: there was to be no state support for those 'lame duck' industries that could not survive in the market place; tax cuts were enacted in order to promote consumer spending and individual choice; and Britain joined Europe, not in Heath's eyes in order to dominate it as of right, but for British industry and Britain to be regenerated through competition and exposure to new ideas and industrial and commercial methods. British central government departments were rationalized and local government reformed and reorganized. Britain was to be an energetic, businesslike country governed by more efficient means and by fewer people.

However, Heath's government was soon blown off course by domestic and external events, thereby abandoning the reforms set in train in 1970 and by seeming to reverse them he was responsible for the creation of a new phrase in the political lexicography of Britain: the 'U-turn'. This change of policy now involved the nationalization of 'lame duck' industries such as Rolls Royce and Upper Clyde Shipbuilders, an Industry Act which gave the state more powers of intervention than any other since the war and the attempt to regulate pay demands not through market forces but through statutory and hence interventionist controls. Consensus politics seemingly returned, but Heath did not: his government lost power in the February 1974 election and a minority Labour government under Wilson returned.

If Heath retreated from a reassessment of the role of the state, the public sector and consensus in British politics, it was not however to be delayed for very long.

While Wilson saw out a period of government which had the appellation of consensus, a blight was already seeping into the vine of the post-war settlement. It was left to Wilson's successor, Callaghan, to begin the change in the approach to the state and the reasons were essentially economic rather than ideological. By 1976 Britain had a major problem with high inflation, partly caused by pay demands but also through the knock-on effect of the oil price rise of 1973–74 to which Britain, not then an oil producer, was vulnerable. Britain was being classified as the 'sick man of Europe'. The value of the pound was tumbling and in order to support it, the Labour Government in 1976 sought a loan from the International Monetary Fund. While this was granted, it was done so only on conditions, the major one being a reduction in public expenditure. This changed the economic priority of the government; in a break with consensus, unemployment would now be allowed to rise and, monetary targets were used as a tool to control inflation, along with an incomes policy through the 'Social Contract'. The IMF loan and conditions were thrust on to the Callaghan government, but there are those who could see the government turning towards a new 'realism' anyway. In 1975 the then Labour Environment Secretary, Tony Crosland, recognized that Labour had to work within the situation it had inherited and that there would need to be, for the first time since 1945, a reduction in the living standards of the British. Local government and, by extension the rest of the public sector, were notified that the party was over (Crosland 1982: 295).

Thus 1976 could stand as the key watershed in British politics, as the beginning of the rejection of the post-war settlement and associated role of the public sector as a result of dire economic difficulties. However, the election of Mrs Thatcher is normally taken as the real point of departure. Why is this? One reason is that while the economic foundations of the post-war settlement were abandoned under Callaghan, this decision was not portrayed as such. In fact Callaghan endeavoured through the 'Social Contract' incomes policy and continued consultation by means of the tripartite arrangements to maintain the illusion of consensus. A second reason is that the change in the approach was forced by circumstances; it was not welcomed with the same zeal that Callaghan's successor Mrs Thatcher, brought to her task. Moreover, the use of monetary targets to dampen down inflation under Callaghan had been just one device in the government's economic armoury: under Thatcher it became the central element as incomes policies were renounced. Thus the election of Thatcher's first government is understandably seen as the real starting point for the permanent dismantling of the post-war settlement and parallel attack on the public sector.

2.4   THE ROLE OF THATCHER AND THE NEW RIGHT

The chance for Mrs Thatcher and her brand of Conservatism came as a result of the two election defeats of Heath in 1974. These left the Party demoralized, with its lowest level of the vote this century. It clearly needed firmer leadership, as well as refocusing, if it were to re-establish its position as the party of government. With luck and some deft manoeuvring Mrs Thatcher was able to seize control of the leadership in 1975 from the Heathites. From the outset it was clear that the Party was to be steered in a different direction from the Conservatism of Macmillan, Butler and the post-war consensus.

Thatcher in fact embarked upon a reconstruction of the Conservative Party reflecting her prejudices and views on Britain's decline, which she saw as her mission to arrest. The origins for much of this were to be found in her background which was, ironically, not dissimilar to Heath's. Brought up in the East Midlands, the daughter of a lower middle-class grocer, her education at Grammar school and Oxford was achieved through merit and not privilege. She was no member of the establishment, Home Counties, professional class. Her background imbued in her the virtues of thrift, hard work, acceptance of individual responsibility and, reflecting her father's influence, the importance of financial prudence: of not spending what one could not afford (see Young 1989: 4–8). To her critics, much of her philosophy appeared homespun and platitudinous. It seemed to smack of the prejudices of the English suburban middle class, but it touched a popular nerve in enough of the electorate and took her to Number 10 in 1979.

Once in power she was quick to denounce both previous Labour and Conservative governments for cultivating the politics of consensus, reserving a special contempt for Heath for having retreated in the face of union power and high unemployment in 1972. She felt that much of Britain's problems had their origins in the post-war settlement which had been built on values irreconcilable with those she held so dear. In particular, she exhibited a hostility towards the public sector and the accepted role of the state in the management of the economy. The public sector she considered inefficient and wasteful; it cultivated dependency, smothered self-reliance, induced anti-social behaviour and spawned a rampant set of restrictive practices within the public sector work-force. For Thatcher and her supporters, these were social and administrative viruses which threatened to debilitate Britain and which needed excoriating.

> Welfare benefits, distributed with little or no consideration of their effects on behaviour, encouraged illegitimacy, facilitated the breakdown of families and replaced incentives favouring work and self-reliance with perverse encouragement for idleness and cheating. (*Thatcher 1993: 8*)

In addition to these, the involvement of the government in the management of the economy had been a factor in the gradual weakening of authority when governments had failed to deliver: it was thus appropriate for government to be withdrawn from the firing line by reducing its responsibilities. This would create 'opportunities for the successful exercise of constitutional powers' weakened under the social democratic settlement (Wolfe 1991: 245). This campaign unsettled some in her Party who were unsure of where Thatcher would lead them but in her defence, if she needed it, she could point to a revival of New Right thinking, reinforcing her approach which set the ideological framework for the public sector after 1979.

The restoration of the Right of the Conservative Party owed much to the precursors of Thatcher, such as Enoch Powell and to the contributions of Keith Joseph who, while the Party was in Opposition in the 1970s, pressed for a reappraisal of Conservative thought and through the establishment of the Centre for Policy Studies provided a think tank to facilitate this process. Other bodies too, such as the Institute for Economic Affairs and the Adam Smith Institute had been beavering away at the foundations of the post-war settlement for some time and provided the necessary intellectual support for what Mrs Thatcher felt emotionally. There was thus for Thatcher and her supporters a happy coincidence between the gut feelings of suburban Britain and the ideological ascendancy of the New Right.

While the ideology of the New Right is a mixture of ideas, the role of the market is pivotal to its thinking. For the New Right, the free market is accepted as a more efficient and productive method of allocating resources in society, protecting and promoting freedoms, and allowing choice than is the state. Thus in relation to post-war British politics, it would take as its touchstone the misconceptions of the social democratic consensus, promoting instead the values of the free market, and not the activity of the state, as the basis of economic and political freedom (Hayek 1944).

While New Right thinkers such as Hayek accept the need for some state action, it is largely of a minimal kind or to set a legal framework in which the market can then operate. Thus the post-war settlement and the role of the public sector in it were clear targets for the New Right for a number of reasons. First, the development of the public sector constituted an intrusion by the state into the market as did the management of the economy along Keynesian lines: the raising and lowering of demand by governments restricted the role of the market. This distorted resource allocation by allowing political and administrative criteria to become dominant (Gamble 1988: 49) and is a particular criticism levelled by Public Choice theorists of the New Right (King 1987: 11). Second, the welfare state, a central element of the post-war settlement was seen as inflationary: it encouraged spending by the state and increased public expenditure. In addition, the welfare state created a dependency culture between groups and the state thereby stifling initiative, independence and choice while supporting interest groups with a stake in maintaining and increasing the level of national resources allocated to it (ibid: 45). Furthermore, it placed excessive tax burdens on the electorate, drained individual incentive and enterprise and was socially and economically debilitating.

The Thatcher government took as its point of departure these central elements of New Right thinking and in a blatantly populist manner Mrs Thatcher was able to infuse the ideology of the New Right 'with her own moral and political values, thus clothing it in a popular idiom which made it sound like the economics of common sense' (Clarke 1992: 302). In particular, Mrs Thatcher's approach to the public sector with her trenchant criticism of waste, inefficiency and lack of choice could easily be supported in the popular mind of both the middle classes and some of the changing working classes in Britain.

Thus, the government was to ensure the maintenance of a tight monetary regime in order to squeeze inflation out of the economy, it would seek to reduce the welfare state as well as reducing direct taxation in order to release funds for private investment and therefore job creation; the state owned industries would be privatized;

choice would be introduced in public services through the introduction of competition; and the removal of public sector inefficiencies would be addressed through the commercial disciplines of the market.

THE THATCHER PROJECT

- The reduction of the welfare state
- Management of the economy: the market to decide
- The privatization of state owned industries
- Consumer choice and competition in public services
- The commercialization of the public sector

2.5 THE THATCHER APPROACH TO THE PUBLIC SECTOR

The most obvious reason for the public sector entering the sights of the Thatcher government related to the problem that had engaged the Callaghan government: it was seen as the major source of inflation, especially through the corporatist relationship between government, interest groups and unions. By 1975, government expenditure was 49% of GNP (Pollard 1992: 342). Thus Thatcher's wish to squeeze inflation out of the economy made public expenditure and public sector practices prime targets. The ground had already been prepared by the Labour government and the International Monetary Fund. In 1974, cash limits had been introduced into the Rate Support Grant for local government, introducing a major new discipline. Moreover, after 1976, it is clear that public expenditure became a target for the Labour Government signifying that the Keynesian legacy was beginning to crumble.

However, Thatcher's appeal was much more far reaching. There is hardly a part of the public sector in Britain which has not been touched by her radical approach. It was wasteful and inefficient, it denied choice and fostered uncommercial, restrictive and thus uncompetitive practices. Moreover, it was not sufficiently accountable for the incoming government's taste. Much could be attributed to the fact that the public sector was insulated from the dictates of the market and hence from commercial disciplines. It is not surprising therefore that the attack on the public sector was so widespread and persistent.

2.5.1 The assault on waste and inefficiency:

The assault on waste and inefficiency was an early mark of the Thatcher approach to the public sector. The source of this attack lay in the New Right view that it was intrinsically prone to overmanning, serving as a haven for restrictive practices built up through the canker of corporatism since 1945 in which public funds were used to keep unemployment levels artificially low. Thus the lethargic public sector needed to be slimmed down to make it more efficient. In addition, the manpower levels in the public sector made the service provision unnecessarily expensive contributing to the problem of the Public Sector Borrowing Requirement. Finally, on a personal level, waste offended Thatcher and ran counter to the fireside homilies learnt in her youth. The central bureaucratic machine was protected from the vicissitudes of an enterprise economy: senior civil servants in Whitehall were cosseted, sheltered and expensive: they had become a protected species with no legitimate claim to that status. Moreover, these same civil servants had been major players in the post-war consensus and had the blood of Britain's decline on their hands. Consequently Thatcher applied a succession of reforms of working practices and customs designed to root out inefficiency, duplication, waste, the dead hand of bureaucracy and inertia.

The Thatcher pruner was taken to both Central and Local Governments and departments or tiers of government either hacked off completely (the Civil Service Department and the Metropolitan Counties) or dramatically reduced in size: the civil service was reduced in size from 734,000 in 1979 to 567,000 by 1990 (Cm 1520 1991: 34). In addition, the Efficiency Unit in Whitehall was launched under Sir Derek Rayner, the Managing Director of Marks and Spencer, itself an organization whose byword was 'value for money'. With its remit to identify and eliminate waste and duplication in Whitehall, the Efficiency Unit did promote a climate of efficiency contributing to the Financial Management Initiative which permeated other parts of the public sector by the introduction of the three 'e's, of efficiency, effectiveness and economy (Chapter 4). Having been spawned in central government, these were to play a major role in the reform of local government under Mrs Thatcher.

Local government was an obvious target for Thatcher. It was seen as wasteful, it bred dependency, denied choice in the provision of services and most heinous of all, it was a challenge to the authority of the national government. The result was a marked deterioration in central-local relations during the 1980s, which took on near warlike tendencies as the central government restricted drastically the powers of local government. The latter began to resemble an administrative Florida coastline: battered annually by a hurricane of reforms. Of particular importance was the creation of the Audit Commission, which in spearheading the drive for value for money and the promotion of efficiency, effectiveness and economy challenged local government and other parts of the public sector to devise performance indicators as measures of the efficient use of resources: the phrase 'best practice' became a mantra in the new public management. These reforms were then extended in the late 1980s as the Conservative government articulated the changed role of local government from being monopoly suppliers of all services to enablers, allowing the market and competition to encroach into this provision (Bulpitt 1989).

2.5.2 Commercialism and accountability

In addition to the attack on waste and the promotion of efficiency, effectiveness and economy, the public sector was infused with a more commercial ethos and with an emphasis on accountability (Chapter 8). These examples of public sector commercialization are now extensive. The creation of agencies out of government departments with their own budgets and management styles; market testing; internal markets in the NHS; the many reforms relating to education (referred to in Chapter 7); competitive tendering especially in local government services; the whole scheme of privatization of state owned industries and the devolution of budgeting throughout the public sector are all indications of the way the commercial ethos has gained ground.

These reforms do however also connect with an emphasis on accountability, a principle central to the definition of 'good' public management (Chapter 8). In the absence of any competition, the provision and administration of services by the state needed to be supported by an effective system of accountability: an objective which was not always met in the period before the new challenge to the public sector. However, rather than a tightening of the sinews of traditional accountability, the 1980s saw the emphasis move towards financial accountability. Hence commercialism in the public sector was designed in part to focus attention on service provision and to sensitize deliverers and budget holders to their market and to the demands of their more immediately visible clients. This was indeed the thrust of the discredited poll tax. Portrayed as the flagship of Thatcherism in local government finance reform, it was devised in order to establish greater accountability for spending commitments in local government: the requirement of some contribution from all adult voters would focus the mind of the local elector in the voting booth on what the bill for political pledges might, in future, entail. However, the emphasis upon the financial elements of accountability still left problems for the public in receipt of services from public sector monopolies: a remedy for which has been sought, although with little success, by Thatcher's successor through the Citizen's Charter with its emphasis on standards and quality and the promise of more 'open government'.

2.6   THE EFFECT OF THATCHERISM

There can be no doubt of the effect of the Thatcher reforms. The public sector of the post-war settlement laid down by Attlee's government and managed within a consensual framework by Labour and Conservative governments was either dismantled or reorganized after 1979. In those parts which did remain public, the injection of a market ethos through commercial nostrums such as internal markets, performance indicators, league tables, devolved budgets and competitive tendering went so deep that a return to the structure and culture prevailing in the 1950s and 1960s was impossible. In addition, Britain's continuing economic vulnerability combined with the social demands on the state ensured that the resources at the disposal of the public sector were utilized to the full, thereby reinforcing the Thatcherite demands for greater efficiency and value for money within it. Thus there was no turning back for the public sector once the Thatcher reforms had been let loose. Yet while the post-war settlement was dismantled under Thatcher, she failed to provide Britain with a new vision of the state and its appropriate role, one on which, as in a previous era, there could be agreement between the major parties and to which the public adhered.

Yet the signs appeared favourable when Thatcher was forced from office by her own party in 1990. The Labour Party, following three successive election defeats, was already in the process of discarding some of its ideological baggage and with it those parts of the post-war settlement to which it had previously been closely wedded, but which appeared to have decreasing voter-appeal. Kinnock's Labour Party was pressed to respond to the conditions established under Thatcher whereby centralism and the pervasive, providing, state appeared anachronistic characteristics of a bygone age: this reorganization occurred at a time when the centrally controlled economies of Eastern Europe were toppling with incredible haste, thereby lending even greater credence to the need to abandon what was increasingly seen as old fashioned centralism. Yet in spite of the changes begun under Kinnock, the Party was still unable to win the 1992 election, evidence of the continuing absence of trust that some voters had towards the Party and its leadership. This was an indication that the Party had still further to travel in its march towards reform, a theme taken up by Kinnock's successors, John Smith and Tony Blair.

In addition to the changes taking place in the Labour Party, Thatcher's removal seemed to offer the prospect of a different governing style, one less confrontational and divisive, under her approved successor John Major. He was keen to see a country 'at ease with itself', an indication that under Thatcher the temper of the country had been less than tranquil. Major's aspiration appeared to present a new style of politics which could nonetheless build on the foundations laid by the Thatcher government and to which all parties would, as with the post-war settlement, need to accommodate. A new consensus on the role of the state appeared possible in 1990 yet failed to materialize. Why was this?

One explanation can be sought in the fact that the Thatcher project for reforming Britain and the British state was never fully endorsed by the whole British electorate. Undoubtedly Thatcher skewed not only the Conservative Party, but also British politics generally to the right. However, the Conservative electoral dominance after 1979 did not indicate an unequivocal acceptance of the Thatcher reforms by the British public. The establishment of the post-war settlement by the Attlee government and its assigned role for the public sector 'was built on a widespread popular commitment to the Welfare State, which was why the Conservatives became so anxious to be identified with it' (Wright 1989: 210). The same could not be said of the revolution undertaken during the Thatcher era. While the Conservatives won four consecutive elections, and certain of their policies had a popular attraction such as the sale of council houses, there is little evidence that Thatcher's reforms were embraced whole heartedly by the electorate. Thatcher and Major were only able to translate conviction into action by using to the full the constitutional structure of a pre-modern, eighteenth century state, whereby governments can effect swingeing, major changes without having a popular mandate to do so: a rather rich irony given that the Thatcher project was built on the virtues of reform of the state and the public sector. The Conservatives averaged in all four elections only 42% of the vote and their electoral dominance owed much to the divided Opposition and the internal feuds in the Labour Party during the 1980s. Nevertheless, under Thatcher and Major Britain, through the vagaries of the electoral system, became a virtual one party state where the Conservative government, assured of a majority, had little need to win arguments.

A second reason for the failure of Thatcherism to lay down a foundation for a new settlement on the role of the state lay in the essential contradictions of the project.

Thatcherism stimulated and in fact relied on the paradox of the free economy and the strong state, of the liberal tradition of conservatism mixing with the Tory one. Thus an inconsistency was created: that while the public sector was exhorted to be more efficient and slimmer, and to be less bureaucratic and to be more sensitive and thus accountable to its customers, many parts of it were subject to centralizing influences and market reforms which had the effect of increasing bureaucracy. In addition, having preached the virtues of accountability in the public sector, Thatcher and Major then exchanged parts of it, such as in local government and the Health Service with an unaccountable, unelected state and the spawning of a 'quangocracy' (see Chapter 10).

A third explanation for the failure to reach a new consensus has highlighted the fundamental destructiveness of the project begun in 1979 (Giddens 1994; Gray 1994; 1996 and Hutton 1996b). In this view, while Thatcherism dismantled and even destroyed many of the post-war fixtures of the British state, it failed to put anything concrete in their place other than an obeisance to the virtues of the market. It has been the very emphasis on these virtues which to some, such as John Gray, has sounded the death knell of the Thatcher project. The ideologically motivated programme of adulation to the free market that has been the mark of Thatcherism, has had a deeply destabilizing effect.

By extolling the value of the market and elevating choice, individualism and rights to ideological pieties, Thatcherism created a situation where not only were many of the traditional institutional fixtures of the British state altered but the adhesiveness of the social glue was diluted and social cohesion suffered. In this explanation, the public sector landscape was shaken by the Thatcherite artillery of choice, rights and commercialism. Local government, the National Health Service, schools, police and the civil service have all had their structures undermined by the barrage of reforms. In addition, the emphasis placed on the rights and freedoms which derive from choice within society has been corrosive of traditional authority and deference which was a central feature of British class culture. The result has been seen in a range of indicators: unprecedentedly high crime figures; a sense of creeping decay and decline in the standards of many public services, an underclass excluded from much of social life and trapped in a cycle of poverty and a sense of 'yobbery' spreading across the nation and throughout the state. The malaise seeped into all corners of the body politic to the extent that sleaze, the decline of public standards and probity became a watchword for the 1990s and the Major government in particular. The catalogue was damning: the increased use of ministerial patronage, the cynical movement of former ministers to the directorships of the newly privatized industries, the indecent pay awards given to these directors and the refusal of government to take the blame for anything but the applause for everything. All led to an impression that Thatcherism had spawned 'private poverty and public sleaze' (Doig and Wilson 1995).

The effect of the neo-liberal, free market ethos of Thatcherism took its toll on the Conservative Party as well. Essentially a party which conserves, and which for so long was dominated by the One Nation tradition which depended on deference and traditional authority structures for its existence, it has, in the post-Thatcher period, realized that Thatcherism and the various ideas of the New Right have been anything but conservative. By embracing them, the Conservative Party has been thrown into a contradiction, 'for nothing is more corrosive of established traditions, habits and forms of social cohesion...than the wholesale cultivation of market relations' (Giddens 1994: 37).

2.6.1 The Conservative Party

The Conservative Party has therefore, after Thatcher, been broadly split into those on the centre/left that wish to return to a stability of One Nation Conservatism which Thatcherism shattered, and those on the right of the Party that wish to push on with the Thatcher project. The centre/left of the Party, having removed Thatcher have sought to reconnect with some traditional Conservative anthems, through an appeal to the creation of good citizenship and strong communities. While recognizing the significance of Thatcherism in stoking the fires of capitalism, some of the Conservative left has been keen to emphasize the importance of people and values and that capitalism cannot exist in a moral vacuum (Hurd 1994). However, it has had difficulty sustaining this note of a traditional Conservative motif for two reasons. First, it has been a willing player in the Thatcher-Major ensemble in its interpretation of a new theme for Britain and more pointedly, appeals to community values and standards have sounded somewhat hollow set against a chorus of a decline in public standards as illustrated by the 'cash for questions' episode in the House of Commons, the vast pay increases awarded to the chairman of the newly privatized industries and the farce of the 'back to basics' campaign which Major launched in 1993 only for it to run aground on the rocks of the personal peccadilloes of a number of Conservative MPs.

The right of the Party such as John Redwood and Michael Portillo wish to extend and even complete the Thatcher project and see further scope for privatizations, greater reduction in public expenditure and further efficiency savings: these were the themes of Redwood's campaign when he stood against Major for the leadership of the Party in 1995. The right has also shown an interest in the restoration of community values as central to Conservative thinking and something not in conflict with the free market (Willetts 1992). However, in practice, there has been the danger for the Conservative Party that appeals for public spiritedness and community action, such as through the Major Government's Street Watch initiative (walking with a purpose), will be seen as a form of social authoritarianism.

Yet by far the greatest division in the post-Thatcher period has been over the very issue which forced Thatcher from office: Europe. The centre/left has been keen for Britain to play a more committed role in Europe, while stopping short of federalism. The right, however, is deeply hostile to any further integration of the European Community, seeing it as riddled with the worst aspects of pre-Thatcherite Britain: bureaucratic, profligate, inefficient and over-centralized as well as being, not surprisingly, staffed by foreigners. It was these attitudes from the right which led to the defection of Conservative MPs Alan Howarth and Emma Nicolson to Labour and the Liberal Democrats respectively. Thus, far from governing a country 'at ease with itself', John Major has been unable to apply that aspiration to his own Party.

2.6.2 The Labour Party

The response of the Labour Party to the divisions within Britain in the post Thatcher period has been to further discard the legacy of the left and to seek to offer a new start for Britain: in effect to offer a new settlement, a unifying theme in the face of the divisions created by the Thatcher project. The process was begun by Kinnock's successor, John Smith, after the 1992 election defeat but accelerated and given greater clarity by Tony Blair following Smith's premature death in 1994. Blair has sought to capture the middle class vote, which appears to have become alienated from the Conservatives, while at the same time needing to maintain the traditional links with a changing working class in Britain. His critics have accused him of a rightward lurch, even of wearing the mantle of Thatcherism (Hay 1994).

Scargill rails against Tory Party Mark II (*The Times, 5 October 1994*)

In his defence he has claimed to offer Britain, 'New Labour', a party that is forward looking and divorced from much of the ideological dogma of the past. To support this he has re-written Clause IV of the 1918 Labour Party constitution, the public ownership clause, a political feat which would have been unthinkable even at the start of the 1990s. Blair has accepted that a future Labour government will retain much of the Thatcher reforms of the Trade Unions and that most of the privatizations will not be reversed, thus acknowledging the Thatcher drive against some parts of the post-war settlement as irrevocable. However, Blair was ardent in his desire to see a state in which much of the social and political detritus of the Thatcher period is expunged, in which there was a sense of justice and fairness and in which every member of society felt included not excluded: a fate which he considered too many suffered under Thatcher and Major. Blair sought to emphasize this in January 1996 through his appeal to the creation of a stakeholder society (Blair 1996), one which utilized the ideas of Etzioni and the reinvention of communities and the acceptance of responsibilities, (Etzioni 1995) which under Thatcher had too easily been marginalized.

2.6.3 A new settlement?

Thus it was clear by the mid 1990s that a new consensus, a new settlement had not replaced the old post-war social democratic one. Undoubtedly Thatcherism had shifted British politics to the right, but this did not provide a common ground on which the political parties could encamp. Under Major, the Conservatives had continued with Thatcherite policies. Indeed, many of the reforms of the public sector while having their roots in the Thatcher period have sprouted and seen the light of day under Major.

> [Thatcherism] has sometimes emerged in its starkest and most uncompromising guise under the Major administration, as for example in the privatization of British rail or the run down of the coal industry (*Sharp and Walker 1994: 397*)

Consequently, it was difficult for Major to reconstruct a new settlement that deviated from Thatcherism without putting strains on the Party. However, by 1994, Major was seeking just that, by putting a halt to the Thatcherite project and claiming the centre ground of British politics. Thus Major sought to use the Thatcher reforms as a point from which a new consensus could emerge and his stress on continuity appeared to portray him as a routine manager of existing policies rather than a visionary: in fact in his speech to the 1994 Conservative Party Conference, he sought to play up the strengths of, as he saw it, the 'action thing' rather than the 'vision thing' (*The Times 15 October 1994*).

If Major retreated from embracing a big idea for British politics, Blair leading the Labour Party did not. Given the seeming impossibility of a return to the post-war settlement, Labour stressed the importance of building a new settlement under the banner of 'Britain as One Nation' thereby occupying traditional pre-Thatcher Conservative ground.

> Now we are the One Nation Party (Tony Blair at the 1994 Labour Party Conference, reported in *The Times*, 5 October 1994)

In addition, Blair's Labour Party alleged that Thatcher and Major had utilized, to the full, an 18th century constitutional structure, comprising a pre-modern and pre-industrial set of political conventions. The consequent malaise of British society and politics which the Thatcher project had created and which Major had failed to address, went so deep as to require a modernization of the British state through an overhaul of the constitution to tackle the questions of, among others, the decentralization of power through devolution, more open government and trust in the electorate through freedom of information and a nod in the direction of modernity by way of a reform of the House of Lords.

Britain thus faces two possible futures as the millennium dawns. One is of a deeply divided society in which the 'haves' and 'have nots' occupy distinct and separate locations: the underclass and the overclass with all the attendant repercussions for employment, health, education and law and order. The other is of a society in which many of the divisions created by the Thatcher project are healed. The challenge for any political party, be it a revived Conservative Party led from the centre/left or a reformed Labour Party, seeking to repair the rents of Thatcherism will be the introduction of a broad settlement which furnishes political reform, social cohesion and economic well-being and creates once more fixtures in the British state and values in the nation of which the broad majority of its people approve.

2.7   CHAPTER SUMMARY

The following key learning points emerge from this chapter:

- The post-war settlement was built on a number of social, economic and political assumptions about the appropriate role of the state and the size and scope of the public sector which was shared by the major political parties.
- The post-war settlement came under strain as a result of changes in society and wider global changes which eroded the ability of governments to deliver the goals of the settlement.
- The election of the Thatcher government in 1979 presaged a reform of the settlement and the role of the public sector. Thatcher was supported in this through the political and economic ideas of the New Right.
- Thatcher's brand of Conservatism was based on the free market as an efficient deliverer of services and a strong state to maintain authority. Thus the public sector was both reduced in scope and subject to the introduction of commercial practices and the post-war settlement was dismantled.
- Thatcherism failed to provide a new settlement: politics shifted to the right yet there has been no post-Thatcher consensus on the appropriate role of the state.
- The Conservatives have been unable to devise a new settlement as the electorate were always deeply divided on the Thatcher project and Thatcherism has thrown up deep divisions in the Conservative Party.
- Major tried to halt the march of Thatcherism but was hindered by demands of Party unity.
- Major's government became closely associated with a decline in public standards.
- Under the leadership of Tony Blair the Labour Party sought not merely to attack Thatcherism and Major's stewardship of it, but to devise wide ranging reforms of the state.

TEXT-BASED QUESTIONS

1.   Discuss the factors which influenced the post-war political settlement in Britain.

2.   What were the New Right's major criticisms of the public sector in the post-war settlement?

3.   How much of a Conservative was Mrs Thatcher?

4.   Why has John Major been unable to build a new post-Thatcher settlement?

ASSIGNMENT

The post-war settlement has gone and cannot be recreated. However, a new settlement is required in British politics if society's divisions are to be healed. Consider a number of different features of reform which you think would lead to a new settlement of political consensus in Britain. For example, it could be along the lines of a Freedom of Information Act and the creation of more open government: would this form of constitutional change assist in the creation of a new consensus and if so how?

FURTHER READING

Beer, S.H. (1982) *Britain Against Itself: The Political Contradictions of Collectivism*, Faber & Faber, London.

Checkland, S. (1983) *British Public Policy 1776–1939: An Economic, Social and Political Perspective*, Cambridge University Press, Cambridge.

Etzioni, A.(1995) *The Spirit of Community: Rights, Responsibilities and the Communitarian Agenda*, Fontana, London

Gamble, A. (1988) *The Free Economy and the Strong State*, Macmillan, London.

Gilmour, I. (1992) *Dancing with Dogma: Britain under Thatcherism*, Simon and Schuster, London.

Gray, J. (1993) *Beyond the New Right: Markets, Government and the Common Environment*, Routledge, London.

Hayek, F.A.(1944) *The Road to Serfdom*, Routledge, London.

Hennessy, P. and Seldon, A. (eds) (1989) *Ruling Performance:British Governments from Attlee to Thatcher*, Basil Blackwell, Oxford.

Hutton, W. (1996) *The State We're In*, Vintage, London (revised edition).

King, D.S. (1987) *The New Right:Politics, Markets and Citizenship*, Macmillan, London.

Letwin, S.R. (1992) *The Anatomy of Thatcherism*, Fontana, London.

Marsh, D. and Rhodes, R.A.W. (1992) Implementing Thatcherism, Policy Changes in the 1980s, *Parliamentary Affairs*, **45**, (1), January pp. 33–50.

Riddell, P. (1991) *The Thatcher Era and its Legacy*, Blackwell, Oxford.

Skidelsky, R. (ed) (1988) *Thatcherism*, Chatto and Windus, London.

Thatcher, M. (1993) *The Downing Street Years*, Harper Collins, London.

Willetts, D. (1992) *Modern Conservatism*, Penguin, London

Young, H. (1989) *One of Us, a Biography of Margaret Thatcher*, Macmillan, London.

MANAGING CHANGE IN THE PUBLIC SECTOR

3

Chris Painter

3.1   CHAPTER PREVIEW

The primary objective of this chapter is to systematically address a theme that runs throughout the book, that is:

- environmental turbulence and what it entails for the management of change in public sector institutions.

Indeed, just as in the private sector, such institutions have increasingly felt the chill winds of downsizing, delayering and outsourcing. There are particular challenges arising out of what many see as:

- a qualitative shift in external conditions – that is environmental discontinuity – and the attendant crisis of the traditional public administration paradigm.

Hence the endeavours to fundamentally re-orientate public authorities. Indeed, one intriguing notion that has gained currency is 'reinventing government' – the idea of shifting from conventional bureaucratic to new 'entrepreneurial' principles. The chapter therefore underlines:

- The **strategic** nature of the changes being undertaken in the public sector.

Hence the appropriateness of a strategic management perspective.

But it is necessary to look critically at prevalent change role models in the public sector and to consider some of their potentially dysfunctional consequences. The internal as well as external dynamics involved in the change process need to be identified, as does the growing importance to government agencies of the skills associated with this process. There are also the prerequisites for successful innovation and obstacles to be overcome, and the chapter therefore highlights:

- The benefits to be derived from adopting a more systematic approach to change management – whilst having regard for the realities of organizational life.

The chapter will conclude by focusing on local government management of change issues and the nature of the responses to environmental turbulence in a particular – but mainstream political – institutional context. It sets the scene for related (more applied) case study material in subsequent chapters.

3.2   CHANGING ORGANIZATIONAL PARADIGMS IN THE PUBLIC SECTOR

3.2.1 The Thatcher managerial reforms in context

When addressing the management of change in the public sector, it is tempting to assume that the challenge only really began with the onset of the 'Thatcher revolution' and that upheaval was consequently something exclusive to the 1980s. Yet, many of the ideas on the so-called 'new agenda' are not entirely novel, something confirmed by the most cursory glance at the 1968 Fulton Report on *The Civil Service*, or indeed by earlier debates in the local government arena (Asquith 1991). The latest phase of managerial reformist agendas in response to growing concern about government performance therefore goes back at least to the 1960s.

Moreover, the 1970s were characterized by momentous external shocks which destabilized the world economy, the resource difficulties experienced leading to retrenchment and the challenges of cutback management in a financially constraining climate. That decade is also associated with major institutional reorganizations throughout the public sector. Given the prevailing belief in the economies of scale, it was after all the era of rationalization, amalgamation and mega-organization. In a study of strategic change in one institutional setting, Hinings and Greenwood (1988) analyse the responses of local authorities in England and Wales from 1972 onwards to a range of pressures to adopt a different design 'archetype' (see below). The 'heteronomous professional bureaucracy', characterized by high differentiation and minimum co-ordination between a diverse array of services, was being delegitimized in favour of 'corporate bureaucracy' with its more integrated structures.

3.2.2 A public service revolution?

Nonetheless, with prescriptions germinating since the 1960s reaching fruition and ideological fervour reinforcing the fiscal pressures building up during the 1970s, the 1980s did mark a significant shift in the direction of reform. One contention is that the 'Thatcher effect' can be overestimated: 'The Thatcherite revolution is more a product of rhetoric than of the reality of policy impact' (Marsh and Rhodes 1992b: 187).

However, reform did assume a distinct thrust in so far as the Conservative government became intent both on reducing the scope and improving the management of the public sector and notably on improving the management of resources; hence the growing fixation with value for money (considered in the next chapter) (Elcock 1991). The momentum behind change in this respect showed every sign of accelerating, adding to the sense of turbulence, with a number of previously mentioned strategies employed to force the pace – notably those of privatization, deregulation, compulsory competitive tendering and market disciplines: 'The overwhelming impression is one of change and the creation of a new agenda for the public sector . . . a fundamental re-assessment has taken place . . .' (Lawton and Rose 1991: 147).

This is a view corroborated from many quarters whether on the 'outside' or 'inside' of the government machine:

> In the United Kingdom, the 1980s saw more administrative reform than any previous decade in the twentieth century – except, perhaps, for periods affected by the two world wars
>
> *(Chapman 1991: 1)*

Parliament's financial watchdog stated: 'All this requires a revolution in the way public services are run and in the way public servants think and act' (National Audit Office 1992: 3). It is both the pace and scale of change that with hindsight is striking. The fate of local government graphically illustrates the point: 'During the 1980s some 40 Acts affecting local government were passed. The scale of the activity was daunting . . . ' (Rhodes 1991: 83). Consequently, this decade 'was probably the most dramatic era that local government has ever faced' (Delderfield, Puffit and Watts 1991: i). More generally, comparison with the pre-Thatcher period is instructive: 'If we look back to the mid-1970s, we find a public sector which had never heard of compulsory competitive tendering, contracting out, internal markets, customer orientation and so on' (Lawton and Rose 1991: 173).

What we witnessed as we moved towards the end of the 1980s arguably was a qualitative, paradigmatic change in the structure and organization of the public sector and hence in the primary means adopted for delivering public services.

This entailed a significant shift away from hierarchical co-ordination. The emphasis moved instead towards market-type transactions, with such principles also introduced for the internal functioning of organizations – notably in health. It was by no means a development confined to the UK:

> The late 1980s and early 1990s have witnessed a transformation in the public sectors of advanced countries. The rigid, hierarchical, bureaucratic form of public administration, which has predominated for most of the twentieth century, is changing to a flexible, market-based form of public management
>
> *(Hughes 1994: 1)*

Networking arrangements too assumed greater significance, including collaborative ventures and partnerships where one agency became dependent on resources controlled from other quarters, particularly in view of the increasing fragmentation of organizational responsibilities (refer to Chapter 10) (Thompson, Frances, Levacic and Mitchell 1991).

As indicated above, the pace of change was just as unrelenting in the 1990s, priority particularly accorded by John Major to improving the **quality** of public services, making them more responsive and accountable through the *Citizen's Charter*, with tough performance targets to be progressively tightened. However, the *Citizen's Charter* immediately illustrates the difficulties that can arise in relation to both the substance and ease of change. The Prime Minister was eager to claim that improvements could be discerned in public service standards and in making these services more user-friendly as a result of his initiative. But to critics it appeared as little more than a public relations gloss, repackaging many established entitlements, and which could prove politically counter-productive by highlighting problems of underfunding. Furthermore, there was said to be considerable disappointment behind the scenes, with some Whitehall departments proving slow to deliver; hence successive attempts to revitalize and put more teeth into the initiative, with regular high-level meetings to monitor developments.

3.2.3 Bureaucratic juggernauts and nimble dancers

Nonetheless, there had been a widely perceived need for changes in the delivery and organizational culture of the public services, particularly for less insularity and greater attentiveness to customer satisfaction. Taken in conjunction with the uncertainties engendered by a rapidly changing environment, this called for a reappraisal of hitherto dominant bureaucratic structures – in favour of more flexible, adaptive and innovative organizational forms (Lawton and Rose 1991). In the civil service context the change has been likened to turning bureaucratic giants into nimble dancers:

> The whole thrust of recent thinking in reforming the civil service can be portrayed as one of getting giants to learn to dance ... the principles of classical Weberian bureaucracy upon which central government departments were founded have given rise to lumbering hierarchies which ... are no longer appropriate ... The call is for ... more nimble organizations which can respond quickly to complex and dynamic environments
>
> *(Colville, Dalton and Tomkins 1993: 549; 550)*

The Next Steps Whitehall reforms exemplified such trends. Thus, one of the largest of the departmental agencies established under this initiative to improve the management of public services – the Benefits Agency – has been undergoing 'a cultural revolution designed to turn the organization which pays social security benefits from a sluggish bureaucracy into a fast-moving customer-friendly service'. Moreover, this has meant that words 'like vision, ownership and empowerment, the common currency of the private sector ... are now being heard in Whitehall corridors' (Cellan-Jones 1992).

These changes may be seen therefore as a symptom of the crisis of traditional bureaucratic techniques of organizational control. Indeed, a striking feature of the emerging post-bureaucratic paradigm is 'regulated autonomy' – the devolution of responsibility down the management line for operational matters within a strategic framework (Hoggett 1991). *The Next Steps* reforms, as well as facilitating organizational design tailored to the requirements of the specific task in hand, clearly conform to this principle of control through the medium of framework documents and hence the trend towards more decentralized management (Common, Flynn and Mellon 1992: Ch. 4).

Moreover, reform has entailed a fundamental reassessment of organizational role. At issue is the extent, for example, to which local authorities should relinquish direct responsibility for service provision, not only to operational delivery units, but also to the private and voluntary sectors, concentrating instead on funding, standards and quality assurance. At the very least, this means abandoning notions of self-sufficiency in favour of partnership and inter-agency collaboration, the management of interdependency underlining the importance of skills in organizational networking. It is in this context that the 'enabling' concept became fashionable, notwithstanding its different connotations (Clarke and Stewart 1988). The Conservative government's aim was clearly for local councils to become buyers rather than providers of public service. The purchaser-provider split is also a cardinal principle driving the reform process in the NHS (refer to Chapter 8).

The scale of the changes taking place in central government too was gradually becoming apparent. The ultimate goal is to 'leave Whitehall as a slimline policy-making directorate . . . ' (Wapshott 1992). Government departments, it would appear, were also to become primarily purchasers/commissioners rather than providers of services. Moreover, following the delegation of executive functions to agencies, the Whitehall 'revolution' entered a significant new phase through the extension of 'market-testing', as part of the *Competing For Quality* initiative launched in November 1991. It meant that 'privatization and "contractorization" is moving closer to the heart of government' (Hirst 1992), even more the case now that some of the *Next Steps* agencies are themselves being prepared for privatization. Many would view this infusion of competition into formerly monopolistic public services as by far the most important post-war cultural change in public administration.

3.3   REINVENTING GOVERNMENT

3.3.1 Entrepreneurial government

The argument that we are witnessing a paradigm shift has been taken up by Osborne and Gaebler – encapsulated in their phrase 'reinventing government'. They address a new form of governance they observe emerging across America: ' . . . we have seen . . . many public institutions transform themselves from staid bureaucracies into innovative, flexible, responsive organizations . . . ' (1992: xxii). The bankruptcy of bureaucratic government was thus encouraging new forms of 'entrepreneurial' government, with an emphasis on opportunity-seeking rather than on the risk-avoiding behaviour so characteristic of the traditional public service culture. They define an entrepreneur as one who 'uses resources in new ways to maximize productivity and effectiveness' (ibid.: xix):

> Our thesis is simple: The kind of governments that developed during the industrial era, with their sluggish, centralized bureaucracies, their preoccupation with rules and regulations, and their hierarchical chains of command, no longer work very well ... Hierarchical, centralized bureaucracies designed in the 1930s or 1940s simply do not function well in the rapidly changing, information-rich, knowledge-intensive society and economy of the 1990s ...

---

1. **CATALYTIC GOVERNMENT**
   – steering rather than rowing (ensuring that something desirable is done but not necessarily doing it directly).

2. **COMMUNITY-OWNED GOVERNMENT**
   – empowering rather than serving (enabling communities to take responsibility for their own affairs, assisted as necessary by 'social entrepreneurs', rather than having services handed down).

3. **COMPETITIVE GOVERNMENT**
   – injecting competition into service delivery (competitive tendering, market testing etc.).

4. **MISSION-DRIVEN GOVERNMENT**
   – transforming rule-driven organizations (focusing on organizational purpose and underpinning values, i.e. a strategic orientation).

5. **RESULTS-ORIENTED GOVERNMENT**
   – funding outcomes not inputs (rewarding success rather than failure and with appropriate performance indicators in place).

6. **CUSTOMER-DRIVEN GOVERNMENT**
   – meeting the needs of the customer not the bureaucracy (a theme at the heart of the UK Government's *Citizen's Charter*).

7. **ENTERPRISING GOVERNMENT**
   – earning rather than just spending (income generation etc.).

8. **ANTICIPATORY GOVERNMENT**
   – prevention rather than cure (being proactive rather than purely reactive).

9. **DECENTRALIZED GOVERNMENT**
   – from hierarchy to participative teamwork (moving decisions closer to point of service delivery; collegial rather than command principle etc.).

10. **MARKET-ORIENTED GOVERNMENT**
    – leveraging change through the market (including use of the price mechanism as in the case of lead-free petrol, i.e. differential pricing).

Figure 3.1 Osborne and Gaebler's Ten Principles of 'Entrepreneurial' Government

Bureaucracies brought the same logic to government work that the assembly line brought to the factory

(Osborne and Gaebler 1992: 11, 12)

3.3.2 Organizational design dilemmas

Osborne and Gaebler's model of entrepreneurial government has attracted criticism and even a heavy dose of scepticism. Despite their claim to be dealing with a global phenomenon, American social and political values intrude. Yet they also imply that some kind of remorseless process is at work, given wider socioeconomic imperatives, rather than political and social choices. This determinism means that little insight is provided into the actual dynamics of organizational change: 'What we have in essence is a variation on the theme of governmental restructuring for a post-Fordist era, where the world of mass production and related hierarchically-controlled institutions is receding . . . '(Painter 1994: 249). Moreover, any set of principles runs the risk of pointing in potentially different directions. The Osborne and Gaebler entrepreneurial principles are no exception: 'The clarity of mission to be derived from breaking up large organizations can, for example, lead to fragmented user-hostile systems unable to cater holistically for the needs of individuals' (ibid.: 249). Institutional design is inevitably confronted with dilemmas. Any set of organizational arrangements is bound to bring drawbacks as well as advantages:

> Osborne and Gaebler's remedy . . . neglects the fact that traditional systems had 'defects' as a consequence of delivering virtues such as reliability, fairness, probity . . . The design of government involves choosing between different packages of costs and benefits . . . it involves trade-offs among desirable goals . . .
>
> *(Jordan 1994: 278)*

Their thesis is also flawed by a logical contradiction: 'The source of the innovations which they extol was the bureaucracy they excoriate' (Rhodes 1994: 289). Moreover, fashions quickly move on and spawn new labels. Reflecting the pressures for fundamental organizational change one such example is 'corporate re-engineering' – defined as:

> . . . the radical rethinking of an organization's purpose, strategies and systems with the express intention of changing the way the organization thinks, learns and behaves . . . The issues for members and managers in local authorities are the same as their counterparts in the private sector . . . Tomorrow's organizations . . . need to be much more adaptive and dynamic, responsive to the environment in which they operate . . .
>
> *(Crosbie and Edwards 1994: 18, 19)*

3.3.3 Reinventing or abandoning government?

But **reinventing government** did strike a chord, with parallels drawn between the UK public service reforms and Osborne and Gaebler's entrepreneurial principles: ' . . . a "paradigm shift" is taking place in government in the US . . . we, too, are caught up in a transformation of government. Monopoly public services and traditional bureaucratic organizations . . . have been challenged . . . The mould has been broken . . . ' (Clarke 1993: 19). Conservative ministers were certainly eager to assert that they too were reinventing government. Indeed, William Waldegrave claimed that 'Britain now has the most comprehensive public service reform programme of which I am aware' (1993: 12). The Cabinet Secretary noted that:

> when Ted Gaebler visited the UK in December 1992, he was sufficiently surprised by the extent to which we had been applying the same approach that he wondered whether we had somehow plagiarized the manuscript. We had not. These ideas had progressively been developed in Britain over the previous decade
>
> *(Butler 1994: 264, 265)*

However, given the neo-liberal ideological position of many Conservatives it can be contended that policies were as much directed at the dismemberment as the renewal of government implied by the term 'reinvention' – given a declared mission to reduce government to its 'inescapable core'. Picking up on the analogy of getting bureaucratic giants to learn to dance: 'It may . . . be that rather than being concerned with the quality of the dancing, the government is more interested in who is doing the dancing . . . private dancing will be by definition excellent' (Colville, Dalton and Tomkins 1993: 564).

Yet, Osborne and Gaebler profess their own deep belief in government as the means for collectively meeting society's needs, the challenge being to make government institutions more effective instruments. With the high quality inputs required by modern corporations to succeed in increasingly competitive global markets, if anything the role of government in training and education, funding of research and infrastructural investment was becoming more important. They accordingly take issue with a privatizing ideology, accepting the need to balance consumerism, choice and competition (the paradigm clearly favoured by the UK Conservative government) with a recognition of the importance of community, citizenship and democracy: ' . . . the arguments deployed in *Reinventing Government* are more subtle than the anti-government rhetoric at the heart of transatlantic politics until recently (Painter 1994: 255).

3.4   A BUSINESS ETHOS AND DYSFUNCTIONAL CONSEQUENCES OF CHANGE

3.4.1 Monstrous hybrids

Apart from a privatizing ideology, the UK public service reforms reflected the perceived virtues of business management methods and values. Indeed, this became the role model to the extent of subjecting 'the public services manager ... to invidious comparison with a purportedly dynamic private sector counterpart ... ' (Harrow and Willcocks 1992: 79). In this respect, a number of the ideas currently in vogue – not least consumerism – have an impeccable pedigree, rooted as they are in market paradigms and private sector management ideas, with the emphasis accordingly placed on individual utilities rather than on collective benefits (the application of a 'consumerist-market' model to one public service is evaluated in Chapter 7). Indeed, so profound are the cultural changes taking place that any differences between the public and private sectors arguably are rapidly being eroded, giving credence to the convergence hypothesis, or at least making it more sensible to think in terms of an organizational continuum than a dichotomy, stressing differences of degree rather than kind (Vinten 1992). One commentator has observed that 'benefit offices may soon resemble the average branch of a bank or building society'. Yet, the continuation of this same account is very illuminating:

> With no control over the type or volume of its customers, an annual fight with the Treasury over funding and the constant struggle to satisfy the minister, the Benefits Agency knows that its destiny is not in its own hands. While private sector techniques are helping to focus minds on where resources are going and how they might be better used, there is a limit to what they can achieve ...
>
> *(Cellan-Jones 1992)*

Moreover, the management of change has often proved problematic in public service settings because of the organizational diversity associated with multiple – policy, management and professional – domains, the conflicting values provoking intense and bitter power struggles (see below) (Willcocks and Harrow 1992). Indeed, a number of factors distinctive to the public sector have previously made it difficult to achieve sustained change (Nutley and Osborne 1994).

Apart from the uncritical adoption of role models which provide hostages to fortune when 'prime private sector managed companies end up failing or being surpassed [so that] yesterday's successes can quickly become tomorrow's has beens ... ' (Vinten 1992: 18), there is the bearing that organizational context has on what is deemed appropriate.

A contingency framework emphasizes how the validity of any prescriptions for reform will depend on circumstances and therefore must be organization-specific, including taking account of the differences between public and private management (*Willcocks and Harrow 1992*).

To the extent that public services (inevitably) retain their distinctiveness, including the high degree of unpredictability and ambiguity that tends to characterize the public policy environment (McKevitt 1992), so doubt is cast on the wholesale transferability of private sector solutions. This includes indiscriminate adoption of consumerist philosophies or insensitive application of performance measurement techniques. Indeed, one contention is that the only consequence of imposing the ethos of commercial organizations on so-called 'guardian' organizations is to create monstrous hybrids. There will be confusion, disarray and corruption of organizational aims – as in the case of performance targets for police forces, temptations to make false arrests, and perversion of the course of justice (Caulkin 1994).

3.4.2 The business ethic and public standards

'One way learning transference' is itself a strange notion, placing the emphasis almost entirely on 'outward' as opposed to 'inward' learning, so devaluing the accumulated knowledge and experience of organizational members (Harrow and Willcocks 1992). In terms of effectiveness, there is much to be said for a more measured approach to change, building upon some of the traditional strengths of public service professionalism as well as developing a capacity to innovate in the face of new challenges (Holtham 1992). Even many of those willing to concede that the Thatcherite legacy to the public services has brought the benefits of greater efficiency and responsiveness express concern about the neglect of traditional public administration values, not least the fundamental importance of public accountability and the safeguards against abuse of office that those accountability structures represented (Elcock 1991) – borne out by some of the recent excesses of the 'quango state'.

Although greater accountability of public services is a professed objective of the *Citizen's Charter*, the managerial flexibility at the heart of the *Next Steps* agency initiative can, for example, only thrive at some price in terms of parliamentary accountability (Greer 1992). A graphic account of the implications for the constituency casework of MPs, again particularly relating to the responsibilities of the Benefits Agency, has been provided by a prominent Labour backbencher – part of a process he describes as 'creeping abnegation of ministerial responsibility . . . ' (Kaufman 1992). Hence apprehension that the essence of recent developments may be a 'manager's charter' to the detriment of democratic values.

Undermining traditional checks and balances, by cultivating a private sector ethos of risk-taking behaviour, could also prove dysfunctional in encouraging self-servingness and opportunism (Willcocks and Harrow 1992). The revelations in connection with the so-called 'Iraqgate' affair – revolving around the sale of arms allegedly in breach of guidelines conveyed to Parliament – that have been investigated by the Scott inquiry, as well as a series of other incidents, certainly aroused anxiety about the standards of conduct being observed in public life by ministers, civil servants and others entrusted with public office. The Prime Minister eventually relented by setting up the Nolan Committee to monitor the position and make recommendations.

In addition, cultural values being imported into public agencies may themselves turn out to be mutually incompatible, as in the case of customer responsiveness and dynamism, if radical options are regarded as disconcerting by service users

(Harrow and Shaw 1992). This is besides the temptations for displays of management machismo and to indulge in short-term fixes under the new public management regime (Hood 1990), or related hazards of jumping on the latest bandwagons and being blindly swept along by what may turn out to be only passing fashions! Change, therefore, is not by definition a positive value. This depends on whether it is an appropriate response to institutional circumstances and on judgements about the costs as well as benefits of what is taking place.

Indeed, it is important to balance change with 'zones of stability' if some kind of equilibrium is to be achieved in organizational life (Nutley and Osborne 1994). There has accordingly been concern about the sheer pace of public service reform and the danger of falling into the 'permanent revolution' syndrome. Yet, at the same time, given recent challenges change has become as imperative for the public sector as for the private sector. It is something that does have profound implications for organizational culture – if the change is to be other than purely superficial – notwithstanding the long timescales involved in turning this around (Asquith 1994; Buckland and Joshua 1992; Thomson 1992).

3.5   ORGANIZATIONAL CHANGE: CATALYSTS AND CONSTRAINTS

3.5.1 Top-down pressures and local mediation

There are factors facilitating and inhibiting organizational change, forces both driving and restraining this process – hence the insights to be derived from 'force-field' analysis (Nutley and Osborne 1994). The impetus for organizational change is frequently generated by environmental turbulence and external pressures. After 1979 the pace was set by national political agendas, in the form of the 'Thatcherite project' and associated legislative programmes. This strong 'top-down' political commitment to change and the restructuring of public institutions (with pressure not only to change structures but also ruling organizational assumptions and public service cultures) might indeed be construed as a form of radical shock treatment (Pettigrew, Ferlie and McKee 1992).

But there were also the wider, more deep-rooted environmental forces at work – economic, technological, demographic and socio-cultural mentioned in Chapters 1 and 2. Indeed, as indicated in the **reinventing government** context, the organizational and managerial changes in the public sector may be symptomatic of broader processes of restructuring in a 'post-Fordist' world, bureaucratic design principles reflecting a passing era geared towards mass production of goods and services for undifferentiated markets, as opposed to specialized production for niche markets (Hoggett 1991; Stoker 1989a). These pressures also explain the increasing tendency to use external change agents and therefore 'the many private consultants now thronging the lobbies of government buildings . . . ' (Cellan-Jones 1992). The 'new blood' syndrome is a related phenomenon. For example, some of the chief executives of the *Next Steps* departmental agencies were recruited from outside traditional civil service channels to provide fresh momentum in changing established organizational cultures. Inter-organizational comparison can have a similar catalytic effect, as in the dissemination of good practice through the local authority networks.

However, organizational change is internally generated as well as externally induced. In local government attention had tended to focus on the challenges presented by the Thatcherite reforms, yet local political mediation can be a significant determinant of local change too. This helps to explain differential responses to external pressures. A case in point was Kent County Council's (KCC) structural, management and cultural revolution as an authority in the vanguard of local innovation. This, to an extent, pre-dated Thatcher's accession to office, although the new national political context provided additional impetus for the forces of reform to prevail over those of reaction. What happened at KCC was indeed in large part attributable to local political initiative, in some respects a local equivalent of the 'Thatcher revolution' nationally: 'Global forces which foster change do not translate automatically, or even readily, into reform strategies at the local level. They must be mediated politically' (Holliday 1991: 456).

In the National Health Service top-down pressures have also been locally mediated, leading Pettigrew, Ferlie and McKee (1992) to contrast 'receptive' change contexts with 'non-receptive' ones. Their research demonstrated the unevenness and variability of change, with national reforms played out in local settings, more radical in their impact in some areas than others. Although top-down pressures were not without significance, they had not produced similar effects across all localities given this differential receptivity. Thus, the simple pressure-response model is too crude. The 'non-receptive' context also highlights that the constraints on change should not be under-estimated.

3.5.2 Precipitating dynamics and enabling capabilities

There are always factors obstructing as well as promoting change and, as with catalysts, these impediments assume both external and internal forms. Institutional inertia and entrenched cultures are perennial obstacles, as is resistance from those regarding change as threatening, the conflicts of interest which are an endemic feature of organizational politics accentuated during a period of major upheaval. In the case of public institutions, the lack of self-evident crisis when there is no financial 'bottom line' has been a further barrier to change, though policies such as compulsory competitive tendering obviously changed the ground rules. Moreover, organizations may not be well equipped to handle change, lacking the necessary competencies. Change, consequently, is not only about precipitating dynamics; there must be an enabling capability for it to be successfully achieved, partly a matter of transformational leadership, but also one of knowledge, expertise and skills (Hinings and Greenwood 1988).

Pettigrew, Ferlie and McKee's (1992) research raised the question of why the rate and pace of change differed across district health authorities. The explanations were manifold, given the multiplicity of driving and inhibiting forces at work in the change process.

The propensity and ability to change is affected by the interplay of many variables. The combined effect of a series of factors will determine whether the forces of stability or reform are likely to prevail.

One framework for systematizing those variables has been developed by Hinings and Greenwood (1988). Contextual environmental pressures undeniably figure in the equation, but so do the actions of organizational members in interpreting the meaning of external changes and deciding on appropriate responses – a function of their values and beliefs. Internally, account must also be taken of political realities, how change is likely to reverberate to the advantage or disadvantage of different interest positions, the outcome in turn dependent upon organizational power structures. To this must be added the necessary organizational capacity to make the transition required by pressures for change. It is these complex interactions that determine whether institutions retain or move away from an established organizational design, indicating why some achieve transformation whereas others are locked within, or struggle to escape from, an established design 'archetype'.

3.5.3 Front-line realities

Even in favourable circumstances there are likely to be some grounds for scepticism about the penetration and durability of reform, especially as changing culture – and therefore values, attitudes and behaviour – can be a protracted process. The impact may be very patchy in the more peripheral parts of the organization and with variations departmentally say in a local authority context (Holliday 1991). Support for changes imposed from the 'top' – a feature of recent public sector reforms (albeit as indicated above with scope for local negotiation and mediation) – may be only token as they percolate downwards, especially where political clout is a substitute for a real cultural revolution. The vantage point certainly makes all the difference to how the change process is perceived, the cynicism often displayed by junior staff creating something of a credibility gap for senior management (Cellan-Jones 1992).

Thus, consumerism can appear in a very different light at the organizational sharp end where front-line encounters with members of the public occur. The need to paper over the cracks because of inadequate resourcing engenders not only staff frustration and dashed expectations on the part of service users, but high stress situations and even client aggression (Harrow and Shaw 1992). Indeed, whereas strategic managers see many opportunities arising from the change process, those further down the line may perceive the consequences of change as pushing the system into crisis, virtual chaos and almost terminal decline, as staff struggle to keep afloat with too few people and too little money (*The Guardian* 1990).

3.6   STRATEGIC ORGANIZATIONAL CHANGE

3.6.1 Transformation and evolution

Hinings and Greenwood view strategic change as transformational, entailing fundamental organizational reorientation, as opposed to more routine adaptation intended to solve essentially operational problems. It therefore relates to a major shift from one organizational design 'archetype' to another, an archetype defined as 'a particular composition of ideas, beliefs and values connected with structural and system attributes' (1988: 18). Alternatively a distinction can be made between changes that redefine existing parameters and those that take place within these parameters (Nutley and Osborne 1994). Others make the contrast between deep cultural change and surface change.

But a recasting of organizational structures and systems in the shape of a new set of ideas and values is not easily achieved. Hence outcomes other than what Hinings and Greenwood (1988) call the successful reorientation 'track'. Inertia may prevail; experiments with alternatives to existing arrangements are discontinued; the organization may be left in a state of almost suspended animation, failing to obtain any clear design coherence. Thus, the attempt to bring about transformation in the public sector by replacing the traditional public service with a new business ethos has often generated enormous tensions, two cultures uneasily co-existing in the same organization.

Nor is change necessarily in a consistent direction, the reality often one of considerable oscillation. Rather than a simple linear progression change is typically messy, precarious and reversible (Pettigrew, Ferlie and McKee 1992). There are elements of trial and error (Nutley and Osborne 1994), although organizational experimentation can be used as a conscious strategy for building critical mass in support of change. The nature of its diffusion is such – recalling the point about differential rates of innovation – that institutions in any sample organizational set (local authorities for example) will be located at different points along a continuum of change, with the pace of reform fluctuating and therefore the existence of laggards as well as innovators (Isaac-Henry and Painter 1991a).

This raises questions about the actual dynamics of organizational change. Even transformational change is likely to be brought about through an evolutionary, gradualistic process. Indeed, the total quality management (TQM) philosophy makes a virtue of continuous improvement:

> In the TQM approach there are no quick fixes but a belief that high-quality change ... is the product of 1–2 per cent of improvements achieved over a wide range of processes on a continuing basis ... small incremental improvements are continually achieved ...
>
> (*Morgan and Murgatroyd 1994: 22*)

It is common for there to be a succession of initiatives to maintain the momentum of a reform process and not necessarily part of some preconceived plan. The reform of Whitehall and the Civil Service post-1979 exemplifies such an approach.

Thus, the 1994 White Paper was 'a continuation in an unprecedentedly long period of administrative reform' (Chapman 1994: 605). What started out as relatively minor

1979:   The Rayner Efficiency Scrutinies launched to carry out detailed investigations of discrete administrative operations with a view to promoting greater cost-consciousness in Whitehall.

1982:   The Financial Management Initiative gets off the ground as a more systematic attempt to raise standards of financial stewardship in government departments.

1988:   The Agency Management Initiative takes reform along the road of major structural reorganization, moving responsibility closer to the point of service delivery, thus reinforcing the trend towards greater devolved management initiated by the FMI.

1991:   The above initiative was also conducive in central government operations to the customer focus at the heart of the *Citizen's Charter* programme.

1991:   Later the same year, the *Competing For Quality* initiative increased the tempo for the market testing of civil servant jobs and in creating external competitive threats potentially an even more fundamental change than the creation of departmental agencies.

1994:   The *Continuity and Change Civil Service* White Paper (Cm 2627), apart from giving departments greater responsibility for determining their own management structures and efficiency strategies to achieve centrally stipulated targets, outlined reforms of the Senior Civil Service, proposing to place top Whitehall officials on written employment (performance-related) contracts, and with provision for open competition from outside candidates for these senior appointments.

Figure 3.2   Civil Service reform post-1979: a tale of successive initiatives

tinkering eventually reached such proportions that there were even those ready to proclaim the death of the Civil Service as we have known it! In retrospect it does indeed amount to strategic (transformational) change.

3.6.2 A strategic management perspective

When all the qualifications have been made, the accelerating pace of technological, economic and social change and the stark reality of a turbulent environment, means that skills in the management of change are now at a premium: 'Today all managers must realize that change is going to be a constant feature of their working lives. Skills in being an effective change leader are at the core of the management competencies needed for the twenty-first century' (Carnall 1991: viii). Given the cumulative effects of radical policy initiatives since 1979 and their underpinning assumptions, the explicit management of change (Thomson 1992) is as important for public sector institutions as in any other organizational context: 'increasingly, the most fundamental role of the public services manager is managing change' (Holtham 1992: 108).

> As the Civil Service example above demonstrates, increasingly **strategic** change management is the issue. Hence the relevance of the insights derived from a strategic management perspective.

A turbulent environment may mean that the organization needs to (re)position itself accordingly (a process evident not least within the Labour Party to make it a more effective electoral force again). The magnitude of the challenges being faced therefore calls for an (outward) environmental orientation as opposed to organizational insularity. This underlines the importance of organizational intelligence and environmental scanning, so that the significance of key trends and developments is discerned. Most important, it is a matter of being proactive rather than simply reacting to events and succumbing to short-term crisis management. As Train and Stewart indicate, the latter danger is one that has been all too familiar to the Prison Service:

> The pressures which are placed upon it are many and varied and there is a risk that in seeking to respond to them the Prison Service could become an entirely reactive organization, constantly changing direction to meet the needs of the moment and without a longer-term vision

(1992: 259)

Identifying issues crucial for continuing organizational success and effectiveness, particularly by making an assessment of PEST (political, economic, social and technological) forces, is integral to the strategic analysis that forms the foundation for strategic choices. These choices, in turn, entail taking a longer-term view about the organization's prospective position, thereby raising 'actors' eyes beyond their immediate preoccupations' (Elcock 1993: 63). It demands a willingness to look afresh at fundamental assumptions.

Putting in place a corresponding strategic framework requires a mission (or position) statement that defines the 'core' business (what the organization exists to do and underpinning values). With this in mind – as well as ministers' wider ideological view on the appropriate role of government agencies – the Home Office has, for example, been undertaking a review of 'core' policing functions. From a mission statement can be derived broad strategic objectives relating to general organizational direction (where it is going). These are then translated into more specific operational objectives for discrete organizational activities. Such objectives will be reflected in organizational priorities and resource allocations, with performance review also a vital part of the process. Thus, the structural changes brought about by the *Next Steps* agency initiative in Whitehall were to enable ministers and departmental headquarters to move away from an operational to a more strategic focus (Morley 1993). However, ironically events in the Prison Service (notably those surrounding the removal of its Director-General, Derek Lewis, in October 1995) – itself with agency status – graphically revealed the difficulties of making this distinction in practice, given the pressures for ministerial involvement and intervention.

3.6.3 Strategic flexibility and implementation

Here we touch again upon the distinctive characteristics of policy making in the public domain. Apart from the lack of political value consensus, it is argued that government is increasingly facing conditions of uncertainty, not least because of the rapidity and complexity of social changes, placing a premium on 'the learning society' (Ranson and Stewart 1994; Stewart 1995b). But this raises the more general issue of the strategic flexibility and strategic learning required in an increasingly turbulent world. Thus, rather than the order and control at the heart of conventional management theory, insights derived from chaos theory may be more apposite: 'Chaos, part of complexity theory, emerged in the natural sciences as an attempt to describe unpredictable, turbulent phenomena (flames in a fire, eddies in a stream) which are resistant to conventional modelling' (Caulkin 1994b). The distinction between 'planned' and 'emergent' strategy (McKevitt 1992: 35) is certainly pertinent. Whereas the former places the emphasis on organizational direction and control, the latter shifts the focus more to organizational learning. It was indeed emphasized earlier just how messy the change process can be.

Strategies must also be grounded in organizational realities and capabilities. Hence the significance of SWOT analyze s – the strengths and weaknesses of the organization in relation to the opportunities and threats being faced. In the case of the public sector many would contend that this must include the characteristics of professional service organizations. The conflicts that have arisen with the expectations of these independent-minded professional groups bring the attendant danger of potential organizational strengths being turned into weaknesses. Here we are dealing with issues of strategic implementation, that is, translating strategy into action. But it is not just about the mechanics of putting in place a strategic framework of the kind described above. It may entail structural, behavioural and cultural changes. There are issues of support and ownership. The active commitment of a number of agencies may be required where there are 'resource interdependencies'. It is in precisely such a situation of increasing organizational interdependence that the significance of the strategic methodology discussed in this section will be illustrated in Chapter 10. But the issues raised above lead us directly back to the skills involved in the management of change.

3.7   MANAGING THE CHANGE PROCESS

3.7.1 The politics of change management

For the reasons stated earlier, effectiveness and performance depend on appropriate application of such skills. This, of course, raises the fundamental question of how change can be successfully brought about. Reference has been made to the importance of leaders with a strong commitment to change, willing to take radical initiatives from the 'top' – albeit subject to local mediation – the role of Margaret Thatcher herself in Number 10 proving crucial to the implementation of management reform in government (Elcock 1990) and a mantle inherited by John Major. Indeed, events following the Conservative election victory of 1979 have been viewed as a battle for political control over the Whitehall bureaucracy, breaking down resistance to cultural change (a private-sector-style ethos and eventually major structural reorganization – in the form of agency creation – very much part of this process). Yet, simultaneously there were benefits to central government in weakening local democracy to reduce the scope for 'recalcitrant' behaviour (Kingdom 1991).

Such constructions on events bring concepts of power and interests to the surface, alerting us to the utility of political imagery in analysing the management of organizational change (Morgan 1986). It is a perspective with surprisingly wide applications, focusing attention for example on narrowly-conceived approaches to the management of technological change (refer to Chapter 6), where the cultural, behavioural and ultimately political dimensions of information technology are overlooked. Ignoring the impact on power structures and status, or perceived threats to the positions of particular interested parties (the fact that change brings its casualties as well as winners explaining defensiveness and sources of resistance) can be fatal in organizations as politically complex as the National Health Service (Willcocks 1992). Indeed, the new managerial ideology has been about strengthening the position of line management relative to that of the health professionals (Pettigrew, Ferlie and McKee 1992). Certainly success in building a power base can have a crucial bearing on the change process. Yet, as previously indicated, there is a distinct danger of being drawn into impositional change strategies where, other than at senior management levels, mobilization of support has an extremely tenuous basis. Taking this into account, the prerequisites for effective innovation, and therefore the main ingredients of successful change programmes, take on a rather different complexion.

3.7.2 Non-impositional change strategies

Apart from building on rather than disregarding established organizational strengths, the emphasis is then on consultation and openness. The object is to promote commitment to and shared ownership of initiatives – albeit not something to which an increasingly casualized and outsourced workforce is necessarily conducive – and above all to build trust. If perceived threats from the change process are to be minimized and a sense of common purpose achieved, overcoming mutual distrust is essential. Keeping staff informed and involving, indeed empowering, them becomes a priority. Hence communication strategies, including the necessary staff feedback mechanisms, are indispensable to success. At the very least, the high-level management tasks involved in change situations include not only the ability to formulate coherent responses to new circumstances, clearly articulating organizational values, purpose and mission. That strategic vision must also be communicated, listening to various stakeholders to establish the degree of congruence between behaviour and statements of intent, so that any disjunction can be acted upon (Thomson 1992).

Change strategies, then, should clearly convey the related objectives, the underlying pattern to the process and the prospective benefits. This is assisted if there is a consistency to initiatives, as well as evidence of tangible achievements. In fact, to build support there is a strong case for starting with initiatives that can produce rapid results, and for ensuring that successes are publicized throughout the organization. Moreover, this raises the issue of changing the framework of incentives and rewards to bring about the desired behavioural changes. There should also be positive steps to provide the support mechanisms and training (or in certain cases dignified exit routes) to help those individuals struggling to cope with what is an unsettling process make the necessary adjustments. It is essential, moreover, that senior managers convey informal signals that are not at variance with the new values and approaches the organization is seeking to cultivate (Carnall 1991; Isaac-Henry and Painter 1991a; Nutley and Osborne 1994).

3.7.3 The efficacy of alternative change strategies

One particularly important issue in the effective management of change is the sequence in which alterations to the constituent elements of organizational design occur, i.e. what should be changed and in which order (Hinings and Greenwood 1988)? How much priority should be respectively accorded to structures, processes, people, attitudes and behaviour and values and culture? There has been repeated preoccupation with structural change as a means of improving public sector performance (Elcock 1991). It has often been used as a solution for all problems, to the detriment of behavioural and cultural approaches to managing change (Nutley and Osborne 1994). What, in fact, is its efficacy given past faith in reshuffling the organization in public service agencies, in contrast to private manufacturing enterprizes which have been much more concerned with product development (Hickson, Butler, Cray, Mallory and Wilson 1989)? It may be a necessary – if not sufficient – condition for success, with a catalytic effect, symbolically concentrating minds and providing tangible manifestation of the need for change. Nonetheless, the extent to which there are differences in how the organization actually functions and in the attitudes and behaviour of staff, is the test in the final analysis (Isaac-Henry and Painter 1991a). Indeed, it is not just a matter of the impact of change strategies on the service deliverers, but ultimately on users' satisfaction and the extent to which they can discern improvements in service standards (Common, Flynn and Mellon 1992: Ch. 5).

There is, moreover, the importance of planning and managing the change process, and need for sensitive implementation of associated strategies. As previously indicated, internal analysis of the organization facilitates diagnosis of strengths and weaknesses, capabilities and resources, thereby focusing on obstacles to improvement, as well as on the scope for exploiting organizational attributes as a platform for change. If the changes concerned are of real significance to the organization, then appropriate priority should be given to overseeing the change process, adopting a project management approach, as exemplified by the *Next Steps* reform programme. The planned changes should have defined objectives, be sensibly phased and timetabled, with accountability for desired outcomes clearly allocated. In addition, effort should be made to empathize with the people who will feel the impact, attending to the anxieties, uncertainties and stress thereby created. Strategies for dealing with the related problems of resistance to change need to be addressed as well (Carnall 1991). In fact, proponents of changing organizational culture stress the need firstly to 'unfreeze' existing ideas and practices given the emotional attachment to established ways of doing things, then to inject momentum into the change process and finally to 'refreeze' thereby consolidating the new patterns (Buckland and Joshua 1992; Nutley and Osborne 1994).

Nonetheless, as emphasized earlier, there is a danger of viewing the change process too mechanistically.

> The fact that successful organizational change is not necessarily accomplished underlines the many pitfalls that can be encountered along the way. What constitutes an appropriate approach to the management of change must also to some extent depend on the prevailing circumstances.

If there is the public sector equivalent of a 'corporate turnaround' situation, with an operation's very survival at stake – as when facing the prospect of competitive tendering or market testing – then the changes obviously have to be achieved with greater urgency than might otherwise be the case. Much also depends on whether there is underlying agreement on the fundamental objectives of change. A consultative, information-sharing strategy will pay dividends in some contexts, but in a highly politically-charged situation an effective strategy is more likely to revolve around bargaining strategies (Nutley and Osborne 1994). Indeed, support for change will partly reflect the clash of ideas and hence outcome of the contest for legitimacy/ hegemony (Pettigrew, Ferlie and McKee 1992).

And although resistance may prove frustrating for strategic organizational managers, the fears and apprehensions of those on the receiving end can indeed be well-founded in relation to their own interests and values (i.e. one must be wary of assuming that negative attitudes towards change are irrational emotions). Moreover, the rapid and smooth progress that is feasible when opposition is muted or even non-existent can itself sometimes spell disaster: 'an ill-considered scheme . . . may be implemented, whose dangers and deficiencies will become apparent only later' (Elcock 1990: 71). Clearly, though, managing change goes beyond technical competence and planning prowess. Process skills – in communicating, influencing or negotiating – are often the key to success (Nutley and Osborne 1994).

3.8　THE MANAGEMENT OF CHANGE IN LOCAL GOVERNMENT

3.8.1　Challenging traditional assumptions

Managing the process of change and keeping up the momentum of reform is becoming a ubiquitous challenge. As we have seen, this applies to Whitehall as much as to any other part of the public sector, and reflected not least – as the Efficiency Unit has emphasized – in the departmental agency reforms:

> Many agencies have embarked ... upon an imaginative range of initiatives ... designed to ensure that change is implemented on a broad front and that they reinforce and complement each other ... though ... a great deal remains to be done to make staff more customer-oriented ... the centres of departments similarly need to ... develop new ways of working ... senior managers must now review their programmes for communicating and supporting the changes in attitude and behaviour needed if they are to make the most of Next Steps ...
>
> *(1991: 10)*

Indeed, a number of these agencies were showing increasing signs of being run like commercial businesses, preparing if necessary for market testing – or for that matter future transfer to the private sector.

However, local authorities form a particularly interesting case study. Their critics maintain that as public bureaucracies they have been slow to adapt, yet reforms in this context are of central importance to the Government's concept of a changed public sector (Isaac-Henry and Painter 1991b). There has in fact been very little respite as the reforming impetus continued to change the face of local government (Isaac-Henry and Painter 1992) and indicating that the challenge may not be so much 'the management of change or the movement from one point of stability to another, but the management of changing' (Clarke and Stewart 1990: 24). Again, recently reform has notably affected the structure of local government, comprehensive reorganizations having been completed in Scotland and Wales, whilst continuing on a piecemeal basis in England under the auspices of the **Local Government Commission**. The extension of compulsory competitive tendering, as well as the transfer of functions to local non-elected agencies has, moreover, further diminished the involvement of local authorities in direct service provision.

Thus, apart from the increasing propensity towards central government intervention in local affairs, some observers lamented 'the differentiation scenario of an ever more fragmented, complex and unaccountable system' (Rhodes 1991: 109). Elsewhere, this has been viewed as the 'Americanization' effect: 'the Conservative government is shifting local government in Britain swiftly towards American models – towards a more fragmented, more privatized, more private sector oriented form' (Hambleton 1990: 7, 8). Because of this fragmentation of institutional responsibility 'local governance' rather than 'local government' is becoming a more apposite description of the changing realities, a development more closely analyzed in Chapter 10.

We are seeing a redefinition of local government's previously established role 'as a prime service deliverer for the welfare state' (*Gray and Jenkins 1991: 465*). Inevitably, this raises fundamental issues about the very nature of the local government system, presenting a challenge to the way in which local authorities have traditionally been organized.

This has been more for the running and local administration of services than for community government. Clarke and Stewart indeed emphasize that in the key choices now to be faced the 'issue at stake is not just the future of local government but how the UK is governed in the changing society of the 1990s and beyond' (1991: 76, 77).

3.8.2 Managerial vitality

Therefore the key assumptions underpinning the local government system have been vigorously questioned: 'In these circumstances, it is hardly surprising that the management of change loomed so large and began to dominate the local government agenda' (Isaac-Henry and Painter 1991a: 69). Apart from inevitable variability given the nature of the change diffusion process, processes of local mediation and negotiation are likely to be particularly pronounced in this context because of the different characteristics of local political systems. Indeed, Chapter 10 will indicate the range of responses to the growth of local non-elected agencies. Nonetheless, the reaction of many local authorities to this period of enormous upheaval remains instructive; '[They] are ... rapidly and radically [changing] the way they manage their business. There is a new ... dynamism ... and a sense of being at a watershed ... ' (Stoker 1989b: 5). One account of a comprehensive programme of reform on Nottingham City Council emphasized however that 'changes have not been easy for the vast majority of authorities who had, over the years, developed into traditional hierarchical bureaucracies ... ' (Buckland and Joshua 1992: 21).

Indeed, another account (Isaac-Henry and Painter 1991a) points to a new uncertainty in some authorities about their primary mission, but more positively the attempts to answer anew the elementary question of any organization, namely 'what business are we in'? Promotion of a less bureaucratic culture and therefore a more managerial ethos could be discerned, so raising sights above the standard operating procedures. The importance of organizational self-appraisal was increasingly appreciated – posing critical and challenging questions about whether the authority is where it wants to be and what it is that is to be achieved. There was a corresponding recognition of the need for a greater sense of direction and future vision, given that mere survival is hardly a positive motivating factor. Moreover, the promotion of learning organizational cultures is symptomatic of an endeavour to change previously insular attitudes.

Strategic management too was being given more priority and in addressing key policy issues arising from environmental change a more proactive stance was being encouraged – strengthening organizational capabilities for shaping the future. As a corollary, there had been a redirection of the main focus of activity in the central core of the organization, with roles reviewed and structures reformed accordingly. Strategic teams were in fact established in some authorities to spearhead the process of change, freed from direct operational responsibilities and as such, able to transcend the demands of departmental routines. The 'new blood' phenomenon has been much in evidence, too, with a growing inclination for chief executive officers (CEOs) to be recruited from outside the appointing authority.

The 'progressive' authorities were therefore developing a more integrated vision and clearer perception of where their organization is going, defining corporate priorities with reference to some sense of overall purpose. In fact, a whole raft of reforms have been required: 'local government has had to develop a stronger sense of strategic leadership, an increased emphasis on performance, quality and better financial management and a greater concern for the consumers of local services' (Buckland and Joshua 1992: 21). It is indeed attempting to meet the demands of change, rising to the challenge of the gauntlet thrown down by central government, as well as responding to the other manifold environmental pressures. This amounts to 'a much more reassuring picture of the system's adaptability in response to environmental turbulence than is usually gleaned from the media's obsession with recalcitrant behaviour and the conflicts bedevilling central-local relations' (Isaac-Henry and Painter 1991a: 87).

Of course, managerial vitality is only one of a number of factors to be taken into account in judging the overall health of local government. At stake in the final analysis is the condition of local political institutions and therefore, as Clarke and Stewart (1991) emphasize, ultimately the democratic strength and constitutional position of local authorities within our system of government. It is a matter systematically addressed by the **Commission on Local Democracy**.

3.8.3 Managing change in a political setting

Nor should we overlook those considerations, highlighted earlier, with a crucial bearing on successful change management. Given that it is not just a matter of willingness to change but the ability to do so, which factors have therefore been critical to the management of change in this particular context? A series of interviews conducted with CEOs in a sample of local authorities during 1989–90 provided insights on the nature of some of those factors (Isaac-Henry and Painter 1991b), many of them evident from the account immediately above.

In relation to the last observation in Figure 3.3, the new competitive disciplines unleashed on local government – notably as a result of compulsory tendering – and the pursuit of a customer care ethos point to the increasing relevance of business analogues (the convergence hypothesis). Nonetheless, as the example of the Benefits Agency cited earlier demonstrates, unique constraints continue to apply in the public sector.

Indeed, senior managers in local government remain very much part of a political process, 'operating in the full glare of publicity, subject to the governmental resource rationing system, the constraints associated with handling taxpayers' money, and with public accountability placing ... limits on the scope for a commercial ethos' (Isaac-Henry and Painter 1991b: 17). These realities are viewed negatively in some quarters, making life more difficult in comparison with management in the private sector. Yet, democracy is absolutely fundamental to local government's claims to independent governing status and to its distinctiveness of mission and purpose, the very thing which those fearful for the future see increasingly threatened – not least through seemingly inexorable centralizing forces. Nonetheless, some encouragement can be derived from the adaptability and resilience of local government in recent years –

- Effective leadership and vision, with clear objectives to pinpoint the direction in which the organization should go – and the greater regard for priorities thereby implied.

  The younger 'new wave' CEOs, many appointed specifically to act as catalysts for reform, increasingly saw their function as that of strategic change managers.

- Turnover of senior officers to convey appropriate signals within the organization, and in recognition of just how important it is for those in strategically pivotal positions to be positively receptive to change.

  However, too great an inclination to recruit key personnel from outside sources is likely to be detrimental to the fostering of managerial talent within the organization.

- An appropriate management framework, to focus attention on such matters as 'institutional values, mission statements, allocation of resources with reference to explicit objectives, and establishing an organization capable of achieving those objectives' (*Isaac-Henry and Painter 1991b:16*)

- Self-sustaining change properties also need to be cultivated – for instance, creating a capability for flexible responses by moving towards a more 'bottom-up' and less 'top-down' organizational design.

- Employee involvement too is a prerequisite for success, staff needing to be convinced of the necessity for change if they are to be favourably disposed – therefore motivated to implement such changes – and feel part of the mission (whilst not forgetting the implications for change management of organizational politics!).

  Hence the importance of human resources more generally, including the contribution that staff development and training can make in equipping people with appropriate skills, confidence and understanding (refer to Chapter 5).

- This highlights the importance of the 'softer' side of managing change, that is of communication, motivational and, again, leadership skills.

- The institutional environment is of significance, notably whether there are established organizational strengths to provide a firm foundation for innovation (linking up with the notion of 'receptive' and 'non-receptive' organizational contexts referred to earlier).

  Those local authorities with a conservative culture were at something of a disadvantage, although paradoxically central government intervention helped to break down resistance to change, allowing management to tackle long-standing problems.

- Therefore successful reform strategies often require a combination of external and internal (managerial) levers for change (Common, Flynn and Mellon, 1992: Ch. 7).

  In the case of a local authority, however, the many stakeholders involved in and affected by change (managers, staff, politicians, citizens, taxpayers, customers and various outside groups and organizations) can make the process extremely difficult.

- Given the nature of local authorities as elected institutions, an effective political-officer partnership is particularly vital to effective change management, so engaging the active commitment of councillors to reform.

- Even in the absence of decisive political leadership and when, instead, reform must therefore be officer-led, account still has to be taken of preparedness to undertake change at this level – underlining the political skills, awareness and sensitivity that such an institutional context demands.

Figure 3.3 Factors crucial to successful change management in local government

even as it goes through further processes of organizational upheaval. Impediments to organizational change in this setting, as in any other, nonetheless underline the priority that should be accorded to formulating coherent strategies for effectively managing the change process. Even then there will be many unanticipated and unpredictable eventualities!

3.9   CONCLUDING COMMENTS

The managerial reforms addressed in this chapter are – at least in part – a manifestation of a particular political environment and set of values about the appropriate role for the state (consult Chapter 2), with related assumptions about what was necessary in order to tackle economic underperformance (Thomson 1992). To that extent, these reforms are themselves contingent. The corollary is that the future direction of the public sector could be affected by any change in this political context (Chapman 1991). The onset of the Clinton Presidency in the United States was taken by some to be an early sign that the political pendulum was beginning to swing again after the ascendancy of the 'New Right'. This was hardly borne out by the sweeping Republican gains in the mid-term Congressional elections. And significantly, Clinton and his Vice-President were themselves zealot apostles of 'reinventing' government.

But the disarray to which the Major government was reduced following the forced exit from the European Exchange Rate Mechanism in autumn 1992 – and from which it never entirely recovered – meant that the British political scene began to show greater fluidity after the long Conservative hegemony. This, in turn, could have implications for the longevity of some of the prevailing values and assumptions of this era, thereby creating new uncertainties for the future direction of public management. Consequently, it may be necessary to start looking afresh not least at some of those panaceas peddled so convincingly by the management consultancy industry as part of a reforming orthodoxy now potentially in difficulty. Change agents in public management will conceivably soon be addressing a different set of challenges. The Shadow Cabinet themselves were being sent on a business school management course. More organizational repositioning. And yes, indeed, the management of **changing** rather than simply the management of change!

3.10   CHAPTER SUMMARY

The following key learning points emerge from this chapter:

- Reform in the UK has increasingly constituted a paradigm shift in departing from the traditional bureaucratic basis for organizing and delivering public services.
- Hence the significance of Osborne and Gaebler's notion of 'reinventing' government and associated 'entrepreneurial' principles (see Figure 3.1).
- Nonetheless the influence on reforms of a business management role model remains problematic in a public sector context.

- There are forces both driving and restraining organizational change in the public sector as elsewhere – emphasizing the utility of a 'force-field' framework.
- The significance of (environmental) political, economic, social and technological pressures for change also point to the utility of PEST analysis.
- Indeed public service reform has been construed as a manifestation of restructuring for a post-Fordist world (bureaucratic design more suited to a passing era of mass production for mass consumption).
- The external pressures for public institutional change have included 'top-down' political influences – yet such pressures are also locally mediated and negotiated (hence the unevenness and variability of change).
- The internal inhibitions on change include conflicts of interest and therefore organizational politics.
- Yet the very notion of a paradigm shift suggests that the challenge facing the public sector has become one of strategic (i.e. transformational) change and entailing fundamental reorientation.
- This explains the relevance of the insights derived from a strategic management perspective – including the significance of SWOT analysis.
- Yet, the dynamics of organizational change are such that even in this context evolutionary processes are likely to prevail – as in the case of post-1979 Whitehall reform (see Figure 3.2).
- Nonetheless, there has increasingly been a premium on skills in the management of (strategic) change in the public sector.
- It is therefore important to identify the main ingredients of successful change management, bearing in mind that what constitutes an effective strategy will depend on the prevailing circumstances.
- Local government provides an instructive case study of such change management given recent challenges to its traditional role and consequently the pressures for fundamental reorientation.
- However, there are renewed (political) uncertainties surrounding the future direction of public management.

TEXT-BASED QUESTIONS

1.   Explain the reasons why change management skills have become imperative in the public services.

2.   What is the essence of Osborne and Gaebler's 'reinventing government' thesis in this respect?

3.   What consequences may be associated with the adoption of a business management role model for public services?

4.   What is distinctive about strategic organizational change? Which insights can correspondingly be derived from a strategic management perspective?

5.   Careful thought needs to go into the planning, managing and implementing of a change strategy if it is to be coherent and effective. But what are the main ingredients that should be incorporated into a successful change strategy?

6. Which management of change issues have arisen specifically in the local government context? What factors are particularly crucial to the successful management of change in this institutional setting (see Figure 3.3)?

ASSIGNMENT 1

Undertaking the following three-part assignment will help to bring together many of the key themes and issues tackled in this chapter:

(a) Identify the principal environmental changes affecting a selected public service organization and the threats or opportunities likely to arise as a consequence;
(b) Indicate to what extent the analysis of the associated trends has strategic significance for the organization – and if so how the organization should (re)position itself bearing in mind its strengths and weaknesses;
(c) Outline which factors should particularly be taken into account so as to manage the associated change process effectively.

ASSIGNMENT 2

An alternative assignment which can help to develop a feel for the nature and extent of change taking place in public sector organizations – together with the associated problems – is to use Osborne and Gaebler's ten principles of 'entrepreneurial government' as a benchmark (See Figure 3.1).

Having compared these principles with those on which public service delivery has traditionally been based, again taking a selected public service organization:

(a) Identify how many of the Osborne and Gaebler principles are now apparent in that organization;
(b) Where this is not the case whether this reflects adversely on that organization's capacity for change;
(c) Alternatively, whether it demonstrates some intrinsic difficulties in applying such principles.

Following on from (c) there is also an opportunity to consider whether this alternative to the traditional bureaucratic paradigm may create as many problems as it resolves.

FURTHER READING

Hinings, C.R. and Greenwood, R. (1988) *The Dynamics of Strategic Change*, Blackwell, Oxford. Develops a framework for systematizing the variables impinging on strategic change, with specific reference to design 'archetypes' in local authorities in England and Wales.

Isaac-Henry, K. and Painter, C. (1991) Organizational Response to Environmental Turbulence: The Management of Change in English Local Government. *The International Journal of Public Sector Management*, **4** (4), pp. 5–20. Explicitly addresses management of change issues in the same institutional setting, based on more recent interviews with Chief Executive Officers in a sample of local authorities.

Lawton, A. and Rose, A. (1994) *Organization and Management In The Public Sector*, Pitman, London. A lucid overview of many of the public sector changes considered in this chapter.

Nutley, S. and Osborne, S.P. (1994) *The Public Sector Management Handbook*, Longman, Harlow. Chapter 12 specifically addresses 'managing during times of change'.

Painter, C. (1994) Public Service Reform: Reinventing or Abandoning Government? *The Political Quarterly* **65** (3), pp. 242–62. Considers the relevance of Osborne and Gaebler in the context of UK public service reform.

Pettigrew, A., Ferlie, E. and McKee, L. (1992) *Shaping Strategic Change – Making Change in Large Organizations: The Case of the National Health Service*, Sage, London. Addresses 'receptive' and 'non-receptive' contexts for change with particular reference to one of the major public services.

Ranson, S. and Stewart, J. (1994) *Management for the Public Domain*, Macmillan, London. A timely reminder of what is distinctive about managing in the public sector.

Train, C.J. and Stewart, C. (1992) Strategic Management in the Prison Service, in *Handbook of Public Services Management* (eds. C. Pollitt and S. Harrison), Blackwell, Oxford, pp. 258–67. Clear account of a strategic framework in another public service, and particularly poignant given recent controversies surrounding the management of the Prison Service.

RESOURCE AND PERFORMANCE MANAGEMENT IN PUBLIC SERVICE ORGANIZATIONS 4

John Rouse

4.1 CHAPTER PREVIEW

This chapter is concerned with managing and evaluating the performance of public service organizations, with an emphasis upon the broader organizational, cultural and political context. The chapter addresses:

- the major critiques which have informed the performance management movement's meaning, content and approach
- the frameworks for addressing performance management and, in particular, a discussion of financial, budgetary, managerial and political interpretations of accountable performance and quality service provision
- an outline of the strategic approach to performance management and a discussion of the factors critical to its successful implementation, with a focus upon performance measurement
- examples of performance indicators and a discussion of some of the pitfalls involved in their implementation

It will conclude by emphasizing the importance of organizational context and culture to the appropriate definition and successful implementation of a performance management approach. It will stress that performance improvement is a journey without an end, a process of continuous improvement, where politics must be treated as integral and central rather than inhibiting and peripheral.

4.2   THE ISSUES

It is a recurrent theme of this book that public service organizations are different from private organizations in a number of important ways and these differences are significant for public managers. With reference to this chapter's concerns, perhaps the most critical issue is that the goals of public service organizations are rarely clear or consensual given the multiple constituencies of stakeholders involved and the complex environments of public service delivery.

> Goals and objectives are most likely to be multiple and complex and outputs difficult to measure, with the consequence that evaluating performance is problematic.

Since the agenda for public managers is frequently set by politicians and the stakeholder base is wide, the key feature is that of complex and extensive accountability. However, private and public organizations have one fundamental thing in common: they use scarce resources, both human and material, to produce outputs which are consumed by their users, clients or customers to achieve valued outcomes. It is this relationship between inputs, activities, outputs and the outcomes (impacts of the service on the wide range of 'users') and the ways its productivity and quality might be improved which is the focus of this chapter. We use the term **performance management** to describe the range of processes, techniques and methods to achieve such an improvement. We begin by examining the development of the performance management movement in the public services sector.

4.3   THE PERFORMANCE MANAGEMENT MOVEMENT

Elsewhere there has been reference to the complex pressures which gave birth to the performance management movement. Hadley and Young (1990) have classified these pressures in terms of three major critiques, each of which questioned the traditional ethos of public service organizations and each of which has informed the particular meaning of performance management and the most appropriate means to its achievement. First, they identify the group that probably had the most influence on the 1979 Conservative Government, the **'marketeers'**.

4.3.1 The marketeers

This critique sprang mainly from the work of the New Right, discussed in Chapter 1 and 2, informed by a number of economic contributions all emphasizing the efficiency properties of the competitive market system. State provided services were seen, by contrast, as fundamentally and inherently flawed due to their organizational characteristics and the structure of incentives which face their managers.

In particular, their statutory protected positions, making them immune from the normal competitive pressures of the market, in conjunction with their need for political, financial and budgetary accountability, caused them to be obsessed with the control of their fixed cash-limited budgets, thereby encouraging an input cost control culture with little emphasis on the customer/client. As virtual monopolies they faced little competitive pressure in the product market since their customers had few if any alternative sources of supply. As state owned monopolies they faced even fewer competitive pressures in the capital market since they did not raise their capital in the open market, have share capital, pay dividends and could not be taken over. It is this attenuation of their property rights which was seen to cause an incentive failure on the part of public managers, since they faced no effective competitive market pressures to maximize performance both now and through time. They had effectively been captured by the special interests of professional supplier groups serving their own interests rather than those of users and the general public. Inefficiency manifested itself in a variety of ways: allocatively, in that the things produced were not the ones most wanted by customers; technically, in that production costs were higher than necessary; and dynamically, in that the organizations failed to be flexible, enterprising and responsive to new opportunities.

From this perspective, the only genuine solution to the 'problem' of public service agencies lay in their complete or partial privatization, thereby enhancing the role of external competitive forces to sharpen managerial incentives. Where such solutions were less possible then 'marketization' (Walsh 1995) of the public services themselves was advocated. This took a number of forms including the introduction of pricing and charging for public services, the use of vouchers and a variety of forms of contract management and the introduction of internal markets.

4.3.2 The empowerers

Hadley and Young (1990) refer to the second set of critics as the **empowerers**. Representing mainly the Centre and Left of the political spectrum they claimed that services produced by a centralized paternalistic state cast the citizen in a passive role since politicians, administrators and professionals decided what they needed and how it should be provided. Bureaucratic professionalism stressed administrative values – doing things right, rather than management values – doing the right thing (Newman and Clarke 1994). There was little opportunity for service users to become involved thereby reinforcing the passivity in service recipients and inefficiency in service providers. These critics stressed the need to reorganize provision **within** the public sector to make services more accessible, accountable and responsive to their users so as to empower rather than disable. From this perspective, appropriate methods could be developed to enhance performance in public service organizations by strengthening internal incentives rather than external market ones. Vital to all their reforms was a need to involve more directly the range of service users through the promotion of active citizenship and more direct forms of democratic participation and community governance.

4.3.3 Organizational reformers

The third group of critics are referred to as the **organizational reformers**, since the origin is largely from the field of organizational behaviour and management. Perhaps of most influence was Peters and Waterman's (1982) *In Search Of Excellence*, particularly its theme of 'close to the customer' as a critical ingredient of excellence in private organizations. Other principles of significance for successful organizations, private and public service ones, included: a bias for action, productivity through people and simultaneous loose-tight properties. More recently the major work of influence for public service organizations has been that of Osborne and Gaebler (1992) with their emphasis upon reinventing government (discussed in Chapter 3). These and related developments, particularly the enquiries of Rayner and Griffiths, led to arguments for a more business like approach and the need for a new performance culture in public service organizations, one driven by vision, learning, empowerment and a results driven customer orientation. In practical terms, it provided intellectual backing for management decentralization, financial devolution, 'new' human resource management, the quest for quality, for strategic thinking in a changing environment, and a more market-orientated approach.

Hence, a number of critiques with quite different intellectual roots were all pointing towards the need for more emphasis on a results orientated performance culture in public service organizations. Carter, Klein and Day (1992), however, argue that though enhancing public service performance became a major political issue in the early 1980s it represented a resurrection of earlier ideas rather than a revolution. It was yet another attempt to move from 'process politics' which tended to 'favour partisans such as agencies, bureaux and interest groups' (Schick 1973) to 'systems politics' which tended to favour 'the central allocators', particularly the Treasury. In an earlier era it was Planning, Programming, Budgeting Systems (PPBS), Management by Objectives (MBO), Programme Analysis and Review (PAR), Fulton and Bains. The 'second coming' (Carter, Klein and Day 1992) of the early 1980s included the 1982 Financial Management Initiative and the whole 'value for money' movement promulgated initially by the Audit Commission. Though this second coming was due partly to the cogency of the critiques above it was largely driven by the increasing fiscal stringency necessitated by counter-inflation policy objectives combined with rising public expectations. This fiscal pressure was to influence both the content and direction of the performance management movement and it was the source of much initial resistance. But what is the content of the performance management movement?

4.4 PERFORMANCE MANAGEMENT

4.4.1 A performance framework

Performance management is essentially concerned with enhancing the **value adding process**: that is, with increasing the productivity and quality of the relationship between organizational inputs/resources, outputs delivered, and outcomes achieved, where the latter focuses upon the impact of the services on a range of users. It is about making the difference between costs and benefits as large as possible. A simple and conventional illustration of the performance relationship is presented as Figure 4.1.

The inputs, for example, could be the teachers or health workers employed, the outputs the children educated or patients treated and the outcomes the increases in the education and health status of the population, valued in terms of their enhanced state of well-being.

However, though this remains a valuable way of conceptualizing the performance management framework it does have a tendency to over-simplify the situation. There are a number of complications which make the concept of successful performance and its achievement highly complex and elusive in public service organizations – far more so than in private ones.

- Public service organizations are characterized by **multiple stakeholders**. These include current users, potential users, voter citizens, elected members (and increasingly, unelected board members of QUANGO organizations), professional groups, front line staff, trade unions and managers. This is far more complex than the private sector where ultimately the owner/shareholder interest must prevail.

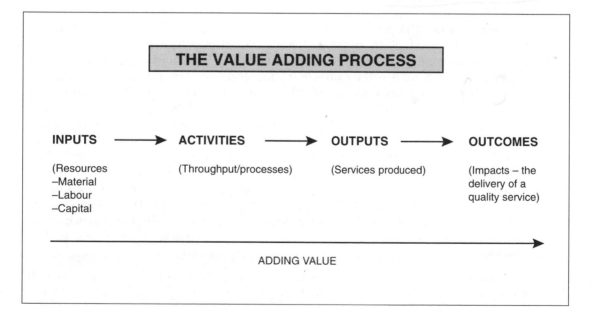

Figure 4.1 The value-adding process

- As a consequence, public service agencies have multiple and frequently **conflicting objectives** since each set of stakeholders may well have a different set of values and a different view on what is appropriate performance.
- A public service agency usually delivers a wide range of complex services and policies in a **non-market or quasi market environment** and is usually in a monopoly position. In such a setting value is not translated via prices into financial returns and must instead be imputed by more indirect means.
- There is the **nature of the public service** itself. Many public services are different from private ones in that, for example, they involve coercive relationships (policing), involve dependency (social security), are non-rejectable (arrest), involve conflict (a contested planning application) and have irreversible impacts (a court case lost). Many are such that outcomes only appear after a long time period has elapsed (education). Most are 'experience goods' rather than 'search goods' (Nelson 1970) since they cannot be investigated prior to purchase and can only be assessed in the process of use. What this means is that it is sometimes hard to distinguish between activities and processes and the output of a service, as the output is also the very process of being served. In a planning application, for example, there are at least two prime customers, the applicant and the public, probably in conflict. Any assessment of performance in this case is better focused on the process/activity rather than the actual outcome. For example, promising the public they will be counselled and their views taken into account, promising the developer they will be kept informed on how things are progressing and identifying a time scale. Hence, in many public services it is the quality of the interchange between provider and recipient which is vital to an assessment of quality performance (Gaster 1995).
- Public services are delivered in a **complex socio-political environment** resulting in considerable **uncertainty** in many public services surrounding the causal relationship between inputs, outputs and outcomes and the extent to which external factors influence the performance of this relationship. Hence, there can be doubt over the 'ownership' of organizational performance (Carter *et al.*, 1992). For example, changes in criminal activity may be the result of joint efforts by the police, probation service, the courts and prison service. It may also be more affected by the state of unemployment and other external events than the policies of any of these agencies.

  In addition this problem is being exacerbated as the public sector is becoming more diverse, differentiated and **fragmented**. Service outcomes are increasingly jointly produced with many other agencies as boundaries overlap and new networks of organizations emerge in place of integrated bureaucratic hierarchies.
- There is a further complication in that public organizations are not only concerned with doing the right thing but also about doing things right. The public is interested in not just outcome but also **process**. The political values of participation, negotiation and democracy may be seen as key ingredients of successful performance.

The net result of these essential characteristics of public service provision is that the meaning of successful performance and quality service delivery has many dimensions and is inherently contested.

> Performance assessment, it must be emphasized, is inevitably a polit-
> ical and value-laden exercise where judgement and, therefore, difference
> is inescapable.

Emphasizing the mutliplicity of stakeholders and the uncertainties and uncontrol-
lability of the essentially political environment ('multiple constituencies and multiple
environments') Moss Kanter and Summers (1987: 227) argue that:

> the significant questions about performance ... are ... not technical but concep-
> tual: not how to measure effectiveness or productivity but what to measure and
> how definitions and techniques are chosen and linked to other aspects of an
> organization's structure, functioning, and environmental relations.

It is argued that performance assessment in the public domain is a judgement that
has to be made politically and that the process of political debate through time will
generate performance criteria which will shift as values change (Stewart and Walsh
1994). To this extent then 'performance assessment is an exercise in political wisdom
not measurement' (ibid: 49). This means that the criteria for performance assessment
at any point in time are at least partly contingent on the prevailing ideological climate.
For Peter Jackson (1993: 9–10):

> Performance evaluation in public service organization is fraught with theoret-
> ical, methodological and practical problems which run deep in any discussion
> of democracy ... [Consequently] the challenges which face public service
> managers are often more daunting than their private sector counterparts and
> require a wider range and greater intensity of skills.

Hence the concept of performance in the public domain is elusive and is inherently political. But this must not be taken as a counsel of despair, only as a warning
against a naïve and simplistic approach. There are a number of levels on which
performance can and has been defined and measured. Each effectively represents a
particular definition of **accountability**. Accountability refers to the demonstration to
someone else of success or achievement. It involves revealing, explaining and justifying what one does, or has done, or how one discharges one's responsibilities. We
identify four levels of performance definition and accountability:

- **financial** accountability;
- **budgetary** accountability;
- **managerial** accountability; and
- **political** accountability.

They are not necessarily mutually exclusive, each one has a number of interpretations, and each requires a different set of information in order to demonstrate
achievement. Each has received varying degrees of attention at different points
in historical time. Until more recently the vogue had been for a rather narrow
definition of managerial accountability premised as a neo-Taylorist approach to

managerialism (Pollitt 1993). There are now some signs of a movement towards a broader definition around political notions of what should be done, premised on a new approach to managerialism (Stewart 1995b; Newman and Clarke 1994). It is a debate also relevant to the growth of the unelected state discussed in Chapter 10.

There are other forms of accountability and one of notable importance in the public services is professional accountability. For professionals it is the professional body that sets the objectives and rules that govern the performance of the individual and it is the profession that defines what is satisfactory performance. Accountability is predominantly outwards to professional colleagues. It has been argued that this accountability has become too strong relative to accountability upwards ultimately to politicians and downwards to customers, to the detriment of a broader performance (Elcock 1991). The medical profession is the classic example.

4.4.2 Financial performance

The narrowest definition of financial performance is that of **probity.** This involves the provision of financial information to demonstrate legality and the accuracy of financial statements. Ensuring probity was the traditional role of the auditor (internal or external). It remains vitally important in public service organizations but alone it has little to do with performance as generally understood. Indeed, if requirements for probity is used to justify tight financial control which, for example, prevents virement across lines within the budget, it may lead to such inflexibility as to inhibit potential improvements and compromise more efficient and effective performance.

Traditionally there has been much less use of other financial performance criteria, such as **financial targets**, in public service organizations largely due to their non-trading status. In the private for-profit sector basic financial statements are used as a measure of performance. The income figure, particularly expressed as a ratio of net investment, has come to be the ultimate test of a company's success or failure and constitutes the popular definition of 'the bottom line' (profit after all deductions). It is the company's achievement of financial targets which provides the market with information on the quality of management and it is the ultimate indicator of performance.

Increasingly, however, a number of public services are required to operate trading accounts as required, for example, by CCT. If the local authority retains the work by providing the competitive contract they have to create Direct Service Organizations as independent units each having a trading account and each required to publish an annual report and accounts, to achieve a certain rate of return on their financial assets employed, to break even in terms of income and expenditure and to adhere to their external financial limits (EFL) for borrowing. Since the growth of contracts and quasi-market agencies has been increasing throughout the public services sector the use of financial targets is now wide-spread. However, as Flynn (1993) warns, care needs to be taken in interpreting financial results as a measure of performance. First, high rates of return may be due to monopoly power rather than superior performance. Second, the rate of return will depend on how assets are valued and how prices are set. For example, a cost-plus contract cannot fail to produce a positive return. Third, we should be wary of financial performance as a measure of the quality of management if managers have little control over their costs such as where national wage rates prevail. Hence, financial targets need to be used with caution and certainly only provide a partial perspective on performance.

4.4.3 Budgetary performance

Adherence by the organization to its annual budget is a traditional measure of performance in public service organizations. However, it is frequently argued that the nature of the public budgetary process in many public service agencies, is such that performance against budget provides insufficient incentives for managers to secure quality service delivery. The traditional budget has been criticized on a number of grounds:

- Given its **annual focus** which permits very limited virement between financial years there is a tendency for managers to spend unused funds towards the end of the financial year often without much regard for their efficient or effective use. Not to spend may mean loss of some of next year's budget but to over-spend may mean more next year.
- Traditional budgets are **input focused** presenting information on the items on which the money is being spent but does not indicate the outcomes of such expenditure in terms of outputs and services delivered.
- Adherence to budget has usually been defined on a **cash basis** rather than an accruals basis. In cash accounting income and expenditure are recognized when they are actually received or paid in cash whereas in accrual accounting expenses are recorded as they are incurred (when the invoice comes in rather than when it is paid) and income as it is earned during an accounting period. Cash accounting does not always present a real indication of resource cost, particularly for capital items, and can encourage 'foot-in-the-door' expansionary tactics since the future consequences of long term expenditures may be discounted.
- Traditional public service budgets have been **incremental** in that the bulk of the budget (the base) remained unexamined and was merely rolled forward each year with an allowance for expected inflation. Scrutiny was confined to the annual increment made possible by additional funds expected from financial sponsors. Without comprehensive scrutiny of budget composition, however, there is a real possibility that the budget reflects past priorities rather than changing needs and priorities chosen by a 'rational' evaluation of options (Wildavsky 1964). Evidence from the more recent era of fiscal restraint, however, indicates that though incrementalism has become 'more managed and less muddled' (Elcock et al., 1989: 188) it continues to exist:

> Bargaining and negotiation, compromise and pragmatism, incrementalism and marginal changes remain the order of the day.

'Public budgets remain essentially a reflection of a political process. The outcome is a reflection of the balance of power between budgetary 'advocates', such as service professionals, street level bureaucrats, clients and users, elected members who bargain and negotiate with budgetary 'guardians', wishing to restrain expenditures, represented by the Treasury and other finance departments (Wildavsky 1964; Elcock 1991). The outcome of this struggle is influenced by a large number of factors, both internal (e.g. the extent of departmentalism, whether the agency is multi-functional, dominated by professional values, its size, its history, etc.) and external. Chief among the latter is the general economic and political climate as reflected in the fiscal condition, increasingly one of restraint. The general conclusions from studies of budgetary behaviour in public service organizations is that the incentives which exist have tended to drive managers towards a budget seeking posture rather than a performance demonstrating one. Success has been measured in terms of the politics of resource acquisition rather than measured performance. Hence Flynn's conclusion that 'adherence to the budget is not necessarily a measure of competence' (1993: 123).

There have been a number of attempts to move the budget towards a more performance demonstrating posture, but they have met with limited success. **Planning Programme Budgeting/Output Budgeting** (PPBS) attempts to relate all cost items to broad functional objectives defined at the outset (output focus) by constructing an organizational framework within which it is clear what resources are being devoted to what ends and with what results, thereby assisting managers in their policy choices. **Zero Based Budgeting** involves a thorough and regular scrutiny of total budget composition in terms of organizational objectives, in contrast to the annual incremental scrutiny of traditional approaches. The latest manifestation of the rational approach to budgeting is reflected in the Government's recent Green Paper *Better Accounting for Taxpayers' Money* (HMSO 1994). This argues for resource based accounting and budgeting, 'priority-based cost management', across all areas of the public sector. First, resource accounting involves moving from cash accounting to accrual accounting since this should provide more relevant management information for decisions. This is already used in much of the public sector, including health, local government and the non-elected agencies. Second, however, the Green Paper is at pains to stress that resource accounting is more than accrual accounting:

It brings with it a framework to capture costs and to match these to departmental objectives and (where appropriate) outputs, and to transmit this information to the relevant management level within the department (*para 2.4*).

With better understanding of the full cost of their operations, departments will be better placed to make decisions on the allocation of resources consistent with their overall priorities.

The key point here is that in addition to the usual accounts required by all companies the Green Paper proposes what it calls a 'main objective analysis' which will show the cost of resources consumed by departmental/organizational objectives, with additional information on out-turn against budget. Lastly, an 'output and performance analysis' is strongly recommended. This compares the full costs of delivering a department's/organization's main objectives with the outputs achieved. This is all remarkably similar to the old PPBS format and approach, offering all the potential advantages and all the potential pitfalls!

The arguments for a more performance-focused budget seem persuasive. However, the reasons for the failure of past attempts must not be forgotten. They failed partly due to technical problems – of defining objectives, measuring outputs, but mainly to organizational ones – they challenged budgetary traditions and vested interests and were resisted (Schick 1973). However, there is a further more philosophical argument which questions the very logic of the rational analytic approach of such budget reforms and provides some justification for traditional incrementalism. Those who advocate a disjointed incremental approach to decision-making (Lindblom 1959; 1979) see positive advantages in 'muddling through' as the best means of securing appropriate performance in the public domain. The rationality model, it is claimed, is based on the false assumption that conflict of interests and values between different individuals and groups can be resolved and a unique and agreed set of objectives agreed, with the latter specified at the outset of the policy process. Critics argue that this is both naïve and impossible. It is naïve because rarely are politicians prepared to be so open preferring ambiguity and vagueness, since this leaves them less exposed to pressure groups and less easily judged. It is impossible because the reality of politics is that ends become clarified as means are selected for their achievement, simply because the world is one of surprise and uncertainty where preferences are learned through trial and error and negotiations in political settings. The attempt to be rational and analytical may well eliminate political review, the very stuff of democratic decision making. It may be better to muddle through generating acceptable outcomes focusing upon means and ends where agreement can be reached (Hogwood and Gunn 1984)

This perspective inevitably provides a very different view of performance in general and the budget in particular. But it is a perspective which is no longer very fashionable. Rationalism has become the dominant paradigm, albeit dressed in the new clothes of managerialism.

4.4.4 Managerial performance

The apparent deficiencies and incompleteness of financial and budgetary accountability and their associated definitions of performance have led to a broader one embracing the 'value for money' (VFM) concept. This requires public agencies to demonstrate their achievement of policy aims efficiently, economically and effectively. **Managerial accountability** is defined by Day and Klein (1987:27) as 'making those with delegated authority answerable for carrying out agreed tasks according to agreed criteria of performance'. It was to secure more results-orientated public services that the government strengthened the national auditing framework in the early 1980s, introduced the Financial Management Initiative (FMI) and *Next Steps* initiative in central government and established the Audit Commission in 1982 specifically charged with auditing for economy, efficiency and effectiveness in local government (and later the NHS and police).

> VFM is most easily defined as the economic acquisition of resources and their efficient utilization in the realization of the purposes of the organization – with the simultaneous achievement of **economy, efficiency and effectiveness** (the 3 Es).

However, other authors include a fourth E, that of **equity** (for example Selim and Woodward 1992, Bovaird, Gregory and Martin 1988), whilst Jackson and Palmer (1993) include **excellence, entrepreneurship, expertise** and **electability**. Fenwick (1995) adds the very last one, **enough**! Focus here is upon the 3 Es. It should be noted prior to each of the definitions which follow that the terms are not entirely discrete.

Economy

Entails the purchasing of inputs, defined as the resources used to produce a service or execute a policy, of a given quality specification at the lowest possible cost. It is the first principle of good housekeeping. A lack of economy would occur, for example, where there is over-staffing or when over-priced facilities are used.

Efficiency

Entails achieving the maximum possible output, which refers to the services produced or delivered, from a given level of inputs, or alternatively, that for a given level of output minimizing the inputs used. It is measured by the ratio of actual input to actual output, or the rate at which actual inputs are converted into outputs. The smaller the ratio, the more output for input and the more efficient the organization. The ratio can be improved by the 'productivity' route (input constant, output increased) or the 'economizing' route (output constant, inputs decreased), with the Government in the 1980s tending to favour the latter (Gunn 1988).

Effectiveness

Is concerned with achieving the top level goals of the organization i.e. ensuring policy aims are being met. Effectiveness is concerned with **outcomes or impacts**, the results obtained or the effects of the service upon clients and is achieved when the impacts of a policy are meeting its policy aims. This is a somewhat broader definition than that of the Treasury which defines it as 'the ratio of output to planned output', which is equivalent to the achievement of an organization's own goals or its intended results. The problem with this definition is that it makes no allowance for the fact that the organization's own goals may not be sufficiently wide or stretching to be fully appropriate, thereby leading to an over-concentration on economy and efficiency. Bovaird *et al.* (1988: 17), emphasizing the wider impact dimension of the effectiveness of a public service, define it as 'the change in community welfare it has brought about' or 'carrying out measures which make the community better off'. Defined in this way it is apparent that effectiveness is far more elusive than the other two Es given the multiplicity of stakeholders that make up the 'community' of public service organizations and the difficulty of specifying precise policy objectives and, therefore, criteria for accountability. Indeed, defined so broadly it could include wider political values discussed in the next section. It follows that this criterion for performance measurement is partly contingent on the prevailing ideological climate.

Hence, economy is about inputs; efficiency about inputs and outputs; and effectiveness about outputs, outcomes and impacts. Each one, however, is of little use on its own. For example, it is not much use to know that something was as cheap as possible (economic) if it does not satisfy the organization's or client's objectives. Similarly, efficiency alone is insufficient since the wrong outcomes may be achieved, albeit at least cost. Again, effectiveness is of limited use on its own: knowing that objectives were achieved irrespective of cost is insufficient. Certainly in early days of implementation, driven by the need for fiscal restraint, VFM tended to be concerned mainly with economy and efficiency and gave insufficient attention to effectiveness. In a number of situations this is still the case.

Hence, the three concepts are essentially interdependent and the relationship between them is shown in Figure 4.2.

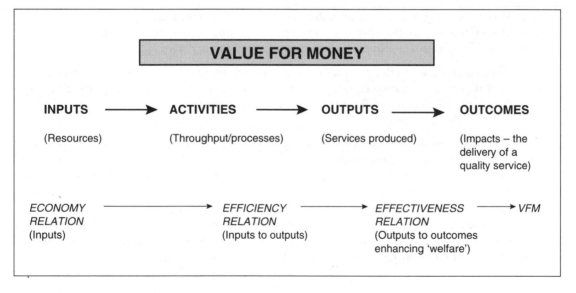

Figure 4.2   The managerial performance measurement

4.4.5 Political accountability

This is the broadest and most elusive concept of performance and accountability and could include all of those already identified above and more besides! Like all concepts of accountability it involves the justification of decisions, but here the justification is in terms of 'the values which are currently supposed to characterize stewardship of the citizens' interests' (Pollitt and Harrison 1992: 3). It is fundamentally about what **should** be done and the **process** by which it is done. Accountability for the performance of a service in this view is to be answerable to multiple stakeholders for the achievement of multiple objectives, including the process of their devising and achievement. It is performance which reflects what John Stewart has called the distinctive purposes, values and conditions of the public domain (Stewart 1995; Stewart and Ranson 1988). The distinctive public service values include equity, fairness, community, citizenship, justice and democracy. The distinctive conditions include the democratic process, public accountability and openness of decision-making. For many, a major key to this form of accountability is accountability upwards through the bureaucratic chain of command and ultimately to elected representatives. The growth of the non-elected agencies has fundamentally compromised this form of accountability with the rise of an unelected elite. Justification is in terms of a new form of accountability, that of acceptability of a public service more directly to its consumers (Waldegrave 1993). Here citizenship relates less to participation in the public realm than to consumption in the private realm (Walsh 1995). This theme is more extensively discussed in Chapter 10.

This is an extremely rich and diverse notion of performance and is much harder to demarcate let alone define in the form of a precise set of indicators. This is, of course, no reason for paying it less regard. As Stewart says:

> The distinctive challenge for management in the public domain .. is to reflect [its] distinctive purposes and values, [and] conditions . . . and, in particular, to build citizenship as well as to respond to customers.
>
> *(1995c: 4)*

It is not entirely sufficient to invent a 4th 'E' called **equity** – defined in terms of justice and fairness, more particularly in terms of the process and outcome of the distribution of policy impacts – and hope that everything not included in the other three can thereby be captured.

Given what is said above, a separate discussion on quality is hardly necessary since quality is simply appropriate performance and, as we have seen, there is no one definition of what that is in a public services context. In any case the issue of quality is dealt with in Chapter 1 and 12.

4.5   ACHIEVING SUCCESSFUL PERFORMANCE

4.5.1 A strategic framework for performance assessment

Successful performance management, it is generally agreed, depends upon having both appropriate technical and procedural practices **and** supportive cultural and attitudinal characteristics within an organization. Its introduction and use can raise important issues in the management of change (Jackson and Palmer 1993).

Jackson and Palmer (1993) argue that the inherent complexity of public service organizations and the difficulties of defining and measuring their performance must be built into any successful performance framework and the only possible way to

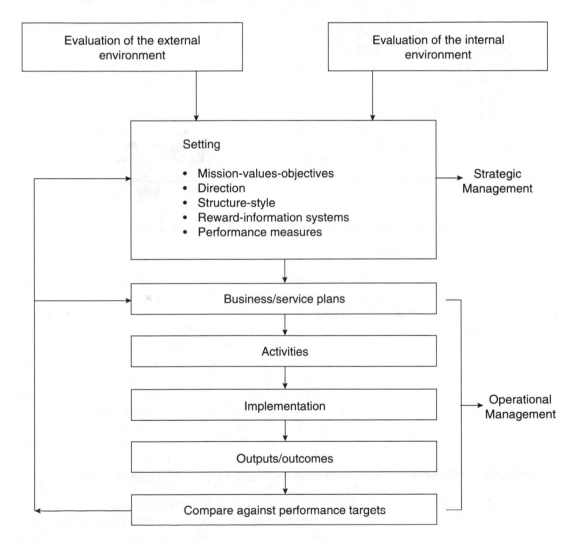

Figure 4.3   Performance in a strategic framework (*Source: Peter Jackson (1993)*)

do this is to adopt **a strategic-management perspective** (discussed in Chapter 3). This is confirmed by the better managed private sector organizations, they argue, but is still quite rare in public services ones. By having a strategic focus fully integrated into the working practices of the organization, a systematic performance framework can be developed which encourages and facilitates organizational learning and a systematic approach to problem solving rather than organizational control. Peter Jackson (1993) provides a useful strategic framework, reproduced as Figure 4.3. It sets out the standard strategic management model but includes an additional feedback loop between the information produced by comparing performance indicators against targets so as to encourage greater learning.

Breaking this down, a systematic performance framework involves the following:

- a system in which managers, at all levels, have **clear objectives**, derived from the organizational **mission**, expressed as precisely and unambiguously as possible;
- emphasis is upon **outputs and outcomes** in terms of specified objectives, rather than simply activities undertaken by the organization;
- objectives are set in terms of **targets or 'measurable' indicators** so performance can be assessed (monitored) and compared with potential, inside and outside the organization (benchmarking);
- each person knows what is expected of him or her and knows that they are responsible for specific results and that these results are achievable but stretching;
- **supportive systems** need to be developed, both 'hard' – such as appropriate management information systems, and 'soft' – such as an appropriate organizational culture or fit.

4.5.2 Performance measurement in private and public service organizations

Critical to effective performance management and the achievement of accountability is the monitoring and evaluation of past and present achievement in terms of the organization's mission and the derived objectives set. To do this it is essential that performance can be measured. Though performance measurement is important in all organizations, private, public and voluntary, in the private sector it is perhaps less complex since market-based accountability prevails. That is, profitability (the difference between the flow of revenue and cost) tends to be used as the over-riding indicator and certainly provides a 'bottom line'. However, even in private for-profit organizations it is rarely that simple, particularly if the organizations are large and complex. Success in any organization is multi-dimensional and a variety of performance measures are needed. Moreover, profit performance and the events that generate profit are not synchronized. Profit is only known after the accounts have been finalized. In the meantime, then, private firms need other indicators (Carter *et al.*, 1992). Jackson (1993) claims that the best private companies use performance indicators closely related to their strategic decision-making cycle. These could include indicators of consumer satisfaction, product or service quality, competitiveness, innovation, flexibility and not just simple financial ratios. The more enlightened might even include non-commercial values such as environmentalism and social ethics! Of course, profit remains the bottom line.

It is apparent that the profitability indicator is less frequently available or appropriate in the public services sector since there is no equivalent flow of revenue related to sales and value created. By the nature of the provider relationship, though this has been changing more recently, the dissatisfied public client usually has few alternatives and hence continues to 'purchase' the service irrespective of performance. Hence, **performance measures or indicators** need to be developed in public service agencies as surrogates for profit and loss. Moreover, the increasing move towards separating purchaser from provider and the subsequent growth of contract culture (both internally and externally) has increased the need to develop performance measures so that contracts can be defined in terms of service standards and compliance monitored.

4.5.3 Critical success factors for performance measurement

Performance indicators (PIs) have two main roles, though these are easier to distinguish in theory than in practice:

- **Internal management**: with PIs assisting in the policy planning and control processes within the organization. They can provide managers at all levels with information necessary to make decisions which reflect, for example, economy, efficiency, effectiveness and quality service provision.
- **Public accountability**: this role is to provide those 'outside' the organization with a basis for judging performance and establishing accountability. These could include council and board members, the auditors and, of course, the consumers and public at large.

In performing both their roles PIs provide a form of quasi-competition with, for example, league tables being used to score different units within the same organization, the same unit at different points in time or the same units in different organizations. It is unlikely, however, that a single set of indicators can satisfy both purposes since the needs of internal managers and the different external stakeholders will vary, with the latter requiring less technical indicators and more high profile ones. Moreover, the same indicators may be interpreted differently by different audiences. Recognizing the tension both between and within the internal and external role of PIs, Jackson (1988) argues for a 'complex mosaic of indicators', comparing performance indicators with mirrors which reflect particular aspects of an organization's activities. However, fashioning a perfect set of mirrors is an impossible aim given the multiple stakeholders, both internal and external, with their varying perspectives. Performance assessment, as we have emphasized, is inevitably a political and value-laden exercise where judgement and therefore, difference, is inescapable.

Though performance measurement will always remain a value-laden exercise there are a number of factors which are critical if it is to have any chance of performing either its internal or external role.

Fundamental to the selection of appropriate PIs is the establishment from the mission statement of the **objectives** of the activity, unit or organization, preferably structuring performance measurement in terms of a hierarchy of organizational objectives.

Performance indicators which, for example, are used because information is currently available, but are unrelated to objectives, are at best irrelevant and at worst positively dangerous since they could mis-direct behaviour. The major implication of this, as we have stressed above, is that top management should have a systematic performance framework and this must be cascaded and integrated top-to-bottom throughout the organization to ensure value alignment. It is imperative to ensure that the purposes for measuring performance are clear and accepted by everyone. Organizational 'fit' is important (Selim and Woodward 1992: 165). It is generally agreed that a commitment culture will lead to greater acceptance and ownership of PIs (as opposed to compliance to PIs) than a control culture. A non-threatening participative environment may well empower managers and motivate them to subscribe to the ethos and practices of performance management. As Selim and Woodward (1992: 163) say:

> where measurement is used consistently, creatively, constructively and positively to help managers improve their performance, implementation and use is more likely to be a success. If systems are designed and used punitively, managers may cheat.

In other words, in an appropriate culture and context the information generated by performance monitoring systems can be a means of organizational learning.

An implication of this for performance indicators themselves is that, to be of value, they must be unambiguous and subject to influence by the managers responsible for them and achievable through reasonable actions. If they are, managers are more likely to accept their findings and change their behaviour accordingly, whereas if they are not PIs will simply generate frustration and counter-productive tactical responses (Pollitt 1989). To be feasible and controllable, of course, means that all PIs need to have contingencies built in so that they are sensitive to, for example, unforeseen and uncontrollable changes in the external environment. The danger is, and it is greater in a control culture, that these contingencies become so elastic as to provide excuses for all deviations from the performance norms established, offering opportunities for counter-productive manipulation by the person or unit being assessed.

Hence, it is vital that PIs are transformed from a 'control' to a 'development' function (Burningham 1990), the former emphasizing their role in identifying opportunities for corrective action and the latter their role as 'part of a learning cycle in a process of intervention and change of management intended to improve performance' (Burningham 1992: 87). In this they act as descriptive 'tin-openers' as opposed to prescriptive 'dials' (Carter *et al.* 1992: 49), helping in an exploratory process of inquiry instead of providing exact numbers for defining unambiguous standards of performance. To do this, of course, may require major management of change initiatives to promote collective understanding and sense of purpose, alignment of the organization top-to-bottom so that people can see value and personal benefit from performance measurement.

The need for supportive systems for performance management includes the need to develop **management information systems** consistent with the performance framework and its associated PIs. It is highly unlikely that existing information systems will be appropriate or sufficient. It is important that those responsible for delivering the various elements of performance at the operational level are involved in designing the information system (Jackson 1993). At least in the short term, the requirement for such systems will cause costs to increase. Improving performance is not a free good and the cost implications will force organizations to concentrate on a limited number of key indices likely to give the highest pay-off. The danger is that concentrating on a limited number of PIs may provide only a partial view of performance, distorting incentives within the organization since 'what gets measured gets done'.

For PIs to be of value in directing attention to areas of potential improvement then the actual achievement which they measure must be **compared** with the possible and the possible defined in a plan capable of achievement (Butt and Palmer 1985). Comparing PIs against some benchmark or target will enable the organization to identify 'performance gaps' and should enable organizational learning (Jackson 1993). A number of possibilities for benchmarking exist:

- **inter-authority** and **inter-sector**: this might be with the private sector or with other LAs, for instance, and examples could include league tables of examination passes, crimes prevention rates, activity completion dates, cost per household of refuse collection, etc. The comparison can be with national averages, yardsticks, standards or benchmarks produced by, for example, the Audit Commission, Government Departments or CIPFA. Relying primarily on moral pressure for its effectiveness, the value of this approach is that it highlights potential issues for action. The real problem with this sort of comparison is there are frequently many reasons which can be given for deviation from the 'average': e.g. non-homogeneous populations served, different accounting conventions. A good illustration is the current debate surrounding league tables of educational attainment based on assessment scores unadjusted for pupils' backgrounds. Ideally then, performance indicators need to normalize for these 'legitimate' differences so that comparisons are those in which performance is measured against the **potential** of the individual unit and its particular objectives rather than the actual achievement of other units in other authorities or sectors, which may well face very different circumstances and have different values. The political nature of this issue is apparent as recent controversy over educational league tables has illustrated so graphically. A recent approach to making comparisons as valid as possible is to form 'benchmarking clubs' with, for example, similar agencies getting together in local or regional groups to set common performance targets, share experiences and outcomes and exchange information. There is, for example, a 5 London Boroughs Group which is set up to develop equality indicators.

- **time or trends** compare, for example, this year's performance with last year's. This method tends to be superior to league tables since it is more likely that like is being compared with like, though in practice many variables are likely to have changed. However, the key question is whether the trend information relates to objectives and to plan. For example, trend information may be provided on the number of police officers in a constabulary over time. The greater police numbers observed through time may reflect success in recruiting and in retaining existing police, but it may still be below the numbers planned for and required. Hence it is important to define a valid benchmark.

- **targets** are used to compare actual performance with some standard desired and, by avoiding the pitfalls of the other two methods, are potentially the most valuable since they force public service bodies to state their aims and objectives in terms of explicit targets against which they can be judged. Examples include cost and economy targets (percentage cost reduction targets), efficiency targets (percentage occupancy rates for residential homes), output or volume targets (number of users of a sports facility), effectiveness, outcome and quality targets (e.g. percentage reduction in customer complaints resulting from faulty work). A major problem is to translate very general statements about aims and objectives into concrete targets, the danger being that those than can be so translated dominate the softer ones that cannot, thereby mis-directing managerial behaviour. For example, schools which meet their targets expressed in terms of exam results may well compromise wider educational values.

One of the most ambitious attempts to use comparative PIs was initiated by the Audit Commission, which in March 1995 published a series of performance tables, based on 70 separate measures, for the 449 English and Welsh local authorities. Figure 4.4 illustrates how easily an exercise which was not intended to encourage spurious comparisons can nonetheless degenerate into crude league table mentality.

The critical factors for successful PIs are summarized in the work of Andrew Likierman (1993). Following feedback from over 500 managers he proposed a list of 20 lessons which describe good practice in the use of PIs in organizations illustrated in Figure 4.5.

4.5.4 Performance indicators: some examples

Economy and efficiency

Economy and efficiency, involving the provision of a specified volume and quality of service with the lowest level of resources, can be measured using a number of

Big differences in efficiency of councils found

Some councils spend twice as much as others on educating secondary pupils, according to figures published today by the Audit Commission, the local government watchdog.

In a wide-ranging survey of council performance, the commission reveals big variations in spending by local authorities and in the inefficiency of the services they provide.

The survey shows that poor performance by councils is concentrated in poorer areas of the country. But it also provides numerous examples of big discrepancies in the performance of neighbouring councils controlled by the same political party. The commission's figures seem certain to fuel the current row over education funding and will provide ammunition for all parties in the run-up to May's local elections.

Among its findings, which form the basis of the first national leagues tables on council performance, are:

• spending per secondary school pupil varies from £4,055 in Conservative-controlled Kensington and Chelsea to £1,535 in Tory Westminster.

• Council houses can remain empty before re-letting for as long as 37 weeks in the Labour-controlled London borough of Hackney. But in many others they are vacant for less than a week.

• Parents in Liverpool are almost twice as likely to get a school place for their three and four year olds than those across the Mersey on the Wirral. Liverpool gives 97 per cent of pre-school children a nursery place, compared with the Wirral's 56 per cent. No single party controls either council.

• In the north-east, Labour-controlled Sunderland has failed to assess any child with special needs within the six months target period set by the government. Neighbouring Durham, Labour-controlled, deals with 72 per cent of children within that period.

The commission's performance tables use 70 separate measures for each of the 448 English and Welsh local authorities. They allow comparison to be made on each authority's record on providing social services, education, housing, council tax collection, and recycling. It is the most ambitious exercise of its kind attempted in the UK and will become an annual event.

Mr Andrew Foster, controller of the Audit Commission, said the indicators would be a "massive catalyst" for the improvement of council performance.

Mr Frank Dobson, the shadow environmental secretary, said the figures showed that the Tories' flagship borough of Westminster provides "some of the worst value for money services in the country". It spends £53.61 per head on refuse collection – the highest in the country – while neighbouring Labour-controlled Camden spends £24.33.

Westminster's street cleaning services were also the most expensive in the country at £38.98 per head, more than double Camden's £14.42.

Mr Eric Pickles, Conservative party vice-chairman, said the indicators showed Conservative councils were "delivering value for money by providing higher quality services at lower cost".

Figure 4.4 *Financial Times* article 30 March 1995

indicators. Measures tend to relate to volume, cost and speed and lend themselves to number crunching. For example: workload and productivity ratios measure the amount of useful work undertaken by staff in a defined length of time such as the number of library books issued per staff hour, the number of claimants/enquiries served by a member of staff in a Benefits Office, or the number of patients seen by the GP and the number of housing repairs undertaken. Each could be expressed as a time target: for example, responding to a distress call within x minutes. Utilization rates measure the extent to which available service capacity is used, such as the occupancy rate of places in schools or the percentage of hospital beds occupied.

Concept

1. Include all elements integral to what is being measured since what gets measured gets done
2. Choose the right number of PIs appropriate to the particular organization
3. Provide for qualitative PIs and develop PIs for quality
4. Reflect the political values and constraints to secure appropriate accountabilities

Preparation

5. Devise PIs through negotiation with those affected to establish ownership
6. Guard against short-term PIs alone
7. Ensure the PIs fairly reflect the efforts of managers
8. Build in contingencies so as to reflect external or uncontrollable changes
9. Use the experience of other organizations/other parts of the organization to compare
10. Establish realistic levels of attainment before the first targets are set

Implementation

11. Value the learning process and be prepared to revise PIs in the light of experience
12. Link PIs to existing management systems
13. Ensure PIs are understandable by those whose performance is being measured
14. Where outcomes are impossible to measure choose proxy PIs carefully
15. Review internal and external relationships alongside the introduction of PIs

Use

16. Ensure the information on which PIs are based can be trusted
17. Use the results to inform discussion, not to provide all the answers
18. Ensure there is feedback and dissemination of findings
19. Prioritize and trade-off PIs since all will not be equally important
20. Present results in a user friendly format, in a timely way

(Source: Likierman (1993: 15.–22))

Figure 4.5 Performance indicators: 20 lessons for managerial use

Perhaps the most popular is the **unit cost indicator**. This measures the actual cost of providing a service or unit of service, preferably compared to a unit, standard or target cost over time or with some other comparable organization and compared with planned or expected unit costs. For example, cost per place in homes for the elderly. For each service it might include net cost per 1000 population and/or manpower per 1000 population. In education an example would be cost per pupil; in highways, maintenance cost per kilometre of road; in housing, construction cost per dwelling completed. Though of some value in raising red flags, in themselves unit costs provide little clues to performance, unless like is being compared with like. There are two further criticisms which warn against using such indicators as a basis for policy planning and control – against confusing *ex post* PIs, useful for monitoring, and *ex ante* PIs, useful for policy planning and evaluation.

● First, since unit costs are measures of **average cost** (total cost of provision divided by the number of units of service) they rarely reflect **marginal costs** (the cost of providing an incremental unit of service). It is, of course, the latter which should influence policy planning. For example, though the average cost per occupied bed-day (total hospital costs divided by total number of occupied bed-days) may provide an efficiency indicator, it may be quite incorrect to use this as a basis for planning since a 10% reduction in length of stay will not reduce costs by 10% if the most costly parts of treatment are concentrated in the earlier parts of hospitalization and the cheaper ones later on. In this case the unit cost figure may over-estimate the potential savings since the relevant cost is the marginal cost, below average cost in this case. The unit cost indicator, used to judge efficiency, may be taken as an erroneous guide to future action thereby compromising efficiency and effectiveness in the longer term. The correct performance indicator is the marginal cost not unit cost of a service.

- Second, unit costs are measured only in financial terms (the inputs paid for by the agency) rather than opportunity cost terms (the full societal sacrifice involved in making a decision). Using a health example again, the cost of early discharge from hospital of bed-ridden patients is a saving to the Health Authority but an additional cost to the domestic carers, to non-hospital health services, voluntary bodies, friends, etc. Whether early discharge is genuinely worthwhile is not clear from the hospital unit cost indicator. The recent controversy over Care in the Community is an excellent illustration of the conflicts. The likelihood of these wider consequences being taken into account is even less likely to result as multi-purpose public service organizations are being fragmented into a range of single quasi-market agencies each concerned with its own performance but with little concern with performance overall. 'Cost shunting' is all too likely. The overall result may be system inefficiencies since important spillovers (externalities) are not accounted for. (Flynn 1994; Stewart 1993a).

Effectiveness

Measures of effectiveness raise even more problems. Effectiveness concerns providing the right quality services to the right people and is ultimately concerned with indicators of **outcome** in terms of the changed welfare status of the range of clients/stakeholders served. The difficulty is that 'outcome' has many dimensions and includes the ramifications throughout society of the relevant public sector intervention. In its broadest sense it can be interpreted as the value placed by society on the activity (Smith 1995). In measuring effectiveness one important distinction is between:

- whether services achieve what they set out to do, referred to as 'service effectiveness'
- whether services achieve what their consumers want them to do, referred to as 'user effectiveness'.

Whereas the former defines effectiveness in terms of the quality of the product, usually in terms of technical dimensions capable of 'objective' measurement, the latter defines it more subjectively in terms of the quality of the service relationship. The former has tended to have an input focus and product determined service standards, whilst the latter has a genuine output/outcome focus and consumer determined service standards (Thomson 1992). We examine each in turn:

- The notion of **service effectiveness** was introduced by the Audit Commission in 1988 and incorporated input and process issues into its analysis of what must go into performance measurement. The 1988 action guide identified a key set of questions for local authorities such as 'Is the service getting to the right customers, in the right way, with the right service, in keeping with its stated policies?'. As Henkel (1992) points out, this makes it possible to use such measures of performance as amount and level of service delivered, opening hours and response times and the number of categories of service users included. Thus service effectiveness merges with the efficiency measures identified previously.

- **User effectiveness** is a far more demanding criterion of performance since it focuses on the impacts of the service on clients, users or customers and attempts to measure changes in their welfare or levels of satisfaction. On one interpretation it involves fully articulating the customers' perspective with results judged not in terms of managerial and professional standards but in terms of what the customer wants. (This user orientation is very similar to the 'public service orientation' (PSO) propounded by John Stewart and the Local Government Training Board in the mid-1980s.) As Henkel points out, however, this is not only difficult to do in operational terms but, most significantly, it may challenge the resource allocation decisions and distribution of power in designing and operating services (Henkel 1992: 82). In particular, there is a danger that 'user effectiveness' is reduced to some crude consumerist perspective, failing to recognize the multiple 'customers' for public services and the complexity of the context in which they make their choices. In local government terms, for example, there is a danger that consumerism devalues the role of professionals, of elected members and the democratic process and the 'public' as a whole, thereby embodying an unduly narrow individualistic view, empowering some – those best able to articulate their wants – at the expense of others.

Of course, this is the very danger of the Government's *Citizen's Charter* initiative with its emphasis upon customer determined services. The Charter is based upon four themes – quality, choice, standards and values – and its intent is to transform public service agencies into learning organizations with a commitment to continuous improvement, moving them beyond simple value for money to building in innovation to produce goods and services which continually delight the customer. The Charter covers all public services and there are a large number of PIs associated with each service-related field. A major criticism, recognized by the Audit Commission itself, is that there have been too many indicators to be of much interest to citizens and very few of them reflect effectiveness, quality and efficiency. Moreover, it can be argued that the Charter contains a flawed understanding of the concept of citizenship, with its emphasis on citizenship in terms of individual rights rather than membership of the community, and thereby a restrictive market-based form of accountability (Walsh 1994). There is also the real danger of central government 'capturing' performance since all agencies are required to achieve centrally prescribed performance indicators irrespective of their relevance to local circumstances, including

It is apparent that effectiveness measures are both conceptually and practically problematic because there is often little consensus as to how outcome is to be evaluated given the complexity of stakeholders and environments.

the local political mandate. Hence central Charter driven performance, with its associated PIs, may not reflect appropriate performance in terms of local citizen preferences.

One rather crude indicator is in terms of throughput of clients (including indirect ones) such as the number of housing repairs completed or number of meals provided to the elderly. But work performed is no guarantee of quality or of welfare increase. A key objective, of course, is to measure changes in client/user/customer welfare or satisfaction. A crude way to do this is through the level of client complaints. However, this is an entirely negative approach and such complaints need to be set in the context of overall satisfaction and methods employed to discover this (Bovaird and Nutley 1989). Systematic market research into customer satisfaction levels is required and increasingly being employed by public bodies. A pioneer in this field is Cleveland County Council which has been conducting annual social surveys since 1975, providing a detailed data base for monitoring and evaluation. Consumer satisfaction surveys, designed to measure the added-value provided by a service in terms of the service users' changed welfare state, must be central, though currently they are in their infancy in most public service organizations. There is a problem, though, in that eliciting user/client feedback can raise expectations as well as discovering preferences, thereby moving the target beyond resource capabilities. As John Stewart (1995c: 9) has said the management of expectations – which frequently means rationing – is one of the most difficult tasks now and in the likely future. Effectiveness measures derived from economics in terms of customers' willingness to pay may also offer great possibilities, but as yet they are largely untried outside the traditional areas where cost-benefit analysis has been applied.

The approach of the West Midlands Police to measuring achievement of one of its five local objectives, illustrated in Figure 4.6, that of improving performance in dealing with criminal investigations is also revealing. There is an attempt to relate PIs to aims and objectives and to set performance within a strategic framework. Again, however, there are few outcome measures.

Though performance indicators of economy, efficiency and effectiveness are clearly partial and incomplete, those which attempt to measure wider political values such as community, citizenship, openness, democracy, etc. are virtually non-existent. Some very limited progress has been made with respect to equity, though there are huge problems given the different interpretations of the concept. Indicators are needed which reflect the potential fairness/unfairness of current practices in terms of policy incidence. The development of indicators to evaluate and monitor equal opportunities effects of policies and equal opportunities policies themselves is one way in which this is being handled. The London Borough of Hackney, for example, has made

CRIME MANAGEMENT

The aim to increase expertise in the investigation of crime and provide an improved quality of service to victims and witnesses. It will forcus on those crimes which cause most concern and ensure staff are trained and deployed to deliver the best possible response.

The aims are . . .

**TO IMPROVE PERFORMANCE
IN DEALING WITH
CRIMINAL INVESTIGATIONS**

To improve its detections in specific crimes	To improve its services to victims of crime

The Police Authority will measure performance by monitoring . . .

- The number of crimes detected, by primary means, per officer
- The % of all crimes detected by primary and other means
- the % of violent crimes detected by primary and other means
- The % burglaries of dwellings detected by . . .
- the % of theft of motor vehicles detected by . . .
- The % of theft from motor vehicles detected by . . .
- The % of files sent to CPS which fail to reach the requisite at first submission
- The % of files sent to CPS which comply with time limits
- The % of files proceeded with the CPS
- The number of 'drug trafficking' crimes
- The number of drugs seizures

- The % of victims satisfied with the police service at the time of initial response to report of violent crime
- The % of victims of violence satisfied with police service at the time of the initial response to report of burglary dwelling
- The % reduction of repeat victimization in respect of violent crime
- The % reduction of repeat victimization in respect of burglary dwelling

Its targets are . . .

To improve on last year's performance	to improve on last year's survey results

Figure 4.6   West Midlands policing priorities 1995

considerable strides in this direction. There remains a great deal of work still to be undertaken in this field and even more in devising a set of PIs which include measures of outcome in terms of the broader notions of political accountability identified earlier in this chapter.

4.5.5 Some dangers of PIs

Though PIs, used both internally and externally, are essential ingredients of attempts to enhance performance management in public service organizations there are dangers too. In changing the motivational set confronting managers Pollitt (1989), in particular, warns of 'gaming' and argues that there is no guarantee PI systems will be improved year by year as they are refined and their users become more skilful. Though training and refinement of the database are both necessary to long term success they are not sufficient. It will depend upon how interested is each of the main actors and how prone the particular system is to 'gaming'. As we have seen this emphasizes the importance of organizational context and culture, and the need for a strategic approach to the management of performance.

To assume that because PIs exist to monitor events in an organization these events are under control is also dangerous. Problems can arise because PIs are not always fully linked into other planning and review systems. Commenting on local government experience Burningham (1992: 90) argues that 'some performance review committees become sidings into which performance indicators are shunted as "background information" rather than junctions through which they pass in a process of real evaluation and decision'. To be operationally effective within public service organizations PIs must be grafted rather than bolted on (Burningham 1992: 94), securing the involvement and support of all concerned in the organization, especially the professionals. A climate of fiscal stringency with its emphasis upon cost cutting is not the most appropriate for their success, particularly in public service organizations which are dominated by professionals devoted to maintaining public service standards.

Finally, there is the danger of 'targetology', where a narrow focus on set targets adversely affects other aspects of service delivery. The danger is that accountability becomes reduced to the meeting of pre-stated PIs and that activity is manipulated to show that these have been met whilst real priorities are neglected. A hospital pursuing a target of decreasing waiting lists for operations could increase throughput by reducing post-operative hospital care thus having a detrimental effect on the quality of health care. Target following can also lead to the neglect of the qualitative in favour of the quantitative together with an unfortunate short-termism. Focus on short term target achievement is most likely where such achievement is related to managers' rewards, contracts are fixed term and there is lack of strategic mission in the organization. The cost of such behaviour may be under investment in innovation, quality improvements and other long-term strategic areas. The real danger is that the systems and data used to produce PIs become more important than the actual significance of the measures themselves. Steve Nicklen (1995) of the Audit Commission, referring to local authorities, warns against the real danger of 'performance monitoring systems that grow like some kind of lurid swamp monster, spreading in all directions as council officers suddenly see PIs as a kind of test of organizational virility and become convinced that council members in particular will see services with the most indicators as the most important'.

Peter Jackson sums up:

Performance indicators are a means of assisting responsible management to make efficient and effective decisions. They are not, however, a mechanical substitute for good judgement, political wisdom or leadership.

(1988: 15)

4.6   CONCLUSION

A most important theme in the current literature on performance management is the importance of organizational context and culture to its successful implementation. We have learned that if the context in which performance management is implemented is one of fiscal stringency combined with a general attack on public sector provision then there will be resistance. We have also learned that developing techniques to implement performance management, though important and challenging, is secondary to organizational behavioural issues. The recent history of the public sector is littered with failed reforms which introduced new 'rational' techniques but which took little account of institutional and political realities, particularly institutional inertia, tradition and resistance: PAR, PPBS and Fulton to name but a few. We have learned that there is a need to 'fit' or 'root' performance management techniques and reforms into the power relationships and core values of the organization and, where this is currently not possible, that appropriate organizational change is critical to success. There are some organizational cultures which are not likely to be compatible with the rooting of performance management. It is perhaps ironic that the import of a 'business ethos' into the public sector has in many situations increased control, disabling front-line staff rather than enabling them. A decentralized and participative culture is most likely to be compatible. The real need, as the private sector is all too aware, is to transform organizations into learning organizations with a commitment to continuous improvement.

Of course, this is something far easier to say than do, particularly in the case of public service organizations where the political context in which this transformation is to take place must remain a central issue in both defining what it means and legitimizing the process. Given the distinctive values, purposes and conditions within the public domain, there is a need for a pluralistic approach to assessing performance. This must attempt to balance the many perspectives, recognizing and incorporating the values of the various stakeholders involved – 'customers', elected members, professionals, interest groups, 'citizens' – as well as the many different public service contexts. Political values must be treated as integral and central rather than inhibiting and peripheral. Complex and extensive accountability is desirable. Achieving it, however, may not be easy in the current ideological climate where there are strong pressures in favour of defining accountability and performance in terms of a narrow customer focus, in an institutional setting dominated by increasing fragmentation and a contract culture in which organizational learning can be frustrated. In developing an appropriate perspective on performance enhancement in public service organizations much more attention needs to be given to the democratic institutions that allow debate about the contested nature of performance to take place.

4.7 CHAPTER SUMMARY

The following key learning points emerge from this chapter:

- Performance management is used to describe the range of processes, techniques and methods to achieve an improvement in the productivity and quality of the relationship between inputs, activities, outputs and outcomes in public service organizations: it is concerned with enhancing the value adding process.
- The pressure for more emphasis to be given to performance and its enhancement was driven by a number of pressures, both intellectual and financial, which questioned the traditional bureaucratic mode of organizing and delivering public services.
- Managing performance in public service organizations is complex since goals are rarely clear or consensual given the multiple constituencies of stakeholders involved and the complex environments of public service delivery. Performance is elusive and is inherently contested and, therefore, political.
- Financial performance criteria such as probity remain very important but financial targets need to be used with caution and only provide a partial perspective on performance.
- Given the nature of the budgetary process in most public service organizations, adherence to the budget is not necessarily a guarantee of high levels of performance and quality service delivery.
- The managerial performance criteria of 'value for money' – the economic acquisition of resources and their efficient utilization in the realization of the purposes of the organization – have proved the most popular.
- Political accountability involves the most elusive concept of performance, one which incorporates the distinctive purposes, values and conditions of the public domain and is about what **should** be done and the **process** by which it is done.
- The concept of quality in public services is as contested as the concept of performance.
- Successful performance management depends upon having both appropriate technical and procedural practices **and** supportive cultural and attitudinal characteristics within an organization.
- Given the complexity of public service delivery and the difficulties of defining and measuring its performance a strategic management perspective fully integrated into the working practices of the organization is required.
- Managing performance requires clear objectives, emphasis upon outputs and outcomes, supportive systems and the ability to measure achievement via PIs.
- PIs serve both an internal management function and a public accountability one. There is likely to be a need for a cluster of indicators tailored for particular audiences.
- For PIs to perform their key role of facilitating organizational learning and development an appropriate organizational culture is required, one which is committed to continuous improvement.

- PIs also require specifically designed management information systems and need to be expressed in a form which facilitates comparison against some benchmark.
- PIs for economy and efficiency are far better developed than those for effectiveness, and there are dangers in using a number of the crude unit cost indicators.
- Effectiveness PIs are more complex largely because it is concerned with outcomes evaluated in terms of the changed welfare status of the wide range of stakeholders served.
- PIs hold dangers too, including mis-directed target following, short-termism and an obsession with the measurable to the exclusion of the qualitative with PIs becoming an end in themselves rather than a means. In the public services where performance can never be finally defined it can never adequately be measured.
- Performance management requires political and organizational skill. It is not easy, nor costless and it takes time. There needs to be permanent evolution if the changing needs of the legitimate political process are to be expressed and supported.

TEXT-BASED QUESTIONS

1. What do you consider to be the key differences between public service organizations and private sector ones? Specify the relevance of the differences identified for the management of resources and performance in public service organizations.

2. How far do you think moves to secure economy, efficiency and effectiveness in public service organizations will come into conflict with

    (i)   equity; and
    (ii) political accountability?

3. What do you consider to be the most appropriate cultural and attitudinal characteristics within an organization to be compatible with the achievement of high levels of performance? How far do the characteristics you have identified describe public service organizations with which you are familiar?

4. What is the relationship between quality service delivery and value for money?

5. Identify how, using examples, performance indicators could assist managers make more economic, efficient, effective and equitable decisions.

6. Who should set standards for performance in public services? Should it be professionals, politicians, or service users?

ASSIGNMENT 1

For a public service with which you are familiar, attempt to establish the extent to which the organization as a whole, or one part of it, is using a systematic performance framework.

In particular try to establish:

(a)   the aims and objectives of the public service you have chosen;

(b)   the inputs used, the activities undertaken by the organization, the outputs delivered and the likely outcomes achieved;

(c)   the extent to which performance indicators are available and whether they measure inputs, inputs in relation to outputs, outputs and outcomes in relation to objectives;

(e)   how the information is used, for example, in terms of benchmarking or monitoring;

(f)   how the organization might improve its performance management system and the quality of its service delivery.

ASSIGNMENT 2

Prepare a 'hierarchy of objectives' for an area of your work, or one with which you are familiar, together with associated indicators by which you can assess the extent of achievement of the objectives.

In particular:

(a)   prepare a flow diagram indicating the objectives of your area of work, arranged hierarchically starting with the mission statement at the top, breaking this down through several layers of the hierarchy into lower and lower level objectives, until you reach operational activities;.

(b)   prepare a set of performance indicators which might be appropriate for establishing whether objectives at the various levels have been achieved;.

(c)   discuss how you will obtain the necessary information on performance with respect to each PI, the frequency of data collection, the appropriateness of targets, the relevant comparisons to be made, how the results will be presented and to whom, and enforcement opportunities;

(d)   provide a critique of the hierarchy of objectives approach to managing performance in public service organizations.

FURTHER READING

Carter, N., Klein, R. and Day, P. (1992) *How Organizations Measure Success: the Use of Performance Indicators in Government*, Routledge, London. Provides a valuable over-view and a number of case studies of performance measurement in both public and private sectors.

Fenwick, J. (1995) *Managing Local Government*, Chapman and Hall, London. Chapter 5 provides a good survey of the whole field of performance management in the local government context.

Gaster, L. (1995) *Quality in Public Services*, Open University Press, Buckingham. An excellent exploration of quality and performance as contested concepts with practical suggestions for their achievement.

Jackson, P. M. (ed.) (1995) *Measures for Success in the Public Sector: A Reader*, Public Finance Foundation/CIPFA, London. A useful collection of articles on performance management which have appeared in *Public Money and Management* over the past few years.

Jackson, P. M. and Palmer, A (1993) *Developing Performance Monitoring in Public Service Organizations*. Management Centre, University of Leicester. A very useful and practical guide.

Likierman, A. (1990) Performance Indicators: 20 Early Lessons from Managerial Use. *Public Money and Management*, **8** (4), pp.15–22. A very good summary paper.

Selim, G. M. and Woodward, S.A. (1992) The Manager Monitored, in *Rediscovering Public Services Management*, (eds L. Willocks and J. Harrow) McGraw Hill, London, pp. 141–69. A good survey with particular emphasis on the wider organizational issues.

Stewart, J. and Walsh, K. (1994) Performance Measurement: When Performance can Never be Finally Defined. *Public Money and Management*, **14** (2), pp. 45–9. A very clear argument as to why perfect PIs cannot be found in the public domain.

CHANGING MANAGEMENT AND EMPLOYMENT IN LOCAL GOVERNMENT

5

Clare Rigg and Kiran Trehan

5.1 CHAPTER PREVIEW

Earlier chapters have examined some of the rapid changes taking place in public sector organizations with local government in the forefront of such changes. It is now almost a cliché to say that management in those organizations is about managing change. An essential ingredient for effective management of change is the approval and (best of all) commitment of those who work for the organization – hence the importance of managing human resources. But the concept of managing people is itself changing. Indeed, the ramifications of human resource management (HRM) and its distinction from personnel management, are still being hotly debated in local government circles. This is against a background of external and internal pressures to cut resources, employ 'new managerialist' practices, and compete for contracts, all of which have intensified work, broadened role functions and rendered jobs less secure. The role and boundaries of middle managers have also been subject to a degree of redefinition.

The objective of this chapter therefore is to explore the current experiences of managing and working in local government by addressing a number of important questions including:

- whether there is a new approach to human resource management in local government, as distinct from personnel management;
- how the new practices and ideas of 'managerialism' are affecting the status and conditions of managers and employees in local government;
- the extent to which the new paradigms are being imbedded in the value systems of those employed in local government;
- how people are being developed and supported in meeting the new demands facing them;
- the extent to which these attempts at management development are meeting the real needs of local government employees.

This Chapter is based mainly on original research and consists of extensive interviews carried out by the authors amongst middle managers in local government.

5.2   WHAT IS HUMAN RESOURCE MANAGEMENT?

HRM is a controversial concept, with as yet no clear consensus over its actual meaning. It is easy to use terms like HRM and personnel management, and yet to define them is to enter murky territory. This has resulted in a proliferation of terms which would be difficult enough if they were all exact synonyms, but the problem is made worse by the fact that authors use the same term to mean different things, and sometimes use different terms to mean the same thing. The only way to tell the difference is to delve beneath the surface to ascertain what is actually meant.

Definitions of HRM abound. Legge suggests that

> Personnel management is concerned with the management of subordinates and non management staff, whereas HRM seems to be about the development of the management team

> *(1995: 34)*

She argues that the role of line managers seems to be different, within personnel management. It tends to be about the implementation of specialist personnel procedures. Under HRM, line managers are at the centre of devising and implementing people management policies which are integrated with business strategy and unlike personnel management, HRM has the management of organizational cultures as a prime activity.

Rosemary Harrison argues:

> Personnel management is about maintenance of personnel and administrative systems. HRM is about the forecasting of organizational needs, the continual monitoring and adjustment of personnel systems to meet current and future requirements and the management of change

> *(Mumford 1994:110)*

Within this debate HRM is seen to be linked to the strategy of the organization and should be judged against criteria of coherence and appropriateness, that is, whether aspects of the employment systems are internally consistent with one another and are aligned with business strategy. This raises the question of whether the HRM function itself has enough influence to transcend its traditional operational role.

Others suggest that the differences between personnel management and HRM are not so clearly identifiable. Fowler (1988) for example, is of the view that substantively there is little new in HRM. Armstrong agrees but states that at least HRM

> has the virtue of emphasising the need to treat people as a key resource, the management of which is the direct concern of top management as part of a strategic planning process of the enterprise

> *(1989: 32)*

Other writers like Guest also argue that the term carries neither particular connotations nor conveys any particular distinctive meaning when placed alongside terms such as personnel management, management of people, or employee relations (1989: 506). He points out that a number of personnel departments have become human resource departments without any obvious change in roles and there is scepticism about there being any substantive difference between human resource management and traditional personnel management.

A sharper critique of HRM is presented by Storey (1991). He argues that the term is not new. For many years it carried no special significance and it tended to be used more or less interchangeably with a whole host of alternative formulations to signal what most would understand as personnel management. However, personnel management has long been dogged by problems of credibility, marginality, ambiguity and a 'trash-can' labelling which has relegated it to a relatively disconnected set of activities, many of them perceived as low status welfare roles. Thus, HRM came to be seen as denoting a radically different philosophy and approach to the management of people at work.

The picture painted by some of the above definitions demonstrates the difficulties associated with the term HRM. It has become difficult to define because it can have a variety of meanings, depending on the context in which the term is being applied. As Guest (1989) argues,

> we cannot really ask what HRM looks like in practice unless we have a model about what it constitutes, otherwise we are in danger of accepting as HRM any practices that are labelled as such, even if indistinguishable from what in the past has been termed personnel management

> *(1989: 507)*

Having introduced debates as to what HRM is, the following sections explore how middle management and senior officer roles have been affected by local government trends, before proceeding to discuss some of the consequences for employees on lower grades, particularly those subject to compulsory competitive tendering (CCT).

5.3   MANAGEMENT PROCESSES AND FUNCTIONS – CHANGES TO MIDDLE MANAGEMENT JOBS

5.3.1 Breadth and intensity of jobs

Local government middle manager jobs have been caught up in such changes as devolved responsibilities; an upsurge of customer responsiveness; tight control of spending and a strengthened line manager function in terms of requirement to actively manage through planning, target-setting and monitoring and appraising performance. Middle manager roles have become more intense, with more to do as a consequence both of devolution and of sharing out the workload of frozen posts. In addition, with increased responsibility, roles have intensified over recent years, with tighter targets, a plethora of initiatives, or increased statutory functions. Our research shows that most employees think it more stressful being in local government now than hitherto.

Some see their role as having expanded, not only quantitatively but also qualitatively, so that they not only have their 'professional' functions to perform, but they are also managing people, budgets, contracts and projects, all of which require changed skills. However, line managers' functions have not always been strengthened. Some feel their role has actually been confined with internal markets, as they become managers of contracts rather than of people or projects, giving them less control over implementation. For those reliant on external funds to develop projects, work has declined as funds have been diverted to quangos such as City Challenge.

A similar pattern exists with decision-making, where some believe they have more autonomy, whilst others feel constrained by the contracting culture, giving them less flexibility than previously. For example, some see themselves as more proactive, able to make decisions, for which in the past they would have had to obtain agreement from more senior staff. For others it is not a case of more autonomy but rather that work has simply expanded. From another perspective, the advent of internal trading contracts has constrained scope for decision-making, where previously if a decision was needed about prioritizing projects, a manager could act almost unilaterally, providing that she had the support from relevant people, whereas now it involves renegotiation of a contract.

5.3.2 Devolved power

Budgets are commonly devolved, with the consequence that team leaders have their own budget, for example, becoming responsible for maintaining a unit's building which was previously paid for centrally. However, although responsibility for accounting for expenditure is devolved, frequently, power to spend more than very small amounts is not, with corporate policy or standing orders still requiring committee approval for larger sums, even for direct labour organizations (DSOs). Even where a staff development budget was devolved to them, some middle managers described being blocked in their decisions concerning their staff by corporate policy on what training was considered appropriate.

There is also widespread devolution of personnel responsibility, so that those line managing are now involved in recruitment, appraisals and disciplinaries. However, some managers have lost responsibility for staffing because of the creation of an internal market and their being classified as being on the client not the contractor side of the authority. They are now more concerned in strategy-making, separated from responsibility for implementation. So for example, it was argued that

> We don't involve central personnel in interviews or things like that, we may involve them in disciplinaries because we need someone from outside or if it's a particularly iffy one on industrial relations, we've got a couple of experts over there, we use them. But on personnel and on welfare we deal with it ourselves
>
> *(Interview by authors)*

5.3.3 Frustrated creativity and enterprise

There is also evidence of frustration amongst middle managers, when on the one hand they are encouraged to think competitively and control resource use, but on the other they are prevented from using organizations other than the internal providers of certain services. This tension is not unexpected. It can exist in any organization when there is the need for entrepreneurship and creativity at the same time as an imperative for control and certainty. However, it is arguably more acute in local government where there are new pressures to be creative and entrepreneurial (in the sense of identifying opportunities and taking initiative) alongside the enduring older constraints of legislation and standing orders, as well as a risk-cautious ethos in that it is public money that any risk-taking jeopardizes. This raises the question of what kind of risk-taking and creativity is desirable in local government and how to avoid losing people who develop the ability, gain a taste for it but end up more deeply frustrated.

5.3.4 Flexibility

Some managers see current practice as offering more flexibility with people working together, going beyond job descriptions and with individuals who are broadly skilled, rather than narrowly specialized, so that they can all undertake any projects a team is pursuing. However, others are not so optimistic. A recurrent complaint is of constraint experienced with CCT and internal markets, particularly a loss of accommodation and adaptation in the way different groups work together. Financial awareness appears to bring retrenched boundaries around groups. These managers' perception is that if they do not anticipate and write in everything they need in a contract at the outset the cost may subsequently rise.

Concerns expressed by some on the client side are not only of a rigidity perceived in contracting, but also of frustration that whilst internal providers are slipping

> Previously I could just go to a member of staff and say I want you to do this project and this is how it needs to be done, or this is what we need to deliver at the end of it and agree how it was going to be done, but that would be on a one to one and there would be no negotiations, there would be no cost attached to it – we would have to work out how much I was prepared to spend and then make sure that they were coming to budget, that they weren't overspending, and all that had been introduced. To me it's a disbenefit. I know that under the previous arrangements I could have got these things done and that's frustrating. It would be important if we truly were in a market situation, but we haven't been market orientated.
>
> *(Source: Interview by authors)*

Figure 5.1   Inflexibility in contract culture

happily into exercising their commercial power of charging and negotiating, for them, the client, it is a **'fake commercialism'** in that they cannot go elsewhere for the work.

5.3.5 Strategy-making

The Management Charter Initiative (MCI) in its definition of and standard for middle management regards strategy as the preserve of senior staff and perceives middle managers and other officers as non-strategic, having no involvement in an authority's strategy-making. We would argue that strategy is the outcome of actions, not of a rational, formal planning process (Whittington 1993), and as such there is evidence of strategic activity by middle managers as, for example, they help determine training policy; develop a market for their unit; direct the pattern of customer relations and feedback and devise specification. Most are engaged in influencing the direction of actions, not merely operationalizing others' plans, although doing this as well.

5.4   BOUNDARIES – CHANGING PATTERNS OF RELATIONSHIPS

One consequence of the changes affecting local government has been alterations to internal and external relationships. In particular, new forms of collaboration are evident, as are ways in which authorities are fragmenting.

5.4.1 Collaboration

The rhetoric for local authorities is that recent trends have encouraged collaborative work and an enabling role. The evidence suggests that this is a partial practice. There appears to be increased external collaboration, as local authority staff seek partnerships to secure finance, working with:

- other regional authorities on policy development and resource allocation;
- the private sector to generate its financial involvement;
- bodies such as the local authorities' women network;
- the voluntary sector.

For some there has been a growth in networking within their department, task groups for example cutting across formal boundaries to develop departmental and corporate initiatives, such as training, project management for new computer systems, quality management teams and equal opportunities. Traditional networking, as a way of developing informal links, is also alive and well. However, cross-departmental collaboration is frequently described as declining, becoming restricted to formal trading agreements, as people redefine interactions as exchanges for financial transaction.

> The motivation for collaboration appears commonly to be the prospect of acquiring finance or business, rather than a belief in enabling others who are better placed as providers.

5.4.2 The shrinking authority

Much writing on organizational futures recommends delayering middle management and it has been argued that organizations are more efficient if pared back to their core business with support activities contracted out to peripheral businesses or individuals (Peters 1992; Atkinson 1984). An anticipated trend for local authorities is that they become more decentralized and fragmented. There is a small, but growing practice of externalization and a high degree of fragmentation with internal markets, DSOs and community care providers as well as decentralization in the form of neighbourhood offices. However, there are also contradictory trends in local authorities trying to remain intact, for example forming 'soft' splits within a department.

(a) Structural fragmentation

Fragmentation describes a process of local authorities disaggregating themselves, moving away from the sixties' and seventies' aspiration of striving to be corporate (Maud 1967) and centrally-located in a prestigious town hall. The form of fragmentation pursued differs between authorities. In some, such as Wolverhampton, Tower Hamlets, Birmingham, decentralization of services geographically scattered around the borough, has been the path followed. The most radical perhaps were Walsall's proposals (1995/96) for 54 neighbourhood councils which would purchase services from a shrunken centre. In many authorities devolution is evident, whether totally as in local management of schools (LMS) or in part by the construction of certain activities as cost centres or strategic business units, with devolution of budgets and certain areas of decision-making.

(b)   Internal markets

In most councils the past five years have seen a hardening of internal boundaries with widespread introduction of internal markets, as authorities re-conceptualize inter-departmental activity as a process of trading, requiring service level agreements and trading accounts.

In some authorities the client/contractor split has been perceived simply as an expedient to avoid anti-competitiveness in complying with CCT legislation. In others the principle has been extended even in the absence of competition, for the purpose of clarifying internal trading relationships through Service Level Agreements (SLAs). In some, but not all instances, this formalization of inter-organizational trading has been accompanied by devolution of budgets, leading to the formation of cost centres or strategic business units.

(c)   Externalization

One response to CCT which is being explored in different authorities is 'external-ization'. As an alternative to setting up as individual business units bidding for contracts, an existing consultant is contacted to take on a number of staff, such as engineering or computer staff, the local authority guaranteeing work for a specified period. The staff are effectively 'floated away' in the market place.

Management and employee buyouts have been other mechanisms used to exter-nalize units. Here the boundaries retain a tenuous connection with the local authority for an interim period of guaranteed work, before being entirely transformed to a local authority – private sector relationship.

(d)   Soft splits

A hard split occurs where departments are completely separated into client and contractor, between whom there is a straight forward business relationship. Some authorities have constructed a soft split where the department is not totally split but there are separate functions, which means that at some point within the manage-ment chain there will be somebody that actually controls both even if this is only at chief officer level.

5.5   EQUALITY – THE IMPACT OF CCT

An Equal Opportunities Commission (EOC) survey (1995) of the gender impact of CCT found that women employees were being adversely affected, both as manual staff in CCT services and as white collar clerical and administrative staff within central support services. In comparison with male dominated areas of CCT such as refuse collection, the survey found greater loss of working hours; higher job loss; increased use of temporary workers; greater loss of pay and reduced benefit from corporate training amongst the predominantly female cleaning and catering areas. The overriding conclusion is that equality policies have been seriously damaged by competitive tendering.

5.5.1 Cost of equality

The cost of equality policies is seen by many local authority officers as a burden in a competitive context, even if they actually support the policies, because of the lack of government and private sector backing for equivalent policies. For example, within competition legislation, aside from costs of employing disabled staff, equality policies are not a legitimate competitive cost to write into contracts. Equality targets are rarely part of senior managers' performance review and many middle managers feel there is a contradiction imposed on them between performance targets and equality (which implicitly they are not defining as part of their performance). Some middle managers feel equality policies may be on the agenda of senior managers, because of their targets and of junior staff, as beneficiaries, but they as middle managers are given different targets – performance outcomes. Yet they are also expected to implement equality policies in terms of how they recruit or release staff for training. The dilemma was highlighted by a middle manager who argued that he:

> . . . was having to compete with outside organizations, they hadn't got the local authority burden on them as far as all this equality stuff, so therefore it's nice to do the nice things, but when you're competing for your job you're down to bottom line stuff, and its all hands to the pumps otherwise we're going to go under and we're going to go on the dole
>
> *(Interview by authors)*

Other managers, in contrast, see no inherent conflict between equality in employment and performance, either because policies such as jobshare enable them to keep women staff or because they believe family-friendly practices, which are flexible around occurrences such as illness, actually lead to people treating work as important. There is also the argument that if equality policies help to get and keep the 'best people for the job' they make good business sense.

5.5.2 Indirect consequences

Two contradictory trends are indirect consequences of present local authority developments. First, devolved responsibility, in exposing middle managers to wider experience, is increasing the profile of women and ethnic minority staff who, though not at the top, have accumulated in the middle range of jobs.

Second, more detrimentally, redundancies and the redistribution of remaining work is changing the workforce profile compared to the late 1980s. Some of those departments that have already been subjected to blue collar CCT, have frozen posts and restructured the remaining responsibilities rather than make people redundant. However, the turnover of posts have largely involved women who are in clerical and administrative positions, so those jobs are being lost. As a consequence the gender profile of the organization is changing. The more this happens the more that people who are prepared to stay long periods are the ones who will occupy jobs and it could be that an authority will shift more towards being a male dominated organization again.

5.6   NEW MANAGERIALIST PRACTICES

'New managerialist' practices include business planning, a consumerist perception and treatment of service recipients, culture change initiatives, performance measures, perception of accountability and use of generic rather than professional managers (See Chapters 1, 3, 4, 7 and 8).

5.6.1 Business plans

Business plans are used widely for a range of purposes, including as:

- a plan of action of how a unit would be turned around in the coming year;
- an examination of the service provided, clients' preferences for the type of design and delivery of services, who the suppliers are, prioritizing the work of a section within the overall objectives of a council, department and division;
- part of a CCT tender submission;
- a strategy for whole department;
- a strategy for a council as a whole.

Awareness of the financial implications of work has become more widespread, enabling staff to price for internal trading or CCT, to assess the external competition, to monitor performance, or to focus on earning income.

5.6.2 Consumerism

Consumerism in the public sector is discussed at length in several chapters of this book (see Chapters 5, 7 and 8). Our study found comprehensive evidence that middle managers have a defined conception of their consumers, whether internal or external and frequently 'talked' the language of consumerism. Many staff are more proactive in their external and internal relations, indicating an awareness of customer needs that goes further than mere use of language. Examples include: going out to speak to the quangos that now receive money previously paid to the council; effectively marketing a section's capability to generate work; and role expansion to embrace customer relations with an open door policy for public grievances.

5.6.3 Corporate culture initiatives

Many councils have some kind of initiative which could be said to be aiming to promote 'new managerialist' practices, such as devolved resource management; training in effectiveness; customer awareness and quality training; use of quality circles. At times training is explicitly used to try to change employees' attitudes and behaviour. Scenario planning is employed in some authorities to generate options for the future, for example, bringing staff together with managers to explore how particular visions could be implemented. Others use what they call 'events' workshops combining customers, staff and suppliers to consider problems.

5.6.4 Setting standards – performance indicators

Performance indicators are widely used to measure and monitor output. Often they are employed in response to the demands of external bodies such as the Audit Commission, DTI or DoE. Sometimes they had been internally initiated when an individual wanted to make changes to work practices, for example, to improve response rates given to internal customers or to focus staff on the quality of work done.

5.6.5 Accountability

Bound up with awareness of customers, competition and finance is a wider perception of accountability. For some this is expressed as a change in organization culture that no longer tolerates sexist or racist behaviour. For others, it is a pressure to perform well, and yet in other instances, it is to have open auditable systems (See Chapter 1 and 4 for further discussion of this aspect of accountability).

5.6.6 Generic management or a new public services managerialism?

There is clear engagement by middle managers in many activities that constitute new managerialism. However, there is continued assertion of public service ethos, not merely commercialism or economism. For example, in a review of job advertisements, community consultation and working within an equal opportunities framework were emphasized as requirements of the post holder.

In local government consumerism is not necessarily a direct transfer from the private sector, as forms of consumer relations differ. For example, events in which service-users are involved in problem solving with staff are not typical of commercial companies, which tend to utilize consultation rather than participation as their mode of contact.

Equality illustrates well the tensions between local government domains of service, policy and management. For many authorities equality in service delivery and employment retains a high profile and for many individuals, particularly those who have benefited, there is still a high value placed on the pursuit of equal opportunities. However, as emphasized earlier, there is also evidence of pressure to cut back on perceived additional costs of equal opportunities in order to meet performance output targets or be competitive in CCT although, as suggested above, this has indirect causes as well as being the direct result of cost-cutting.

This example of tensions between the domains could be characterized as one of public service new managerialism, where the management domain is more dominant than in the past, but the policy and service domains remain buoyant. However, the position is also fluid and the balance between the domains is likely to continue to alter.

5.6.7 Different values and beliefs – how deep does it go?

If there is evidence that local government jobs have broadened and encompass new managerialism, how deep have the values underlying new management practices penetrated? Do people really believe that customers come first; or that they should be constantly proactive, or vigilant about resource savings? Or do they merely comply with the new routines?

In our study a majority of interviewees were themselves supportive of many of the new developments in local government, although this was usually a moderated rather than an unqualified judgement. However, their comments also indicate that 'new managerialism' is not embraced by many of their colleagues and that a scepticism about culture change initiatives pervades the workforce. When people feel they have not been valued in the past, they are dubious about new cultural messages promising to value and invest in staff. They fear that such promises may be no more than means to extract more work from them.

Local authority employees are adopting varying strategies to respond to current trends. Some recognize the permanence of changes, both in terms of demands at work and the comparative insecurity of employment. Their response is to take control and avoid becoming over-specialized, or to develop transferable skills that could make them employable in the private sector. Others shore up their position by strategies other than development or adoption of 'new management' practices. These included the renowned ostrich strategy: hoping change will go away, or that a Labour government will turn back the clock. Some cultivate a political armour, hoping to survive

> . . . because they are politically capable, they know the right people in the city, some of them are very good with politicians so they're bullet proof really; no matter how bad they perform

> (*Interview by authors*)

5.7   EMPLOYMENT TERMS AND CONDITIONS

5.7.1 Impacts of CCT

Evidence emerging suggests that employment terms and conditions have been adversely affected by CCT. Contractual hours of work, levels of employment, pay rates and conditions such as sick pay, annual leave and pensions have all been adversely affected in a significant proportion of cases. As Kerr and Radford argue:

> Subjecting public services to competitive tendering was intended to encourage competition . . . leading to better managed, more innovative and more respon-sive services. . . . it was envisaged that these changes would result in greater efficiency and lower costs. . . . studies suggest that savings . . . have arisen as a result of contractors imposing job losses, and inferior pay and conditions on employees, most of whom are women

> *(1994: 37)*

Table 5.1   Comparisons of pay and conditions for a street sweeper

	Local Authority	Contractor
Weekly earnings	£182.94	£146.75
Bonus	44% basic	None
Hours of work	35 per week	40 per week
Holidays	20 days (1st year of service)	15 days
Pensions	Local Government Superannuation Scheme	None
Sickness	1st year of service: 1 month full pay and (after 4 months' service) 2 months' half pay	1–13 weeks' service: Statutory Sick Pay
	2nd year of service: 2 months' full pay and 2 months' half pay	14 weeks – 1 year service: 1 week half pay
	3rd year of service: 4 months' full pay and 4 months' half pay	1–2 years' service: 2 weeks half pay
	4th and 5th year of service: 5 months' full pay and 5 months' half pay	3–4 years' service: 3 weeks half pay
	After 5 years of service: 6 months' full pay and 6 months' half pay	

(Source: DoE 1991)

(NB Local authority earnings include average bonus, London weighting, average overtime and cleaning money)

Contractual hours have decreased by 25% in building cleaning and by 16% in education catering, but have remained the same in refuse collection, although actual hours worked by full-timers have increased. Female part-timers in catering and cleaning have been most affected by a decline in hours, placing an increased number below the National Insurance Lower Earnings Limit.

CCT has also affected the levels of local authority employment, with a fall of 22% in female employment and 12% in male in the first round of tendering (EOC 1995). Between March 1989 and March 1992, the LGMB (1993b; 1992) estimate a loss of 28,192 full-time equivalent posts, particularly affecting building cleaning and refuse collection, although also catering, leisure management, street cleaning and vehicle maintenance. Most authorities in the EOC (1995) study have increased their use of temporary employees, primarily in cleaning, catering and community care services.

Basic pay rates in refuse collection actually increased during the first round of tendering, but remained static or declined in catering and cleaning (EOC 1995). However, take-home pay has been reduced by changes to or abolition of bonus schemes in about 50% of services (Kerr and Radford 1994). Other conditions of service have also declined (e.g. shift patterns, alteration to sick pay schemes), as DSOs lower their costs in an attempt to compete with private sector bids. As Kerr and Radford state 'the private sector will generally offer lower pay rates and poorer conditions such as holidays, sickness pay and benefits' (ibid.: 38). Table 5.1 above offers a comparison of pay and conditions in a local authority and a private contractor.

Jobs: retention of the existing workforce - all those employed at the time of transfer must be employed by the new contractor

Pay and conditions: existing terms and conditions must be preserved, including rate of payment, holiday and sick leave.

Pensions: Pensions are not transferable, but the new contractor must make alternative, broadly comparable arrangements.

Length of service: time spent with the authority counts towards length of service with the new employer.

Unfair dismissal: this can be claimed except on the grounds of 'an economic, technical or organizational reason entailing changes in the workforce'.

Union Recognition: existing arrangements transfer to the new employer.

Collective agreements: including grievance and disciplinary procedures transfer to the new employer.

Consultation with the workforce: the employer has an obligation to inform and consult with recognized trade unions

---

Figure 5.2 Transfer of undertakings (protection of employment) regulations 1981 (TUPE)

5.7.2 Transfer of Undertakings (Protection of Employment) Regulations (TUPE)

When the government introduced CCT legislation it assumed that when work was contracted out contractors could take on some or all of the previously local authority-employed on reduced terms and conditions. However, decisions taken by the European Court of Justice have led to the inclusion of TUPE in the Trade Union Reform and Employment Act 1993, so that the definition of an undertaking is extended to include those that are non-commercial (see Figure 5.2 above). Terms and conditions of local authority employees have therefore, to some extent, been protected by TUPE, but continuing controversy around the extent of its application and outstanding court decisions, help explain why terms and conditions have deteriorated in many instances. In addition, of course, TUPE does not protect local government employees working for DSOs, if pay and conditions are downgraded as the DSO seeks to win tenders by reducing costs.

5.8   THE PERSONNEL FUNCTION

The service provided by personnel management units during the next few years is likely to play a significant role in achieving change. In the 1990s local authorities have been under increasing pressure to become competitive, to provide cost effective services or commission them from the market place, with financial constraints being at the forefront. Local authorities have been faced with a seemingly endless stream of government legislation and the realities of the commercial approach have brought about dramatic changes in the way some departments operate, and the demands made on managers. It is of interest, therefore, to examine how the personnel function has been shaping up to meet the challenge.

In some authorities the perceived role of the personnel function is as supportive of management and must transform itself as management changes to meet new service delivery requirements. Thus as one personnel manager observed,

> In the past, because of the way in which the organization is structured, Personnel was seen as a control function . . . we acted like the village bobby and the village grocer. That may change

> *(Interview by authors)*

Managers are also having to take on increasing responsibility for their own personnel decisions, such as employee planning, recruitment, training, development and appraisal. The personnel function provides the vehicle, support and training to enable this to happen. In the past there has been a tendency for managers to be dependent upon personnel professionals for decision-making in a range of areas and this relationship is now being altered. For example, it has been argued that:

> The policy of devolving decision-making to managers has involved a shift in power from the personnel specialist to the line manager. As a result, personnel

units are under increasing pressure to ensure that their own staff are properly trained, and updated to assist in the change process, whilst at the same time remaining cost effective

(Interview by authors)

The role of the central personnel function has been to prepare strategies and policies which facilitate better service delivery. The role of departmental personnel units has contributed towards the formulation of this policy and its implementation through line managers in departments. This has formed a link between service delivery and personnel policy formulation.

It is important to acknowledge the variety of services delivered to the community by departments and how this is reflected in the organizational, cultural and environmental differences between them. This is expressed in the different expectations of Chief Officers for their departmental personnel officer. These differences have increased with the impact of current legislation and an increase in decisions at the local level.

To implement change and new policies have also required a high quality training function in the organization. Departmental personnel units are well placed to assess and meet training needs in consultation with line management. Whilst line managers have been encouraged to contribute within the training process and to play a far more active and flexible role in the career/personal development of employees, central services are likely to continue to provide common skills training and training arising as a result of policy initiatives in response to demand, acting in a consultancy capacity to departments.

In some areas of decision-making, line managers' dependence on personnel is restricting and does not afford the opportunity for personnel practitioners to optimize their skills. Trends are for the personnel management function to complement and integrate with the service delivery function, rather than having separate identity.

Within local government the degree of change in the field of personnel management has been subject to much debate. There are, in essence, two interpretations; one view suggests that the degree of change has been exaggerated and any claim to major transformation is a myth and the other is that there have indeed been changes in the nature and role of personnel management.

This can be seen via the emergence and development of the line managers' role as key players in devising, driving and delivering new HRM initiatives. They are encouraged to place the emphasis on unlocking the potential of their human resources through a distinctive set of techniques (paying close regard to motivational aspects, communication, development and managerial leadership) against a background where the emphasis is also placed on the quantitative, calculative and business strategic aspects of managing and planning the headcount in as 'rational' a way as any other resource.

5.9   MANAGEMENT DEVELOPMENT

5.9.1   Patterns of development

The emphasis of development processes in most organizations, if there has been any at all, has been on formal, planned activities, epitomized by the existence of courses or workshops. Up to the mid-1970s these could be characterized as systematic in the sense of being formal courses, but participation tended to be ad hoc, there being no strategy on who is to be trained, or even in what area. This was the outcome of individual staff requests or who happened to be free to attend a particular seminar (Pedler *et al.*, 1991).

Into the 1980s interest rose in both organization development and self-development, though still these were frequently local rather than strategically integrated. More recent works, for example, by Pedler *et al.* (1991) maintain that the future of management development is bound up with organizations becoming a learning company: 'an organization that facilitates the learning of all its members and continuously transforms itself' and is 'capable of adapting, changing, developing and transforming themselves in response to the needs, wishes and aspirations of people, inside and outside' (ibid.: 1). For these authors, learning is facilitated by the structure and culture of an organization, not from exigent training activities.

The concept of the learning organization is an ever-shifting model. The notions of continuing change, evolution and development are both its central theme and its most fundamental characteristics. In itself it is not merely an approach to training and development, it is a concept of organizational and personal growth. Peter Senge describes the learning organization as one:

> where people continually expand their capacity to create the results they truly desire, where new and expansive patterns of thinking are nurtured, where collective aspiration is set free, and where people are continually learning how to learn together

> (*Mumford 1995: 89*)

Further understanding of a learning organization requires an analysis of how it has arisen and a study of its characteristics.

The learning organization approach has developed as traditional approaches to training and development have become less effective, ceasing to provide organizations with the competitive advantage they seek. The search began to establish how organizations can develop in an environment of fast, difficult to predict and complex change. From this have emerged new perspectives of the organization and new practices which enable it to cope with such turbulence. To survive, organizations need to be able to adapt at a faster rate than previously. To do this, staff must be aware of the realities of their environment, learning and adapting continually. It therefore follows that there is a need for an organizational culture which will create and sustain this continual learning and adaptation. A learning organization displays the characteristics listed in Figure 5.3.

1. Strategy-making is seen and used as an opportunity for experiment and learning.

2. Participative policy-making, involving all those affected.

3. IT is used to inform and empower people.

4. Systems of accounting are used to assist learning.

5. There is internal exchange, with an internal market, yet also collaboration so that all parties remain aware of corporate purposes – a win:win situation;

6. Reward systems reward flexibility.

7. Enabling structures – loose roles where departmental boundaries are seen as temporary and fluid. Opportunities exist for individual and business development.

8. All those with contact at the organization's boundaries are seen as scanners who can feed information back.

9. Inter-company learning exists with external collaboration from which learning is sought, e.g. bench-marking.

10. A learning climate exists, where managers facilitate staff's experimentation and learning from experience; feedback is sought.

11. Self-development opportunities are made available for all, e.g. courses, work-shops, seminars, self-learning, development groups, one-to-one coaching and mentoring, peer counselling.

(Source: Pedler M., Burgoyne J., Boydell, T. (1991) The Learning Company, Macgraw Hill, Basingstoke)

Figure 5.3 Eleven characteristics of a learning company

5.9.3 Models of management development

Approaches to management development within organizations have followed various models. Figure 5.4 summarizes the argument that management development can derive from three sources: informal, accidental processes, opportunistic, but integrated means, and formal, planned activities.

Writers such as Mumford (1988, 1989) and Revan (1980) argue that management development is most effective when rooted in helping managers to work through real experiences, so that it is both much more than undirected, ad hoc learning from experience, but also is not simply knowledge-based as in most formal off-the-job training and education. For Mumford, management development should embrace 'practical processes for integrating real work processes and formal schemes of development (1994: 569). He argues that if there is no intervention 'in those informal accidental day-to-day activities through which managers learn, their effectiveness is both reduced and partial.' (1994: 560). These views are echoed by others such as Snell (1990) in whose view 'management developers would better prepare managers for their learning careers if they were to encourage strategy and opportunism in context' (1990: 17) and Davies and Easterby-Smith (1984) who maintain that managers develop primarily through confrontations with novel situations and problems where their existing repertoire of behaviours is inadequate.

Type 1: 'Informal Managerial' – accidental processes

Characteristics: occur within managerial activities
explicit intention is task performance
no clear development objectives
unstructured in development terms
not planned in advance
owned by managers

Development
consequences: learning is real, direct, unconscious, insufficient

Type 2: 'Integrated Managerial' – opportunistic processes

Characteristics: occur within managerial activities
explicit intention both task performance and development
clear development objectives
structured for development by boss and subordinate
planned before hand or reviewed subsequently as learning experiences
owned by managers

Development
consequences: learning is real, direct, conscious, more substantial

Type 3: 'Formal management development' — planned processes

Characteristics: often away from normal managerial activities
explicit intention is development
clear development objectives
structured for development by developers
planned beforehand and reviewed subsequently as learning experiences
owned more by developers than managers

Development
consequences: learning may be real (through a job) or detached (through a course)
is more likely to be conscious, relatively infrequent

(Source: modified from Mumford, A. (1988) Developing Top Mangers, Gower, Aldershot.)

Figure 5.4   Models of types of management development

According to writers like Margerison and Mumford, good practice in management development would draw on Type 2 processes as well as the traditional Type 3 and would encompass the following policies and practices:

- integrated to required skills and jobs
- linked with promotional routes and rewards
- related to business plan
- planned, not ad hoc
- a day-to-day issue, led by line managers, not separated out to training departments

- involve managers in diagnosis of needs
- work-related activities
- output-orientated
- early leadership experience

Argyris and Schon (1974) go further in arguing that management development must show double-loop learning in the sense of not only learning from experience about how, for example, to solve a particular problem, but also learning how to learn.

5.9.4 Management development in local government up to the mid 1980s

Development in local government up to the 1970s was defined as formal training, primarily concerned with the achievement of professional qualifications by examination and for white collar staff with little attention to manual employees (Fowler 1980). Responsibility for providing development was perceived to lie with professional associations and individuals as much as with local authorities. This education/training focus was formalized in the 'purple book' or National Joint Committee (NJC) scheme which laid out priorities of:

- induction
- day-release for 'O' and 'A' levels and preliminary stages of professional qualifications
- assistance for preparing for qualifications recommended by the NJC for promotion purposes
- facilities which help to equip an officer for better performance of his existing or possible future responsibilities in the service

(Fowler 1980: 184)

Emphasis on training for exams began to be supplemented by short general management courses and the promotion of diplomas in management, in management development in the 1970s. This was reflected in the name change of the Local Examination Board to the Local Government Training Board (LGTB) in 1968, (now in the 1990s the Local Government Management Board (LGMB). It is also interesting to note the changes in courses of the LGTB, which in the 1970s included a Certificate in Municipal Administration (comprising public administration, economics of public finance, local government administrative practice and social policies) and a Diploma in Municipal Administration (encompassing local government law and finance, social administration, personnel practice and local government administrative practice).

By 1980 these courses had been replaced in popularity by the Diploma in Management Studies and the Institute of Chartered Secretaries and Administrators' Diploma. Fowler suggests that prior to 1980 there was already talk of generic management but that in terms of comprehensive management development:

It seems that full-scale management development is still relatively rare in local government. Some authorities have introduced staff assessment systems, some make a planned use of management training courses, some regularly review their management resources and forecast future needs, some have developed forms of internal training, some have encouraged their senior managers to use on-the-job coaching methods to train and develop subordinate staff, some have experimented in self-assessment systems, some have applied the target-setting and review principles of management by objectives. Few have linked all these activities in one integrated development program.

(*Fowler 1980*).

This suggests that in the 1970s management in local government was perceived as an administrative function, but that by the end of the decade some people were talking of generic management and integrated development, including the work-based learning environment. However, practice in management development, though going beyond exam-orientated courses, remained fragmented. Willcocks and Harrow (1992: 77) reported that even where the concept of organizational learning was talked about in local government, attention was on 'outward learning' – looking for ideas and models externally, whilst 'inward learning' tended to be ignored in that there were rarely mechanisms for recording, storing, reviewing or communicating learning from internal experiences.

This section so far has traced perspectives on management development and suggests that in local government two patterns can be discerned: first, conception of development has evolved from preparing people to be administrators to being managers; second, development in local government generally has been *ad hoc* and has emphasized and valued the formal processes.

Development in the 1990s in local government highlights that one of the strands of 'new public managerialism' is an increased valuing of generic managers in preference to professionally specialist managers.

5.9.5 Organization support for development

Typically, authorities have a central personnel unit responsible for co-ordinating staff development and in some instances there are departmental officers as well. Some councils have an internal management development programme of Certificate in Management (CM), Diploma in Management Studies (DMS) and Master of Business Administration (MBA). The view in other authorities is that such in-house development is limited because it does not give exposure to people from differing sectors and experiences. Another approach is to have an in-house training programme of short courses that are MCI accredited. In addition to these programmes, most authorities have regular internal short courses on a range of issues (e.g. CCT, recruitment and selection).

Some authorities have concerted policies of putting everyone through some type of training as a part of a customer-focus strategy. Others have corporate policies of encouraging the development of women and ethnic minority staff. Still others have sought Investors in People (IIP) status either corporately or through individual departments. But there are also examples of continuing traditional practice in management development such as 'promoting the best surveyors to manager even though they hadn't got any management ability' (*interviews by authors*).

5.9.6 Does development meet staff needs?

The early part of this section introduced views on management development practices and approaches that may be considered good practice. Within local authorities
it would appear that management development is formal education and training.
Comprehensive management development is still relatively rare in local government.
Whilst some authorities have introduced corporate development policies, in-house
training, staff assessment systems and have encouraged their managers to use on the
job coaching methods to train and develop staff, few have linked all these activities
in one integrated development process. Evidence from some authorities suggests that
management development, where it occurs, is top down and centrally determined,
underplaying middle managers' self-defined needs. Interviews suggested that even
in authorities with formal management development programmes staff found new
skills were demanded of them, for which they had no organizational support. For
example, although 'customers' and customer care had a high profile in many authorities, practical support to enable staff to develop markets or work with 'customers'
was rare.

The official British governmental response to developing managers since the late
1980s has been the competence route, led by the Management Charter Initiative (MCI),
where competence can be defined as the demonstration of appropriate knowledge,
ability and skill to do a particular task to a determined level. However, it has been
argued (Talbot 1993; Farnham and Horton 1993) that generic management competencies are inadequate for public sector managers. The principles of trying to define
what managers do and the activities and processes they engage in, are accepted as
useful, but MCI standards are for example divorced from a process of helping people
to define what they actually do and what they need, a process that is fundamental
if individuals are to take ownership of their development. Also, by being so reduc-
tionist, they offer little insight for organizational learning in identifying how and in
what direction to try and develop people. By ignoring the context, the MCI activities of middle managers do not relate to what specific managers do in their particular
context and there is no inclusion of political awareness.

MCI competencies are not considered irrelevant as such, but inadequate. A more
useful approach would be for each organization to devise its own strategy, building
on existing frameworks, but tailored to the activities and strategy of the specific
context. Furthermore, if a form of competencies is used, they can be no more than
part of a management strategy.

So, despite the fact that some local authorities are extensively engaging in such
activities as management development, training, making managers more business-
like, adopting HRM policies, encouraging cultural change and devolving personnel
and financial functions to line managers, in reality it would appear that practice is
varied, with contradictions between rhetoric and practice. This has meant that development processes have often proved to be inadequate for either preparing managers
as new managerialists, or helping them manage the new demands they are experi-
encing.

There are examples of contradictions in development between the espoused values
of the organization and what staff experience. For example, even where there is
funded training and management talk of valuing staff, in the new resource con-

strained and flat organization, the lack of career progression leads to the demotivation of staff.

> The conclusion is that management development in local government needs to be critically evaluated. In some local authorities it is both inadequate for preparing middle managers to meet the new managerialist challenges that result from their jobs and does not match the best practice of 'integrated managerial' development as advocated by Mumford, or of encouraging people to learn how to learn.

So, whilst authorities may have a vision and several policy initiatives, both corporately and departmentally, these policies are not always translated into action and are not always seen by staff as helping them meet the demands of their job.

5.10   CONCLUSION

The experience is that employment in local government has become generally more intense and less secure. Roles tend to be broader with devolved responsibilities. New skills, not simply professional competence, are now demanded of officers – the abilities to manage budgets and information; to be politically astute; to be entrepreneurial; to manage a variety of hierarchical and lateral relationships; and to manage projects and contracts as well as ongoing services.

Staff and management development in local government suggest that two patterns can be discerned. First, conception of development has evolved from preparing people to be administrators to being managers. Second, development has mirrored that more generally in Britain, being ad hoc and valuing formal processes. In the 1990s, development in local government highlights that one of the strands of new public managerialism is the elevation of management above professional specialism. It is suggested that the generic MCI competencies are inadequate for public managers because the activities of local government middle manager roles are distinctive. Even if a form of competencies or qualities is used, it can be no more than part of a management development strategy.

Some local authorities have tried to take a more integrated approach to management development, as a starting point towards creating a learning organization, although achievement of the ideal is likely to be environmentally constrained. Furthermore, whilst authorities may have a vision and policy initiatives for the future, these are not always translated into action and are not always seen by staff as helping them meet the demands of their jobs.

To the extent that authorities have devolved personnel activities to line managers and are attempting to tailor staff development to strategic organizational objectives, there is evidence of a new approach to HRM, as distinct from the personnel management of the past.

5.11 CHAPTER SUMMARY

The following key points emerge from this chapter:

- Jobs on career grades and in middle management have generally become broader and more intense to combine a wider range of roles and activities. However, some feel more constrained by the contract culture.
- A key influence has been devolution of responsibilities, such as budgeting and staff management, to middle managers.
- Staff are being asked to be creative and entrepreneurial in seeking funds or finding solutions, but the legislative framework and a risk-averse cultural ethos can create tension.
- Internal and external relationships show new forms of collaboration in some instances, particularly between local authorities and external bodies and retrenched boundaries in others, particularly across internal departmental boundaries
- New structural forms are being explored as different authorities pursue one or more of decentralization, internal markets, externalization and soft splits.
- Equality practice and policies tend to have been significantly damaged by competitive tendering, both indirectly and directly as equality is widely seen as a cost that is in tension with other performance measures.
- There is evidence that the management domain in local authorities is growing in relation to the policy and service domains. In particular there is an upsurge in new managerialist practices.
- However, continued assertion of public sector values such as community consultation and equality suggests that local government management is characterized by a new public services managerialism, rather than a generic commercial managerialism.
- There is also evidence that despite cultural change initiatives and a changed external financial and political environment, change in some employees' minds is surface.
- Employees in services subject to CCT have generally been adversely affected in their job terms and conditions. Pay has largely declined; numbers of jobs have fallen; and sick pay, holiday pay and pensions are typically inferior. Women workers have been most harshly affected.
- TUPE has offered some protection for terms and conditions of employees transferred from local authority employment to private contractors, but not to employees remaining in the employment of DSOs (direct service organizations).
- The degree of change in personnel management is subject to debate:
  - (a) one view suggests that the degree of change has been exaggerated and any claim of major transformation is a myth;
  - (b) an alternative view is that there have been real changes to personnel management, with the emergence and development of line managers as key players in devising, driving and delivering human resource management initiatives;
  - (c) there is greater emphasis placed on thinking strategically about the numbers, skills and roles of staff.
- Development and resourcing policies are being integrated into the broader aims of the organization.

- Conception of development has evolved from preparing people to be administrators to being managers.
- Development has been ad hoc with the emphasis placed on formal processes.
- One of the strands of new public managerialism has been an increased valuing of management, at the expense of the values of professional specialism.
- The competence route led by the Management Charter Initiative should be no more than part of a management development strategy. They may be the modern replacement or supplement for qualifications, but they remain within the domain of formal types of management development.
- Some authorities have tried to adopt a learning organization approach as a means of human resource and organizational development, although environmental constraints limit achievement of a learning organization.
- Whilst authorities may have a vision and policy initiative for the future, these are not always translated into action and are not always seen by staff as helping them meet the demands of their jobs.

TEXT-BASED QUESTIONS

1.   What have been the key influences on middle grade/middle manager jobs in local government in recent years?

2.   Discuss the extent to which management practices and cultural values in local government have really changed in the past five to ten years.

3.   What sorts of skills and qualities are required to manage the changing type of boundaries and collaborative relationships in local government?

4.   How appropriate do you consider a competence-based approach to be in developing managers to meet the demands of working local government?

5.   What kinds of tension exist in implementing equality policies in a competitive context and how would you recommend these are managed?

6.   To what extent do present developments in human resource management in local authorities differ from the traditional local government personnel function?

ASSIGNMENT

A new human resource/personnel officer has joined your organization/section. In order to get a feel for training and development in the organization section over the past three years he/she has asked each employee to prepare a paper on their training which should include the following:

- an outline of the staff training (in the broadest sense) received in the last three years;
- discussion on the role the employee has played in the planning and deciding on such training
- evaluation of effect of any or all of such training on the employee's job and/or on the employee's attitude to his/her job;
- suggest improvements which could be made to such training.

As an employee prepare your paper.

FURTHER READING

Armstrong, P. (1989) *People in Organizations*, Elm Publications, Cambridge.
Equal Opportunities Commission (1995) *Gender Impacts of Compulsory Competitive Tendering* EOC, Manchester.
Fowler, A. (1988) *Human Resource Management in Local Government* Longman, London
Leach, S *et al.* (1993) *Challenge and Change*, Local Government Management Board, London.
Margerison, C (1991) *Making Management Development Work*, McGraw-Hill, Basingstoke.
Pedler, M. Burgoyne, J. and Boydell, T. (1991) *The Learning Company*, McGraw-Hill, Basingstoke.
Pedler, M. Burgoyne, J. and Boydell, T. (1994) *A Manager's Guide to Self-Development*, McGraw Hill, Basingstoke.

MANAGEMENT OF INFORMATION TECHNOLOGY IN THE PUBLIC SECTOR 6

Kester Isaac-Henry

Even more than in the past IS/IT in government will be the medium which reconciles the reduction of resources with the potential for improved service delivery

(*CCTA, Annual Report 1994–95: 1*).

6.1 CHAPTER PREVIEW

Information technology (IT) is so dynamic and fast changing, that it is in an almost constant state of revolution. It is having an enormous impact on management in the public sector and consequently on how services are delivered. The impact will become even greater as the technology advances; as managers become more aware of how the technology can transform organizations and as the technology becomes better managed. This chapter therefore explores:

- the development and use of IT in the public sector;
- the forces that are driving and restraining its use in that public sector;
- the problems public sector organizations face in their acquisition and use of IT;
- the attempts being made to overcome such problems.

A critical examination of the key aspects of the changing structures and processes of the public sector is a principal theme of this book. Most of these themes have put an emphasis on quality information and its management. Hence the chapter also explores:

- the importance of information to the effectiveness and efficiency of the public sector;
- how information in the sector could be better managed;
- the need to manage both information and information technology together as a resource ;
- the problem of managing a technology which is in a constant state of change.

The chapter also emphasizes the importance of managing effectively, what has become, in addition to information, a major corporate resource of organizations and the difficulties presented to management by turbulence both in the changes being wrought by the development of **'new public management'** and the rapidity of change in information technology.

In the exploration of these management issues a number of case studies have been used.

6.2   THE CONTEXT

The speed of change makes it difficult to define but by IT we refer to the use of computers and telecommunications equipment to record, process, calculate and transfer information in the form of data, image and voice from one place to another and at great distances. The power of the technologies has been enhanced by their being integrated and by the spread of IT infrastructures through networks and recently by the open inter-connectivity of the hardware. Information technology is regarded as a key strategic resource helping organizations to gain a competitive edge and is increasingly becoming indispensable to organizations both in the private and public sectors.

Until recently, in the public sector at least, the 'technology' rather than the 'information' was the driving force in the activities and strategies relating to IT. This is understandable, given that the earliest use of IT in the service sector was to support 'structured' activities such as ordering, purchasing, payroll, accounting and stock-taking (O'Brien 1989: 194). Developments in the last two decades have resulted in IT doing the same things better, doing more things and doing new things. The technology is increasingly being used for unstructured activities such as aiding analysis, developing strategies, decision-making, planning and information management. It is increasingly being argued that IS/IT strategies should be driven by the information needs of the business. Information is a major resource of public sector organizations. Quite often it is their raw material, their processes and their end products. The public sector creates, processes, stores, acts and reacts to information. In pursuing the democratic/ political processes, in managing resources, executing functions, measuring performance and in service delivery, information is the basic ingredient. In local government information is said to be

> central to the workings of local authorities . . . to the provision of local authorities services, to achieving value for money, to competitiveness and to the workings of democracy. It is central as a resource, as a service, as a window on the authority and as a medium of influence and for enabling. It is central to the day-to-day operations, to management, to strategy, to politics.
>
> (*Local Government Management Board 1990: 3*)

A technology which aids the production, management and control of information should widely be used by, and be an influence on, public sector organizations.

However, IT should be used for much more than providing efficient services. For some, it has the potential to transform organizations and their activities. The government, for example, has conjured up a vision where, by using IT, it will become more responsive, accessible and will offer vastly improved services to citizens at less cost while allowing the latter a greater say in decision-making on matters affecting their lives (CCTA 1995b: 10). It is a vision which will be realized by the use of the information superhighway where people will use (and are using) the technology to:

- talk to each other – telephony
- talk to each other and be seen by each other – Video conferencing
- send messages to each other – faxing
- work from home or choice of location - the electronic cottage

(HC Deb., Col 913, 13 March 1995)

> But more importantly, people can join together to do all these things and can do so from different parts of the world. The internet – a global inter-communication network – will be the slip road on to the information superhighway which places information and its management in the fast lane of the developing technology.

6.3   USING THE TECHNOLOGY IN THE PUBLIC SECTOR

The public sector has long been a leader in the development and use of computer technology (Frissen 1992). As early as the 1950s, the social security task was aided by computer technology helping to carry out routine operations and keeping personnel and client data. The existence of the National Police Computer, the use of computers in the armed services supply systems and in the drivers and licence sections of the Ministry of Transport, all testify to its early use by government.

A critical examination of key aspects of the changing structures and processes of the public sector is a principal theme of this book. Most of these changes have put a premium on quality information and its management. Indeed 'a common dimension of recent initiatives to improve management in government is that it amounts to a new agenda on information in public administration' (Bellamy 1994: 55). Many government policies are now predicated on the basis that IT will be used to plan, deliver and control services. The public sector faces the problem of how to plan for and use IT effectively, when changes in the sector are endemic and when the future of some of these bodies is so uncertain. For example, in the years between 1992 and 1996 local authorities had to plan and develop IT strategies, against the background of the developing concept of new public management encompassing fragmentation of responsibilities and services (CCT, quangos, opting out of schools etc.) as well as against the uncertain future of their existence as a consequence of local government restructuring. At the same time the technology was 'moving so rapidly that no one can easily define, let alone reach, their goal. In this sense management was forever 'chasing a rainbow' (Audit Commission 1995: 76).

Although the extent and sophistication of use varies, most departments of government are heavily involved in the use of IT, many viewing it as critical to their effectiveness. As to be expected, the early use of IT concentrated on office automation involving the use of word-processing, spreadsheets, databases and electronic mail. However, as integration between the various uses has taken place and, as networking gathers pace, there is a rush towards office systems providing for management information, IT infrastructures and corporate databases. The Government Information Service, for example, created in 1994 with a view to making government information more widely available and holding information on over sixty government organizations, is growing rapidly and is accessed by over 80,000 subscribers each week (CCTA 1995b: 10).

6.3.1 IT in central government

Central Government's expenditure on IT for non-scientific and non-military purposes amounted to about £2000 million in 1993 (Willcocks 1994: 13), with related IT assets of over £7000 million. Some departments have developed very large systems based on the nature of their functions. The Inland Revenue, responsible for processing the returns of 28 million tax forms in 600 offices, computerized its PAYE system in 1988 at a cost of nearly £350 million. The Ministry of Defence spent about £200 million on IT in 1989–90 (on non-military office support systems) with the objectives of

- supporting managers and commanders at all levels of decision-making;
- carrying out tasks which cannot be undertaken efficiently or effectively or not at all without involving IT support;
- providing required information where needed at the right place, time and cost;
- helping to contribute to the defence objectives within available resource (NAO 1991b).

The Department of Social Security presents an example of one of the largest information technology projects ever undertaken by (civil) government in developing 'Operation Strategy' (see Case Study 6.1). The project is illustrative of the use to which IT can be put in government and the problems which may arise from such developments.

The NHS spent around £600 million in 1992 (Willcocks 1994: 13). The development of IT in the NHS and the problem that development has confronted epitomise the development of IT in most parts of the public sector. Until the 1990s it had no overall IS/IT policies on the use and acquisition of IT and a state of anarchy appeared to have existed and where

> there are hundreds, if not thousands, of departmental mangers both medical and non-medical who have acquired their Apricot, Apple, Acorn, or some other bit of fruit, who are happily building their own independent system without

CASE STUDY 6.1   Operational Strategy in the DSS

In 1982 the Department of Health and Social Security embarked on 'Operation Strategy', a development of an integrated system designed to computerize its operations. The system began operating in 1991. The fascination of this development lies in the

- size of the project;
- gigantic escalation in cost;
- concept of the 'whole person';
- implications for structural changes;
- the problems in encountered with staff.

The DSS is responsible (now through its various agencies) for paying out many benefits including those for pensions, widows, incapacity, unemployment and income support. Traditionally these were paid separately and generally at different counters in a social security office. 'Operational Strategy' was designed to computerize the operations of a service which in 1982 paid out £45,000 million in benefits (about £71,000 million in 1991) employed 108,000 staff and at the outset was to cost £713 million pounds to develop. In 1995 the DHS was said to possess 70,000 terminals, 184 mainframes produces each year 85 million girocheques, 57 million order books, and 155 million printed items (H.C Deb, July 12 1995: col. 187). Between 1982 and 1989 the cost of the project rose (at 1989 prices) to nearly £2000 million. At the same time the estimated net savings fell from £915 million to a rather optimistic £175 million in 1990 (Margetts 1991). In 1995 the Chief Executive of the Information Technology Agency (of the DSS) stated that 'Operations Strategy' cost about £2.5 billion pounds to develop but was in 1995 responsible for savings of abvout £3.3 million (Social Security Committee, DSS, ITSA, Minutes of Evidence H.C Deb. May 24 1995: 1).

The 'whole person' concept is one in which an individual's claim for different benefits can be dealt with at a single point by one civil servant. This is done by integrating the information available on the individual. The 'whole person' concept should be regarded as an important development in customer relations, saving customer time (and dignity), staff time and office space, although this concept has not yet been fully implemented.

Organizational change is another feature of 'Operation Strategy'. A distinction has been made between the 'front' and 'back' office staff. The former refers to those who work in the local office with on-line computers dealing directly with the customer. The latter provides the support service. Traditionally they were located in the same office. However, by networking, the two offices can be physically separated. The DSS has taken the opportunity of moving its support staff out of high cost areas (such as London) into lower cost and high unemployment ones.

The DSS's strategy also provides an acute example of how the introduction of new technologies can go wrong. Although one of its objectives was to provide more staff satisfaction, two years into the 'Strategy', the department was faced with a lengthy strike of computer staff, which delayed the development and increased the cost as well as causing a great deal of inconvenience to the public. The DSS's response was to transfer the development of strategy from in-house specialist civil servants to consultants, on the grounds that the development of the system and its maintenance should not again be compromised by such actions. The result was, as the National Audit Office's (NAO) thinly veiled criticism suggested, that the DSS was paying consultants four times more than it would cost to remunerate civil servants undertaking similar tasks, while with better staff relations the whole development would have been considerably cheaper (NAO 1989b).

any thought of compatibility, whether of hardware or, much more importantly, of data.

(*Abbott 1986: 2*)

Some of the most spectacular failures involving IT have occurred in the NHS including those related to the West Midlands Health Authority, Wessex Health Authority and the London Ambulance Service (LAS). See below for further discussion on the NHS.

6.3.2 The use of IT in local government

In 1990 the Audit Commission argued that without IT local government 'staff could neither manage the growing demand nor indeed provide for the present level of service' (1990a). Reports from such bodies as Audit Commission and Society of Information Technology Managers (SOCITM) indicate the extent of its use and impact by and on local government. Not surprisingly the last decade and this have witnessed a steady rise of local government investment in IT as indicated by Figures 6.1 and 6.2 below.

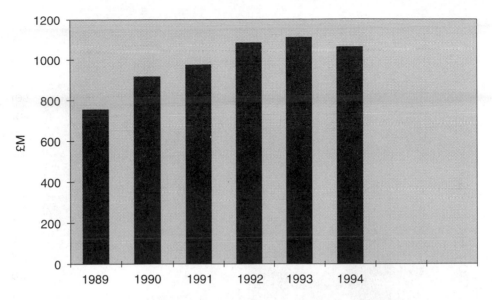

Figure 6.1   Annual expenditure on IS/IT by local authorities in 1994/95

Source: SOCITM IT Trends in Local Government 1994/95

Computers and IT are now used in almost all aspects of local government work and although local authorities have had their problems in acquiring and using the technology the Audit Commission argues it would be difficult to imagine:

- a community care programme without the development of an IT system to record client needs and monitor budgets;
- delegated school budgets operating without supportive IT finance system;
- council tax implemented without an appropriate IT system;
- census analysis without an effective statistical package

(1994b: 4)

As in other parts of the public sector local government use IT in a variety of ways. For example in Figure 6.3, a local authority is developing a project which will make innovative use of IT in road management of traffic and transportation.

6.4   CHAOS IN TIMES OF PLENTY

In 1990 the Audit Commission (1990a: 3) warned that the IT challenges facing local government in the 1980s would pale into insignificance when compared to those of the 1990s. This was, perhaps, an overstatement but the view was that, given the lightening pace of development, the technology might slip out of control. The technology itself and the changes it induces must be properly managed if the potential benefits are to be reaped. This was true for the whole of the public sector. The 1980s witnessed a rapid development of IT, offering to those public sector bodies possessing the vision, the will and the resources, opportunities to exploit it to their advantage. In that period

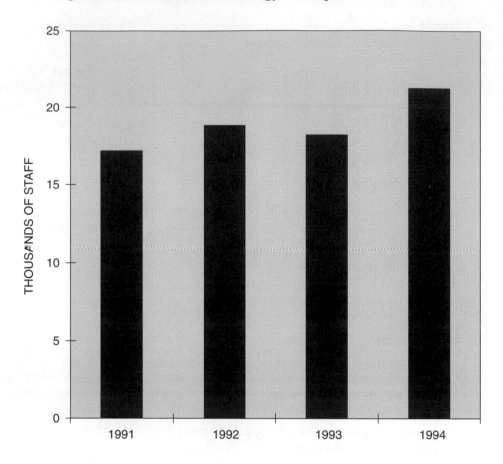

Figure 6.2 Total IS/IT staffing trends in local government 1994/1995

Source: SOCITM, IT Trends in Local Government 1994/95

(as at present), while there were positive forces pushing the public sector towards exploitation of IT, there were also negative forces inhibiting its effective use – see Table 6.1.

6.4.1 Driving forces

The forces encouraging the exploitation of IT included, first, a number of develop-ments profoundly affecting its use. The most important of these was the development of the microchip and the resultant micro-computers. At the same time a new industry was being spawned: the production of 'off-the-shelf' sophisticated software for all types of computers. Simultaneously, the cost of computers was declining. Organizations faced with much more powerful and sophisticated hardware at a rela-tively rapidly decreasing cost and the availability of appropriate software were thus

Southampton, in conjunction with Hampshire and two other cities, Cologne and Piraeus (Greece), supported by the European Union (EU) are working together to develop systems, strategies and solutions to their diverse traffic problems which, it is hoped, will be able to be applied across the countries of the EU. The project hopes to

- influence travel behaviour
- increase the use of public transport
- improve the efficiency of the transport networks
- provide high quality information for use in strategic decisions relating to transport and traffic
- provide accurate and timely information to the public.

ROMANSE consists of a number of mini projects amongst them is STOPWATCH.

STOPWATCH

Exploiting advances in new technologies, STOPWATCH is designed to fit bus stops with electronic signs giving minute-by-minute information to travellers about approaching buses. Waiting passengers will be able to see the route number of the nearest three buses, their destination and the estimation of the time when each bus will arrive at the stop. At some bus stops voice synthesizers will be installed to help those who have difficulty reading the signs. The key to the system is a small computer fitted on each bus which picks up a signal from road side beacons which can place the bus within 10 metres of its real position. Importantly, operators of the system will be able to see where delays are occurring, the reasons for the delay and can intervene to correct the situation, for example, by manipulating traffic signals.

(Source: Scope 1992–94, Hampshire County Council and Southampton City Councils 1994)

Figure 6.3   ROMANSE in Southampton

Table 6.1   Force field analysis

Driving forces	Resisting forces
Technological developments	Speed of development of the technology
Lower cost of the technology	Lack of IT knowledge and awareness by managers
The new public management	Disorganized acquisition
The explosion of information	Lack of evidence of benefits
Financial Restraint and push for efficiency	Lack of specialist skills
Government legislation assuming use of IT	Lack of proper management of IT
Growing public expectation	Lack of appropriate criteria for measuring performance

encouraged to acquire and exploit this technology. In addition, computer hardware was becoming increasingly compatible with each other, which made for competition as well as ease of networking.

Second, the boom in the home computer market resulted in widespread awareness of the capabilities of IT, leading to a lessening of the awe in which computers and computer specialists were held. Departments began to acquire IT equipment to enhance administrative tasks without having to go through the central bureaucracy.

Third, the 'new public management' stressed concepts such as economy, efficiency, effectiveness and responsiveness with emphasis on service delivery and on consumer orientations. Accountable management in the form of decentralization and devolved management is fragmenting public sector organizations. Neighbourhood Offices, Trust Hospitals, Next Step Agencies, contracted out and opted out services, the split between producer and purchaser and internal markets all emphasize this trend. As a consequence, public sector bodies needed improved, increased and more widely shared information if co-ordination was to take place and changes effectively managed. The emphasis on measuring performance also put a premium on accurate, timely and appropriate information. At the same time they were operating under severe financial restraints. This necessitated using resources even more economically and efficiently, giving value for money and to many this pointed in the direction of increased use in information technology.

Fourth, given the veritable explosion of information and communication in local government, some local authorities have identified as a matter of some urgency, the need to manage effectively internal and external information.

Fifth, the Government's influence on the public sector's use of IT has often been more direct and there is now a tendency to take the use of IT as given. So, for example, the poll tax could only have been effectively administered by using computers. But there have been many other legislation which demanded its use. The NHS's attempt to introduce general rather than professional management and common data practices across the whole service, the Resource Management Initiative (RMI) and the concept of separating purchaser from provider, all appeared to be dependent on the exploitation of IT.

Sixth, there is a growing expectation from the public to have up-to-date information, to be informed and to receive better service as a result of better use of information. They are confirmed in this by the use being made of information in some private sector organizations. The Audit Commission argues, for example, that

> [P]atients increasingly (and rightly) expect more from the health service. They want to be told what is available, what they can expect and when they can expect it. The Patient's Charter meets some of these expectations . . . All of this creates new demands for accurate and timely health information.
>
> (*Audit Commission 1995: 9–10*)

But expectations come from other quarters too, expectations which sometimes put undue pressure on organizations to move more quickly on the IT front than perhaps they should. Thus, although the London Ambulance Service (LAS) Inquiry Team criticized LAS managers for attempting to introduce and implement its IT system too quickly, the Team acknowledged that the managers were under such pressures from the Regional Health Authority, MPs, the public, health service consumers and the media that even if they wanted to adopt a more leisurely pace, they might not have been allowed to do so (South West Thames Regional Health Authority 1993: 7).

6.4.2 Resisting forces

There were, however, inhibiting factors. First, some organizations inherited an unenviable legacy because

> most of the major computing developments at that time [1970s] were bespoke departmental systems. Some of these were huge and represented many years of development and yet had, in some cases, little hope of success and eventual implementation'.
>
> *(Local Government Management Board 1988: 8).*

Such an 'historic commitment to increasingly redundant technology' (Anderson and Sims 1990) rendered organizations ill-placed to launch necessary IT changes. It was difficult to convince senior managers and politicians to discard systems which had cost a great deal of money to develop and which had been expected to last a long time. This state of affairs resulted (and is resulting) in inflexibility (older systems being more difficult to modify); increased running costs; increased burden of learning for users (older systems are less user friendly) and 'technological lock-out' (where older systems precluded the use of new technology) (Audit Commission 1995: 26). Organizations new to the field often appear to be better placed and the technology is such, that new users often make up ground quickly on those using the technology for a much longer period.

Second, managers and politicians lacked the understanding of the technology and an awareness of its potential for increased efficiency and effectiveness. Its development was often left to third and fourth tier managers, resulting in the lack of a 'product champion' drawn from the higher reaches of the managerial hierarchy. The potential for transforming the organization by integrating IT strategy with the business strategy was neither perceived nor realized. Left to the specialists, much of the emphasis was placed on the technical aspects and on structured activities. Lack of managerial awareness, understanding and failure to manage the development were the sources of many of the problems of implementation.

Third, by the beginning of the 1990s, the use and management of IT in some public sector organizations were in a chaotic state. Application of the technology was often uncoordinated and disorganized with different sections and individuals using different hardware and software which were not compatible with each other, rendering networking difficult.

Fourth, a common concern was that in a large number of cases IT systems did not deliver the anticipated benefits. It must be said that this is not a problem peculiar to the public sector. Although huge sums are invested in IT in the private sector, when it comes to the bottom line there is no clear

> evidence that these new technologies have raised productivity (the ultimate determinant of our standard of living) . . . In fact precisely the opposite is true.
>
> *(Scott Morton 1991: vi)*

One observer has suggested that in the UK about 20% of expenditure on IT is wasted, while another 30–40% yield no benefit (Willcocks 1994: 14). Some developments were abandoned even before they were installed, at great expense to the organizations concerned.

Here the public sector may have particular problems when compared with most of the private sector because, according to Collingridge and Margetts (1994), some of the projects are very large ones and have the characteristics of

- long lead times (e.g. operation strategy took over ten years to be implemented);
- large unit size ('Operation Strategy' of the DSS);
- capital intensity (where, as in Operation Strategy, large sums are sunk into projects);
- infrastructure support (where dedicated hardware and software systems are needed for the project which is not resaleable).

Collingridge and Margetts postulate that such characteristics lead to 'inflexible technology', where the organization cannot learn from its experience, where mistakes are likely to be costly because little can be done to remedy them. In such situations, development of projects is based more on an act of faith rather than on the well defined, costed and widely discussed and analysed choice of objectives. It is also argued that the large number of legislation demand new applications to be developed, quite often at short notice, forcing public sector organizations to react to new legislation rather than plan their own speed of development (Prachett 1994: 86).

Fifth, a constant theme in the evaluation of IT in the public sector is the lack of proper management in the area. It is a failure to understand how to manage and how to manage projects. It is a failure to have a vision, to set clear objectives and performance measures and to manage properly the human resource involved by getting their commitment. It is suggested that the failure starts from the fact that senior managers still do not themselves understand the value of information and the capability of the technology and thus fail to show proper leadership and obtain the commitment necessary for success (Audit Commission 1994b; 1995). The majority of systems in local and central government were not delivered on time, cost tended to escalate quite rapidly from the one agreed at the start of a project; there was failure to evaluate alternative systems; project management was poor and exhibited a lack of appropriate personnel and technology skills. Quite often too the users and potential users of systems were not involved in their development. Thus the expected benefits failed to materialize (Audit Commission 1990a; National Audit Office 1989b). It was a situation well illustrated in the much publicized IT failure in the London Ambulance Service (LAS) in 1992.

Sixth, it was difficult to find a method for appropriately measuring returns on investment in IT. Managers and politicians wanted

> to understand in clear terms, the contribution IT is making to the performance of their authority. Stated simply they want to know if they are getting value for money
>
> (Hill 1990)

But gaining such understanding is not easy. As the use of IT moves from structured to unstructured activities, measurement becomes more difficult. IT is being used

What is clear from the Inquiry Team's investigations is that neither the Computer Aided Despatch (CAD) system itself, nor its users, were ready for full implementation on 26 October 1992. The CAD software was not complete, not properly tuned and not fully tested. The resilience of the hardwarre under full load had not been tested. The fall back option to the second file server had certainly not been tested. There were outstanding problems with data transmission to and from the mobile data terminals. There was some scepticism over the accuracy of the Automatic Vehicle Location System (AVLS). Staff, both within the central Ambulance Control (CAC) and ambulance crews, had no confidence in the system and were not fully trained. The physical changes to the layout of the control room ... meant that staff were working in unfamiliar positions, without paper backup and were less able to work with colleagues with whom they had jointly solved problems before. There was no attempt to foresee fully the effect of inaccurate or incomplete data available to the system. ... The decision on that day to use only three computer generated resource allocations (which were proven to be less than 100% reliable) was a high risk.

(Source: South West Thames Regional Health Authority)

Figure 6.4 Report of the Inquiry into the London ambulance service, February 1993, p. 3

increasingly to provide information for politicians, for aiding decision-making and for building a technology infrastructure to benefit the whole organization. To measure such use by the rate of return on investment or by cost benefit analysis is inappropriate. Expenditure was and is quite difficult to justify to politicians and to Boards and it becomes a matter of judgement (House of Lords 1985: 33).

Seventh, a common and continuing problem is the lack of IT specialists in public sector organizations. As the use of IT expanded, the competition to recruit and retain skilled staff became intense. Unable to match the pay and conditions of the private sector, such organizations simply lost out. Some of the shortcomings mentioned above were undoubtedly a consequence of this.

6.5   ATTEMPTS AT RATIONALIZATION

6.5.1 Rationalizing the Centre

By the end of the 1980s, there was a growing concern to rationalize the use and acquisition of IT. Attempts at rationalization centred around:

- developing IT strategies which, for some local authorities, included taking a more centralized approach to development of systems and procurement of equipment and setting criteria on which bidding for IT investments could be evaluated. The NHS appeared to have combined both approaches where a national strategy was agreed but the implementation was left to the districts (and now Trusts). Central government adopted a more decentralized approach with departments able to decide IT policies in their own area;

- adopting a more decentralized approach with departments able to decide IT policies in their own areas. The NHS appeared to combine both approaches where a national strategy was agreed but the implementation was left to the districts' (and now Trusts') local government. It was a more centralized approach to the development of systems, procuring equipment and setting authority criteria on which bidding by departments for IT could be evaluated;
- developing a more cost conscious approach to the acquisition and use of IT and encouraged to do so by the Audit Commission;
- separating the producer from the user of the technology;
- using facilities management or 'outsourcing' to provide part of the IT service.

The Central Computing and Telecommunications Agency (CCTA) has played a major role in bringing rationality to central government use of IT. Set up as the Central Computer Agency in 1972 under the aegis of then the Civil Service Department, 'Telecommunications' was added to its title in 1977 to reflect the developments in new technologies. (The CCTA is now called the Government Centre for Information Systems and is located in the Office for Public Service and Science.) Its role at the outset was to advise government departments in their planning and implementation of IT strategies, to work on key issues which were of collective interest to the government, to develop and manage inter-departmental communication and to procure IT goods and services for all departments. Its control seemed powerful since it owned all the computer equipment and could decide on the type and make of computers to be used.

Thus the management of IT was centralized from the beginning. In 1984 a review of the role of the CCTA was undertaken resulting in departments taking full responsibility for developing and implementing IT solutions 'without interference and second guessing from the CCTA' (CCTA 1984), decentralizing in line with the philosophy of Financial Management Initiative (FMI). Its role changed to that of helping departments with their strategies, projects and strategic planning.

Paradoxically therefore, when compared with local government (see below), rationalization in central government led to decentralization rather than centralization. However. the CCTA still had important co-ordinating and corporate roles to aid the management of IT in government. It was responsible for addressing inter-departmental and corporate issues and for helping to improve effectiveness and efficiency in the Government's use of IT, disseminating good practice and setting guidelines for departments on matters such as investment appraisal (1990), project management (1988 and 1990), customer liaison (1990) and facilities management (1991). It has no executive powers but its reputation as a body which set standards which even the private sector uses as hallmarks of good practice, has aided its influence. It also has allies in the form of the NAO and the Public Accounts Committee. Those bodies periodically review the use of IT in Government Departments and one of the criteria they often use to determine good practice, is to see whether guidelines set out by the CCTA have been followed or whether the CCTA has been consulted. The Public Accounts Committee, for instance, having noted that IT projects which do not follow guidelines set down by the CCTA are at greater risk of failure recommended that for all future projects, in Great Britain and Northern Ireland, full use should be made of CCTA's advice and support to ensure that contracts with suppliers are effectively managed and controlled, and that if CCTA's advice is not followed the reasons should be recorded in writing

(CCTA 1995a: 3)

By the beginning of the 1990s government departments were responsible for administering their corporate IT strategies, their IT infra-structure, their in-house developments and their contracts with other agencies or private sector suppliers. However, the changes brought about by the implementation of the 'next steps 'agencies' are fragmenting departments (Muid 1994: 117). At the same time business managers of agencies need to manage and be in control of such an important resource as information systems and information technology (IS/IT) if they are to meet performance targets. To some extent this has been recognized in some spheres of government by the sharing out of the IT budget amongst agency managers who then become the customers of the department's directorate for IT. Returning to the example of the DSS, 'Operation Strategy' was developed in a unified department. Since then the DSS has been split into six agencies in addition to the remaining core. One of the six, the Information Technology Agency (ITSA) set up in 1990 with a budget of over £430 million and about 4000 staff, had a remit to 'implement and maintain the hardware, software, networks and telecommunication which runs the department's (DSS) technology' (DSS 1995). In 1994, following the trend for devolution and decentralization and as a logical response to the creation of agencies, the finances spent on IT in the DSS were transferred to the agencies. They are now truly (external) customers of ITSA (DSS 1995: 6). This has resulted in the introduction of 'hard charging' and the greater visibility of ITSA's costs. Information Technology in government is thus increasingly being decentralized.

6.5.2 Rationalization in the NHS

This state of anarchy mentioned above has not disappeared in the 1990s and the Audit Commission in 1995 bemoaned the fact that Trust hospitals are still using outdated systems and software. Some users in the health service were forced to develop their own systems because of the lack of networking and because of the bias towards administrative and financial systems, as opposed to those systems which would improve the care of patients (Audit Commission 1995: 25). The changes in the service in the latter part of the 1980s and the early 1990s resulted in the use of IT coming to the fore. The first formal hint of rationalization came in 1984 with the publication of the Kröner Report which (inter alia) recommended that

- data should be collected within particular sections, such as acute hospitals, to a common set of definitions (over the whole NHS)
- local and national statistics should be provided

(DHSS 1984)

Although doubt has been expressed as to the usefulness of such statistics to hospitals and doctors, the collection and dissemination of such statistics did propel

> - information will be person based
> - systems may be integrated
> - information will be derived from operational systems
> - information will be secure and confidential
> - information will be shared across the NHS
>
> *(Source: Audit Commission, For Your Information, 1995: 17)*

Figure 6.5   NHS information management and information (IM&T) strategy December 1992

information and IT on to the NHS management agenda (Gowling 1994: 32). This was further endorsed by the Resource Management Initiative which included the developing of new IS/IT strategies for 'managerial' and 'clinical' decisions. In 1992, following the post-Griffiths changes in the NHS (see Chapter 8), the NHS Management Executive (NHSME) set out its vision for IS/IT in the service, as shown in Figure 6.5.

The investment and financing for the strategy has been delegated to individual hospitals.

Some observers harbour considerable doubts as to whether the NHS IM&T strategy is working or will ever work. Their doubts are fuelled by:

- lack of clear objectives as to whether the strategy is to (a) improve patient care, (b) build an infra-structure of IT, (c) inform or educate patients;
- conflict between the needs of NHSME for IT and those of the individual hospitals operating in a competitive environment, which may want to demonstrate their independence from the centre (Keen 1994a: 25–6);
- focus of the strategy is still on the technology rather than on the information or the needs of the business (Audit Commission 1995: 40);
- data collected has often been inaccurate and are not trusted by the operational side of the service;
- political conflict between the managerial and clinical side of the service seems not yet to have been resolved.

Given these doubts and the uncertainties which exist in the NHS one observer has voiced the opinion that extensive computerization of the NHS is not justified because
there is little point in implementing systems to achieve particular objectives if those objectives are changed or rendered irrelevant before the system is in place; and on going attempts to change systems to meet new demands will result in considerable long-term redesign costs. The NHSME might draw the conclusion that now is not a good time to be making major capital investments – but is in fact making them.

(Keen 1994a: 51)

6.5.3 Rationalizing in local government

By 1993 over 94% of local authorities possessed an IT strategy or were in the process of preparing one (SOCITM 1994). The strategies usually involved the setting up of a central IT department responsible for project approval, acquisition of hardware and software, development of systems and factors relating to control over corporate as well as departmental systems. (In recent years this trend has been reversed with departments in larger authorities assuming responsibility for their IS/IT systems which relate to their field of management and operations.) In addition, an increasing number of local authorities have been separating the user and producer functions, as well as introducing procedures for costing of IT use and development. A strongly influencing factor has been the threat of CCT extending to the IT services. An increasing number of authorities have gone even further by using facilities management – a process of contracting out services to private and other sectors – to provide their IT requirements.

Case study 6.2 provides an insight into how a large local authority attempted to rationalize its IS/IT needs and develop a strategy.

The problems faced by Birmingham in developing and managing IT were, on the whole, typical of those faced by a large number of other authorities. One major difference was that it was one of the few authorities which encouraged both centralization and decentralization as a means of achieving rationality. In 1992 it abandoned centralization and devolved most of the IT functions (including budgets) remaining with the City Council to departments. Only expenditure relating to the corporate services continues to be funded centrally (Birmingham City Council 1992).

One suspects that where Birmingham is leading others will follow eventually. The accountable management culture is in the ascendancy. The Audit Commission is of the view that decentralization should gather pace so as to empower the users of IS/IT (1995: 1). In any case there is a view that local government will go the way of central government. The existence of a contract culture and the specifying and commissioning of services conjures up a similar relationship to that of government departments and next step agencies. Business units delivering services under contracts will want to be responsible for controlling their own IS/IT systems as the next step agencies are doing. Nevertheless, local authorities appear to be remarkably resistant to the splitting of the producer/ contractor function and outsourcing when it comes to IT. In 1994, only 27 of a sample of over 250 authorities (SOCITM 1994: 6) had made the split, despite the then beckoning finger of CCT. Again, in 77% of the sample IS/IT in the authority was delivered by the central unit. Centralization of the IT services was still the norm.

6.6   MANAGING IT

There is general agreement that efficient and effective use of IT will only come about where it is properly managed. Only about 7% of project failures in IT spring from failure of hardware or software. Weak management is usually the cause. It is the failure to understand and manage change. The LAS Inquiry Report, for instance, spent more time dealing with the management structures, objectives and especially

CASE STUDY 6.2 The anatomy of a strategy – Birmingham City Council

The City of Birmingham was a pioneer in the use of computers in the 1950s and 1960s. By the 1980s it had developed over 40 major systems including city accounts, rates and housing allocation (Isaac-Henry 1987: 11). In 1983, Birmingham decided that it needed a strategy for managing the development of IT, not only because the acquisition of hardware and software was piece-meal, but also because the use of the technology was too narrowly conceived. In an attempt to rationalize the use and acquisition of equipment, an Information and Services Division (ISSD) was created as a section of the Treasurer's Department. The ISSD was divided into four sections, namely:

- Operation division – providing a variety of services to departments including monitoring of performance and finding solutions to operational problems;
- Systems and programming – helping departments in their development of systems;
- User services – promoting and supplying the use of computer facilities throughout the Council;
- Computer centre – reviewing projects and providing consultancy on project management.

Two other important policies emerged from the strategy. First, a determination to involve users and even non users in the development of IT. Second, there was to be systematic training of all staff within the authority although this would take some time.

Departments were encouraged to set up their own computer/systems sections and to develop their own IT strategies. However, departmental bids for any major acquisition or development had to satisfy the ISSD and Management Committee that they would:

- result in improvement in service to the public;
- provide information relevant to the needs of other departments;
- meet statutory and city needs;
- provide benefits which outweigh cost.

In 1987 the strategy was again reviewed. The number of computers in the City had doubled between 1983 and 1986. The authority had now to consider the:

- increased potential of the new technology and the awareness of officers of such potential;
- rapid advance of micro computers in departments;
- imposition of financial restraints pushing them towards obtaining greater
  efficiency.

Between 1983 and 1987 the old systems were modified and new ones installed. The development of IT was not spread evenly across the departments. Whereas the Housing Department was very much involved in the development and use of IT, Social Services and Education lagged behind – a case of decibel planning, where those who shouted the loudest received most of the resources.

A most important influence on the development of an IT strategy from 1984 was the Labour Party's policy of decentralization in the form of Neighbourhood Offices. The implications of the policy were that staff in these offices needed to have:

- local information system for clients in their area;
- access to departmental transactions;
- the means to process departmental transactions;
- the need to communicate with other Neighbourhood Offices;
- access to City-wide information;

Technology was to be the key (Birmingham City Council 1986).

The strategy of 1987 separated users from providers with the latter (the Information Technology Division) given direct labour organization (DLO) status and was made responsible for:

- development of central and departmental systems and the communication network;
- managing (through facilities arrangements) departmental equipment;
- providing support for assisting effective use of IT services.

IT planning and strategy development was now the responsibility of the Management Information Systems Division which represented the client (the local authority). This division was responsible for helping departments develop their IT strategies and their bids for their programmes as well as co-ordinating the investment in and development of the City's IT plans. The Head of user services was to be responsible for the City's IT development and was now attached to the Chief Executive's Department and not to the Treasurer's.

In 1989 the City was again in the throws of modifying its IT strategy. It was argued that the pressures from Government legislation (e.g. the poll tax) and other sources, meant that the City could not guarantee the level of investment needed to sustain existing IT resources, that it was also difficult to retain highly skilled staff and that their rapid turnover meant fluctuating workload and difficulties in achieving objectives. In any case there was a strong possibility that the IT services would be the subject of compulsory competitive tendering (now a reality). Creating a DLO did not solve the problem and the producer role went to a private sector organization because it allowed;

- for savings through rationalization and taking advantage of competitive tendering;

- the City to determine the level of information technology without being restricted by the existing in-house resource level;

- the provision for career paths for existing information technology staff but retaining access to their skills and knowledge.

The City reluctantly turned to the private sector for the solution, outsourcing the provision of IT in the authority.

human resource management than on the technological aspects. In 1990 the Audit Commission (1990a, pp. 7–9) suggested that efficiency and effectiveness (and therefore better management) could be achieved in IT if the organization stressed the importance of

- understanding the IT customer
- setting clear IT objectives
- assigning clear IT and management responsibilities
- communicating effectively about business needs and IT
- monitoring results
- adapting quickly to change

It was the same recipe that the Commission had advocated for the general management of local government (1988a), but this should cause no surprise since management of IT is about managing change and as discussed in Chapter 3, concerns changing behaviour, culture, structures and dealing with organizational and process issues. Setting IT policies and implementing them is also concerned with missions, objectives and strategies. Introducing, implementing and properly managing the IT service in an organization has parallels with managing the organization as a whole.

For such activities to be effective they have to have the commitment of top manage
ment as well as involvement and participation of staff further down the line. However,
experience suggests that in the public sector (as perhaps elsewhere) the management
of IT is still in the hands of the technologists and that even when top management
is involved, this relates to senior officers with politicians excluded, or if involved,
playing a minor role (Audit Commission 1995: 41).

Many managers still cling to the automation version of technology justifying investments on immediate returns and efficiency gains, such as staff cuts, which leads to
short-termism and a denial of the fact that IS/IT is an enabling technology and an
important part of an organization's infrastructure (Gowling 1994: 43).

Successful implementation of IT strategy is said to be particularly dependent
on paying proper attention to the human factor involved as matter of strategy
(CCTA 1992a). Staff commitment appears to be a prerequisite to successful change and

> staff are likely to be more committed, motivated and productive if they play
> an active part in the process of change. So staff should be involved throughout
> the planning and implementation of IT systems.
>
> *(CCTA 1992a: 9)*

As with management of change generally, training and development are also important ingredients of effectively introducing and implementing an IT strategy.

The political context will also have to be managed. Information is by general consent
a source of power. Introducing IT and new information systems and information flows
render individuals and sections more or less powerful. Effectiveness of introducing and
implementing IT into organizations can quite easily flounder on the rocks of political
conflict. Gowling highlighted such conflicts between the different perceptions and cultures of medical staff and 'managers' in the health service suggesting that it

> has long been part of the game for doctors and management (with information
> staff in tow) to sit on opposite sides of the table and describe each other's infor-
> mation as rubbish.
>
> *(Gowling 1994: 38)*

Not only must political forces be recognized but they must also be harnessed to
ensure success of implementation.

Other managing and management factors have also to be considered if IS/IT is to
be successfully managed. One such factor is that the technology strategy has to be
aligned to business strategy if the benefits of IT are to be fully realized. Here, some
parts of public sector face a major problem. In local government only about 51% of
authorities possess a formal business plan (for the whole of the authority) despite
every reason, its seems, for their doing so (SOCITM 1993). (Departments in local
authorities are, however, more prone to develop a business plan, with over 78% of
them doing so in 1993.) Only 50% of those possessing both business and IT strategies attempted to integrate them (SOCITM 1993: 10). Central government departments
are much better placed since agencies, which are proliferating, are obliged by their
contracts to produce such business plans.

Another factor which could aid the success of IS/IT strategies is the representation of 'a deep technical understanding of IT needs at highest management levels'
(Scott Morton 1991). Top management must have enough appreciation of the

technology to realize its potential for business, how it might transform the organization and how it can best be implemented. At the same time, if the IT manager is to help in alignment he/she must in turn also have a deep understanding of how the business works. However, it still remains the situation that senior managers have little or no experience or real understanding of IT (Benjamin 1987: 18; Harvey, 1992: 4). The often repeated suggestion for improving the situation is to develop the 'hybrid' manager, a 'twin tracker', a manager who possesses:

- technological competence to recognize opportunities when they present themselves or even to create them;
- business confidence so that an application opportunity can be recognized and a case made for it;
- organization skills to manipulate people, time and other resources so as to get things done (Earl 1989: 205).

Management practices and ideas, as well as IT, are however changing so quickly that it would be difficult for a manager to devote enough time to business matters while keeping abreast of the changing technology. On the other hand there are encouraging signs that the top echelons of public sector organizations are viewing IT less as a technical support and more as an important and valuable corporate facility. Information Technology managers are often now reporting directly to chief executives and management teams.

A third factor which impacts most importantly on the effectiveness of the management of IS/IT is that such policies must be driven by the information needs of the organization and must be aligned with and driven by the information strategies and policies.

6.6.1 Information, information management and information strategy

In examining the role of information and information management in the public sector two factors stand above the rest. First, an increasing number of public sector organizations are regarding information as a major organizational resource to be put alongside people, finance and property (Wedgwood Oppenheim 1990; CCTA 1990b; Birmingham City Council 1992; Hampshire County Council 1992 and 1994; Westcott, 1993). Departments such as those of Trade and Industry, the Inland Revenue and Customs and Excise have adopted this approach, echoing the Chairman of the Training Agency in 1985 when he argued that 'information is a key resource and should be managed as effectively as we manage other key resources such as money and staff' (CCTA 1990b: 33) because it is essential to the advancement of government business and is obtained at a cost. The move towards treating information in such a way is also gathering pace at the local government level.

Second, there has been a veritable explosion of information in the public sector in recent years. This has been the result of the development of the 'new public management' as well as the wider climate and culture in which the public sector now operates. Such information has to be properly managed if organizations are to be both effective and efficient. Such management is concerned with how and why information is collected, how it is held, used and disseminated in furtherance of objectives and business and who is responsible and accountable for such activities. The management of information stresses the need to develop an information culture in which information is viewed as a corporate resource, is highly valued, where provision for staff, politicians and the public (customers) are considered and where it is maintained in a form in which it can meet many different and varied demands made upon it (Wedgwood Oppenheim 1994). Indeed, for it to be well managed there must be an information strategy or at least strategic thinking on the matter. Importantly such a strategy should come from the strategic plans of the organization and should emerge as a result of answers to questions such as:

- What are the organization's aims and objectives?
- What information is needed to achieve them?
- What information is available in the organization?

The effective management of information in organizations necessitates the use of computers and IT. But many organizations in the public sector do not possess an information strategy, as a result of which the technology drives information and not vice versa. There are still relatively few local authorities (about 20%) with such a strategy (SOCITM 1992; 1993). The most effective approach of managing information needs of the organization is to develop an information strategy. The strategy should be based on the strategic needs of that organization with an information technology strategy a subset of the information strategy. In this way information can be made to be the driver of IT strategies.

CASE STUDY 6.3   Managing information in Hampshire

Hampshire County Council is one of the leading local authorities in the field of information management and uses IT extensively to manage information. Importantly policies and strategies concerning information are the responsibility of a sub-group of the Chief Officers Group so that responsibility for information strategy is sufficiently high-level within the organization to demonstrate the importance given to it. There is an Information and Strategy Group providing direction and support for departments, and supported by an Information and Technology Forum (consisting of representatives of all departments). In addition, each year each department has to produce an information strategy. It is these strategies which drive the technology used. The values on which the information strategy are based state that information must be:

- fit for the purpose for which it is intended;

- regarded as a corporate resource and is not seen to belong to any one department;
- widely known and available to all departments (subject to the data protection act, security and the necessary confidentiality);
- maintained in a form that enables it to be aggregated in different ways to meet different needs;
- clearly be the responsibility of an individual or section, who is accountable for its maintenance.

But the information strategy and IT strategy are not designed merely for internal use. They are geared to provide 'effective' information to and from external customers. Hampshire CC has developed HANSNET a computer based information system on which there

- is a directory to every department's information;
- is a database of employers provided by the Careers Service;
- are committee agendas, minutes, reports;
- is information about members;
- is information on foreign language speakers within the authority;
- are electronic mail, diaries, meetings organizer;
- is information about local organizations;
- is relevant information from sources such as newspapers and Hansard relating to the authority.

Using HANSNET, the County Council has developed local information points (LIPs) designed to give easy access to information about all its services. These LIPs, located across the county, are placed in locations such as community schools, libraries, local councils (community and parish) and social services area offices and accessed by the county council staff on behalf of the public – Hampshire CC feels that few people are confident enough to use a terminal in the high street to get information from HANSNET (interview 1994). Not only does it mean that information about all the Authority's services can be accessed from the one point but information will also be available on a large number of other public and voluntary bodies.

As the county council admits, the technology is not revolutionary. Nevertheless, its use is innovative and springs from the fact that it is the information which is driving it. HANSNET and the processes involved are said to be engineering cultural change within the county council. Traditionally, information was developed for inside use and customers faced major problems in accessing it. Hampshire's information policy and HANSNET have ensured that information is developed for use outside the organization and can be accessed easily from any where within the county. Second, the information policy is bringing groups closer together (an inter-agency approach is being taken) where pooling of information for the community is taking place as well as improved co-operation against a background of increasing fragmentation of services.

(Hampshire CC 1994)

6.6.2 Privatizing public sector IT

The trend to seek private sector solutions in operating and developing (and sometimes managing) IT systems is on the increase. A number of factors are pushing in this direction. First, under the 'market testing' scheme of the government, public sector bodies are obliged to identify areas of their work which might be privatized and IT has become one of the prime candidates. A large number of government departments have earmarked IT for market testing (Margetts 1995: 97). Second, development of the Next Step agencies is exerting pressures for outsourcing by making IT divisions of departments agencies in their own right and emphasizing the client (customer) contractor (the IT agency) split. This renders such IT agencies ripe for privatization and a number of them have taken that route, including the IT division of the Department of Transport (DVOIT) and the Information Technology Office of the Inland Revenue. But even where the IT arm of agencies remains in the public sector there is pressure (from government policies and attitudes and from the point of view of profit making) to involve the private sector as much as possible. In the case of ITSA, for example, the policy now is

> to outsource nearly all our IT, so that the IT agency is going to be a small unit which is responsible for the integrity of the system, professional advice . . . and helping people with how you do the contracts and procurement.
>
> *(House of Commons, 28 June: 142, para. 430)*

Third, the use and understanding of IT on a large scale has become a highly specialized function and for the organization to attempt to undertake all of it might distract attention from core activities.

In local government there appears to be a greater reluctance towards outsourcing. However, the practice is very much on the increase and under both CCT legislation and market testing local authorities will increasingly have to look to the private sector.

There are problems with outsourcing as Birmingham recognized in 1989 when, even though it then opted for bringing in the private sector, it acknowledged that it would lose control of its network facilities and valuable technical skills and that

> information systems are the key to the success of any organization and therefore the selection of a third party to process and man these systems can give rise to many business risks and no method of selection will remove all these risks
>
> *(Birmingham City Council 1989)*

Indeed, information technology has become of strategic importance, and can be highly integral to an organization's business (Bellamy 1994). In addition, given what has been said above concerning IT awareness and commitment by top management, there is a fear that awareness as well as 'core skills' may be lost, adding to the problems of effectively managing information and IS/IT. The client side of IT contract might quickly lose touch with IT developments rendering it less able to play the role of the intelligent customer. There is a need to keep enough experts to define what is needed technologically and to assess the performance of, and preserve some independence from, contractors. There is also the problem of managing IT based on a client contractor relationship (Willcocks 1994: 21). This relationship is normally conducted on an arms length basis so as to preserve independence on both sides, ensure proper competition and lessen opportunities for breaching probity. There are some doubts, however, as to whether such a relationship is conducive to the flexibility and sensitivity required for managing a core function and resource within organizations.

6.7   CONCLUSION

This chapter suggests that in the use of IT and in the attempt to manage information the public sector has not had a smooth passage. The same, incidentally, could be said for the private sector. In introducing and implementing IS/IT strategies the public sector faces turbulence in the general environment and extreme turbulence in the development of 'new public management', as well as in the rapidly changing powerful technology. Nevertheless, IT can be harnessed for providing better planning and control in internal operations, for measuring, monitoring and controlling for efficiency and quality in performance and as interface between public organizations and citizens in service delivery. The chapter also suggests that there are failures on a grand scale. It is therefore not surprising that the Audit Commission should entitle its handbook on management of information technology *High Risk/High Potential*, arguing that despite its use in improving services, for many managers 'information technology looks like a *snake pit* in which risks and danger far outweigh any benefits' (1994a: 4).

> Despite this, IT has become an indispensable factor of management in the public sector. It is has proved not to be a passing fancy, but an enduring yet rapidly changing factor which already has had an enormous impact on the public sector up to the present but in the future it is expected to transform organizations in ways, some of which we cannot yet imagine.

Certainly there is a view that its role in enhancing democracy has not even properly begun to be addressed in this country (Bellamy, Horrocks and Webb 1995). Given the present penchant for fragmentation, IT might rightly be described as the glue which is likely to hold the public sector together (Audit Commission 1994: 76).

To be effective, IT must be properly managed. Management should be based on a strategy of information management and on emphasizing human resources, taking into consideration ' the organization, people and skills'. Its proper management is central to the management of change, in part the subject of this book. IT is not only a facilitator of change but it is also itself part of the change.

Yet despite the great hopes it holds for the present and the future (taking into consideration factors such as the development of the information superhighway), it should not be regarded as a panacea for coping with the ills or for solving all the problems of public sector organizations caught up in environmental turbulence. The changes and transformations necessary for effective government and management will not automatically spring from the use of such technologies. Other factors need to coalesce with information technological advances. Importantly, the political will to use the technology, to provide the resources and to inaugurate other changes in processes, structures and behaviour in order to ensure its effectiveness is of the essence. Thus for the technology to fulfil its capabilities managers (including politicians)

> must take an active and intelligent role in the strategic use of the technology. They can use the technology either to reinforce the status quo or help to bring about a new and better order. The direction taken will depend on the insights and skills of the modern 'princes' and on their willingness to lead the introduction of change.
>
> (*Kraemer and King 1988:24*)

6.8 CHAPTER SUMMARY

Chapter 6 has argued that IT is having an important effect on the organization, processes and performance of public sector bodies and its use is widespread. The following key points emerge:

- The technology is in a constant state of revolution which presents public sector organization with high potential for advantageous change but also as the Audit Commission (1994) suggests high risks as well.
- The development and use of IT in the public sector has not always gone smoothly and a period of disorganized acquisition and use in the 1970s and early 1980s led to a move for rationalization in the late 1980s and 1990s.
- Rationalization took different forms in different parts of the sector with central government opting for decentralization, local government for centralization and the NHS a mixture of the two.
- A number of problems face the public sector in its effective use of IT. Among the most important are the constant state of change in the technology and the lack of proper management, especially in relating IT strategy to that of the business strategy.

- Given the explosion of information with which the public sector has to deal under the 'new public management', management of information is now of the essence.
- Increasingly, public sector organizations are regarding information (as opposed to IT) as a major resource alongside those of finance, people and land buildings.
- Proper management of information is said to include changing the culture of the organization so as to ensure that information is considered to be important and valuable by all employees
- A good example of an attempt to manage information is discussed in the case study on Hampshire County Council.
- Although an important resource, there is now a trend to 'outsource' the IT function.
- Finally, IT is not a fad but a technology which will increasingly play an (even more) important role in the public sector and will do so in ways we may not yet be able to imagine

TEXT-BASED QUESTIONS

1.   Outline the arguments you would use for suggesting that acquiring, using and generally managing Information Technology in the 1990s are 'high risk/high potential' activities.

2.   What is an information culture?
      Why is it important to develop an information culture in organizations?
      How can such a culture be developed?

3.   What are the main arguments for treating information as a major resource alongside others such as finance, property, people and information technology?

4.   In much of the debate concerning the use of Information Technology, efficiency and effectiveness hold sway with usually very little attention paid to the pursuit of improving the democratic process. In what ways could (or can) the new technology aid the democratic process in government (central, local, or all together)?

ASSIGNMENT 1

Using your own organization (or parts of it), or one with which you are familiar and can obtain access, investigate

- the use made of computers and IT
- any conflicts caused by the introduction of IT and how they have been resolved (if at all)
- how IT might develop in the organization in the next few years
- the way IT has influenced the organizational structure or caused it to be changed

ASSIGNMENT 2

Write a report of (1500–2000 words) on the advantages and disadvantages of outsourcing the information technology functions of your organization with which you are familiar and can gain access to IT information.

In producing your report

(a) try and obtain use of any official reports or policies on IT relating to your organization (IT and information policy documents, briefing papers, minutes of discussion and debates);

(b) approach the IT manager (of your department, authority or section) and find out how he/she views outsourcing in relation to whether it helps or hinders proper management and use of IT.

(c) a definition of the term 'outsourcing would be helpful.

FURTHER READING

Audit Commission (1990) *Preparing an Information Strategy: Making IT Happen*, HMSO, London

Audit Commission (1990) *Knowing What IT Costs*, HMSO, London.

Audit Commission (1990) *Acquiring IT*, HMSO, London.

Audit Commission (1994) *High Risk/High Potential – A management handbook on information technology in local government*, HMSO, London.

Audit Commission (1995) *For Your Information: A study of information management and systems in acute hospital*, HMSO, London.

Bellamy, C. and Taylor, J. (1994) Introduction: Exploiting IT in Public Administration: Towards the Information Polity. *Public Administration*, **72** (1) pp. 1–12.

Bellamy, C., Horrocks, I. and Webb, J. (1995) Exchanging Information with the Public: From One Stop Shops to Community Information Systems. *Local Government Studies*, **21**(1), pp. 11–30.

CCTA (1990) *Managing Information as a Resource*, HMSO, London.

FITLOG (1992), *Fit for Business : the management and practice of information technology in local government*, SOCITM.

Keen, J. (1994) *Information Management in Health Services*, Open University Press, Buckingham.

Wedgwood Oppenheim, F.(1994) *Making Information Management Work*, Local Government Management Board, Luton.

Westcott B. (1993) *The Fifth Resource – Information*, LGTB.

Learning Resources
Centre

EDUCATION AND CONSUMERISM: MANAGING AN EMERGING MARKETING CULTURE IN SCHOOLS

7

Chris Barnes and Keith Williams

7.1 CHAPTER PREVIEW

This chapter will:

- Trace the origin of consumerism and marketing in education in England and Wales and explain the realignment of power between local education authorities, the teaching profession and parents following the educational legislation of the 1980s and early 1990s.
- Explain the explicit and implicit assumptions on which key education reforms since the 1980s are based.
- Offer a definition of marketing in which the characteristics and values of the education profession are accommodated.
- Identify the various discrete stages in the marketing process and position those schools surveyed in the maintained and independent sector accordingly.

- Reveal the attitude and receptiveness of those heads and deputy heads surveyed towards marketing education services.
- Use an adapted conceptual model based on Tannenbaum and Schmidt's study to gauge 'management styles' in schools; the implications of the findings here for education marketing and associated activities will be described and critically assessed.
- Describe and comment on the perceptions of senior members of the teaching profession about the future of marketing activities in education services; in this context, the optimum organizational and managerial conditions needed for successful marketing will be illustrated and critically assessed.

7.2 INTRODUCTION

By the mid 1980s '. . . the stage had been set for the most radical phase of Thatcherite education policy' (Tomlinson 1989). This included a commitment on the part of decision-makers to promote the '. . . individual choices of those in the market', for in so doing, it would '. . . produce a more satisfactory result than the rational plans of either politicians or bureaucrats' (Tomlinson 1989). Consumerism and marketing had come to epitomize the very essence of the educational values espoused by the Thatcher administration.

In the context of education, these developments imply that parents/pupils are able to influence the shape of 'products' offered them by competing schools. As consumers in a marketing culture, it is assumed that parents/pupils are empowered to exercise choice, enjoy access to the physical and information aspects of education, actively participate in some school decisions, and benefit from an educational system whose *raison d'etre* is to provide a responsive public service.

But is consumer sovereignty in the education marketplace more apparent than real? Evidently, the infusion of marketing into education offers both producers and consumers considerable benefits: it helps schools influence consumers' perception of them, facilitate consumer-awareness of their offering, and, in a quest to maximize efficiency and effectiveness, enables educational institutions to adopt proactive (rather than reactive) management strategies. Notwithstanding the obvious benefits of marketing, the government's attempt to impose consumer-dominant values on schools is fraught with difficulties. In order to assess the practicability of incorporating consumerism in education, answers to a number of key questions must be sought: are the assumptions on which the government has based its consumer/marketing reforms sound? How responsive are schools likely to be to the planned changes? Are the merits of marketing as self-evident to those responsible for delivering educational services as they are to ministers? Will the newly acquired status given to consumers of education services offer genuine choice?

Clearly the impact of recent education reforms, compounded with demographic and economic forces, is likely to be far reaching and the attendant pressure for change on the organizational structure and behaviour of schools irrepressible. An emerging consumerism is manifest in which the principle of the free market in education and associated notions of competition, choice and efficiency, are poised to dominate (Tomlinson 1994). In short, marketing, which might be defined as '. . . effective management by an institution of its exchange relations with its various markets and publics' (Kotler and Fox 1985) forms a vital component of modern school management.

This chapter describes the salient features of these developments, traces their origin and critically evaluates their likely influence on schools and the education services they offer. The assumptions on which the education reforms are based are exposed and subjected to close scrutiny.

7.3   IMPETUS FOR CHANGE

Before the Thatcher era schools did not have to market themselves since they had a more or less guaranteed supply of pupils. The local education authority (LEA) operated a policy of pupil allocation to their schools by means of catchment areas, thus obviating the need for schools to be competitively minded, or indeed to give any regard to the needs and wishes of the parents. The schooling process was controlled very much by the educational establishment, with the LEA providing the resources, and the head and senior staff determining curriculum policy; to 'outsiders' schools were very much closed institutions.

This post-war arrangement began to be challenged not by the Thatcher policies but by demographic change; between 1964 and 1977 the birth-rate fell nationally by about 30%, creating an era of declining school population where surplus places in schools became more prevalent. Consequently, parental choice became a reality, thus forcing schools, particularly in urban areas, to become more outward looking and market conscious.

The 1970s witnessed a succession of Black Papers on education which criticized the failures of 'progressive' educational ideas; in 1974–5, the William Tyndale dispute also erupted, leading to the dismissal of the head and five staff members (Gretton and Jackson 1976). The Taylor Report of 1977, on the reform of governing bodies, further signalled the awareness of the government and the DES that changes in school management were needed. These ideas were persuasively articulated in Prime Minister Callaghan's speech in October 1976, in which he called for a debate on a number of key educational issues (Tomlinson 1989).

At the same time the energy crisis of 1973 had created a deteriorating economic situation so that public expenditure control became increasingly important as spending policies came under scrutiny. Critical HMI surveys of primary and secondary education in 1978 and 1979 further contributed to the volume of criticism of the state of education. Thus by the end of the 1970s the politicization of education had become a reality, caused by a combination of demographic, economic and educational factors.

Into this rapidly changing environment came Margaret Thatcher in 1979, whose 'parent power' had been a campaigning slogan. The Education Act 1980 was the first step in opening up school management to wider influences by enabling parents to be elected to governing bodies; it also required local education authorities to publish much more information about schools including admission arrangements, the curriculum and significantly, examination results, as well as introducing the concept of the Assisted Places Scheme. The 1980 Act began the process of ensuring that parents could obtain information concerning the quality of education provided by local authority schools. It was however the Education (No 2) Act 1986 which made the important advances in school accountability, by increasing parental representation on the governing body and by introducing community representatives including those from the business community. The Act also required the governors to produce an annual report and hold an annual parent meeting. The protracted teachers' dispute of 1985–7 further diminished the standing and authority of the teaching profession, enabling the government to impose the Teachers' Pay and Conditions Act 1987.

The educational policies of the first two Thatcher administrations were piecemeal movements in the direction of greater accountability, openness, choice and competition, but arguably the essential power structure of the post-war period remained intact with the DES, parents and the business community being marginalized and the LEAs and teaching profession still very much controlling the system, to the disappointment of the radical Right. It was Sir Keith Joseph's replacement as Secretary of State by Kenneth Baker in May 1986 which began the process of fundamentally restructuring the education system. In October 1986 the latter announced his policy for the City Technology Colleges, but more importantly during 1987 he signalled the intention of a major shake-up of education for the third Thatcher administration.

> The resulting Education Reform Act 1988 has created, for individual schools, a climate radically different from that established by the Education Act 1944, by introducing a much more market-driven educational system, in which survival will depend upon the ability of school managers to sell their product in a competitive environment.

The Education Reform Act 1988 allows schools to opt out of the local education authority (LEA) to become grant maintained schools, provides for school budgets to be delegated to governing bodies, requires LEAs to pursue open enrolment policies and imposes on schools a national curriculum with associated testing and assessment policies. The management of these major changes has been a dominant theme for all those concerned with educational policy-making during the 1990s.

To provide further challenges to the schools the Education (Schools) Act 1992 requires the publication of all examination results – GCE 'A' level, GCSE, and Standard Assessment Test (SAT) results for Key Stages 1, 2, 3 and 4, as well as information concerning other performance indicators such as staying on rates, truancy and attendance rates. The 1992 Act also radically changes the inspection system for schools by restructuring the HMI and introducing a four-yearly cycle of inspection: the results of such inspections could well form a key part of the marketing strategy of schools. A driving force underpinning these particular changes has been John Major's *Citizen's Charter* and the striving for a better quality of public Service (Kavanagh and Seldon 1994).

For sixth form and further education colleges the Further and Higher Education Act 1992 set them free from local education authority control in much the same way that the Education Reform Act 1988 did for polytechnics and colleges. Scope for change and innovation is therefore provided for these institutions to provide a greater diversity of provision, competing much more vigorously with each other.

The challenge to educational policy-makers, especially at the institutional level, is to respond to these changes in such a way that they have a clear sense of mission and purpose which can be justified when subjected to public scrutiny. The marketing of schools and colleges will therefore become an increasingly important aspect of educational management as competition is encouraged and becomes more intense. In Birmingham, for example, the changes of recent years has seen choice at the secondary level widen substantially, since as well as the local authority comprehensive schools, church schools and selective grammar schools, there now exist eighteen grant maintained schools and one city technology college (although the CTC is just outside the boundaries of the authority). Other local authorities such as Lincolnshire and Wandsworth have set up 'magnet' schools – institutions which specialize in particular subject areas such as science and technology (*TES* 1992). More recently, the Secretary of State at the Department for Education and Employment has pursued a policy of approving diversity of schools by encouraging them to bid for resources to become technology colleges and language colleges; so far 101 technology colleges have been established and 16 language colleges (*TES* 1995). Such choice and competition is likely to increase throughout the 1990s, despite the considerable slowing down in the number of grant maintained schools being established. But perhaps more importantly for all schools, both primary and secondary, is the requirement of publishing performance indicators, since this will allow comparisons to be made between all schools within a locality on a continuing basis. Many schools and colleges have responded to these challenges of effective marketing in recent years, but more will have to be done in future, a marketing strategy becoming a key element of school and college management.

7.4   EDUCATION REFORMS: RATIONALE

The education reforms and the objectives they are designed to accomplish, are based on a number of explicit and implicit assumptions:

- that schools (producers) are capable of successfully marketing their 'products' to meet the needs of pupils and parents (consumers), and the legislation will encourage them to do so;
- that the promotion of informed consumer choice and a diminution of producer power is an overriding objective in a quest to achieve higher quality education services;
- that it is possible (and desirable) to establish perceptible, independent choices between competing schools, thereby enhancing the quality of the offering;
- that near perfect market conditions are attainable by the intensification of competition between schools; that an effectively managed school will provide essential organizational/decision-making pre-requisites for successful marketing.

7.4.1 Schools' capacity for marketing

There is considerable prima-facie evidence that schools are increasingly active in promoting their services and more willing to accommodate consumer demands (Barnes 1993). Indeed, some schools have been overzealous in marketing, giving rise to concerns about the need to constrain the worst excesses of such activity (NAHT 1990). But the diversity of the organizational characteriztics of educational institutions and the markets they serve, and the distorting tendency of media coverage of schools' frenetic public relations and publicity campaigns, suggests it is credulous to infer from this evidence alone that marketing has made profound inroads to the culture of education.

A survey undertaken in 1990 into marketing in LEA schools in Solihull, and a representative sample of independent schools, provides more objective evidence for assessing the actual and potential impact of the education reforms on relations between producers and users of education services (Barnes 1993: 147–72).

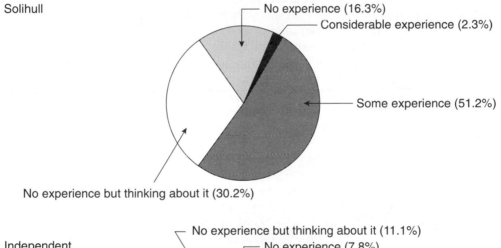

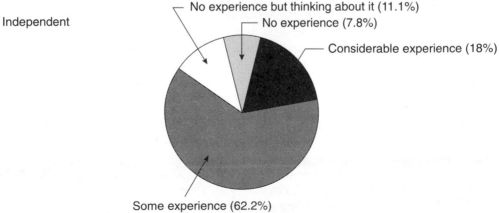

Figure 7.1   Schools' experience of marketing *(Source: Barnes 1993)*

In undertaking the survey, account was taken of the likelihood that teachers may subscribe to differing even conflicting notions of marketing. Indeed, ignorance of the defining characteriztics of the activity is not uncommon amongst senior personnel in many private sector organizations. (The findings expressed in Figures 7.7, 7.8, 7.9 and 7.10 are derived from an 'open' question used in the survey, i.e. respondents' replies were relatively spontaneous.)

Notwithstanding the non-profit culture in which schools operate and the possible antipathy of the profession towards marketing, virtually all heads and deputies surveyed offered strikingly similar definitions of the term to those given by Kotler and others (Kotler and Fox 1985). A consensus emerged that the meaning and function of marketing is:

> ... to cover that which schools consciously do, to identify the needs and wishes of the communities they serve, to publicise the ways in which they respond to these needs, and to promote a public awareness of the quality of the education which is provided.

(NAHT 1990)

Clearly, effective communications between head/staff and consumers are vital if schools are to successfully market themselves. To what extent, then, are schools sufficiently adept to undertake marketing?

The survey reveals that, predictably, independent schools are established marketers (see Figure 7.1). Surprisingly, marketing has permeated many maintained sector schools in Solihull (see Figure 7.1). Though few LEA schools surveyed claim to be accomplished in marketing – only 53.5% describe themselves as 'experienced' in this respect compared to 81.1% of independent schools – their virtual unanimity in ascribing a seminal role to marketing in the future is revealing: less than 3% believing it to be 'not at all important' (see Figure 7.2).

Unequivocally, both sectors recognize the importance of marketing, though independent schools have, as expected, undertaken more of it (see Figure 7.3). Though marketing activities are not always divisible into discrete, sequential stages (conceivably, a school might undertake a number of them simultaneously), usually a planned approach is adopted involving a series of logical steps. But most of Solihull's maintained sector schools are in the initial stages of marketing (i.e. 'thinking' about it) whilst for independent schools the converse is true.

Creating a 'consumer-orientated' culture in schools presents a formidable challenge to heads and governors. To achieve this objective, the process of change must be effectively and sensitively managed by the institution's decision-makers. Theoretically, this involves the forces of change (i.e. head, marketing development officer and governors) attempting to counteract the endeavours of those who might threaten to resist change (e.g. traditionalists amongst the teaching staff) (Kotter and Schlesinger 1979). But how likely is it that staff will resist initiatives which they perceive as threatening the status quo? Clearly, the method and approach by which a school's decision-makers manage the change process will ultimately determine how successful they are in inculcating a marketing culture.

Staff attitude towards marketing is a useful indicator of likely resistance to change. The survey findings in Figure 7.4 indicate that, as one might expect, independent school staff are more disposed towards marketing education services than their

Solihull

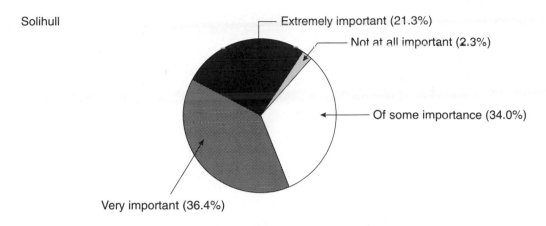

Extremely important (21.3%)

Not at all important (2.3%)

Of some importance (34.0%)

Very important (36.4%)

Independent

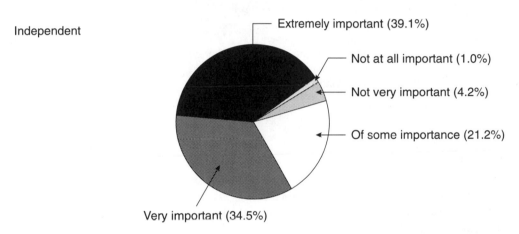

Extremely important (39.1%)

Not at all important (1.0%)

Not very important (4.2%)

Of some importance (21.2%)

Very important (34.5%)

Figure 7.2   Relative importance of marketing to schools *(Source: Barnes 1993)*

counterparts in the maintained sector. Whereas most respondents in the independent sector considered their staff to be responsive to marketing (29.9% being 'extremely/very receptive' and 49.0% 'somewhat receptive'), staff in the Solihull maintained sector were relatively less keen on the activity (14.0% are described as 'very receptive' and 58.1% as 'somewhat receptive', but a resounding 21% are considered 'not very/not at all receptive' to marketing). On balance, the survey indicates a relatively high level of receptivity in both sectors towards 'consumerism'. This suggests that staff are sensitive to the changing climate in which schools operate. Their heightened awareness may be due as much to the intensification of competition in education, following the introduction of recent legislation, as their appreciation of the inexorable impact on enrolment of demographic and economic factors.

Where a dramatic change in school's organizational culture is sought, then a number of recognized mechanisms are available to achieve this. According to Kotter and Schlesinger (1979), six alternative strategies are available for managing change in

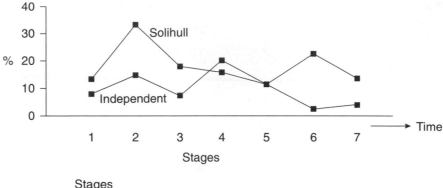

Stages

1 Not contemplating marketing school
2 Thinking about marketing
3 Establishing marketing team
4 Undertaking review
5 Setting objectives, selecting strategies
6 Implementing strategies
7 Monitoring and reviewing strategies

Figure 7.3 Discrete stages in the marketing process *(Source: Barnes 1993)*

organizations, ranging from 'education'/'communication' and 'participation'/ 'involvement' at one end, to 'coercion' at the other. On this scale, the former approaches are considered the most effective for managing change, coercion the least effective in this respect (Chell 1987). Evidently, staff involvement in the school's decision process, from determining its corporate mission to deciding relevant marketing strategies, is a key to success in managing change:

> In deciding where we should go, we have to transfer 'ownership' of the direction by involving everyone in the decision. Making it happen means involving the hearts and minds of those who have to execute and deliver. It can not be said often enough that these are not the people at the top of the organization, but those at the bottom.
>
> *(Harvey-Jones 1988: 48)*

So, a school's style of management reflects its willingness and/or capacity to respond to the change demanded of a responsive organization. To what extent does this reflect customer and practice in schools?

Using an adaptation of Tannenbaum and Schmidt's (1958) model, the survey gauged the appropriateness of current management styles in schools to successful change management, see Figure 7.5. On a scale authoritarian/democratic, over half the schools in both sectors described their management style as 'consultative'. Interestingly, Solihull maintained sector schools reported a markedly higher degree of delegation to staff than that found in the independent sector; 26.2% and 12.9%

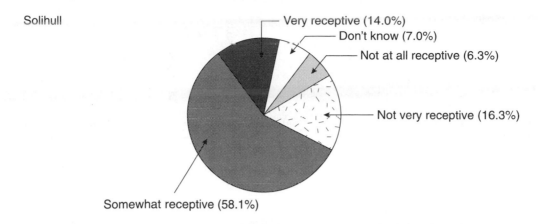

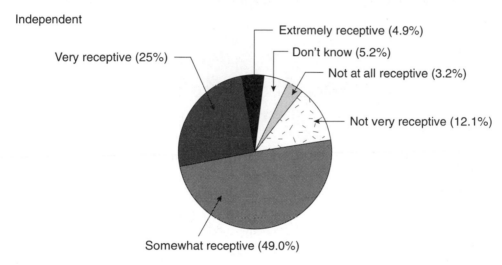

Figure 7.4   Receptiveness of school staff to marketing *(Source: Barnes 1993)*

respectively. Independent schools, compared to those in Solihull, appear manifestly more authoritarian in terms of management style. This apparent difference in leadership style in the two sectors may reflect differences in the ratio of female to male staff, especially in positions of seniority (Chell 1987); more women than men are employed in LEA schools, while the converse applies to the independent sector.

In apparent contradiction to the above, in matters relating to marketing both sectors are relatively authoritarian (see Figure 7.6). The research did, however, elicit a rationale for this phenomenon. In Solihull schools, this is a consequence of the infancy of marketing; many heads there intend involving staff more actively in marketing when objectives and strategies are established, thus freeing teachers to concentrate

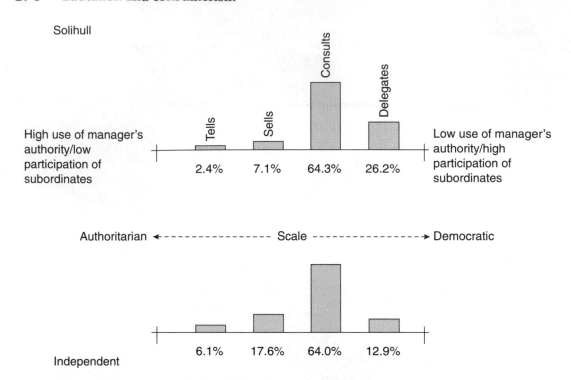

Figure 7.5 Categorization of management styles in schools *(Source: Barnes 1993)*

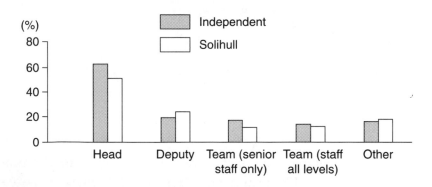

Figure 7.6 Identification of staff most closely involved in school marketing *(Source: Barnes 1993).*

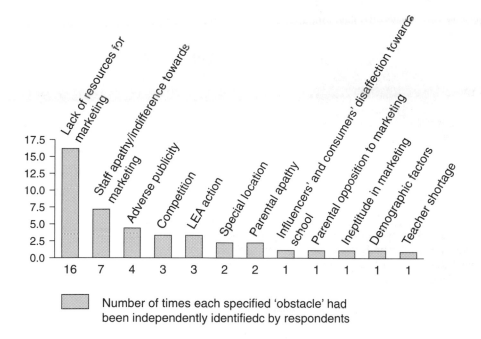

Figure 7.7 Perceived obstacles to effective marketing: Solihull schools survey findings
(*Source: Barnes 1993*)

on the national curriculum and SATs. In the independent sector, marketing has traditionally been the responsibility of senior staff.

These results obviously record the perceptions of respondents – heads and deputies – and may not necessarily reflect the views of teaching staff about their role in the school's decision process. Though further research is needed, the results do at least reflect a recognition on the part of senior managers of the importance of consultation, thus vindicating the theory on effective change management.

If schools are successfully to undertake marketing, then adequate resources must be available for the purpose (Barnes 1993). Indeed, the schools' survey reveals the extent to which respondents considered marketing success to be largely dependent on time, training to compensate for lack of marketing expertise amongst staff, and funds for implementing marketing strategies (see Figures 7.7, 7.8, 7.9, and 7.10). (This represents the conclusions from a survey of companies undertaken by the British Institute of Management (BIM) in 1970. The BIM found that 58% of respondents defined marketing 'incorrectly', 17% omitted to define the concept and only 25% provided an 'acceptable' definition of the term.)

So, how well placed are schools likely to be in terms of resource provision for marketing? A recently published report provides few grounds for optimism:

The pressure with LMS for schools to compete for pupils will result in a fragmented and considerably diminished education service, especially when

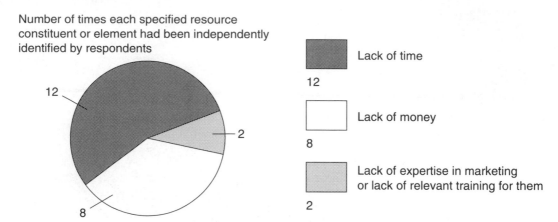

Number of times each specified resource constituent or element had been independently identified by respondents

Note. though 10 respondents independently identified this 'obstacle', some of them listed more than one constituent or element under the head 'lack of resources'; hence total of 22 citations.

Figure 7.8 Solihull schools and 'lack of resources': dissection of this perceived obstacle to effective marketing

combined with the budget reductions currently being experienced in many LEAs.

(IPPR 1992)

These conclusions suggest that schools in both sectors have adopted responsive strategies in their dealings with consumers. Now consumer sovereignty seems a more apt characterization of the prevailing relationship between parents/pupils and schools than one in which education provision is determined exclusively by producers of the service. This emerging consumer-orientated culture in schools suggests a prolonged and accredited role for marketing. The extent to which underfunding and lack of adequate resources threatens this development remains to be seen.

7.4.2 Consumer choice

A principal intention behind the education reforms is that consumer choice should be paramount. But the declaration to foster almost unfettered parental choice at all levels of education is unrealistic. Certainly, the idea of consumer choice is meaningful at secondary level and beyond, where the provision of education services is more prolific and consumers have a greater propensity to move between sectors (i.e. from LEA schools to independent schools) and to travel considerable distances. At primary school level, however, the exercise of parental/pupil choice is strictly circumscribed

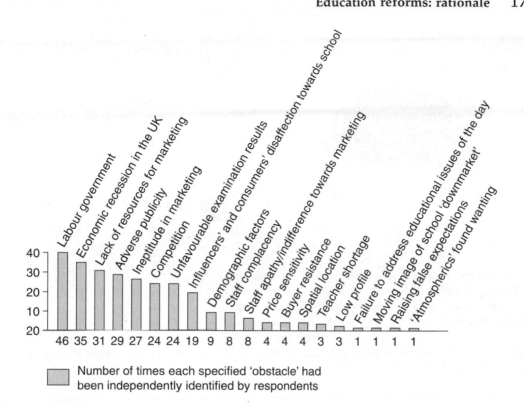

Figure 7.9 Perceived obstacles to effective marketing: independent schools survey findings (*Source: Barnes 1993*)

by the availability of local institutions, given the understandable reluctance on the part of parents to permit their young children to travel long distances to school – the market is therefore an extremely limited one.

Even where a reasonable degree of choice of school exists, a recent study has found considerable 'class-based differences in family orientations to the market both in terms of parental inclination to engage with it and their capacity to exploit the market to their children's advantage' (Gewirtz, Ball and Bowe 1995: 181). The study sees the market as 'a middle-class mode of social engagement' where knowledge of, and understanding of, the local education market provides distinct advantages in enhancing the life-chances of children. The authors distinguish between 'privileged/ skilled choosers', 'semi-skilled choosers', and the 'disconnected'. Although the study is limited to an investigation of three London boroughs, its findings cast considerable doubt on the workings of market forces in education.

Implicit in the case for promoting meaningful consumer choice, is the view that schools should between them provide a reasonable variety of forms of education from which parents might choose, but much of what is offered by schools is heavily circumscribed by the national curriculum. The Dearing Report 1993 reduced to a

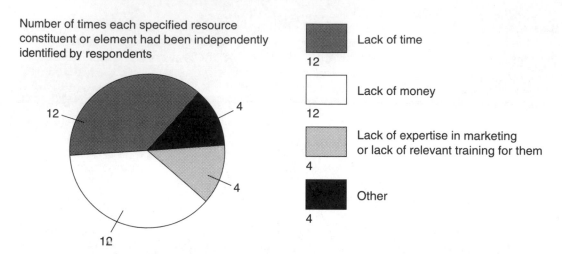

Number of times each specified resource constituent or element had been independently identified by respondents

Lack of time
12

Lack of money
12

Lack of expertise in marketing or lack of relevant training for them
4

Other
4

Note: though 31 respondents independently identified this 'obstacle', some of them listed more than one constituent or element under the head 'lack of resources'; hence total of 32 citations.

Figure 7.10 Independent schools and 'lack of resources': dissection of this perceived obstacle to effective marketing *(Source: Barnes 1993)*

certain extent the constraints of the original ideas, but there still exists a relatively limited variety of product. Standardization and nationalization. These are the key characteristics of the recent reforms. Moreover, key aspects of the education reforms have tended to undermine the concept of 'perfect' competition: the establishment and generous funding of city technology colleges and grant maintained schools, for example, has resulted in an 'imperfect' (rigged) market. The concept of meaningful consumer choice is further eroded.

A further difficulty is that marketing, far from fostering greater consumer choice, actually militates against it: marketing enables schools to target selected consumer groups whom it wishes to attract, intentionally discounting other potential users of its services (not least because of the implications for published examination results). In this respect, marketing is essentially a selective process. Here, choice is illusory. Thus, the second assumption on which the education reforms is based is problematic.

7.4.3 Performance indicators

The introduction of performance indicators of the kind envisaged by the Education (Schools) Act 1992 (refer to Chapter 4) in order to help consumers compare and contrast rival schools in terms of output or outcome (examination results), seems potentially self-defeating. In offering a rationale for this mechanism for promoting consumerism in schools, a former Secretary of State for Education argued: 'I intend to take the mystery out of education by providing the real choice which flows from comparative tables setting out the performance of local schools' (Kenneth Clarke, *The Independent* 10 October 1992), but compulsory publication of examination results seems to run counter to the promotion of parental choice since fear of low ranking in league tables has prompted many schools to 'choose' pupils, not the other way about! Indeed, the culture of league tables is overshadowing other accomplishments and values, as examination results '... become the advertising copy of the (school's) publication department's glossy brochure, which is the main tool to support the marketing function' (M Carney, *The Guardian* 17 April 1990). That published examination league tables enhance the rationality of parents' choice is doubtful: a recent study by the LSE Centre for Educational Research and the South Bank University found that just over half (51%) of parents interviewed said that their knowledge of examination results did not affect their eventual choice of school; 38% said it did and 11% were undecided (*TES* 17 November 1995). Moreover, league tables based exclusively on raw data can be misleading because they fail to measure like-with-like or express strengths and achievements not reflected in formal examination results and this goes to the heart of the limitation of this performance criterion as a mechanism for promoting informed consumer choice: many parents consciously select schools on the basis of criteria other than academic excellence, such as atmosphere and ethos, discipline, uniforms, etc. (*The Independent* 1992).

Only when constructed sensibly, and applied sensitively, are league tables meaningful indicators of relative performance and therefore of practical value to parents and pupils alike. The potential merit of league tables is exemplified by the Tyne and Wear Schools' experiment and the recent incorporation of 'value-added' to raw examination results. In the early 1980s a consortium of like-minded schools in the Tyne and Wear locality operated a scheme to measure and compare 'A' level results. ALIS, the acronym by which the scheme is known, involves each member school entering its annual examination scores against an allotted code number known only to the organizers of the scheme and the institution concerned, thus ensuring anonymity. Subsequently, results are weighted to take account of the heterogeneity of 'intake' or differing pupil abilities, collated and circulated only to participating schools; none are published or made known to parents. The schools involved report that the scheme is of inestimable value to them in improving the quality of their service. (BBC, 12 October 1992). Indeed, so successful is ALIS that it now monitors performance in almost 400 schools, and uses data collected for the Secondary Heads Association in 500 more. (*The Times* 21 August 1995; *TES* 14 July 1995). As a consequence of the adverse publicity surrounding the publication of raw examination results, the government commissioned the School Curriculum and Assessment Authority (SCAA) to investigate the possibility of including 'value added' data to the league tables. The SCAA Report entitled *Value-Added Performance Indicators for Schools* published in 1994, provides a comprehensive survey of research which has been conducted by research organizations and LEAs into 'value-added' across the whole school range from 5–18; a total of 49 examples of value added experiments are listed in Appendix 4 of the SCAA Report. Perhaps the most interesting example provided is that of Solihull LEA which is attempting to construct a profile of all pupils from 5–19 working with YELLIS (Year 11 Information Systems) and ALIS ('A' level Information System) at Durham University. It is clear from the variety of this on-going research that to incorporate the findings into national league tables is extremely difficult, but on the other hand individual schools and local authorities are finding this data helpful in monitoring the progress of pupils, away from the glare of often unwanted publicity.

Notwithstanding the limitations of the raw data provided by the league tables, they are a fact of life for school managers and will remain so for the foreseeable future. If the image of the school is going to be affected by the publicity surrounding the publication of examination results then sensible Heads will try to ensure that the best possible interpretation will be put on the results and indeed the results will be presented in school literature in the most favourable light, for example by selecting the highest percentage of passes whether this is the overall pass rate, or the level of As obtained, or A and Bs etc – manipulation of the pass-rates becomes inevitable. Similarly, suggestions are made that schools will not enter those pupils who may have an adverse effect on the pass-rate and that schools' efforts at GCSE level are concentrated on those pupils capable of obtaining a grade C or above; schools may target pupils who will boost their rankings and of course it makes sense for schools to 'select' pupils with a view to improving examination performance. The 1995 examination results certainly drew comment on the fact that the percentage of pupils obtaining no GCSE passes at all rose slightly to 8% in England and 11% in Wales, giving rise to the concern for a 'long tail of underperformance'.

> But for many Heads the league tables have provided them with clearer strategies for implementing school improvement policies, that is, to improve their position in the league tables.

Some schools have achieved considerable success in raising the percentage of pupils gaining 5 GCSE's at C or above which is the DfEE yardstick for comparative purposes; for example, Noadswood School near Southampton increased its pass-rate from 50% to 75% in the 1995 examinations (*The Times* 24 November 1995); St Saviour's and St Olave's School in Southwark increased its pass-rate from 17% to 42% in 1995 (*TES* 24 November 1995). Such success clearly provides a stimulus to the school and its pupils and provides a positive image for the local community, as well as providing an example to other schools. Specific elements of school improvement policies include homework clubs, extending school library hours, mentoring for pupils in Years 10 and 11, setting targets for improvement for individual pupils, involving parents more closely in the work of their children, Easter revision help, etc. Tables of improving schools published by the quality press help to draw some attention away from the highly selective schools in both the state and independent sectors which inevitably dominate the upper levels of the league tables. Conversely, schools which are failing have nowhere to hide – the Amy Johnson School in Humberside, for example achieved a pass rate of 0% of pupils obtaining 5 GCSEs in 1995 out of 137 pupils; in 1994 the figure was 6% out of 138 pupils. The ultimate sanction of school closure is a greater reality now than in the past where a school is judged to have 'failed', as in the case of Hackney Downs School in 1995. In marketing terms the reports of OFSTED inspections similarly may have an effect, either positive or negative, on local perceptions of school performance; the public listing of 'outstandingly successful schools' by the Chief Inspector of Schools in February 1996 also provides a high seal of approval – what one might call 'OFSTED OSCARS'!

7.4.4 Competition

The view that recent reforms might foster 'healthy' competition between schools, thereby enhancing the offerings available to a discriminating consumer, seems unlikely. Many schools will be placed in the invidious position of competing with each other in a strictly finite market: the 5–16 age group is a relatively static quantity since all children must attend school, in contrast to the 16–19 age group which includes additional potential recruits (i.e. those contemplating staying on at post-16, or those who might be induced back into sixth form or similar study). In circumstances such as these, one school's gain is another's loss, possibly leading to unethical behaviour (Barnes 1993). In Norfolk this concern has already materialized where:

> schools are running campaigns of 'deliberate disinformation' to stop pupils leaving for rival institutions at 16 . . . and further education colleges are retaliating by offering unusual A-level subjects not available to local sixth-forms with the promise of free taxis to and from home to tempt them away.
>
> (*TES 16 October 1992*)

The application of the competition argument to education is problematic on another count: key elements of the education reforms have clearly militated against the operation of market conditions, as attested by the impact of CTCs, grant maintained status and 'opting-out' in many LEA schools.

7.4.5 Effective management: optimum conditions for marketing

An implicit assumption on the part of ministers since 1979 has been that 'effective management' in schools and their capacity to undertake 'successful marketing' are somehow inextricably linked (Downs 1989). But how established is the connection between these attributes?

In a major study of 24 schools, all of which had been categorized by HMI as 'effective', it had been observed that each had different ways of making decisions relating to resources, finance, timetables, curriculum, staffing, job descriptions, teaching methodologies and schemes of work (Torrington and Weightman 1989). Though each school had been described as 'effective', they were not all managed and organized in the same way, nor had identical cultures, attitudes or histories. But would they

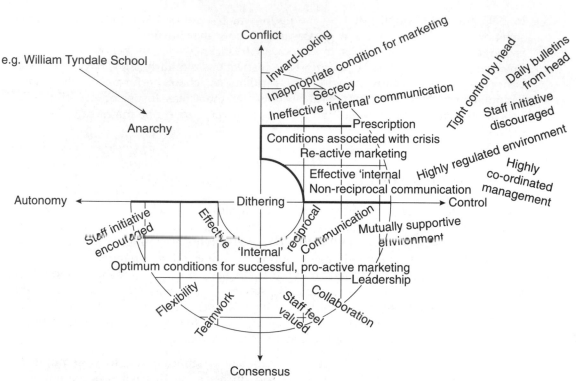

Figure 7.11   Management styles and the optimum conditions for successful marketing

all be equally adept at marketing? Does 'effective school management' entail 'successful school marketing'?

Figure 7.11 identifies where, in terms of a number of organizational and decision-making dimensions, 'effectively managed' schools are to be found. Superimposed on the model are the relative positions from which a school is most likely to launch a successful marketing campaign based on the definition given earlier (i.e. where optimum organizational and decision-making conditions for marketing are to be found). A school's success in marketing is largely determined by the presence of a number of key attributes associated with effective internal and external communication, shared values, etc, not the bestowment of 'effectiveness' by OFSTED. That a school is deemed 'effective' does not entail that its marketing will achieve its desired objectives.

Recent government legislation, especially those aspects concerned with governing bodies, may have had the unintended consequence of making organizational cohesion more difficult to achieve. Well-publicized conflicts between the chairman of governors and the head of Stratford School in East London would not have helped the school to project a positive image in marketing terms. Similarly, Woodroffe School, Lyme Regis, attracted adverse media coverage following the suspension of its head by the governors there (*TES* 1992).

7.5   CONCLUSIONS

This chapter has been concerned with examining a cultural change in the education service, that is the emergence of a marketing culture. Schools have responded to this challenge in a positive way in an attempt to meet the demands for a more consumer-oriented education system. However, problems exist in judging how far substantive change has occurred in enabling consumers to have a greater influence in schools; for example, the acquisition of considerable powers by the Secretary of State in key areas of decision-making – curriculum, examinations, assessment, finance, inspection – suggests that government rhetoric concerning consumerism, choice and competition needs to be tempered in the light of recent experience. Increasingly the evidence is suggesting that the schools are selecting pupils rather than parents selecting schools on behalf of their children. Nevertheless, information is now available to consumers of education on a scale inconceivable before the Thatcher/Major era, but whether choice has been extended as a result of this must seem uncertain. The considerable slowing down of the grant-maintained school policy is clearly a great disappointment to the government; just over 1000 grant-maintained schools have been established out of a total 25000, suggesting that the vast majority of parents are content to send their children to local education authority schools. Local schools therefore may well find that their marketing strategies will focus on those aspects of policy-making over which they still retain a degree of discretion, such as discipline, uniform, extra-curricular activities, cultural pursuits, etc. where the ethos of the school can be publicized.

Can other public services learn anything from this education case study? Are the emerging characteristics in this area of activity relevant or appropriate for social services, the NHS, police, housing, etc? Developments in the last decade or so in some of these areas indicate that the application of consumerist thinking has been attempted, for example, the 'opting out' of hospitals within the NHS, the establishment of Housing Action Trusts etc. But this case study has thrown up doubts as to the degree of change that has been achieved so far in the education service; indeed there is arguably an element of tokenism concerning many of the changes. There is a suspicion that those who understand how markets operate will be able to use them to their best advantage and those that do not understand them will be disadvantaged – knowledge is power. The one indisputable fact since 1988, is that it has been the Secretary of State for Education and Employment who has acquired enormous powers and responsibilities rather than the consumer, and that the 'nationalization' of education is a more accurate description of the changes, rather than the empowerment of parents.

7.6   CHAPTER SUMMARY

- Schools in England and Wales have undergone a dramatic cultural change in which a consumer-orientated education system has emerged.
- Recent experience suggests that the consumer of education services is seldom sovereign: developments in curriculum, examinations, assessment, finance, inspection and league tables sometimes proffer an illusion of informed choice. Parents

with knowledge of the education system are likely to enjoy better access to schools than those less familiar with the service.

- Many head teachers and other senior staff now consider marketing and associated activities vital to the future survival of their schools not least because of the policy of school improvement.
- Educationalists surveyed were generally well disposed towards marketing and recognized its positive contribution to better informed management decisions.
- Schools surveyed had adopted responsive marketing strategies in their dealings with consumers.
- A school's success in marketing is largely determined by the presence of a number of key attributes including effective internal and external communications and shared values.

TEXT-BASED QUESTIONS

1. Identify the reasons for the development of a marketing culture in education.

2. In what sense does a 'consumer-orientated' culture in schools present a formidable challenge to heads and governors?

3. Explain the importance of a school's 'style of management' to its marketing success.

4. Why is a marketing strategy an important element of a school's/college's management?

5. In the context of marketing in schools, examine the concept of choice, performance indicators and competition and explain the connections between them.

6. Identify the optimum management conditions for successful, proactive school marketing.

ASSIGNMENT

In Figure 7.9, reference is made to the 'perceived obstacles to effective marketing'. Study the findings in Figure 7.9 carefully and compare and contrast with the research-results expressed in Figure 7.7.

a)   In this context, it can be observed that independent schools considered a Labour government to represent the greatest threat. In view of the Labour Party's professed priorities in education, to what extent is this concern on the part of the independent schools justified?

b)   The issue of the Labour Party apart, critically assess the principal differences between the findings in the two figures.

FURTHER READING

Barnes, C. (1993) *Practical Marketing for Schools*, Blackwell, Oxford.

Gewirtz, S., Ball, S.J. and Bowe, R. (1995) *Markets, Choice and Equity in Education*, Open University Press.

Tomlinson, S. (1994) *Educational Reform and its Consequence* Rivers, Oram Press.

PATIENTS, POWER AND POLICY: NHS MANAGEMENT REFORMS AND CONSUMER EMPOWERMENT

8

Chris Barnes and David Cox

8.1   CHAPTER PREVIEW

This chapter will

- Review some important recent developments in the NHS. The impact of recent legislation and reforms will be discussed and critically appraised.
- Describe and comment on the emergence of a 'managerial' culture in the NHS and the imposition of an 'internal market' in health care.
- Outline the origins of the consumer movement in the NHS. In this context, the **individual consumer** and **collective 'consumerism'** in the NHS will be critically examined and its implication for patients explained. Included will be critical commentaries and reflections on 'consumer empowerment', 'consumer surveys' and the *'Patient's Charter'* initiative.
- Critically evaluate the contribution of community health councils (CHCs) to the consumer movement in health care. Here, illustrations from case studies and

findings from a recent empirical survey (see acknowledgements at end of the chapter) will be utilized to provide new insights to the operational activities of CHCs in promoting consumer interests.

8.2 SETTING THE SCENE

The management of health care throws up particularly important and distinctive issues which reflect many of the themes in this book but which have a special and added resonance because of the features of organized health care as a managed public service. There is an abundant specialist literature on the politics, management and organization of the NHS in the UK and of private and public health services throughout the world.

The distinctive features of health care include the prominence of the medical profession with its control over the nature and immediate delivery of many forms of health intervention, the ethical issues involved in a life and death service which touches on the most critical of human experiences and the political salience of health care to the population. Within the UK the role of the health service as a flagship of the post-war welfare state, the determination of successive conservative governments to reform the management of the NHS and the dominance of health matters in the public consciousness, the media and political debate have created a challenging and unique environment for exploring public service management. Furthermore the size and scope of the NHS in terms of budget and its impact on people's lives – from the cradle to the grave – means that commentators, practitioners, citizens and politicians can regard the world of health care as unique, moving to its own rhythms and imperatives, separate from both the private sector economy and the other public services. It is these distinctive features that persuaded the Labour government to keep large sections of health care from being subsumed within local government in 1948.

An important element of the Government's drive for reform has been to challenge this aura of untouchable distinctiveness and bring health care into the wider debate about public money, efficiency, managerialism and comparisons with the private sector and even privatization. Challenging medical power and the notion of the unique nature of health service administration has been an enduring theme of successive government interventions (Harrison and Pollitt 1994).

Throughout the world, industrial and developing countries are wrestling with the problems of providing for the health needs of their populations. The optimism of the World Health Organization's Health for All agreement (WHO 1985), emphasizing health promotion, public health and health care as a human right, has been replaced in the run up to the millennium with pessimistic concern about the alleged exponential costs of health care, ageing populations (in the developed world) and medical innovations which offer disproportionately costly solutions to disease and ageing (for example Health Care 2000 1995).

8.3   NHS REFORMS

The British National Health Service was founded in 1948 as part of a broad programme of post-war social reconstruction. While continuing to be widely popular, the service has invariably suffered from underfunding and regional and sector disparities in resources. Over the last twenty years, health service organization has become a major focus of policy and public discussion in which concern about resources has been countered by an accelerating search for organizational and managerial solutions. Major organizational changes were introduced in 1974 (DHSS 1972), 1982 (DHSS 1979) and, following the Griffiths Report, in 1984 (DHSS 1983).

Whereas many politicians and commentators would see a lack of economic resources as the central concern of health service policy, the government, while maintaining and enhancing levels of spending in practice, have asserted that ultimately spending on health is not a bottomless pit and that a prime requirement is more efficient management of the NHS to maximize the use of current resources. The first major reorganization in 1974 was introduced during a period of corporate rationalization which affected many other public services (Hunter 1988: 539). Three managerial tiers at regional, area and district level were established and local authority community health services were brought under NHS control. Health authorities at each level were large (up to 20 members) and broadly representative of local interests, including local authority nominees and professional representatives. The new community health councils were designed to represent the interests of users especially those like the elderly, mentally ill or those with learning disabilities who might be relatively inarticulate, powerless and often in the 1970s, institutionalized.

The 1974 Act built on the previous professional structures of the NHS where 'management' was to be provided by 'consensus' teams consisting of a medical representative, a nursing officer, an administrator and a treasurer. In 1978 a Royal Commission was established to look again at the organizational structure of the service and this resulted in the 1982 reorganization, which abolished the area authorities, emphasized the role of districts and advocated delegation as far as possible of decisions to the hospital and community 'unit' level.

The structural changes did not meet the Thatcher government's requirements of controlling the overall costs of the NHS and introducing modern management methods and systems from private industry. Within a year of the 1982 reorganization Mrs Thatcher asked Roy Griffiths, from the Sainsbury retail chain, to look at the NHS and recommended changes in management arrangements and the control of staffing costs in this labour intensive industry.

This Report, a short twenty-three page letter to the Secretary of State (DHSS 1983), was published in the Autumn of 1983 and enthusiastically endorsed by the government. Over the next three years it produced a number of significant changes to the NHS management. Its underlying theme was to bring to the health service some of the principles and culture of good private sector management. The report's recommendations included setting up a supervisory and a management board at national level, the appointment of one accountable general manager 'regardless of discipline' at regional, district and unit level, an emphasis on delegation, the introduction of management budgeting, the involvement of doctors in management and, finally, greater emphasis on consumer needs and satisfaction.

For Griffiths, a managerial approach involved planning, setting targets, managing implementation and monitoring performance against pre-set criteria. The objective was a much more informed and determined approach to setting and keeping to budgets and in labour intensive health care this meant a stricter control over professional and manual labour costs and performance (see Harrison 1986 and 1988; Cousins 1987). The recurring themes of Griffiths' managerialism are action, effectiveness, thrust, urgency and vitality, management budgeting, sensitivity to consumer satisfaction and an approach to the management of staff which would reward good performance and sanction poor performance with dismissal. The appointment of general managers, coming so soon after the enforcement of competitive tendering for ancillary services, was part of a new and more intensive form of managerial intervention. Whereas earlier reorganizations had brought some management techniques for planning into the NHS, the government was now trying to change managerial behaviour and introduce an approach to control and labour discipline derived from the competitive private sector.

Griffiths brought significant changes to the managerial organization of the NHS, but by 1989 the Thatcher government was concerned to introduce a much more radical agenda of change (Hoggett 1990). The 1989 White Paper *Working for Patients*, was followed by the *NHS and Community Care Act* of 1990 and introduced the 'NHS Reforms' which centred around the notion of an 'internal market' for the delivery of health care.

The large inflexible 'bureaucracy' of the previous NHS was broken down somewhat into **purchasers** and **providers**. Purchasers like District Health Authorities do not manage hospitals and community units. They decide what services their population needs for the coming year and purchase these services under contract from 'providers' which are independent **NHS** Trusts. DHAs are not obliged to purchase from one supplier, nor to use their local trusts if another one gives better value (and patients can or are prepared to travel). The contracts (correctly termed service agreements – they are not contracts in law) specify what health care is to be purchased, how much of it (acute hospital treatment has been measured in 'finished consultant episodes') and include quality standards (e.g. waiting times or facilities needed for sick children). Provider units or NHS Trusts compete in the internal market on costs (defined by price as they cannot make a profit), quality and timeliness and locality of service. Minor shifts of 'business' at the margins can be powerful incentives to Trust managers to improve services or cut costs. This arrangement is further complicated by GP Fundholders who can purchase a growing range of hospital and community services for their patients and thus are another source of uncertainty and force for change. Many GPs are forming purchasing consortia to increase their bargaining power.

The move to internal markets is widespread in management practice as is the 'outsourcing' of supplies and services. It is partly a reaction against the sheer scale of bureaucracy and the frustrations of direct control. Organizations are disaggregating and de-institutionalizing. By encouraging competition and allowing for more specialist consultancy and contracted out services, management seeks to exert control indirectly through contract specifications, competitive tendering and careful monitoring of contract compliance. This is a form of 'hands off' management control and, of course, is not new – many industries started like this. Contracting out cleaning, catering, market research, fleet management has been a long established practice. The specialist firms are more efficient and, for a price, remove peripheral concerns that take up management time. Contracting out core business such as health care for the NHS is a much more radical step.

Handy (1989: Ch. 4) writes of the way traditional pyramid organizations are being replaced by what he calls the 'shamrock' organization. In this structure there are three key groups. The purchasers are the designers, marketing experts and quality monitors – they draw up specifications and keep up to date on what is needed, they can be a very small group of highly paid staff. Next come the sub-contractors, 'providers', competing for contracts to supply the purchasers. They produce to specification at a keen price. The third 'leaf' in the shamrock is the 'flexible labour force'. Because contractors only want staff when they win a contract – no one has a job for life. Staff need to be flexible and respond to demand. They will not have permanent contracts or even necessarily full time ones for one organization, they will need to make their own arrangements for pensions and such like. Many may end up being 'self-employed'. Labour only contracting (called the 'lump' in the building trade) is the logical extension of this idea. This has been canvassed as an idea for the NHS and can be seen in the spread of agency nursing and locum service for doctors.

Like all management strategies, going down the internal market route has its own costs and problems. Contracts are not that good a method of control for many services as things can be overlooked and circumstances change. Purchasers may not have a very good idea of what is needed. Many early purchasing plans were essentially replicas of what the new Trusts did last year. Quality monitoring is not easy and can be expensive. GPs can switch their patients but many services have to be provided locally where one provider may have a monopoly even after the internal market 'reforms'. The legalistic powers to enforce contracts even in private industry are difficult and expensive to use in practice. In the NHS Regional Offices will arbitrate (see Robinson and Le Grand 1994). Any real responsiveness to end users or consumers of the health service is still very indirect in this 'quasi-market' (Le Grand 1990). District Health Authorities may do some consumer research and can collaborate with Community Health Councils (CHCs) to do this through surveys, public meetings or focus groups. GPs do have close contact with their patients and this may be expected to be reflected in their purchasing of acute services. However, many patients may have doubts about their GPs and any CHC or Family Health Service Authority (FHSA) will have a regular series of complaints about a minority of GPs themselves. Purchasing Authorities and Regional Offices will use their Patient Charter standards as criteria for the quality monitoring of contract performance and patients, those on waiting lists particularly may directly benefit from this top down management pressure.

A major matter of contention has been the increase in **transaction costs** that this mode of managing causes. Contract managers, accountants, purchasing teams, marketing teams, information officers, audit teams all struggle to achieve the cost savings/quality improvements required but they are not caring for patients directly and they all require salaries, cars, computers, clerical support and so on.

Many people are worried that the impact of these changes will be to destroy the collaborative spirit that has characterized the NHS since its inception. For all the status seeking, professional rivalries, lack of cost and performance data and sometimes indifference to clients and patients, the NHS enjoyed a level of staff loyalty and commitment which any private sector organization would have envied. Certainly, there has been a great deal of both professional and public opposition to these changes but they have been vigorously defended and pursued by the Government.

8.4   ORIGINS OF CONSUMERISM IN THE NHS

8.4.1   Central concepts: 'consumer', 'consumerism' and 'empowerment'

The term 'consumer' is a modern concept which is derived from economics and the retail trade. It is now a constituent of public sector vocabulary and refers to both recipients of monopoly state services and those who have choice between competing and alternative public offerings (see Chapter 1). It has been a useful corrective to traditions of organizational indifference to service users to compare standards of organizational treatment – reception areas, information booklets, opportunities for redress etc. between the best commercial retail organizations and the worst public services. Hospital out-patient waiting rooms and DHSS offices in the 1970s were illustrations of this.

The concept of 'consumerism' is about information, choice and standards of service and refers to the collective power of consumer organizations such as the Patients' Association and the Consumers' Association. Thinkers on the 'political right' see consumers as **customers** (implying the right to purchase) and prefer market or quasi-market systems where the consumer/customer is 'always right' and can exercise 'consumer sovereignty'(see Chapters 1 and 2). Critics on the 'political left' are less happy with the term and the implied market ethic. Stacey (1976) points out that we produce our own 'health' we do not simply consume health care, while others argue that for many 'users' of public services there is no choice as to which services they receive.

The notion of consumerism applied to public services has been a powerful corrective to the indifference of patronizing professionals and unhelpful bureaucracy that was undermining public confidence in 'their' public and welfare services. But it does tend to reinforce an individualistic and collective passivity. Consumer sovereignty implies choosing between two or more providers with the option of taking your 'business' elsewhere. This gives the consumer no control over the provider organization nor the policies that govern it. In reality there may not be much of a choice: the local hospital, community trust, social service department may be all that is available. There is a debate even in retail economics about how far consumers are manipulated by advertising, have a real choice in mass produced products or get much genuine satisfaction from mass marketed goods and services.

> Entailed in the concept 'consumer' in health
> care is **choice, information and responsibility**

> In the context of health, the term empowerment refers to a ... process [or processes] of giving people the knowledge and skills to make it possible for them to become active partners with the profession in making informal decisions/choices about their own treatment and care; and of enabling communities to exert informed influences on NHS service planning, development and delivery.
>
> *(Farrell and Gilbert 1995: 7)*

It is argued that the two most important factors contributing to the empowerment of patients is the **attitude of health professionals** and **availability of relevant information**. The former condition includes listening to the patient, willingness to share information and decisions and respect for patients' rights and views. The latter includes information which is clear and comprehensible and deals with things such as treatment outcomes, risks and benefits (ibid.). Additionally, patients need support and resources

---

The two most commonly identified factors in the empowerment of patients are:

attitudes of professionals and information for patients

By what mechanism or mechanisms might consumer empowerment in health treatment and care be fostered? A number of factors have emerged from recent research inter alia: audit, monitoring and reviewing health provision and providing feedback on outcomes; effective complaints system; staff training to emphasize the importance of listening to patients; and effective Community Health Councils (ibid.).

Empowerment of patient is facilitated by, inter alia:

   monitoring of health provision;
   effective complaints system;
   staff trained to listen; and
   effective Community Health Councils

8.4.2 Emerging consumer culture in health

Commenting on consumerism in general, Borrie and Diamond observe that consumers '... have always, almost inevitably, been unorganized and relatively inarticulate' (Borrie and Diamond 1973: 33). In the context of health provision in the post-war era, this is especially apt. Here, the organizational strength, established status and prevailing ethos of the medical profession created an almost impenetrable barrier against patients' views and opinions which challenged the medical orthodoxy. Until the 1974 health reforms, patients' interests and concerns were largely interpreted and articulated on their behalf by decision-makers and advisory bodies. (Butler and Vaile 1984: 108) These included hospital administrators, health authorities and various quasi-medical bodies whose perspective on health matters tended to be that of the professional rather than the patient, with whom their capacity to empathize was inevitably limited. The paternalistic and centralist nature of the NHS policy community proffered scant opportunity for direct public involvement in health management and decision-making.

By the early 1970s, the public participation movement had gathered momentum and demands for greater patient involvement in health matters had become irrepressible. In an attempt to reconcile the 'currently fashionable rhetoric' with central planning, the government created new Community Health Councils whose *raison d'être* was formally to represent patients' views and articulate their concerns to decision-makers. (ibid.). Essentially, CHCs were independent of the NHS management structure and as such reflected the government's intention that neither they nor the patients whom they represented should actively participate in management and decision-making. The CHCs' role was confined to **responding** to health decisions, not to get involved in their making; in effect, a reactive (as opposed to proactive) relationship with health decision-makers. Thus, the inception of CHCs in 1974 marked the beginning of formal recognition of the 'consumer' in health matters. For the first time patients had, working for them exclusively, an independent statutory body whose functions were to represent their interests in the health service and provide '... a separate channel for the expression of [their] views distinct from the health authorities'. (Levitt 1980: 9)

The presentation of health legislation in the 1980s further underlines the central position of the consumer and consumer choice in health care provision. The 1989 White Paper *Working for Patients* emphasizes this very point: 'We aim', states the Prime Minister's Foreword, '... to extend patient choice ... All the proposals in this White Paper put the needs of the patient first'.

8.4.3 The Patient's Charter

With its publication in the early 1990s, the *Citizen's Charter* offered further empowerment to the citizen as consumer in relation to all public services (see Chapters 1, 3 and 5). It had been the intention that each service would subsequently produce its own charter. In the case of health services, this duly occurred in 1992 with the launching of the *Patient's Charter* which aimed to further enhance the consumers' 'voice' in health matters; charter standards were established in April 1994.

The *Patient's Charter* reaffirmed seven existing consumer rights. These included giving patients 'a clear explanation of any treatment proposed, including any risks and any alternatives, before . . . (agreeing) to the treatment' and allowing them 'access to (their) health records, and to know that those working for the NHS will, by law, keep their contents confidential'. The Charter also introduced additional rights and highlighted performance standards by which the quality of health service management can be judged. Here, patients are promised 'detailed information on local health services, including quality standards and maximum waiting times . . . from (the) health authority, GP or Community Health Council', and 'to have any complaints about NHS services . . . investigated' (*The Patient's Charter*). In April 1995, the Department of Health issued an update to the *Patient's Charter* which bestowed on the consumer further benefits including guarantees that waiting times for admission to hospital for surgery will not exceed 18 months; cancellation of an operation entitles a patient to readmission to hospital within one month and that patients can choose a single sex ward.

The *Patient's Charter* is arguably the best known of the various Citizen's Charter initiatives, but to what extent has it perceptibly furthered consumer rights? The argument that the Charter genuinely advances the consumers' cause must be based on the patient's awareness of his/her rights and entitlements. In the view of one CHC chief officer, the *Patient's Charter* '. . . has raised awareness and expectation and triggered more queries and complaints' (authors' research). And as Buckland suggests, it would appear that the Charter has '. . . encouraged consumers to be more critical of services and less accepting' (Buckland 1992: 10). Now, ministers are exercised perceptibly to diffuse patients' concerns and are increasingly sensitive to adverse media coverage which accrues from them. This may partly explain the increase in consumer complaints which CHCs have taken up on patients' behalf (see Figure 8.4). An investigation into three hospitals in the West Midlands, however, found that in two of them only 33% of patients had been made aware of their *Patient's Charter* rights, while in the third hospital, the figure rose to 64%. These findings are probably not untypical (East Birmingham CHC Quality Report No 5 1995). One CHC chief officer also expressed reservation about the Charter:

> The *Patient's Charter* has made people more confident of raising their rights – we've got to respond . . . Despite all the patient's charters in the world, individuals are still vulnerable to the might of the NHS.
>
> (*Authors' research*)

Another factor militating against the Charter's effectiveness in supporting consumers is continual underfunding of the NHS. At a recent meeting of South Birmingham CHC, it was agreed that they '. . . cannot see how providers will maintain and extend standards with decreasing funding' (South Birmingham CHC, Draft Response to B'ham Health Authorities' Draft Purchasing Plan 1996/97). Notwithstanding these problems, the *Patient's Charter* is perhaps the only Charter initiative which has, in specific instances, enhanced consumer power.

8.4.4 Consumer empowerment

The emergence of consumerism and a supporting infrastructure such as CHCs, the *Patient's Charter* and associated NHS reforms suggest an evolving empowerment of the consumer in health matters.

The extent to which recognition of the patient as consumer represents genuine empowerment, however, is problematic.

Ostensibly, the *Patient's Charter* and the purchaser-provider principle offers the individual consumer greater choice and guarantees of quality in health care. In reality, however, both initiatives appear wanting in a number of particulars.

The concept of the patient as consumer entails **choice**: namely, that the individual is free to select between alternative providers of health care. How this principle could work in practice is hard to fathom. Most users of hospital services, for example, are seldom in a position to exercise choice. Instances of this include people with acute illnesses requiring urgent treatment and patients needing specialist medical services where there exists only one such provider in each city. Indeed, patients who do have some choice in hospital treatment (for example, elective surgery for non-life threatening diseases), comprise a small proportion of total patients; a surgeon in one hospital has suggested that this represented about 9% only of all patients there (Devlin 1990). A further difficulty in sustaining the consumerist argument is that the patient, under the provider-purchaser arrangement, is strictly not a consumer of health care services but more accurately an **end-user**: the purchaser (for example, GP fundholder) decides on behalf of his or her patient. In this context, the GP's 'control' over health provision is considerable, especially in relation to decisions regarding the 'financial currency' of different groups of consumers. According to research by The Association of Community Health Councils in England and Wales ACHCEW in 1994, the majority of people removed from the GP's list were mostly 'old and chronically' sick. It seems that the NHS's structure and the types of services it now provides are difficult to reconcile with patient choice and the individual consumer appears to be a marginal factor.

In the context of **collective consumerism**, 'consumer' groups have had limited direct impact on the formation of **national** health policy. There are some notable exceptions: the mental health charities MIND and MENCAP, for example, played a critical part in public discussion and passage of Parliamentary legislation reforming mental health laws in 1981–82 (Alderman 1984: 31). Collective consumerism suffers from a political system which is seemingly pluralistic but in reality is essentially corporatist, with 'producer' groups tending to dominate an exclusive policy community. These groups, which include DHAs and NHS Trusts, are able to impose sanctions against government and are in possession of vital expertise and informa-

tion needed by decision-makers. This assures them of close, continuous and ubiquitous consultative relations with the Department of Health. The relationship between
'producer' groups and health officials is characterized by negotiation, partnership,
reciprocity and mutual dependence in the formation and implementation of health
policy. 'Consumer' groups, by contrast, have little to offer decision-makers and their
interaction with policy officials is correspondingly limited. These representative associations have an 'arm's-length', formal linkage with the Department of Health, relying
more on contacts with Parliament (especially the House of Commons' select committees on health and social services) and mobilizing public opinion through media
coverage to influence policy outcomes. As the chief officer of ACHCEW commented
in an interview, what they can achieve at national policy level is to help set the tone
of the health debate.

In the context of **national** health policy decision-making, then, **collective
consumerism** is largely illusory. But in the localities consumer groups do seem better
able to promote their members' interests and tend to exert some impact on the policy
process. Generally, local health issues are subject to wider debate amongst relevant
representative associations than is the case nationally. At this level, established
consumer groups are valued by local decision-makers because they can help gauge
public reactions to health initiatives and assist in implementing health care
programmes. Indeed, health consumer groups seem relatively active at the local level.
Newton found that health pressure or consumer groups operating in Birmingham in
the 1970s were amongst the most politically active though numerically represented
the smallest number of voluntary associations there (Newton 1976: 38). A cursory
survey of voluntary groups now active in the Birmingham area reveals a dramatic
increase in their number. It is reasonable to infer from this evidence that consumer
groups are now more closely involved in challenging the local health agenda. This
does not imply, however, that voluntary groups in Birmingham or elsewhere are
necessarily representative of the health consumer in general. Indeed, organized interests tend to promote the sectional interests of the already highly articulate and
well-represented middle class consumer (see Chapter 7). Furthermore, several large
and important voluntary organizations have become significant **providers** in the
'market' for care and receive contracts for a variety of care services funded by health
and local authorities. Thus their independence as a 'consumer voice' may be compromised. It follows that patients in other socio-economic categories are likely to be less
well served by, and 'dislocated' from, collective consumerism than better placed
members of society. A further difficulty for the 'underrepresented' is that some of
the recent structural changes to the NHS seem to militate against public involvement
in local health policy making, as a CHC chief officer put it:

> Trusts [are] not required by statute to consult public on proposed changes in
> service . . . The larger unified health authority may not be best placed to deter-
> mine what amounts to a substantial change in service for local users.
>
> *(Authors' survey)*

But to what extent are these 'dislocated' sections of the health community likely
to secure better representation by other means such as consumer surveys?

8.4.5 Consumer surveys

So far, it has been argued that the terms 'individual consumer' and 'collective consumerism' in the reformed NHS are somewhat misleading because in the context of health, consumer choice is largely illusory and consumer groups tend to exercise only limited, indirect influence on policy outcomes. Following the 1990 health reforms, democratic representation suffered a further set-back when local authority elected members were removed from DHAs.

By 1990, however, health authorities and policy makers began drawing on public opinion to gauge the **quality** of service provided and encourage **feedback** from the community. Since then, the Health Authorities Commission, for example, has undertaken annual opinion polls, consumer surveys and organized public meetings on a regular basis. These findings are complemented by the British Attitudes Survey which expresses public views about the NHS. In the localities, DHAs and CHCs frequently carry out consumer surveys. In the early 1990s, for example, East Sussex Health Authority conducted a major market survey entitled 'The Public as Customer' which resulted in changes in services (Wellesley and Tritter 1995: 5).

More recently, public opinion polls have been used by decision-makers to help **prioritize spending** on health. A technique known as QUALY (Quality Adjusted Life Year) has been developed for the purpose (Ham 1992: 253). In this case, an assessment is made of the benefits of medical intervention in terms of saving the number of years of life and the quality of life. The first highly publicized application of the QUALY approach occurred not in the United Kingdom but in the State of Oregon, United States of America. Known as the Oregon 'experiment', decision-makers there used the technique '. . . to define a basic package of care to be provided as part of the funded health programme'. (ibid.: 253) The 'experiment' was, in effect, '. . . the first attempts to develop an explicit system of rationing health care' (Klein 1991). Local residents' values on health care were sought using telephone interviews and, based on the findings, a list of spending priorities were subsequently published in May 1990 amidst considerable controversy (Ham 1992: 253).

In early 1993, results from the largest survey on health care rationing ever undertaken in the United Kingdom were published (Kings Fund College; see also *The Independent* 12 March 1993); part of the findings are shown in Table 8.1. The survey which was organized by the BMA, the BMJ, the King's Fund College and the Patients' Association, used a representative sample of 2012 members of the public, 2000 consultants and GPs and 450 senior hospital managers. The findings reveal some shared views amongst respondents about health care priorities but significant differences, too (see Table 8.1). Perhaps the most significant revelation from the consumers' perspective was that 51% of public believed that the NHS should have unlimited funds but only 17% of doctors and 2% of hospital managers agreed; 97% of managers and 78% of doctors thought that budgets must be set. Moreover, when asked who should decide on priorities, the public's first choice was hospital consultants (61%), and second choice GPs (49%); but only 6% of the public thought that politicians should decide priorities.

Table 8.1 Health Service Priorities (*Source: Kings Fund College*)

Rank	General Public	Doctors	Managers
1	Childhood immunisation	Childhood immunisation	Childhood immunisation
2	Screening for breast cancer	Care offered by GPs	Care offered by GPs
			Education to prevent young smoking
3	Care offered by GPs	Support for carers of elderly Education to prevent young smoking	
4	Intensive care for premature babies		Support for carers of elderly
5	Heart transplants	Hip replacement for elderly	Screening for breast cancer
6	Support for carers of elderly	Treatment for Schizophrenia	Hip replacement for elderly
7	Hip replacement for elderly	Screening for breast cancer	Treatment for Schizophrenia
8	Education to prevent young smoking	Intensive care for premature babies	Intensive care for premature babies
9	Treatment for Schizophrenia	Heart transplants Cancer treatment for smokers	Heart transplants
10	Cancer treatment for smokers		Cancer treatment for smokers

(*Source: Kings Fund College*)

Only 6% of the general public think that politicians should decide health spending priorities

---

Public surveys such as these seem to suggest that consumerism may be a developing influence in health decisions. Indeed, these prioritizing exercises are now undertaken on a regional level in Somerset, for example, where representative consumer panels have been used to prioritize health care there. (Channel 4 'The Pulse' 22 February 1996). Evidently, the Oregon experiment informed decision-makers regarding public preferences in health care provision. But a cursory examination of the background to Oregon's health care programme and the use to which the prioritized list of treatments had been put, reveals that some of the most inarticulate and disempowered groups in the community, i.e. low income women and children, might eventually suffer further discrimination in health provision (McBride 1990). And the United Kingdom's comparable survey in 1993 did much the same for decision-makers here. In reality, exercises of this kind seem to do more to aid policy makers and producer groups than significantly promoting consumer choice. In both the surveys cited, the outcome is likely to be used to **legitimize ministerial decisions** on health matters or advance sectional interests than enhance consumer preferences. Findings from the United Kingdom survey, for example, appear to have been 'exploited' by its commissioning agents, i.e. the BMA and others, to support their demands for more resources from government: the title given the report by the BMA *et al.* is, aptly, *Public Calls for More Money for the NHS* (Press Statement, BMA 11 March 1993).

From the patient's perspective, whatever the shortcomings of consumer surveys, the activity has exposed associated issues to greater publicity, leading to better informed public debate about health priorities and cost implications. Indeed, the establishment of the purchaser-provider principle may have achieved much the same. At one time decisions regarding the distribution of health care were perceived and accepted as a matter of clinical judgement, but now, it seems, that '. . . political and managerial resource rationing priorities will . . . be visible instead of being largely hidden under the cloak of professional practice' (Klein 1991).

8.5   COMMUNITY HEALTH COUNCILS

Community Health Councils (CHCs) are statutory bodies originating in the 1974 reorganization of the NHS. They are now the only body set up at that time to have survived with their role and function largely intact. Their purpose has been reaffirmed recently in Executive Letter (94) 4 January 1994: 'CHCs exist to represent the public interest in the health service in their districts. This is an independent role given to them by Parliament' (National Health Service Management Executive 1994). More specifically, the object of CHCs '. . . is to monitor standards of NHS care from the viewpoint of the consumer, to use this information to inform purchasing plans and to provide advice and information to the public' (East Birmingham CHC Annual Plan 1995/6).

Successive reorganizations of the NHS have, as indicated earlier, changed the management structure of hospitals and community services, introduced internal markets and eliminated the representative role of management boards at regional, district and trust level. These boards now comprise experts in finance and management, bringing expertise from the business and private sector and operating like boards of commercial companies. Paradoxically, as management control of the NHS has become centralized and become more business-like, the CHC's role in providing a measure of **local democracy, accountability to the public** and as a **consumer voice** for the patient has become more important. This has been especially true as concern about the future of the NHS and the level of provision in local areas has become a dominant theme in the media and public debate.

The CHCs' powers are specific and limited. They have a **statutory** right to be consulted on any major changes of service in the NHS (Butler and Vaile 1984: 108). These include closure or opening of hospitals and clinics, relocation of services and rationalization of wards. Since the introduction of the internal market in 1990, CHCs have had a critical role in consultations on DHA purchasing plans. The CHCs have the right to object formally to major changes or 'substantial variations in service', and ensure that these are referred back to the proposing health authority. If this happens and the issue cannot be resolved locally, changes are delayed for some months while the Regional Office considers the issue and ultimately it is determined by the Secretary of State for Health. CHCs have negotiable rights to visit health service premises. These used to be a statutory right but with the setting up of semi-independent NHS trusts, specific rights of access have to be negotiated with each trust management board. In practice, the right to visit has generally been maintained. Finally, and importantly the CHCs have the **duty to advise** NHS consumers and patients about health service matters and **support individuals who have a complaint** or issue that they wish to raise about their treatment or the service they have received from NHS hospitals, community services or general practitioners. With regard to the latter function, CHCs' work is complemented by the efforts of the health ombudsman.

> Through the CHCs, local health issues can be subject to a wider debate amongst relevant representative associations and members of the general public through open meetings. Specifically, CHCs are actively involved in **planning** health care services such as influencing DHAs' purchasing decisions, **consulting** with DHAs and Trusts in matters such as ward closures, **visiting** care centres and hospitals, **pursuing complaints** on behalf of patients and **facilitating public access to information** on health care issues.

CHCs vary tremendously across the country depending on local context, urban, rural or regional politics; on the approach adopted by current members to collaboration or conflict with the local NHS management and on the specific interests represented by members. However, there are some characteristics which are built into their statutory basis which are common and affect the reality of CHC working. Typically a CHC will have a small office with a chief officer and one or two additional professional staff. Larger CHCs have a deputy who will often concentrate on casework with individual complainants. About half of the officer's time will be spent on individual issues which do not directly involve the members because of confidentiality. The office will ideally be accessible to the general public and contain a collection of files, information and reports about the NHS. The formal membership of the council will normally be about 18 local people who are all volunteers. They will have been nominated from three sources: the local authority, the regional office and local voluntary bodies. CHC members come from a variety of backgrounds and they usually have a special interest in health care or some aspect of it, although others will be nominated by a local authority because of other expertise or because of party contacts. Because there is no obligation on employers to release staff for CHC business, members are disproportionately drawn from the retired population (in this respect they do represent many NHS consumers). Membership is limited to two terms of four years although when CHCs are reformed after reorganizations membership can start again. Many CHCs have a small group of stalwart members and a changing population of nominees who do not get involved or who do so for a while and then find it difficult to manage CHC work alongside other activities. CHCs have their regular (usually monthly) meetings in public and set up specialist sub-committees on key areas like mental health or care for the elderly. Increasingly, they will be in contact with local media and during times of major change will hold public meetings to enable a wider discussion of issues. CHCs send observers to DHA meetings and to public and sometimes private meetings of trust boards.

Above, the various statutory activities of CHCs are outlined. But in practice, CHCs spend most time helping patients resolve issues, usually concerned with complaints arising from communication difficulties with clinicians or hospital managers. It seems that these more routine, practical matters are generally of paramount importance to patients. In this regard, CHCs are often highly effective and general improvements may follow from individual complaints. East Birmingham CHC, for example, recently secured significant improvements to the X-ray department at a major Birmingham hospital thereby providing patients with greater dignity. (East Birmingham CHC Annual Report 1995).

8.5.1 Types of CHCs and their priorities

An earlier study by Buckland (1992) found that CHCs could be classified in one of five categories: independent challenger, DHA partner, independent arbiter, patient's friend and consumer advocate. But Buckland's typology is wanting in at least two respects: it pre-dates important reforms which have subsequently impacted on the activities and relationships of CHCs, thus restricting the range of categories into

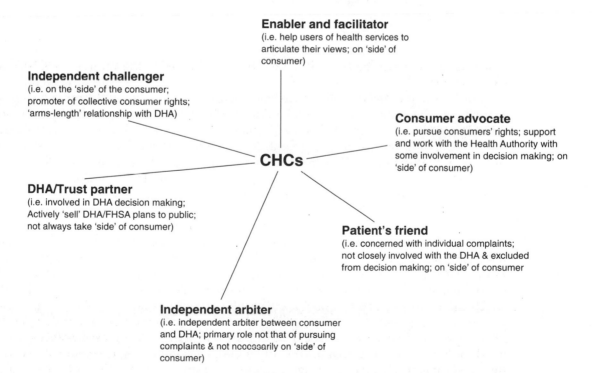

Figure 8.1a Typology of Community Health Councils (*Source: adapted from Buckland 1992*)

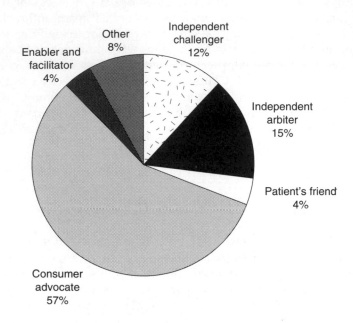

Figure 8.1b   Number of CHCs in each category *(Source: Barnes and Cox)*

which these statutory bodies fall; and it does not quantify the number of CHCs in each category.

In order to accommodate the post-1990 changes to the NHS and profile CHCs in more detail, the authors have modified Buckland's typology which is shown in Figure 8.1a. The authors' recognize that CHCs may assume a number of roles simultaneously depending on the issue to hand; for example: **officer function** may embrace the role of 'Patient's friend' or 'Enabler and facilitator', but where a more direct, less diplomatic strategy is required (for example, to overcome DHA resistance to something), then the role of 'independent challenger' may be appropriate. The author's adaptation of Buckland's typology is designed to categorise each CHC surveyed according to the functions and roles they perform most frequently. The findings, which are based on chief officers' self-assessment, are shown in Figure 8.1b where the number of CHCs in each category is revealed. From this it can be observed that most CHCs (57%) perceive themselves as 'consumer advocates' and virtually all consider that they 'take the 'side' of the consumer'. The results also indicate that all CHCs are to some extent involved with health authorities and the decision process. Research findings expressed in Figures 8.2a + 8.2b reveal something about the **quality** of relationships between CHCs and DHAs, i.e. that they are, in most instances, 'very good' or 'good'. As a panacea to ameliorate the shortcomings in its consumer agenda, the government intends to foster a closer working relationship between CHCs and health authorities. But if CHCs and DHAs appear already to enjoy 'good' working

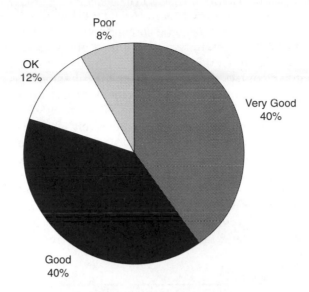

Figure 8.2a CHCs' assessment of the quality of relations with DHAs
(*Source: Barnes and Cox*)

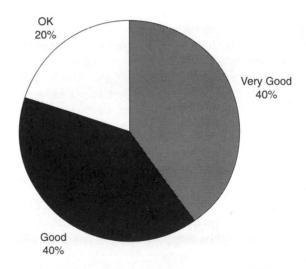

Figure 8.2b CHCs' assessment of the quality of relations with NHS Trusts
(*Source: Barnes and Cox*)

relationships with each other, with CHCs at times becoming almost part of the **policy community** rather than sources of independent consumer power (see Section 8.5, and Figure 8.2a and Figure 8.2b), the Government's strategy for encouraging greater consumerism in health matters may not have the impact intended.

Community Health Councils, it seems, do enjoy an espirit d'corps. Chief officers keep in regular contact through their own professional association which provides them, inter alia, training and development programmes. They also benefit from support given them by ACHCEW. The latter body is principally concerned with assisting CHCs' members who meet collectively at ACHCEW's annual conference. Moreover, ACHCEW encourages CHCs to adhere to common performance standards and a published code of conduct endeavours to achieve the same. In practice, however, these statutory bodies are markedly dissimilar because of multifarious social conditions, variations and unequal distribution of funding between regions, and differing patterns of health needs of the communities they serve. Accordingly, each CHC must, and is permitted to, set its own agenda: it will prioritize its work and formulate objectives and tasks which reflect the perceived health requirements of its constituents.

Local circumstances largely determine the work that each CHC under-takes; **diversity of priorities and behaviour is a striking characteristic of these statutory bodies**. And this is important for patient involvement in health matters for as Blaxter argues '. . . consumer participation implies local diversity' (Blaxter 1995: 18).

Although CHCs are characterized by diversity of activities, the full-time officers' working day is usually dominated by **pursuing complaints** on behalf of patients and **providing information** for them and the public generally on health services. Both these functions are especially critical to the promotion of consumer interests. The number of complaints about NHS services has increased dramatically in recent years (Levitt et al., 1995: 253–7). On this issue, one CHC officer commented:

> It's just increased so much really [assisting with complaints] . . . sometimes it feels quite overwhelming . . . [the] complaints side is really out of proportion to the other side . . . by which I mean the planning and monitoring of services.
> *(Buckland 1992: 10).*

Regarding the latter preoccupation of CHCs, it is self-evident that the better informed is the patient the more genuine will be his or her status as consumer. Public choice, however, is largely determined by what is in effect available (Blaxter 1995).

CHCs expend most of their energy pursuing complaints by patients against providers and providing information

---

8.5.2 Public contact and performance indicators

If CHCs are to articulate effectively the consumers' views on health matters, then public awareness of them and the work they do is vital: patients must be voluntarily induced to make contact with their district CHC. In many respects, CHCs appear to be gaining public recognition. According to the authors' research, the interaction between CHCs and the public had increased dramatically during 1994 – 95: 40% of CHCs reported increases of between 25% to 49%, 32% recorded rises between 50% and 74%, while 16% had experienced increases of 75% and above; see Figure 8.3. But to what is this increase in public contact with CHCs attributable?

From the findings expressed in Figure 8.4, it is evident that 'helping complainants' is considered **the most relevant factor** to which this increase in contact between the public and CHC is attributable. This is closely followed by 'consultations on major changes to NHS', 'changes to NHS' and 'CHC initiatives'. It appears that much of the CHCs' 'success' in this regard accrues from **their own actions**, especially pursuing patients' complaints and initiatives such as advertising, publicity and establishing a patients' information service.

The CHCs' interface with consumers is important because it enables them to gauge the local community's opinions about the health service and from this perform another key role: to **monitor the performance** of purchasers and providers of health services. Many of the specific activities listed in Table 8.2 serve much the same purpose, especially the 'drama workshop' and 'interviews with head teachers'. But CHCs also work with many other participants and facilities to ascertain local views about the quality

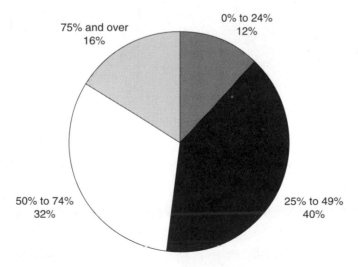

Figure 8.3 CHCs' assessment of increase (%) in public contact since 1994
(Source: Barnes and Cox)

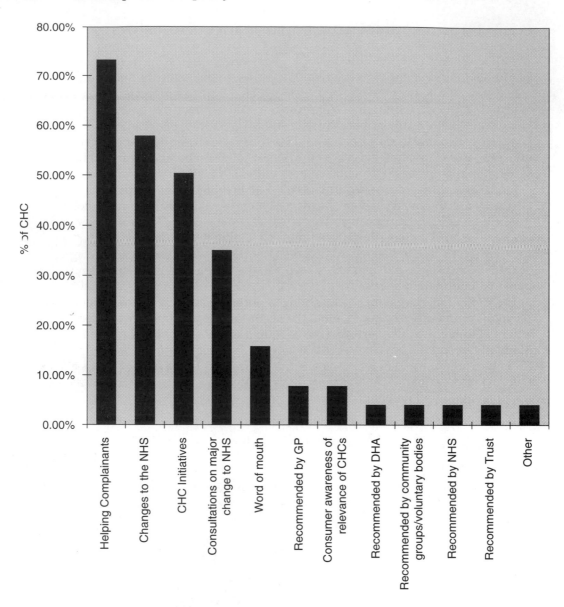

Figure 8.4   Public contact with CHCs during 1994/95: factors giving rise to increase
(*Source: Barnes and Cox*)

Table 8.2 Activities/initiatives most frequently used by CHCs in promoting consumer interest (*Source: Barnes and Cox*)

Activity/initiative	Very frequently	Frequently	Infrequently	Never	Did not answer
Conducting own survey-based research	23.1%	46.2%	23.1%	0.0%	7.7%
Conducting surveys with DHA & provider units	0.0%	46.2%	46.2%	0.0%	7.7%
Working with community groups	15.4%	46.2%	26.9%	0.0%	11.5%
Holding public meetings	23.1%	26.9%	38.5%	0.0%	11.5%
Monitoring service quality	42.3%	50.0%	0.0%	0.0%	7.7%
Working with GPs	7.7%	38.5%	46.2%	0.0%	7.7%
Accompanying consumers to discussions and hearings	46.2%	42.3%	7.7%	0.0%	3.8%
Visiting hospitals, clinics	38.6%	46.2%	7.7%	0.0%	7.7%
Helping complainants	76.9%	19.2%	0.0%	0.0%	3.8%
Working with DHA/ Trusts	46.2%	38.5%	7.7%	0.0%	7.7%
Regular, informal NHS officer contact	53.8%	30.8%	0.0%	3.8%	11.5%
Providing advocacy services	26.9%	30.8%	19.2%	11.5%	11.5%
Providing information services	61.5%	26.9%	3.8%	0.0%	7.7%
Working with media	15.4%	46.2%	23.1%	7.7%	7.7%
Other activities	3.8%	3.8%	0.0%	0.0%	92.3%

of health care. These are specified in Table 8.3. The findings here show that 'conducting surveys' and 'dealing with complaints' constitute the **two most helpful** methods by which CHCs acquire consumer feedback on local health services; 92.3% and 96.2% respectively. It is striking that some of the most commonly used means for ascertaining consumer views gain a score on the 'unhelpful to some extent' category: community groups, public meetings, and CHC members' views. Part of the explanation for this may be that, first, these participants may have their own, personal or sectional agenda and, second, that there exists an inverse correlation between the 'negativeness' of the issue discussed at a public meeting and level of turnout. That CHCs find consultations with RHAs 'unhelpful' in gauging local opinion (57.7%) is not surprising: the remoteness of this tier of the policy/management process makes it generally ill-equipped to empathize with consumers; RHAs, which currently fund CHCs, are to be abolished in April 1996, when they will be replaced by Regional Offices of the NHS Executive.

In general, CHCs are able to use consumer feedback to help monitor health care provision. At a meeting of South Birmingham CHC, the record of minutes taken confirm that a member of the public's expressed concern had received due attention:

Table 8.3 Activities CHCs found most/least helpful in gauging local opinion about health services (*Source: Barnes and Cox*)

Activity	Extremely Helpful	Helpful	Unhelpful to some extent	Extremely Unhelpful	Did not answer
Meeting Community Groups	46.2%	38.5%	11.5%	0.0%	3.8%
Visiting hospitals, clinics & community services	34.6%	50.0%	11.5%	0.0%	3.8%
Consulting with national groups	3.8%	53.8%	23.1%	3.8%	15.4%
Attending public meetings	15.4%	50.0%	23.1%	3.8%	7.7%
Taking account of CHC members' views	38.5%	46.2%	7.7%	0.0%	7.7%
Conducting surveys	73.1%	19.2%	0.0%	0.0%	7.7%
Dealing with consumer complaints	57.7%	38.5%	0.0%	0.0%	3.8%
Consulting with DHA	11.5%	50.0%	26.9%	0.0%	11.5%
Consulting with RHA	3.8%	30.8%	38.5%	19.2%	7.7%
Consulting with Trusts	23.1%	34.6%	30.8%	0.0%	11.5%
Talking with NHS managers	19.2%	50.0%	19.2%	0.0%	11.5%
Meeting GP's	11.5%	73.1%	7.7%	0.0%	7.7%
Monitoring media coverage	3.8%	65.4%	23.1%	0.0%	7.7%
Other activities	11.5%	3.8%	0.0%	0.0%	84.6%

Mr . . . notes that the Acute Unit was not conforming to Patient's Charter standards due to its failure to display information upon the number of complaints received and the response time to such enquiries. He sought support from the CHC that they would raise this as a matter of concern. The Chair assured him that this would be raised with the Acute Unit

(South Birmingham CHC minutes of meeting 15 March 1995)

8.5.3 Promoting patients' interests: mechanisms and actions

The authors' research found that CHCs used a plethora of mechanisms and actions to achieve their objectives. The findings also show that some approaches were employed more frequently than others. In Table 8.2 the results from this enquiry are expressed. It can be observed that 'helping complainants' is an activity which is 'very frequently' used by CHCs followed by, in descending order: 'accompanying consumers to discussions/hearings', 'conducting own survey-based research' and 'providing information services'.

- Initiated project into acute hospital services for 16–65 age group which involved visits to wards and interviews with staff in three hospitals
- Conducted drama work shops to ascertain young peoples' views about health services
- Observed maternity and children's ward at one hospital
- Interviewed head teachers to gauge their views about health services provided for their schools
- Inspected chemists in district
- Investigated access for NHS services for patients with special needs
- Studied day case surgery and after care in the community
- Surveyed GPs for their views on the discharge arrangements for their patients
- Investigated acute mental health services by visiting new units.

(Source: East Birmingham CHC)

Figure 8.5 A CHC's project programme during 1994/95

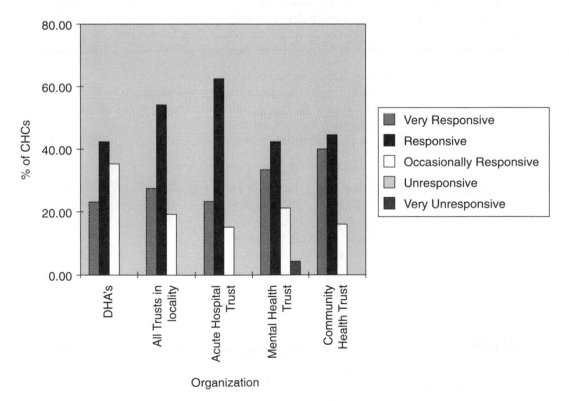

Figure 8.6 CHCs' suggestions for improving health care services: responsiveness of purchasers and providers (excluding GPs) *(Source: Barnes and Cox)*

In order to gain insights into aspects of these activities in more detail, a CHC's programme for years 1994 and 1995 were examined. Figure 8.5 lists **key projects** the organization set itself during that time; these illustrate the nature of 'conducting own survey-based research' and 'providing information services':

How useful are these mechanisms/activities to CHCs in their endeavour to promote consumer interests? To what extent, if at all, are providers and purchasers likely to accommodate CHC demands? The authors' research revealed a varying pattern of responsiveness to CHC in this regard. The findings in Figure 8.6 show that key providers of health care, i.e. hospital trusts, were considered to be generally 'very responsive'/'responsive', and in few instances, 'occasionally responsive'. The mental health trusts alone were judged by some CHCs to be 'unresponsive', but even then by only 4.2% of them. In the case of DHAs, however, the responsiveness rate suggests that in many instances, CHCs do not always find them as accommodating: 34.6% of CHCs surveyed considered that DHAs were only 'occasionally responsive'.

8.5.4 CHCs and politics

Earlier, it was shown that on the whole CHCs enjoy 'good' working relationships with DHAs. Sometimes there are, however, manifest tensions between them. In the West Midlands region, for example, there were concerns on the part of CHCs that DHAs had not always consulted them on major changes to services. In consequence, four CHCs in the area moved to clarify the position:

> ... the four Birmingham CHCs were seeking a joint definition of 'substantial variation in service ... [It] would be put to the Joint Committee of Birmingham and Solihull CHC's with a view to this definition being accepted by April 1996 when the new Birmingham Health Commission was launched ... [Mr ...] expressed the hope that this definition could be used by the existing DHA'

> *(South Birmingham CHC minutes of meeting 19 July 1995)*

Sometimes the tensions between CHCs and DHAs are overtly political and potentially more damaging to the parties concerned. An illustration of this occurred when one CHC had allegedly become a 'radical political forum' in a series of disputes with its DHA and RHA. A close study of the minutes of the CHC's meetings exposes growing alarm on the part of members at the time towards funding cuts. At a meeting on 15 February 1995, members '... expressed concern that monies under the Waiting List Initiative were being spent in the private sector and at facilities that were not in the region'. And a meeting on 21 June 1995 reported that the region had '... seen an 18% reduction in bed numbers (as against 14% nationally) and a cut of 8% in Acute beds (6%) nationally. It was agreed to raise these issues of patient care with the DHA and RHA'. It appears, however, that the members' expressed intention of seeking consultation and discussion with local health authorities to resolve the issue was subsequently abandoned in favour of a direct media campaign:

> (The chair) ... said the CHC faced a choice as to whether members wished to have an active and clear public image, conveying the Council's views ... to the

public and media. Whilst a balance must be struck, where policies and discussions made at local or national level affected the service provided ... then the Council should respond and should make its concerns known ...

... the research element of the Council's work ... was important in influencing its contacts with media.

(The Chair) saw the issue as a question of democracy , and believed that progress was achieved through open and frank discussion, and not through obfuscation.

(The chair proposed) ... a training day using a professional involved in the media ... a written report on media contacts be prepared for each CHC meeting.

These tactics, it seems, evoked disquiet amongst some of the CHC's members, as the following extract from the minutes of a meeting on 15 November 1995 attests:

... the question was about the style in which the CHC carried out its work ... He (CHC member) found it difficult to work within the model currently adopted by the CHC, which was based upon a confrontational stance ...

... It was proper for the CHC both to take up individual cases and to examine and challenge the policies which lay behind these. The CHC should not be deterred from stating its views on policies and on matters of concern ...

Mrs ... was concerned that the CHC should not be diverted, as a result of taking up individual issues and media pressure, from pursuing its agreed priorities ...

Mrs ... said it was necessary to strike a balance between deferential and a confrontational approach.

Evidently, the 'balance' between **deference** and **confrontation** had not materialized subsequently: 'Three senior members of a ... community health council have quit amidst allegations that it has wrongly become involved in political battles', reported a local newspaper. Two of the resigning members were respectively chairman and chief executive of MIND and Age Concern while the third was a former regional director of public health. In an interview with a newspaper reporter, the latter is quoted as saying that 'There is a particular political emphasis which was not very mainstream ... For the voluntary sector a political stance is not acceptable in any case. The CHC's role should be to represent the needs of patients locally'. To which the other erstwhile members added: 'The current CHC style is ... confrontational . .. It seems to have got involved in national issues to do with the financing of the NHS. It has made it very difficult to raise the sort of issues that concern MIND with the health authority'.

Amidst recriminations and threat of a public inquiry, four experienced members of the CHC resigned. At subsequent meetings, although the resignations were regretted, members seemed to have established a new consensus and balance of views and formal and informal relationships with the DHA continued.

8.5.5 Chief officers' assessment

Although CHCs are characterized by diversity owing to the differing nature and needs of the communities they serve, it has been shown that in many key particulars they are strikingly similar: more than half of those surveyed, it will be recalled, perceived themselves as 'consumer advocate' (see Figure 8.1b above) and most devoted the majority of their working day to pursuing complaints, providing information and monitoring services (see Sections 8.5.1 and 8.5.2 above). Moreover, most CHCs seem to encounter similar frustrations which tend to undermine their capacity to help patients.

The chief officers surveyed were asked to indicate 'which **single issues** or factor has been **most unhelpful** to (their) CHC in promoting consumer interests?'

Some of these concerns expressed by chief officers focused on the adverse impact on their work of recent health reforms:

The internal market.

The NHS Community Care Act of 1990 and the introduction of the internal market.

Resources and finance led attitudes/services.

. . . recent changes in NHS structure, etc. (e.g. market forces, purchaser/provider split, contracting for services).

Other chief officers identified lack of resources as a factor most likely to impede their ability to help consumers:

Changes in service [at local hospital] resulting from national shortage of paediatricians . . .

Financial constraints on developments in health care.

Inadequate funding, particularly with regard to the ever-increasing workload.

Organizational and logistical problems arising from recent health reforms were also cited by chief officers as factors undermining their ability to help patients. Comments on these issues include:

> Introduction by one Trust of car parking charges!!
>
> Acute Trust's desire to relocate all services to one site outside city centre.
>
> Time taken attending 'merged' Region meetings a great distance away.

Other concerns articulated by chief officers surveyed, reflected inadequate involvement of CHCs in the purchaser-provider decision process:

> Professional barriers: 'I'm a doctor, I know best for **my** patients'.
>
> Not having a statutory right with regard to social services and their contractual arrangements
>
> Overlap of roles with HA has meant that they give greater weight to the work they do. They tend to use 'safe' groups who re-inforce their views.
>
> Lack of meaningful consultation and dialogue from the DHA.
>
> Not being invited to . . . Hospital Trust Board meetings.

Only a few chief officers considered that lack of public recognition had impeded their ability to promote patients' interests:

> Local public perception of health care in our own area through national media reporting. Lack of public awareness of the services available and undertaken by CHCs. Work on raising profile of CHC needs to be continuous.
>
> Lack of knowledge by the public of the CHC's existence.

One chief officer considered that the tactics adopted by members were detrimental to consumers:

CHC Chair and members pursuing an overtly political confrontational agenda. Not necessarily in patients' interests.

8.5.6 Limitations of CHCs

CHCs, then, are formally constituted statutory bodies that, inter alia, represent and articulate consumer views. Complemented and supported by activities of local voluntary groups, public consultation exercises undertaken by DHAs and investigations by the health ombudsman, CHCs are the consumers' 'voice' in local health issues. Moreover, CHCs are principal conduits in the exchange of information and opinion between local health policy makers and patients and consumers. But the formal role and responsibilities of these statutory bodies exaggerates their impact on the health agenda generally. A number of factors common to most CHCs tend to undermine their capacity to effectively promote consumer interests.

First, CHCs have, as indicated earlier, experienced a dramatic increase in demand for their services in recent years (see Section 8.5.2). This rise in public contact has not been matched by corresponding increases in human and financial resources; as one CHC chief officer complained, typically, his organization had suffered '. . . inadequate funding, particularly with regard to ever-increasing workload', while another chief officer remarked that the real problem was a '. . . lack of resources to publish a regular newsletter, and not enough staff to do everything we want to' (Authors' research). Evidently, without a realistic allocation of funds, especially for staff training, and a reversal of the hitherto over-dependence on the commitment and goodwill of voluntary members, CHCs will be less able to influence **policy outcomes** in the interest of patients. In consequence, consumers might be further discouraged from participating: '. . . the public has an incentive to be involved only if their choices will actually affect local services' (Blaxter 1995). All too often, consultation between CHCs/DHAs and the public do not translate into visible benefits demanded by patients, especially areas concerned with medical working practices or attitudes (ibid.)

Second, the statutory rights enjoyed by CHCs (see Section 8.5) do not in practice amount to much relative to the formal power of the medical profession (Butler and Vaile 1984: 108–9). The difficulties that CHCs in the West Midlands encountered in establishing their entitlement to be consulted by a DHA on purchasing plans, attests to this. Moreover, '. . . GP Fundholding units are required to produce their own purchasing plans and to consult with other purchasers, but not with patients or with CHCs' (South Birmingham CHC, Response to Draft Purchasing Plan 1996/97). We have also seen how inadequate funding of the NHS generally can generate tension between the health authorities and CHCs (see Section 8.5.4) where the latter is almost powerless to challenge the former's rulings. Moreover, the statutory rights that CHCs do enjoy are demonstrably inadequate at times to overcome professional barriers of clinicians, as one chief officer stated above (see Section 8.5.5).

Third, it is not clear that CHCs are able to accurately elicit and reflect public views on local health needs and outcomes. CHCs do work closely with local voluntary bodies which articulate their members' opinions and concerns on health matters. But it is uncertain if such groups are sufficiently representative of the community at large. Indeed, voluntary bodies increasingly use CHC meetings as forums to promote their own agenda. Moreover, public interest in much of the important but routine work of CHCs is usually minimal. It is often the case that only 'negative' issues, such as the threat of a hospital closure, galvanize sufficient numbers of the public to CHC meetings; too little interest is shown in other matters for truly representative views to emerge.

> Additionally, the rather frenetic nature of CHCs' 'gatherings' seems to militate against ascertaining community views with any accuracy, often relying on anecdotal, individual interaction with members of the public:

Unfortunately we get bogged down in trying to sort the thing out amongst ourselves, in the limited time that people have to discuss the issues, that we don't really consult with the public enough. Again I would say our consultation with the public is very much on the informal level. It might be a member attending a day centre as a volunteer, chatting about what is going on and hearing how people react to this, but it's very much on an informal basis.

(Chief Officer quoted in Buckland 1992: 14)

In this context, a further problem CHCs face in attempting to assess patients' reactions to services, is that the type of surveys frequently used by them are often inappropriate. This is especially true of satisfaction surveys where respondents in inpatient questionnaires, perhaps in gratitude for care received, tend to over-praise the service (Blaxter 1995). Moreover, it is often impracticable to undertake valid surveys in hospitals or when patients have returned home. Considerations such as these threaten the credibility of CHCs' survey work and the findings gleaned from them.

Fourth, it seems that while CHCs have been given formal, statutory powers, in reality they have inadequate resources to effectively challenge the principal purchasers of health services, i.e. the DHAs and GPs. CHCs appear highly effective in pursuing a local agenda where **pursuing patients' complaints** against hospitals, **providing information** and **monitoring services** comprise their *raison d'être*. Essentially, their influence over the health debate is more manifest where they reinforce and underpin the prevailing values and actions of health authorities. But where they mount a direct challenge to DHAs authority, their lack of political 'clout' is palpably evident (see Section 8.5.4 above).

Finally, CHCs' members, though invariably dedicated to the promotion of patients' interests, are too often ill-equipped or lacking in relevant expertise or knowledge to effectively resist or challenge the formidable and highly informed provider-purchaser community, especially senior participants in DHAs and Trusts; their debates can often seem amateurish in the face of medical and managerial authority. Indeed, it has been estimated by one respondent that in about 33% of health districts, local voluntary groups such as Age Concern and MIND are better able to influence the DHAs and Trusts than the CHC. The latter are sometimes perceived by senior clinicians and managers as erratic, parochial and indifferent to the overall strategic implications of their demands. Perhaps this is not surprising: CHCs are, after all, principally committed to arguing the case for their constituents rather than unreservedly supporting DHAs and hospitals; it is shown earlier in Figure 8.1b that most CHCs (57%) considered themselves to be 'consumer advocate'. Clearly, some CHCs are less fundamentalist and adopt more accommodating approaches in consultations with DHAs and Trusts. One Birmingham CHC, for example, will support closure of hospital wards if it thinks the case for doing so is proven. The findings expressed in Figure 8.1b suggests that possibly 15% of CHCs may act in a way similar to this Birmingham CHC in this respect, i.e. consider themselves to be 'independent arbiter' between consumer and DHA where their primary role is not that of pursuing complaints and not necessarily on the 'side' of consumer. If CHCs generally are to enhance their competence and 'vision' to 'match' more closely those of senior staff in DHAs and Trusts, then, as the CHCs' representative association, ACHCEW, has suggested, a systematic programme of formal training and closer scrutiny of the process of selection will be required (Authors' research).

8.6   CONCLUSION

This chapter has argued that NHS reforms and attendant initiatives have not brought meaningful consumer empowerment. The public appear less than convinced that the government's consumer agenda is effectively working for all patients. Indeed, *The Guardian* appears to have accurately captured the citizens' cynicism in this matter:

> Communication between the public and the NHS has come to resemble Monty Python's semaphore version of Wuthering Heights, where Cath and Heathcliff attempt to convey their passion by frantically signalling to each other from separate mountain peaks.
>
> (*The Guardian 1 November 1995*).

It has been shown that the necessary conditions for a genuine consumer culture in health is for the patient to be sufficiently empowered to **exercise choice**, **gain access to relevant information**, and to **take some responsibility** in health matters (see Section 8.4.1, first box). It has been argued that the attainment of these conditions by patients has been patchy and in most instances, negligible. Moreover, the statutory bodies concerned with articulating consumer interests, the CHCs, are inadequately resourced for the purpose and often without sufficient power in their dealings with DHAs. At the national level, CHCs' representative body, ACHCEW has limited impact on health policy; at best, it can merely influence the climate of opinion. Where patients or consumer groups have successfully gained empowerment, it is has usually occurred as a result of a determination on their part rather than charters or structural organizational changes to the health service; for example, the extent to which patients' demands have been met in connection with maternity services is an illustration of this (Channel 4, 'The Pulse' 29 January 1996).

At the time of writing, the NHS is about to undergo further reforms. The planned changes involve the abolition of RHAs (the body currently responsible for funding CHCs) which will be replaced by Regional Offices with CHCs coming under direct control of the Department of Health. It is the Government's intention that these latest structural changes will, inter alia, consolidate patient involvement in local health care discussions and, as the Secretary of State for Health, Stephen Dorrell, recently emphasized, to '. . . ensure that the patient's voice is heard alongside the accountant and clinical expert'. Indeed, a principal objective of NHS decision-makers for 1996/7 is to give consumers 'a greater voice and influence' in health issues generally. An even more explicit declaration of the government's apparent commitment to consumer empowerment and the role of CHCs as principal agents responsible for delivering this commitment, is revealed in the Priorities and Planning Guidance for the NHS: 1996/97'. This is reproduced in Figure 8.7. It will be observed that under these proposals, it will be incumbent on DHAs to actively consult and communicate more effectively with relevant interests, especially CHCs, in order to offer patients 'choice about treatment options'. This shores-up earlier guidelines in March 1992 and January 1994 in which CHCs were given extended consultative status with both providers and purchasers.

There are, of course, a number of practical strategies that the government could pursue to deliver its consumer agenda; for example, by establishing realistically resourced consumer forums of the kind once considered in town planning. But the health minister's eye is focused on CHCs as the vehicle for achieving greater patient

---

Priority D:

D.1	Health Authorities should have a strategic plan for, and should be engaged in, systematic and continuing communication and consultation with local people, representative and voluntary groups (particularly Community Health Councils) in respect of the development of local services, purchasing plans, specific health issues and health promotion as appropriate. Particular attention should have been paid to addressing the concerns of those with special needs.
D.2	Health Authorities and providers should be able to demonstrate how consultation and dialogue with GPs and local people or groups, including those with special needs, has influenced the development, planning and purchasing of services; and feedback to local people on the outcome of consultation.
D.3	Purchasers and providers should be able to demonstrate that they have a systematic programme in place aimed at achieving active partnership with individual patients in their own care, in particular seeking to improve the quantity and quality of information given to enable patient choice about treatment options.
D.4	Purchasers and providers should have complaints systems in place which reflect the revised procedures stemming from the Government's response to the Wilson Complaints review "Acting on Complaints".

(Source: Department of Health 1995/96)

Figure 8.7 Priorities and planning guidance for the NHS: 1996/97

involvement in the issue. In this sense, the Community Health Councils will have, when the 1996 reforms are in place, a secure future as the consumer's champion. But unless the practical shortcomings of the existing arrangement under which CHCs operate are addressed, consumer empowerment in health service provision will be very limited.

8.7   CHAPTER SUMMARY

- The *Patient's Charter*, which was launched in 1992, enhances consumers' status in the delivery of health care services, grants them a number of rights and entitlements and introduces performance standards against which the quality of health service management can be measured.
- Producer groups exercise more influence in the national policy process than consumer groups; the latter have more impact at local level.
- Consumer surveys have been used to gauge public opinion on rationing health services. The consumer benefits from such exercises are, however, problematic: survey findings appear to help health policy makers legitimize their policies rather than create better informed decisions.
- Community Health Councils (CHCs) are the only statutory body responsible for articulating patients' concerns. But they are supported in this endeavour by voluntary groups and consultations exercises undertaken by District Health Authorities and other health agents.
- As currently constituted and resourced, CHCs are ill-equipped to promote consumer interests.
- The 1996 Health Reforms envisage a greater, more formally recognized role for CHCs as the 'official' 'voice' of the consumer.

TEXT-BASED QUESTIONS

1.   In what ways does the internal market affect the delivery of health services?

2.   What do we understand by the terms 'consumer', 'consumerism' and 'empowerment'?

3.   Make clear the distinction between 'individual' and 'collective' consumerism.

4.   What is the *Patient's Charter*?

5.   Assess the value of consumer surveys to
      (a)   NHS decision-makers,
      (b)   politicians
      (c)   patients and citizens.

6.   Describe the role and functions of CHCs.

7.   Examine the claim that CHCs, as currently constituted, are limited in their ability to effectively promote consumer interests.

8.   Outline the main features of the NHS reforms which will come into force in April 1996.

ASSIGNMENT

Critically examine the findings from the survey on rationing in the NHS (Table 8.1). Now answer the following questions:

1. Very briefly, describe, compare and contrast the methodologies of the United Kingdom and Oregon health surveys.

2. What are the salient features of the United Kingdom health survey?

3. To what extent will the survey lead to better informed health decisions? Give reasons for your answer.

FURTHER READING

Levitt, R. (1980) *The People's Voice in the NHS*, King Edward's Hospital Fund for London, London.

Levitt, R., Wall, A. and Appleby, J. (1995) *The Reorganized National Health Service*, Chapman & Hall, London.

Robinson, R. and LeGrand, J.(eds) (1994) *Evaluating the NHS Reforms*, Kings Fund Institute, London.

ACKNOWLEDGEMENTS

The authors wish to thank the following people for their invaluable assistance in the research for this chapter: Ian Martin (research assistant), Sarah Head (Chief Officer East Birmingham CHC), Toby Harris (Director, Association of CHCs in England and Wales) and the many chief officers of CHCs who participated in the survey. All errors and inaccuracies are the authors' responsibility.

The research survey into community health councils (CHCs) on which part of this chapter is based, constitutes Phase One of a national survey which is currently being undertaken by the authors. Findings in Phase One are derived from interviews and survey of nearly 70% of CHCs in two regions.

MANAGEMENT AND ACCOUNTABILITY IN PUBLIC SERVICES: A POLICE CASE STUDY

9

Barry Loveday

9.1   CHAPTER PREVIEW

The police service appears to be the last to have experienced the reforms sweeping through public sector organizations in the 1980s. In the 1990s, with the unions subdued, the crime rate soaring, the government's popularity beginning to wane and its image of the party of law and order fast fading, the police service was to face a full frontal assault on its management and other practices in the name of efficiency, effectiveness and market forces in an attempt to reduce the 'crime rate'.

This chapter examines and evaluates:

- government attempts to introduce changes to the police service in the 1990s and the opposition from and conflict with police bodies;
- the changes which have occurred and their impact on the structure and processes of policing in the UK;
- the role of the private sector in competing with police in crime protection and the tensions which have emerged as a result;
- the extent to which the changes of the 1990s in the police service have affected the concept and practice of accountability in this most sensitive area of public life.

9.2   INTRODUCTION: THE END OF THE HONEYMOON PERIOD

Since the publication of the White Paper on Police Reform (Home Office 1993) and the Sheehy Inquiry into Police Responsibilities and Rewards (Sheehy 1993), the police service has been subject to systematic pressure to introduce efficiency gains by way of introducing social market strategies. The Royal Commission on Criminal Justice \and the later Review of Core and Ancillary Duties (HMSO 1995) recommended a number of reforms and organizational changes.

Yet it was the same police service which had loyally served the Thatcher government during the 1980s, in the course of which it was used to confront and overcome industrial strikes which, had they succeeded, might have brought down her government. The miners' strike of 1984–85, was only the biggest challenge to the government in a decade which Hugo Young suggested could best be symbolized by the image of the raised truncheon (1989: 368). What had changed so much that the government of John Major felt able to withdraw support from the police service and subject it to the market reforms imposed on other public services?

Howard Davis, a former controller of the Audit Commission, provides a some what cynical explanation when he states that:

> until the end of the miners' strike in 1985 there was perhaps a sound political reason for leaving the police undisturbed ... the industrial relations confrontations of the early 1980s placed a high premium on the maintenance of unquestionably loyal, disciplined and strike free police. Subsequently the logic of non-intervention became less clear

> (1992: 28)

There is no doubt that as Home Secretary, both Kenneth Clarke and initially Michael Howard, were entirely persuaded by the 'illogicality' of non-intervention in the police service. The Sheehy enquiry was indeed to rock the police service to its foundation. The service suddenly learned that it would cease to be treated preferentially.

The change in government attitude came as a surprise to many in the police service. Thus the recent history of government and the police is one in which apparent perfect harmony was to end in acrimonious divorce. The threat of the collective resignation by Chief Constables should the Sheehy proposals have been implemented in their entirety in 1993, proved to be a prelude to the breakdown of that relationship. As the government opinion poll ratings plummeted, Mr Howard's attempt to patch up the quarrel appeared not to have erased from the service the memory of the government's earlier rejection.

9.3   THE SHEEHY INQUIRY 1993

In what appeared to be a calculated decision to de-stabilize the police service, Kenneth Clarke, soon after becoming Home Secretary, established a review team to consider the pay and responsibilities of the police. This was to be led by a dynamic international businessman, Patrick Sheehy. The Sheehy Inquiry team included the personnel director of the NHS, Mr Eric Caines who, with Kenneth Clarke, had been earlier responsible for introducing the marketized health reforms into the Department of Health and NHS. No police officers were co-opted on to the Inquiry, which was given a wide ranging remit to make radical recommendations to improve the performance of the police service.

In June 1993, the Sheehy Report was presented to the Home Secretary. The report recommended a complete break with existing management and pay structures and represented the most substantial blueprint for reform of the police service since its creation in 1829. The report recommended, inter alia, the elimination of three supervisory ranks (Chief Inspector, Chief Superintendent and Deputy Chief Constable). All police officers would be required to sign new contracts of employment for an initial period of ten years, renewable thereafter on a five yearly basis. Contract renewal would be decided by senior officers on the basis of officer performance over the preceding contract period. Sheehy also recommended the abolition of index linked annual pay awards. In its place, it recommended that pay should be decided according to skills and experience, measured on a 12 point matrix. Automatic pay increases would be ended. No increase would be given to officers whose performance was considered unsatisfactory. The report also recommended the abolition of overtime and the end of all allowances including that of housing. Of the 272 recommendations made in the Sheehy Report, the most significant related to the introduction of compulsory severance on structural grounds. The report recommended that the power to terminate an officer's appointment during the currency of a contract should be introduced. Opportunities should also be made available for management to adjust by structural severance, the age profile of the force and manpower levels. The proposals would have ended any concept of the police job being 'a job for life'. Local wage bargaining was also to be implemented at a later stage.

The Sheehy Report reflected a common approach to all public services and argued that the police service should not be seen as a 'race apart'. For example, pay would be awarded on the basis of performance. One member of the inquiry, Mr Eric Caines, argued that there was a 'tendency on occasions to claim special status for police officers, when this was not justified' and suggested that a major value of the report was that it made it unambiguously clear that there could be no pay increases for unsatisfactory performance in the police service and, ultimately, no job for poor performance (*The Guardian*, 2 July 1993).

9.3.1 Reaction of the police service to Sheehy

The reaction of the Police Associations to the report was swift and well organized. In July 1993 the Police Federation organized a mass rally at Wembley to demonstrate their opposition. More significantly, the Report generated opposition across police ranks and police associations. There was a public declaration by Chief Constables to consider collective resignation if the report was implemented. In an unusual twist for a public service, Chief Officers publicly refused to accept the bribe of huge pay increases offered by way of performance related pay, to persuade them to accept the inquiry's proposals.

> Their refusal contrasted strongly with the alacrity with which many managers in other public services accepted performance pay increases to implement government policy.

Police opposition and the departure to the Treasury of Kenneth Clarke undermined the Sheehy Report. Michael Howard proved less committed to the Sheehy programme than his predecessor and quickly rejected a number of its major proposals. Contracts for all police officers were abandoned as was the introduction of local wage bargaining. The use of a matrix of indicators to judge individual police performance was also rejected by the Home Secretary. Mr Eric Caines, publicly lamented the government's abandonment of the decision to radically overhaul the police, arguing that the Home Secretary was too easily intimidated (*The Guardian* 2 July 1993).

9.4   CORE AND ANCILLARY DUTIES

The government's perception of the police service demonstrated considerable naïveté in the relationship between the police and crime control. High crime rates were, effectively, the fault of the police service, which did not direct sufficient attention to 'crime fighting' – its primary role. It believed that a performance culture linked to financial reward could direct the police towards crime fighting activities, which would necessarily reduce the crime rate. To encourage it to do so, a further inquiry was established to review police core and ancillary duties. Adopting a social market approach to the police service and encouraged by the Audit Commission, the government requested the review to identify core duties and those which were secondary to policing. The objective was to eliminate any duties which could be carried out by alternative providers, thus directing police activity more towards 'crime fighting'. Any support within the police service for such a clear delineation of their role began to fade when it was discovered that significant reductions in police duties would lead to a corresponding reduction in police establishment. It also became clear that the government expected the private sector to assume many of those duties cast off by the police. Although denying it the Home Secretary, at a British Security Industry Association meeting in 1993, was reported to have stated that the private security industry could expect to benefit from police reforms. For the government, further privatization in the police and criminal justice field was to be encouraged by both the 'Core and Ancillary Review' and successive legislation, particularly the Criminal Justice and Public Order Act (1994).

For a variety of reasons, the impact of the final Core and Ancillary Task Review was minimal. From a mountain of activity there came a mouse. The Review recommended the removal of a limited number of duties to other providers. These included the policing of 'wide loads' on motorways and a number of similar and uncontested duties. The severe limitations of the Review may have been explained by the capture of the Review process in its final stage by the Association of Chief Police Officers (ACPO). Following a decision to establish an ACPO Advisory Panel to the Review, it became clear that any radical departure from a very limited set of proposals would be unlikely. In the event most duties will continue to remain a monopoly of the public police while police establishment will in fact be increased.

9.5 REFORM OF THE POLICE 1993–1994

9.5.1 White Paper on police reform (1993)

The Sheehy Inquiry was not the only reform programme pursued by the Major government. Arguably of much greater significance was the publication of the White Paper on Police Reform (Police Report White Paper 1993 HMSO). This threatened overtly to centralize control of the police and provide a platform for further radical change in the provision of police services at a later date. As in its other prescriptions for the police, the government defended its reform programme by reference to the apparent inefficiency of the service. Overwhelmingly, the government's aim was to direct police activity towards 'crime fighting'. This was to be encouraged by a mixture of new contract arrangements (via Sheehy) and the creation of quango-like police authorities, whose management ethos would encourage the police service to 'fight crime' with greater efficiency and to more effect. Basing plans for police authorities on something similar to hospital trusts, the central element of reform was to be the substitution of nomination for election in determination of membership of new police authorities. These were planned to be much more powerful police authorities than their predecessor bodies. As the Home Secretary argued at the time, the kinds of powers he proposed to give police authorities were of such an order that they 'could not be trusted with an elected body' (House of Commons Debate March 1993).

The nature of the reform proposed by the Government threatened to undermine the tripartite structure established between Chief Constable, Home Secretary and Police Authority under the 1964 Police Act. In the White Paper, and later Police and Magistrates' Courts' Bill (PMCB), the Home Secretary was to be given powers to appoint half the membership of 'reformed police authorities' (including the chairperson), while ending the right to hold local enquiries before the amalgamation of police forces. The new police authorities, effectively extensions of the Home Office, would be reduced from 43 to 22 in the first instance as the number of police forces was cut by amalgamations. It was also expected that the retention of elected members on the reformed police authorities would only be for a limited period, reflecting the ongoing commitment of the Conservative government to reduce substantially local government responsibility for services by the creation of quangos or by privatization (Jenkins 1995). Despite a sharp response to the White Paper on police reform and evidence of substantial opposition, the PMCB faithfully reflected the government's original plans in the White Paper. It appeared that another public service was about to succumb to the government's social market reforming zeal.

9.5.2 Police and Magistrates' Courts Act

As a consequence of government misjudgement, luck and the departure of Kenneth Clarke from the Home Office to the Treasury, the police service was not, in the event, to experience the full rigours of reforms planned for it. The government's decision to initiate the Police Bill in the House of Lords proved to be a serious misjudgement. It became apparent early on that many peers across the party divide would not accept the PMCB as originally conceived. No fewer than four former Home Secretaries, as peers of the realm, rejected outright a clause giving the Home Secretary direct power to select all chairpersons and other nominees to the new police authorities. Lord Whitelaw, a former Home Secretary in the Thatcher government, refuted the case for the political centralization of control of the police which such nomination powers represented. In a series of amendments, their lordships substituted indirect nomination, a requirement for a simple majority of elected members to remain on police authorities, the selection of chairpersons by the police authority not the Home Secretary and a requirement that for purposes of the precept, more than half the number of members setting it were to be elected. Elsewhere the government's proposal to abolish the rank of Chief Inspector was also rejected.

In what might be described as a desperate attempt to evade electoral accountability and placate the peers, the government proposed that lord lieutenants would, instead, identify nominees to the police authorities. It quickly became apparent that neither their lordships nor the lord lieutenants, were overly enamoured with this curious proposal. Instead an elongated, complex and arcane selection system was to be devised which satisfied no one but which allowed only indirect influence to the Home Secretary. In an influential alliance between ACPO and local authority associations, the more extreme centralizing clauses were amended. Because the first reading of the PMC Bill and subsequent committee stages occurred in the House of Lords, it also became apparent that the amendments were not expected to be challenged in the House of Commons and in the event they were not.

The Police and Magistrates' Courts' Act (PMCA 1994), although lacking the degree of radical change originally planned by government to the tripartite arrangement, will certainly alter it. Under the Act, the police authority has become a corporate body with its own funds independent of local government. Police grant now goes directly to the police force and is no longer subject to public virement by the local authority. The average membership of the local police authority (LPA) has fallen from around 35 to 17. Of these nine are elected members, five are independent nominees and three are magistrates. In a limited number of LPAs the size of the authority is greater so as to accommodate a larger number of local districts (Greater Manchester; Devon and Cornwall). In place of direct ministerial nominations, local panels (consisting of an LPA member and a Home Office nominee, who together choose a third of panel members) are responsible for drawing up a short list of possible nominations to independent places on the LPA. The short list is then forwarded to the Home Secretary who is then required to select no more than ten names from the original list of nominees. The 'shortened short list' is then returned to the local panel which becomes responsible for selecting the final five independent members. As was argued in the House of Lords, this cumbersome procedure is not designed to last. It did however, demonstrate the difficulty the government experienced in negotiating amendments proposed by opponents of the original PMC Bill.

9.5.3 Independent members

In his ACPO local authority association speech at Birmingham in 1993, Michael Howard argued that LPAs needed to be made more representative of the local community and needed to include 'teachers, farmers and shopkeepers' if they were to be seen as being properly representative. This claim was almost immediately rebutted by a local authority survey of LPA membership in 1994 which demonstrated that all three occupations were already well represented on existing LPAs. Following the passage of the PMCA, the joint LPA and Home Office panels were required to identify suitable nominees. In a survey conducted in 1994, the backgrounds of the independent members were established over a representative number of LPAs (University of Portsmouth Survey 1994). Contrary to the self-expressed objectives of Michael Howard, shopkeepers, teachers and farmers did not loom large in the overall selection of independent members. Although some independents did come from education or agriculture, overwhelmingly those selected were drawn from the private sector as either professional salaried employees or self-employed (County News 1995a). Moreover, those who survived 'Home Office weeding' of initial nomination lists tended to be white middle class males (County News 1995b). Evidence suggested that females and those from ethnic minorities appeared to have been rejected by the Home Office (County News 1995a). In Warwickshire, it was discovered that the list of nominees had been scrutinized by government 'business managers'. A complaint from the county's Chief Constable concerning the removal of nominees by the Home Office from the original list was to be ignored by the Home Secretary. The selection process led, in most cases, to the appointment of businessmen, many of whom would have had little previous connection or contact with the police. Yet the near oracle status accorded businessmen by the present government, along with its stated commitment to creating more 'business like' police authorities, meant that probably they would inevitably loom large in the final selection process.

It is at this juncture difficult to assess the likely impact of independent members on the work of the LPA. It has been argued by some Chief Officers that a noticeable change has already occurred in the work of the LPA. This is now considered to be more focused and inquisitorial and less overtly politically partisan. Elsewhere, Chief Officers have not, however, noticed any significant difference in the conduct of police authority business or the level of debate. What is clear is that the independent members can be expected to assume a more influential role in the work of the LPA as time progresses. Independent members may well assume chairs, as elected members cannot always be expected to vote on bloc for an elected member to chair the LPA. Long-term, therefore, clerks to LPAs expect the independents to assume a greater salience in the work of the authorities (County News 1995c). This could make the link between the LPA and the local authority more tenuous than already exists as a consequence of the PMCA. However, the requirement of the majority of elected members to vote for precepting could be the source of contention if the nominated members (independents and magistrates) pursue policies which are unacceptable to elected members.

9.5.4 Responsibilities under the tripartite structure

The reformed LPAs have been given a range of new responsibilities although they lose responsibility for the provision of many services (building maintenance, vehicles, etc.) and are no longer ultimately responsible for hiring or firing civilian staff. They retain, however, a final responsibility for development of the local policing plan (LPP). Even here the immediate responsibility for developing the plan falls to Chief Constables. They retain responsibility for setting precepts (PMCA Section 28b) and have the duty to secure the maintenance of an **efficient** and **effective** police force for their areas (PMCA Section 4(1)). Under the PMCA an LPA will be able to set local objectives and performance targets which will be linked to the objectives with the final draft of the LPP its responsibility.

The local plan is intended to reflect local opinion and priorities determined by consultation arrangements established under Section 106 of the Police and Criminal Evidence Act 1984. The plan will also identify LPA priorities, the financial resources expected to be available and the allocation of resources to achieve the objectives set. Additionally the LPA will be required to:

- provide an annual report detailing the extent to which local plans for the year have been implemented and forwarding a copy to the Home Secretary;
- negotiate new fixed term appointments of four to ten years for officers of ACPO rank;
- set performance related pay for Chief Officers.

The PMCA, as well as changing the grant system to police forces, has increased responsibilities of Chief Constables. Under the Act the Chief Constable will:

- continue to be responsible for the direction and control of the force;
- have responsibility for preparing the draft of the LPP to be submitted to the LPA for consummation and approval;
- be responsible for civilian staff who will now be under that officer's control (including appointment and dismissal);
- act as disciplinary authority for both police officers and civilian staff.

In addition, under the new grant system based on a standard spending assessment, detailed central controls over spending have been relaxed. In future it will not require the initial agreement of the Home Office to increase police establishment. This will be entirely the responsibility of the police authority and its Chief Constable who may determine spending priorities within the constraints of the standard assessment set centrally.

The Home Secretary gains the most in terms of additional responsibilities. He has the power to:

- determine and set annual objectives for all police authorities;
- set performance targets (related to national objectives) for police authorities;
- give direction to police authorities following any adverse reports from Her Majesty's Inspectors of Constabulary (HMIC);
- issue a wide code of practice relating to duties and functions of police authorities;

- direct that a police authority's budget should not be less than the amount he has specified.

The above powers represent significant increases in the ability of the Home Secretary to influence local planning activities and priorities of the LPA. HMIC's powers have also increased to the extent that they are given the responsibility to report on the LPAs planning processes (Colpa 1995).

9.6   THE TRIPARTITE STRUCTURE AND LOCAL ACCOUNTABILITY

9.6.1 Local accountability

The reforms in the tripartite structure were originally predicated upon the ability of the Home Secretary to select the chairman of the LPA. The new powers given to LPAs, for example, would have been wielded by the Home Secretary although ostensibly the responsibility of the police authority. The government's surrender to pressures in the House of Lords has meant that planned centralization of policing has proved to less extensive than was originally intended. Now, however, it remains unclear who will determine local policing priorities. Central to this question will be the status and specificity of the national objectives set by the Home Secretary along with the performance measures identified by him as 'targets'. The wider and more general the national objectives are, then the more flexibility will be given to local police authorities and Chief Officers. Tight and specific national objectives can be expected to impact across 'local' policing and may be expected to inform all local objectives. Setting specific targets for nationally set objectives could also be expected to influence police prioritization. If, thereafter, police efficiency is identified by means of targets achieved and also by way of comparative data on police forces, then it is likely that national objectives will become the major objectives of police forces. This may be the case if only because Chief Officers and LPAs will recognize that over 80% of police finance now comes from the centre.

Yet Chief Officers are themselves not agreed on the necessity of developing 'costed' police plans. Nor is there an overwhelming commitment to national target setting (Loveday 1996). At a local level the areas of responsibility shared between Chief Officer and LPA remain confused. Is the LPA the budget holder or is it the Chief Officer? If the Chief Officer is the budget holder, then the purchaser/provider split, a division which has been required in other public services, cannot pertain in local policing arrangements. If the LPA does not control the budget, it cannot purchase anything at all. The PMCA may give strategic financial responsibility to the LPA but everyday responsibility for the budget appears to fall to the Chief Constable alone. The ability of the LPA to employ staff to service its activities, also appears to be constrained. As the Act makes clear, before the LPA can employ anyone, prior agreement from the Chief Constable will be needed and/or in the absence of agreement, 'may be determined by the Secretary of State' (PMCA Section 10/3). The ability of the LPA to provide itself with a secretariat to evaluate the local policing plan and other performance data, is of some significance. For the LPA to exercise any independent judgement, it should not be entirely dependent on information from the chief constable and the police force.

9.6.2 The local policing plan (LPP)

The LPP might be seen as the crucial fulcrum of local accountability being a shared responsibility between the Chief Officer and police authority. In the first instance, the LPP will be drafted by the Chief Officer who then submits it to the LPA for its consideration. Consultation will thereafter take place on the plan which will presumably reflect local opinion from Section 106 Police Consultative Groups, along with the views of police authority members. This process could generate possible conflict. Although the LPA is responsible for the final content of the plan, the Chief Officer is not bound rigidly to it. In developing the plan, the Audit Commission has already identified a consultation process for Chief Officers and the LPA (Audit Commission 1994a) and argues for a shared understanding between LPA and Chief Officer and the need to establish a 'joint approach' to the LPP. Realistically, it recognizes that on occasions there may be difficulty in achieving a joint agreement and 'protocols' may need to be identified when differences between the Chief Officer and LPA arise in relation to the plan. It may be the case that changes to the draft plan proposed by the LPA are seen to impinge on the operational autonomy of the Chief Officer, who might refuse to accept them. Here a real difficulty arises since, as the Act makes clear, the policing plan is ultimately the responsibility of the LPA (PAMC Section 4b(1)). Home Office Circular 27/94 'Policing Plans', states that it is open to the Chief Officer to depart from the plan, if for operational reasons he believes it necessary to do so. But as the Audit Commission argues, there could be conflict and confusion on 'the ground' about the ownership of the plan and:

> the issue is not one of mere semantics. Where there has been effective public consultation and agreement reached on the plan, accountability to the community will be more visible. Where there is no such agreement, accountability will be more opaque than at present
>
> *(Audit Commission Paper 1994a: para 86)*

One consequence of this possible impasse could be the need to establish protocols 'to ensure that departures from the plan are joint rather than unilateral decisions'. Three possible outcomes may arise from the planning process therefore. The LPA may accept the draft plan and issue it as its own. Alternatively the Chief Officer may agree to a revised version of the plan. Finally, no agreement may be reached on the plan, between the LPA and Chief Officer. This could prove to be problematic if only because there is, as the Audit Commission notes, 'no statutory mechanism for resolving such differences' (*Audit Commission 1994a: para 85*). The requirements of the LPP are outlined in Figure 9.1.

The responsibilities which fall to the Chief Officer are substantial. That officer will be required to provide a costed policing plan indicating what resources are available. Thereafter it is expected that the Chief Officer will develop a more sophisticated system of costings to show the distribution of resources by output (Home Office

1. Draft plan prepared by chief constable for police authority to consider.
2. Draft plan includes a statement on the financial resources expected to be available and the proposed allocation of those resources.
3. The Plan specifies the Authority's priorities and objectives for the year having consulted the local community on what the objectives should be.
4. The Plan would include the Home Secretary's policy of policing objectives.
5. The Plan will give details of any performance targets set by the Authority.

(Source: Audit Commission 1994, Paper 13, Checks and Balances, HMSO)

Figure 9.1 LPP requirements

Circular 27/94). If in the past police budgeting has been largely confined to inputs, then the new planning process will increasingly identify 'outputs' achieved by the police force as primary measures of efficiency and effectiveness.

9.7 MANAGERIAL ACCOUNTABILITY AND THE POLICE SERVICE

The local policing plan (LPP) symbolizes the commitment of the government to improved efficiency in public services by the application of a new public management ethos and managerial accountability. In requiring police forces to identify costed policing plans, Chief Officers and LPAs will be required to conduct activity analysis to determine how resources are distributed between what are classified as the police forces' main functions. The long-term aim of the Home Office is to ensure that the local policing plan links resources to outcomes and also identifies the cost of policing by output. To encourage this, the Home Office believes that local policing plans should tell the public what policing services and standards they can expect. The

Table 9.1 HOW LIKELY IS IT . . . ?

	Very or fairly likely	Not very or at all likely
That if your house was broken into the police would catch the thief	22	74
. . . you would get your possessions back	8	88
That if your car was stolen the police would catch the thief	22	76
. . . you would get your car back	56	42
That if your car was vandalized the police would catch the vandals	9	89
That if you were mugged the police would catch the mugger	26	69
. . . you would get your possessions back	11	86

Source: Daily Telegraph 1993

process will also encourage performance monitoring by the Chief Officer, police authority and Home Office. In this context, setting targets for objectives determined either centrally or locally becomes a major responsibility for both the LPA and Home Office. This is because performance measurement and comparative data generated by such information, will enable the public to make some judgement about the relative efficiency and effectiveness of their local service. Ultimately, therefore, the Audit Commission will be responsible for an annual publication of a performance league of police force performance data, using a range of performance indicators identified by the police authority and Home Office. An annual report from HMIC will also seek to identify performance levels of police forces.

The Audit Commission itself has developed a range of performance indicators for measuring police efficiency. There will, therefore, be a veritable avalanche of information relating to a wide variety of performance indicators which will extend from police response times through arrest rates and detections to 'percentages of victims of crime satisfied with police performance'. In the 1995 HMIC report on West Yorkshire, no less than 60 performance indicators were to be logged and these ranged from station enquiries 'percentage satisfied' through to percentage of 999 calls answered 'in target' time (HMIC 1994). The limitations of performance indicators have however also been identified by HMIC when:

> he stressed that performance indicators do not on their own give a full picture of performance. They show what differences exist between forces but they do not explain why these differences arise'

> (HMIC 1995a: para 31)

The Audit Commission itself recognized the difficulty in measuring the variety of police activities. Perhaps the most central, that of police patrol, appears to be least susceptible to effective measurement. As the Audit Commission noted, in terms of improving police information on costings and outcomes 'a lot of work remains to be done especially in important but intangible areas such as public reassurance' (1994: para 102). The issue of what constitutes useful performance indicators has also been most recently addressed by Bayley (1995). He concludes that indirect indicators such as response times, arrest rates, clearance rates, speed in answering telephone calls, numbers of neighbourhood watch etc. are of only limited value. More useful indicators will be the identification of direct performance indicators for purposes of evaluating overall police effectiveness and would include inter alia crime rates, criminal victimizations, real estate values, commercial activity, public utilization of common space, and the number of community problems solved.

In developing performance indicators, the problem may be compounded by the inability of the police to influence factors which are extraneous to them and over which they have no control. Crime rates may be influenced by a variety of factors which may have more to do with social and economic issues than with the crime fighting ability of the police. Moreover, public perceptions about what the police can achieve, particularly in the area of opportunistic crime may be entirely accurate. As a recent opinion survey demonstrated (see Table 9.1), the public may make a precise judgement about the limits of police effectiveness in relation to property and/or personal crime.

Additional problems in relation to police performance may be generated by reference to managerial accountability. In relation to 'outcomes' this may be particularly problematic. While the police act as significant gate keepers to the criminal justice system, they no longer exercise great influence over the outcomes of cases which enter the system. Since, for example, the Prosecution of Offences Act 1985, the Crown Prosecution Service decides whether there will be a prosecution and if so what charge will be laid. Nor do the police have the ability to influence significantly the kind of sentences handed down by the courts since this will be a decision for the courts.

Recognition that while the police may determine who enters the criminal justice system, they do not influence eventual outcomes, needs to be stressed when the overall effectiveness of the police in terms of crime control is under consideration.

9.8   POLICE AND CRIME CONTROL

If, under the PMCA, the government expects the police to direct more of its attention towards crime fighting, the general ability of the police to significantly influence levels of crime must be assessed. Here the government has some difficulties in explaining the causes of crime. Successive Conservative Home Secretaries have exhibited a remarkable inconsistency in terms of explanations for criminal behaviour. In the 1980s the Thatcher government argued that the individual was alone responsible for criminality; the criminal made a conscious choice to offend. By the later 1980s the argument had changed significantly, with the explanation for criminal activity appearing to be inextricably linked to the concept of the 'a welfare dependent' underclass. This highly deterministic explanation of crime has continued to gain ground within both the government and the media, although now for the Home Secretary it competes with bad parenting, bad teachers and probation officers as an additional cause of crime (BBC Radio 4 Analysis, March 1995).

These wholly self-contradictory explanations for crime presented by the government are open to challenge. Other than by way of the 'underclass' concept social, economic and environmental factors do appear as possible explanations of crime among Conservative government spokespersons. Yet a range of data suggests that environmental factors could be highly influential. Simon Field has argued that changes in the business cycle may well influence the types of offence committed (1990: 10). Recently Wells has suggested that property crime appears to be closely linked to the state of the labour market (1995: 4). The argument presented by Wells follows on from that of Dickinson who detected a close correlation between the incidence of unemployment among males aged between 16 and 25 years and conviction rates for burglary. Dickinson found that burglary convictions and conviction rates for men under 25 years of age closely followed the economic cycle, with the offence rate declining during years of recovery. Conviction rates correlated with unemployment among this group, although the conviction rate was increasing over time for a given unemployment rate.

The peak offending age for males in England and Wales is now 18 years, with over 80% of known offenders of that age. It is therefore interesting to note that between 1991 and 1994 the percentage of young males aged between 16 and 19 registered as unemployed rose by 5.5% to a total of 21% in 1994 (Social Trends 1995: para 4.26). Of equal interest, data indicates the existence of marked differences between ethnic groups in terms of long-term and total unemployment rates. In 1994 whites had the lowest rates for both long-term and total unemployment. The long-term unemployment rate is highest for those from black ethnic groups (Social Trends 1995: para 4.28).

For those who do offend and who are prosecuted and thereafter given a custodial sentence, the final outcome may not be particularly encouraging either. Of those who are received into prison service establishments, the highest number will be aged between 17 and 20, standing at 45 per 10,000 population (Social Trends 1995: para 9.25). Of those offenders aged under 21 who are placed into immediate custody, 71% will have been reconvicted within two years of completing their sentence. Additionally, of those aged under 21 who are placed on either probation or community service, between 63% and 65% will have been reconvicted within two years. The reconviction rate only begins to fall substantially thereafter, which reflects the age of successive cohorts (Social Trends 1995: para 9.16).

This data questions the ability of the police to significantly influence the crime rate. Moreover the re-offence rate of those with previous convictions suggests that the criminal justice system itself may be inadequate as a deterrent while also failing to rehabilitate. Once again, these may be viewed as outcomes over which the police have little control. It is, however, the current Home Secretary's conviction that prison works and performance targets set for the police will inevitably impact on the arrest rate if not the crime rate. Interestingly, given the targets set for police forces, the recorded crime rate in 1995 began to fall by around 5% for the first time in 16 years, a fact to which the government has drawn attention at every opportunity.

Michael Howard's continued commitment to incarceration as a deterrent will be reflected in future criminal justice legislation. In a new sentencing package, identified in 1995, he intends to introduce the American concept of 'three strikes and you are out'. After three convictions repeat burglars or drug dealers will face an automatic prison sentence if they are over 18 years of age. Serious violent offenders, rapists and attempted murderers who are convicted a second time will receive mandatory life sentences. Parole or early release from prison will be subject to reform. Automatic early release from prison will end. This has been contested by senior members of the judiciary. This programme, along with the introduction of American style 'boot camps' for young offenders, appears to constitute the present government's solution to the crime problem.

9.9　POLICE ORGANIZATIONAL CHANGE

The 1990s have proved to be significant to the organizational structure of the police service. In 1995 it was finally agreed by Home Office and ACPO that a national operational detective force should be established. The new national force is expected to be based upon the existing National Criminal Intelligence Service (NICS) and will also incorporate the existing six regional crime squads. These will have a national co-ordinating centre in London. The new police unit dubbed Britain's 'BFI' is expected to be given greater powers to carry out operations and mobile surveillance. All NICS officers may also be given arrest powers which will provide the operational arm to the new service. As yet, it is unclear whether NICS and its successor body will be removed from the Home Office and given the status of a separate and new police force with its own Chief Officer and a national police authority (*The Independent* 5 October 1995). One matter of great concern to Chief Officers has been the future role of the security service in relation to the new police unit. The end of the Cold War has meant that the security service (MI5) may have lost an empire (Soviet) but has yet to find a role. Under the aggressive leadership of Stella Rimington the largely unaccountable and secretive MI5 will be primarily responsible for all 'Irish' terrorism, not the Metropolitan Special Branch. Under terms apparently agreed with ACPO, MI5 officers will in future also work within the planned national detective agency. In evidence to the Home Affairs Committee (HAC), a police spokesperson argued that only a national force could be expected to successfully counter 'organized crime'. It will therefore be a matter of interest to discover the extent to which the planned national force will be infiltrated by 'security officers' and how they and the police force are to be made accountable for what they do (*The Independent* 5 October 1995). It would appear, however, that Chief Officers are adamant that anyone involved in criminal justice should be accountable. This could therefore have some unusual implications for 'security service' personnel who may act operationally within the proposed national police unit.

Further evidence of the loss of empires by big spending bureaucratic departments occasioned by the end of the Cold War came with the bid by the Ministry of Defence to move into 'crime fighting'. The apparent end of the Northern Ireland conflict and the end of the Cold War have presented a major threat to the continued existence of large defence forces. For the MOD, finding a new role, has taken the form of discovering the potential threat from 'heavily armed international drug cartels' where the use of defence forces maybe appropriate. In a speech to experts concerning 'security in the year 2010', the Defence Secretary Michael Portillo argued that drug trafficking and international organized crime would be seen as a greater threat to national security even than they were at the present time.

This involvement of the security and defence departments may yet represent a direct challenge to the police service and to the accountability of those agencies. How successful, therefore, ACPO proves to be in protecting police interests and police supremacy will be of some considerable interest to both observers and practitioners.

9.10 PRIVATE SECURITY AND THE MARKET PARADIGM

9.10.1 The private security industry

Private security has been the fastest growing industry in Britain in the 1980s and 1990s. The British Security Industry Association (BSIA) estimates that a total of about 126,000 personnel are employed in the industry but a Policy Studies Institute (PSI) Report suggests that there are about 5520 companies with a figure of around 300,000 employed if all categories of security were included. Indeed, the PSI report anticipates further expansion because, in a increasingly voluntary surveillance society, the private sector is able to provide a 'range of protective' functions extending from shopping malls to street patrols. In what might be the biggest challenge to the public police services, private security companies have been employed by local residents, often in high crime areas, to provide protective patrols, which apparently the public police have been unable to offer.

> The surrender of what remains the primary function of the police, which is visible uniformed patrol, to private security companies represents the most direct challenge to contemporary policing in Britain.

This surrender may partly be explained by the increased demands and work load on the police force. It is also partly due to the government's commitment to deregulation and to market forces.

ACPO has voiced its fears at aspects of the expansion of the industry and has attempted to stop further expansion of patrols employed by local authorities more especially when such patrols make use of uniforms and vehicles which closely resemble those of the public police. Yet the absence of public police officers on regular patrol has generated a demand which, it appears, only private or local authority patrols can now meet. It is, however, the case that private security companies rather than local authorities, at least in England and Wales, are overwhelmingly providing patrol officers as an alternative to the public police service.

In 1992, the Adam Smith Institute argued that private sector patrols should be provided in high crime council estates (Adam Smith Institute 1993). More recently, a report for the Institute of Economic Affairs (IEA) reiterated the value of 'consumer sovereignty' in the purchase of protective patrol services. These private sector protective services could, the Report argued, be provided on Council estates and paid for directly by residents, thus guaranteeing not only better quality service but also providing an effective check on cost (Pyle 1995). Remarkably in 1994, the Home Secretary (Michael Howard) argued for rolling back the state and encouraging voluntaristic collectivism where individuals assumed greater responsibility for public security in the streets (Disraeli lecture 1994). Such statements serve to emphasize the continuing commitment to private sector provision and market solutions to which the Home Secretary (and the government) remains committed.

9.10.2   To regulate or not to regulate

Objection to the expansion of private security comes not only from the police and it is not based merely on an objection to competition. Evidence to The Home Affairs Committee of the House of Commons (HAC) and that Committee itself have together voiced a number of concerns. They include:

- The fear that some organizations are little more than protection rackets in which many of the employees have extensive previous convictions.
- The low pay endemic in the industry. In the West Midlands for example, the Low Pay Unit found that pay for security officers stood between £1.79 and £4.35 per hour. A consequence of this is high staff turnover, low quality recruits and excessive working hours to make up pay. Rates of pay were low enough to encourage contract staff to 'sign on' for unemployment benefit at the same time (HAC 1995: para 38/39).
- The use of so many personnel in surveillance programmes raised civil liberties issues.
- The lack of accountability mechanisms for companies operating in a variety of locations.

To each of these concerns could be added others.

Police pressure and criticisms from HAC are seen as a challenge to the government. A clear argument for a regulatory structure for the private security industry was being presented. In its 1995 Report, HAC concluded that the standards provided by the industry fell far below what the public were entitled to expect and what the public interest demanded. HAC argued for the creation of a specific agency to vet individual applicants and to be given access to national criminal records. It recommended that the private security industry should be exempted from the Rehabilitation of Offenders Act 1974 where 'spent convictions' do not have to be identified for purposes of employment. It has also argued for the introduction of a licensing system to regulate in particular the manned guarding sector. The vetting agency could also act as the licensing authority. This would have an immediate responsibility to license both companies and individuals in the manned guarding sector. The vetting agency should:

- act as the licensing authority;
- be made accountable to Parliament via the Home Secretary;
- have clear links with the police;
- be independent of the private security industry (a characteristic which the HAC claimed was not achieved by BSIA)

It is yet to be seen whether the combined pressures of the ACPO and HAC Report will force the government's hand in terms of regulating this industry. Yet the overwhelming pressure within the government is to encourage further deregulation rather than tightening government control over services. This was discovered by HAC itself in evidence given to it by the Home Affairs Minister, David Mclean. BSIA had tried to raise standards by voluntary regulation. Yet the Home Office does not have a policy of only using BSIA companies. As the Minister stated, to the surprise of the Committee, he would not 'freeze out' competent companies merely because they did not belong to the BSIA. The position adopted by the Home Office made the policing of voluntary regulation virtually impossible.

9.10.3 Market failure?

The evidence accumulated by ACPO and HAC suggested that the government's commitment to unregulated expansion of private security provision had actually provided an interesting example of market failure. Private customers and security industry services appeared to encourage the abuse of state welfare payments to ensure low prices. Self regulation had failed comprehensively. Meanwhile, the quality of security personnel employed in the industry continued to fall. 'Market forces by themselves were not proving effective in the large and growing manned guarding section of the industry'(HAC 1995: para.40).

If there was a message here, it appeared to be that reliance on the market could be ultimately self-defeating as the state would necessarily be required to regulate it.

THE COMMUNITY	
Local council police forces	40%
Private security patrols	23%
Citizens' patrols	19%
	(Source: Mail on Sunday 1994)

Figure 9.2   Who will stop the crime wave?

In a revealing summary of public preferences, a national newspaper sought to identify types of protection which might be offered in addition to that of the police. Only a small minority appeared to favour private security patrols and even fewer were happy with the Home Secretary's own preference for citizen patrols (Figure 9.2).

9.11 POLICE EFFECTIVENESS

Successive opinion surveys demonstrate that the public wants to see more police officers on the beat. Responding to this demand remains the most critical current issue for public policing. So far, the variety of measures introduced – amalgamating police forces to create bigger police units, a solution identified in the 1960s and early 1970s – do not appear to have met with any great success (Loveday 1990). A recent 'leaked' Audit Commission Preliminary Report entitled 'Enhancing Police Patrol' has provided some additional evidence of the need for further internal police reform (*The Guardian* 24 October 1995). The Report questioned police claims that they gave priority to putting officers on the beat. It argued that while police forces stated that 55% of their strength was 'the frontline public face of the police', in practice, only 5% of police strength was out on patrol at any one time. In a police force with an average number of 2,500 officers, only 125 could be expected to be committed to be on street patrol at any time. In addition, many of those involved in beat patrols were inexperienced, badly briefed and ill-trained. More significantly, it was to conclude that working the beat was close to the bottom rung in the 'police status ladder'. This conclusion may have been reinforced by 'satisfaction survey' of police work conducted among police officers (see Figure 9.3). This suggested that the very function demanded most frequently by the public generated the least satisfaction amongst those required to provide it. Indeed, the degree of negative dissatisfaction clearly differentiated this duty from all others required of the police.

> The evidence appears to be that, as the Operational Policing Review found earlier, while police officers are attracted to 'action orientated' crime fighting duties, the public gain greatest reassurance through the presence of uniform patrol (Operational Policing Review 1990).

The case for more police officers appeared to have been conceded when the Prime Minister announced to the Conservative Party Conference of 1995 that 5000 additional police officers would be provided by 1999, (a pledge which was confirmed by the 1995 November budget of that year). This sudden commitment to massive spending on police establishment appeared to contradict all that had been propounded by the government concerning police inefficiencies and the lack of value for money, only a short time before. An explanation for the collapse in government interest in improved efficiency may be found in the argument that:

> For the first time in living memory, the polls showed Labour was regarded by the electorate as the party with the best policies on crime ... It was all too much for the Conservatives in and out of Parliament and now with the Prime Minister's pledge on the police numbers, the Conservatives hope that they have shot Mr Blair's fox even if they suspect it belonged to them in the first place
>
> (*Police* 1995)

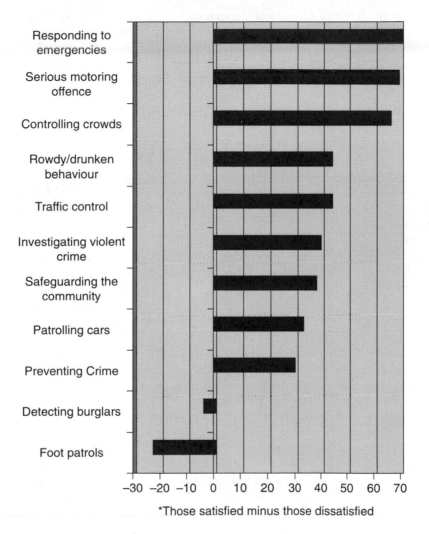

SATISFACTION
Net satisfaction with police work*, by type, by per cent

*Those satisfied minus those dissatisfied

Figure 9.3   Net satisfaction with police work

9.12   CONCLUSION

For a variety of reasons, the overt centralization of police planned by the Major government, by way of ministerial determination of chairpersons and independent members of LPAs, was not to be implemented. Additionally, some of the more extreme tenets of neo-Taylorian management theory identified in the Sheehy Report were also to be rejected. A combination of parliamentary opposition eliminated the more contentious centralizing clauses of the PMCA while the threat of resignation by a number of Chief Officers sank most of the Sheehy proposals. One consequence of this has been that the LPA and its relationship with the Chief Officer remain unclear. It will be a matter of discovery as to whether the new LPAs prove able to act in a more business like way and whether responsibility for the policing plan will be, for the LPA, anything more than formal and symbolic. The ability of the LPA to act as an effective purchaser of service could ultimately be dependent on its ability to establish a secretariat independent of the police which is able to analyse and evaluate police proposals while offering independent advice to the LPA on policing policy.

In one crucial area, the claims made for the PMCA are already being challenged. In the vital area of police community consultation the evidence suggests that there is much that still needs to be done, even if local authority elites have exercised some influence. Police Consultative Groups, (PCGs) statutorily established under Section 106, PACE (1984), have failed by every measure to effectively represent or engage community views on policing (Savage 1984; Morgan 1986; Stratta 1990). Largely dependent on the presence of numerous police officers for their continued survival, the PCGs are characterized by a membership which is biased towards white, middle-aged and middle-class males (Stratta 1990). People from these backgrounds are only rarely likely to come into contact with police.

Evidence suggests that PCG meetings provide very largely, an educative role where police representatives explain to PCG members the limitations of police activity. (ibid.). Moreover, anything less than positive support for the police from PCG members appears to generate a degree of hostility among other members (ibid.). Yet it was the value of police community consultation mechanisms which provided (at least in part) a rationale for the government's reform of police authorities. The reduction in elected members on the LPAs was defended by reference to local police community consultation. The significance of consultation to the arrangements established by the PMCA cannot be over-emphasized. The consultation process is designed to inform the identification of local objectives within the local policing plan and policing activity which the police authority has a statutory responsibility to monitor. In 1993 a Home Office official applauded the apparent success of existing police consultation arrangements and argued that they demonstrated a clear need to translate community interests into police priorities (West Midlands Police Headquarters Lloyd House Conference 1993).

Yet on the ground, the reality has been one of almost universal failure as consultative arrangements have utterly failed to engage the community or public interest. In a number of police authority areas public attendance at PCG meetings has often been noticeable by its absence. Described as the equivalent of 'walking wounded' the PCG arrangements appeared destined to limp on into oblivion. Yet it was precisely this structure which was used to justify the elimination from LPAs of so many of their elected members. The inadequacy of current consultation arrangements has been already identified by HMIC. As one HMI report was to comment:

> the current consultative arrangements are considered to be in need of review. HMI welcomed the proposals put forward by some of the groups to be more dynamic in approach ... however while the PCGs are providing a useful form for communication as they currently operate, they do not alone provide a sufficiently rigorous demanding or representative mechanism for adequate local consultation.
>
> (*HMIC Report 1995: para 7.3*)

It will be, therefore, a matter of interest to discover whether the current failure of statutory arrangements for police consultation groups can be rectified. Some police authorities are already exploring new initiatives. In Northamptonshire, the Chair of the police authority has encouraged the introduction of Community Safety Committees at district authority level. These could, as an elected bodies, provide the authority and legitimacy which are denied to entirely nominated bodies. Moreover, because these committees are an extension of the local district authority, they will provide an opportunity to effect real change in policy. If the police consultative groups are, as has been argued, 'toothless and invisible' then community safety committees provide an attractive alternative:

> Now the demands of local people for better police lighting, security doors on council flats, more visible police patrols can have a real focus and some practicable end results can be seen'.
>
> (*Dr M. Dickie, County News 1995b*)

The development of such safety committees may also serve to re-establish links between police authorities and local government. These links have, of course, been made tenuous by the PMCA which established police authorities as corporate bodies independent of the County Council. Yet evidence suggests that effective 'crime fighting' will necessarily involve the local authority in developing comprehensive crime prevention strategies (Morgan 1991). While crime prevention continues to enjoy a low status in the police service, it is clear that situational and social crime prevention measures may long-term prove more significant than police powers or police numbers in influencing the crime rate. Providing a voice for the people and a channel through which to influence policy may also be a more effective means of 'fighting crime' than either the recruitment of businessmen to LPAs or the identification of national policing objectives and performance targets. It may, however, prove difficult for a government committed to managerial and contractual accountability to accept that performance measures will not provide an effective substitute for public accountability through the ballot box.

Responsibility for re-establishing a more democratic foundation for policing in England and Wales is therefore likely to fall to a government which is committed to **including** rather than **excluding** the people from such processes.

It will be a future responsibility of government to re-emphasize the local nature of policing and reverse the centralization of the police service which has proved to be the final memorial of Thatcherism in this, as in many other, public services (Jenkins 1995).

9.13 CHAPTER SUMMARY

It has been argued in this chapter that:

- The police service escaped the reform of the 1980s because its support was needed for the implementation of some of the government's major policies involving public order.
- By the 1990s, with industrial peace making the police truncheon less necessary and with the apparent failure of the police to curb a burgeoning crime rate, the government turned its attention to reforming the police.
- The radical nature of some of the reforms proposed was lessened on implementation as the police service with allies, for example the House of Lords, lobbied to good effect.
- Nonetheless, reforms were made to the service which impacted on its processes and which increased the centralizing aspects of the service and gave more powers to the Home Secretary.
- The major problem for the government in relation to the police service appears to be a flaw in its thinking when it over-emphasized police powers in crime fighting as the most effective means of reducing the crime rate.
- To be effective in reducing crime, the economic, social and other factors will have to be considered, as well as the structure and process of the criminal justice system; factors over which the police service has little or no control.
- The police service, in the 1990s, faced competition from the fast growing unregulated private security industry and local authority security patrols. Regulation of the industry is made more difficult by the government's commitment to deregulation and the concept of private security fitting with its cherished 'market forces'.
- The police service also faces competition from another source – the attempt to involve the security forces and defence forces in police work as the cold war disappears and Northern Ireland settles into a period of relative calm.
- It is in the field of police accountability that the greatest concerns are raised. Many of the changes in the 1990s – more powers to Chief Constables and to the Home Secretary, the reduction in numbers and membership of police authorities, the added emphasis on business people as members of the police authorities – have reduced the influence of elected members. The traditional tripartite concept and system has been dealt a severe blow.
- Worryingly, consultative arrangements between police and the community have failed, yet much of the justification for the reforms was predicated on the success of such consultation.
- The provision of community inputs into the policy processes of policing may be a more effective way of reducing crime than many of the measures introduced.

TEXT-BASED QUESTIONS

1. Evaluate the extent to which the government has been able to impose its preferred policies on the police service.

2. To what extent can it be said that the changes to the police service in the 1990s have resulted in a national police force?

3. Discuss methods by which the police service could be rendered more accountable.

4. To what extent is the concept of the market appropriate to the police service?

5. 'The wholly self- contradictory explanations for crime presented by the government are open to challenge'. Discuss this statement by setting out

   (a) the government's stated reason for the causes of crime;
   (b) the factors that you consider are important in causing criminal behaviour.

6. How much importance should we attach to the development of the local police plan. To what extent will this serve to enhance the accountability of the local police force

---

ASSIGNMENT

In groups of four or five decide on a list of 15 performance indicators you think would be appropriate for your local police force taking into consideration:

a) any criticisms of your force's performance in previous years;
b) the objectives of improved effectiveness and efficiency;
c) the importance of producing a quality service;
d) any joint actions you would attempt to undertake;
e) explanation of how you would attempt to ensure that such measures involve accountability to the public;
f) the difficulties you envisage in achieving these measures.

(It may be helpful to go back to Chapter 4 to refresh your memory on some of the arguments and concepts.)

FURTHER READING

Jones, T and Newburn, T. (1995) How Big is the Private Security Industry. *Policing and Society*, **5** (3) pp. 233–48.

Loveday, B.(1994) 'Police Reform' in Strategic Government. *ACC Policy Journal*, **2** (1), pp. 7–23.

Loveday, B.(1995)Contemporary Challenges to Police Management. *Policing and Society*, **5**, pp. 281–302.

Marshall and Loveday, B. (1994) 'The Police' in *The Changing Constitution*, (eds J. Jewell and D. Oliver) OUP, Buckingham.

MANAGEMENT BY THE UNELECTED STATE: THE RISE OF QUANGOCRACY

10

Chris Painter

10.1 CHAPTER PREVIEW

Epitomizing many processes and conflicts accompanying the development of 'new public management', the growth of the unelected state brings into sharp focus a number of themes already discussed in this book, notably:

- accountability;
- the threat to traditional public administration values such as equity and probity;
- managerialism;
- fragmentation of local services;
- dominance of private sector ideas;
- managing of change by public sector bodies such as local authorities.

In this chapter it will be argued that:

- the growth of non-elected agencies is not a new phenomenon, their proliferation a source of concern even prior to 1979;
- their development in the 1980s and 1990s has taken on a new dimension in posing an increasing threat to local government;
- the relationship between non-elected bodies and local authorities has therefore become absolutely crucial for the effective delivery of local services;
- such relationships nonetheless vary considerably and are conditioned by a number of factors;

- if the local authority is to build effective working relationships with non-elected agencies, where they can influence the policy and operations of these bodies, it must take a strategic view of such relationships.

10.2   QUANGOCRACY PRIOR TO 1979

10.2.1   Non-departmental public bodies

The growth of the unelected or 'quango' state is not just a recent phenomenon. In the 1970s one academic noted:

> The keenest of observers might have detected the earliest beginnings of the term in the course of some Anglo-American discussions which began in 1969. Now, like the frogs of Egypt, quangos suddenly seem to be everywhere.
>
> *(Hood 1979)*

Thus, an adequate understanding of the central government apparatus could not be gained simply through the study of Whitehall departments, given the existence of an intricate maze of non-departmental public bodies (NDPBs) – boards, committees and tribunals. Stanyer and Smith consequently drew attention to the advisory, quasi-judicial and supplementary executive bodies arranged around individual ministries 'as clients, satellites, or allies' (1976: 53). The labels used to describe such agencies also multiplied at a bewildering pace, including special purpose bodies, *ad hoc* appointed authorities and arm's length government, as well as the fashionable term of QUANGOs (quasi-autonomous non – or national – governmental organizations). More recent rivals in the acronym stakes are EGOs (extra-governmental organizations) and NEPSOs (non-elected public service organizations)!

The growing complexity of the government machine meant that increasingly there were 'communities' of multiple agencies in any given policy field, making co-ordination of the overall system extremely difficult. Indeed, Doig noted instances of 'contrary decisions by different bodies in relation to the same government policy . . .' (1979: 326). However, the formal organizational autonomy associated with NDPBs has to be balanced with a recognition of the significance of the informal networks that can operate through the patronage and appointments system.

Moreover, accurately estimating the size of the 'quango population' is problematic to say the least, especially given disagreement on precisely what to include or exclude and the tendency therefore to use 'different sets of qualifying conditions' (Johnson 1979: 380). Numbers are likely to be swollen if advisory and quasi-judical (tribunal) agencies are included as well as those of an executive type. Conversely, many of the 'new wave' quangos (Gay 1994) – in the form of local non-elected agencies – are excluded from the official Whitehall count of NDPBs. The fundamental problem is that the quango label is 'essentially an umbrella beneath which a tremendous variety of organizations shelter' (Greenwood and Wilson 1989: 209). Put another way, we are dealing with 'a zoo which contains many different types of animals' (Hood 1979).

10.2.2 An anti-quango spasm

Nonetheless, in the light of current developments, it is easily forgotten how during the course of the 1970s – under a Labour government – quangos had become a political 'hot potato'. This 'anti-quango spasm' (Barker 1982: 23) was not simply attributable to the emergence of a strong anti-state streak within the Conservative Party. It was also a reaction against the growth of unaccountable institutional power and the piecemeal nature of the increase in quangocracy, justified as it was on a case-by-case basis and without any general rationale – Johnson referred to 'pragmatism run wild' (1979: 384). Hence the many different reasons for the growth of these non-elected agencies.

One set of explanations stress the managerial flexibility afforded, including the scope to adapt the organization to the requirements and demands of the task in hand. Such motives were to strike a chord as the 'new managerialism' gained momentum during the 1980s and 1990s. But these agencies have also been convenient organizational forms for reasons of political expediency. Ministers were able to distance themselves from contentious issues by disposing of a 'poisoned chalice', or alternatively co-opt support through using the patronage associated with the appointments system. Moreover, they can provide a means of by-passing democratically elected but potentially recalcitrant local authorities – something else that began to take on increasing significance as the Thatcher era proceeded.

This anti-quango spasm contrasted with the very different climate prevailing in the late 1960s and early 1970s, when the preferred policy seemed to be that of 'hiving off' responsibilities from Whitehall departments. Why therefore the growing unease with quangocracy? First, it was felt that ministerial appointments were reaching alarming proportions, regarded in some quarters as a development reminiscent of the eighteenth-century patronage state. There were opportunities to abuse this power for crude party political advantage, especially as the selection procedures were often arbitrary and secretive – with demands consequently made for a public service commission to standardize and open up the process of appointment. To disarm the critics, a public appointments unit was established within Whitehall, compiling a central list of suitable names on a more systematic basis, though there was no obligation on individual departments to draw upon this list when making appointments to agencies falling under their wing.

A related objection was that the growth of agencies operating at arm's length undermined the control of elected representatives and political accountability, marking a retreat from nineteenth century democratic principles. Moreover, the temptation for ministers to resort to unacknowledged intervention and informal pressure, to compensate for their limited formal powers, simply confused the lines of responsibility (the agencies disclaiming responsibility in such circumstances and with ministers sheltering behind the facade of formal impotence). Certainly, the charge that NDPBs were more faceless even than civil service departments tended to stick because of their ambiguous constitutional position. However, the appropriateness of taking the nineteenth century democratic model as a yardstick might be questioned, given the contention that it is naïve in the 'extended state' to propose indiscriminately substituting the elective for the appointive principle (Wright 1995).

10.3   EARLY THATCHERISM AND QUANGOCRACY

Given the pronounced 'anti-quango' climate of opinion that had emerged by the end of the 1970s, NDPBs were potentially prime targets for a Thatcherite government intent on cutting back the public sector. When it instituted a special review the scene seemed set for a 'quango cull'. The Pliatsky Report on *Non-Departmental Public Bodies* (1980) urged caution in establishing agencies of this kind, given the difficulty of striking the right balance between managerial autonomy and political control (a problem indeed that helped to create the conditions for the privatization of public enterprises).

Nonetheless, actual cuts were less draconian than many had envisaged. Far from being major surgery they amounted to no more than cosmetic changes or token sacrifices: 'In spite of pre-election rhetoric, the major features of the landscape of non-departmental bodies in practice remained untouched after the Conservative government's first year in office ...' (Hood and Wright 1981: 119–20). How do we explain what to 'quango hawks' must have seemed a bitterly disappointing outcome?

With regard to patronage, that which in Opposition appears as unacceptable abuse can in office become a golden opportunity, especially for a Government wanting to preside over a political and cultural revolution – something that became the hall-mark of Thatcherism. This institutional form also was increasingly in tune with the managerial ethos permeating the public sector – especially as the emphasis progressively shifted from traditional notions of citizenship to the customer model prevalent in the private sector. Additionally, local government was itself potentially a brake on the forward march of the Thatcher revolution. Revealingly, though the official count of NDPBs did fall following the publication of the Pliatsky Report, this was to be more than outweighted by a proliferation of local non-elected agencies not so classified. And to some observers it is symptomatic of the growing significance of 'third sector' organizations:

> Arts organizations, trade unions and churches are now being joined by colleges, training and enterprize councils, schools and hospital trusts which are loosening their connections in the public sector and need to be managed as semi-independent, non-profit making bodies.
>
> (*Hudson 1995*)

However, as indicated in the next section, what is striking is the varying formal status of the agencies concerned.

10.4   THE RISE OF THE LOCAL UNELECTED STATE

10.4.1   The 'new wave' quangos

Given that Margaret Thatcher initially seemed intent on reversing the trend towards appointment rather than election, there is a certain irony in the fact that those same concerns have returned with a vengeance – with the particular twist that quangocracy is now seen particularly as a threat to local accountability and representative democracy (Davis 1993; Davis and Stewart 1993; Stewart 1993; Stewart and Davis 1994). Stewart has identified three broad trends at the local level:

- The separation of activities previously the responsibility of local authorities;
- The termination of local authority representation on non-elected agencies;
- The separation of institutions from other public authorities formerly responsible for their functions (something evident in the case of health given the organizational division of the purchasing/commissioning and provider roles) (1995).

Spending nearly £50 billion of public money by the early 1990s, on the most conservative estimates with the new 'local magistracy' outnumbering local government councillors by over 2:1 (Weir and Hall 1994), this new wave of local (non-elected) public spending bodies (LPSBs) is seen in many quarters as epitomizing the culture of unaccountability that has been one of the prices paid for implanting a business ethos in the public sector.

Some indication of the bodies involved was given in the previous section. They have included health authorities and trusts, training and enterprise councils (TECs), urban development corporations (UDCs), housing action trusts (HATs), city technology colleges (CTCs), grant maintained (GM) schools and further and higher education corporations. Given the move away from local authorities to housing associations as the main suppliers of social housing, many would include these also in the list. Such has been the cumulative effect of, what again, is a piecemeal process that it was necessary to survey and map the shadowy terrain of the unelected state. This has been done nationally (Weir and Hall 1994) and for particular geographical regions as in the West Midlands (Davis 1993). It has proved quite a task even to establish who sits on these agencies because of the reluctance of the Government to publish a national directory of appointees. The *ad hoc* nature of the process is also underlined by the fact that the agencies concerned vary even in terms of their basic organizational status – some are formally public bodies; others are charitable associations; yet others are registered companies. What they have in common though is their intimate involvement in the delivery of public services, pursuit of public policy goals and spending of public money.

10.4.2 Public safeguards

The transfer of responsibilities from local authorities to local non-elected agencies contains another irony. While these agencies have been proliferating, the Conservatives introduced new rules to force local government to be more open and responsive – in short, to be more democratic. Under the 1985 Local Government (Access to Information) Act the public has the right in advance to inspect the agenda of any council, committee or sub-committee meeting. They have the right not only to see agendas but also any reports and background papers which are being submitted. Moreover, the agenda of full council includes the minutes of all committee and sub-committee meetings held during the cycle. These meetings, in turn, will have been open to the public.

Other significant statutory regulations applying to local government include the availability for public inspection of the register of council members' interests. The local ombudsman investigates complaints of alleged maladministration by a local authority. Councillors can be surcharged and banned from holding office for any misdemeanours. The Audit Commission have a responsibility to satisfy themselves of financial propriety on the part of the local authority and that it has made appropriate arrangements for securing value for money in the use of its resources. Additionally, all local authorities must appoint a monitoring officer with the duty to report any cases where the council, a committee or sub-committee, or an individual officer has or is about to commit an act that is unlawful or improper. And, of course, the most important requirement keeping councillors accountable to their local communities is that they are regularly subject to electoral scrutiny and can be removed from office accordingly.

This amounts to a formidable array of constraints on the abuse of public power and with specific sanctions available should such abuse nonetheless occur. Thus, it has been possible to pursue the allegations of gerrymandering levelled against Westminister Council through the mechanism of the district auditor. It could not be taken for granted that similar requirements for access to information, openness of meetings, redress of grievances, monitoring, or independent audit applied to local non-elected agencies. Indeed, an influential report referred to earlier emphasized:

> the inadequate official framework for [non-elected] public bodies ... their varying status and inconsistent arrangements for accountability, scrutiny and openness.
>
> (*Weir and Hall 1994: 42*)

However, **accountability** is a theme on which we need to pause at this juncture.

Accountability is potentially a problematical concept. We may be talking at cross purposes unless it is clear what an organization is expected to be accountable for and to whom it should be accountable.

The difficulties can certainly be exemplified from the position of local non-elected agencies (NEAs).

10.5   THE UNELECTED STATE: ACCOUNTABILITY AND MANAGERIALISM

In one sense these agencies would claim to be highly accountable.

NEAs have become increasingly performance-driven. Addressed in the previous chapter in the context of the Local Policing Plan, this relates to managerial accountability which, in the words of an interviewee participating in a recent Local Government Management Board research study of local authorities and non-elected agencies emphasizes 'using resources more efficiently and thinking more strategically' (Painter, Rouse, Isaac-Henry and Munk 1995: 24).

Echoing what was stated in Chapter 4, the research study cited above indicates that:

> On the ground it means having a mission statement, a set of operational objectives and targets, programmes and projects aligned to such objectives ...
> In addition it means having a performance culture, these objectives and targets 'owned' within the organization through the alignment of staff to organizational goals and a propensity to monitor and take appropriate corrective action where needed in order to secure continuous quality improvement. It means emphasizing results rather than simply going through due process.
>
> *(ibid.: 24)*

The senior agency executives interviewed all agreed that performance and quality management had become the key priority, in accordance with the changing public management ethos of the 1980s and 1990s. Confirming other evidence (Stewart, Greer and Hoggett 1995) the above study also revealed the extent to which the performance outputs of NEAs are prescribed, with missions and objectives largely determined centrally, as are in many cases performance measures and indicators.

There are also the difficult issues arising more generally in the context of performance management and public services referred to in Chapter 4 – including that of defining appropriate performance measures and the danger of the quantifiable driving out the qualitative dimensions of performance. In a fragmented institutional structure 'even if "technical" efficiency is enhanced, this may be at the expense of "allocative" or "system" efficiency. An optimal use of resources in a single-agency context may not be so within a wider framework of choices' (Painter, Rouse, Isaac-Henry and Munk 1995: p.29). Thus, as indicated in Chapter 4, costs can be 'externalized' or 'shunted on' to other organizations.

Emphasizing results rather than due process can have implications too for such traditional public service values as probity. Hence the 'quango scandals' that have aroused the concern of the House of Commons Public Accounts Committee (PAC).

Although procedures have been tightened up in the light of these well-publicized scandals, as recently as June 1995 the PAC was criticizing GM schools for the ineffectiveness of their financial controls. There is the impact moreover on equity (fairness). With NEAs particularly pressurized to perform in a more 'business-like' manner, priorities can become resource-driven rather than needs-driven, generating some friction between equity and efficiency.

10.6   THE WIDER ACCOUNTABILITY EQUATION

10.6.1   Non-elected agencies and community links

Following through a major theme addressed in Chapter 4, managerial concepts of accountability are narrowly focused.

> **Wider concepts of public accountability** imply accessibility, a predilection to be open and sensitivity to a range of public service stakeholders.

The associated tensions are also evident from the recent developments in the police service discussed in the previous chapter. With NEAs the picture, as it relates to openness, is a distinctly patchy one. Most of the agencies included in the LGMB study held their board meetings in public and held more than they are required to do. To improve accessibility one rural health agency even rotated the geographical location of these meetings. Yet:

> commercially sensitive information, frequently cited in the case of economic development and training agencies, though increasingly in health bodies too – especially the NHS trusts – can create real obstacles to a culture of openness.
>
> (*Painter, Rouse, Isaac-Henry and Munk 1995: 36*)

Many local NEAs have also exhibited a narrow stakeholder base. Of those agencies included in the LGMB sample, national government was frequently regarded as the major stakeholder (not surprisingly given the extent of central prescription and control). Direct service users also figured prominently – consistent with the philosophy underpinning the **citizen charter** movement of making public services more directly responsive to their 'customers'. So too did the claims of the private sector, notably in economic development and training agencies. The corollary of being so preoccupied is neglect of the legitimate interests of other stakeholders, particularly those of the community at large.

Nonetheless, a more open consultative style of decision-making is being developed by at least some of these agencies, with a corresponding desire to strengthen community links. One family health service authority (FHSA), on being advised that several millions of pounds was to be made available to deal with primary health care needs, set up so-called **constituency action teams** – including representatives of local authorities, the voluntary sector and doctors and nurses – to agree on the real nature of those needs (Painter, Isaac-Henry and Chalcroft 1994). An agency cited in the LGMB study, at their mid-year review with the Department of Environment, supplemented technical reporting with a community video and invited 'local voices' to speak of their experiences.

Some health authorities are also engaging the public in health purchasing by experimenting with discussion groups – reflecting the socio-economic composition of the local population – and primed to address the sensitive matter of health priorities and rationing (Brindle 1995). Hence new forms of public consultation and community participation are emerging. Some are impressive; others inevitably smack of tokenism. Indeed, there may be scope for local authorities to draw lessons from these innovative practices, notwithstanding the non-elected status of the agencies concerned. From the community empowerment perspective, local government has in the past itself perhaps been too prone to a 'top-down' style of decision-making.

10.6.2 A variety of practices

But the crucial point in relation to wider notions of accountability is the sheer variability in the practices adopted by NEAs. This partly reflects the formal requirements of these agencies. Thus, the rules applying to meetings and public rights of attendance have varied according to the stipulations of the relevant legislation. Yet, the formal position is not always a good guide to how these agencies actually operate and therefore the realities on the ground. Whereas some of them fulfil only their minimum statutory or contractual obligations others – as we have seen – are being innovative in their endeavours to involve the public or empower the community. Thus, even agencies ostensibly of the same type can exhibit marked differences, reflecting their specific institutional, geographical and historical circumstances (Painter, Isaac-Henry and Chalcroft 1994). The differences of approach can be observed in the board composition and relationship with local authorities of two development corporations in the West Midlands. Half of Birmingham Heartlands Development Corporation's board consists of local councillors, reflecting the fact that the City Council itself was instrumental in setting it up. This is in stark contrast with the often difficult relationship between the Black Country Development Corporation and the neighbouring local authorities on whom it was foisted.

What is particularly evident is that though some NEAs are adopting a more open and consultative ethos, others remain narrowly task-orientated – focused maybe, but also with the consequence of perpetuating a closed decision-making style, consultation viewed almost as an unnecessary distraction. It is this lack of consistency that has been the catalyst for some interesting initiatives to promote greater codification of agency practices.

10.7   CODES OF PRACTICE

10.7.1   The West Midlands initiative

In 1993/94 the West Midlands Joint Committee – comprising the seven metropolitan councils of Birmingham, Coventry, Dudley, Sandwell, Solihull, Walsall and Wolverhampton – commissioned research from the University of Central England on appointed agencies and public accountability. The research findings highlighted the wide variety of agency styles and the fact that good practice is likely to happen as much by accident as design (Painter, Isaac-Henry and Chalcroft 1994). As a consequence, in September 1994 a major policy initiative was launched by the Joint Committee (Cheeseright 1994). Its ten-point code became known as the *West Midlands Code of Practice* (Painter and Isaac-Henry 1994; Local Government Information Unit 1995: 25–6). The intention was to persuade NEAs operating in the conurbation to endorse the *Code*, as a mark of their recognition of what constitutes good practice for organizations in the public domain. It was therefore a matter of establishing a framework of general principles and standards to which these agencies could reasonably be expected to conform, inducing the laggards to follow the example set by their more innovative counterparts – a form of 'benchmarking'.

Launched jointly by the Leaders of a Labour-controlled and Conservative-led authority, the attempt to 'sell' this *Code* is unique in that it was the response of several authorities working together. Apart from forming the basis for national lobbying on NEA accountability, invitations to abide by the *Code* have achieved tangible returns, some of the agencies approached agreeing to open their meetings to public scrutiny for the first time. And a conference convened at Birmingham Council House in January 1995 to discuss the initiative, attended by representatives of many of the principal agencies in the West Midlands, generally saw a constructive response from those present.

10.7.2   The Nolan reform agenda

Significantly, a trend is now unfolding towards greater codification on the part of the NEAs themselves, as they take steps to put their own house in order (whether or not under ministerial pressure). Hence the codes of conduct and accountability for the boards of health authorities and trusts. The TEC National Council's code of practice is a framework of local accountability for training and enterprize councils. Following allegations of mismanagement and conflicts of interest, another code of conduct has been drafted by the College Employers Forum for further education governors. A pattern – if piecemeal – is becoming evident.

Even more notable is the Nolan Committee's First Report on *Standards in Public Life*, published in May 1995, urging that consideration be given to producing a more consistent legal framework for propriety and accountability in public bodies. Investigating universities, FE colleges, GM schools, TECs and housing associations as part of its second inquiry, in response to continuing demands for greater account-

Local non-elected agencies should conduct their business with reference to the following:

1. HOW THE AGENCY IS ESTABLISHED

    The agency should explain in a form available to the public the legislative background to its establishment, its formal status and remit, and the date on which it came into operation.

2. WHO THE MEMBERS ARE

    A full list of board members and arrangements by which members can be contacted by the public should be published.

3. HOW MEMBERS ARE ELECTED OR APPOINTED

    The public should be informed of how members of the agency are elected or appointed, by whom, with what selection criteria and for what period of tenure, and also how the chairman is appointed.

4. OPENNESS OF MEETINGS AND ACCESS TO DOCUMENTS

    The dates and venues of meetings of the agency should be published in advance and, wherever practicable, meetings should be open to the media and public. Arrangements should be made to enable the public and media to access appropriate reports before as well as after the meeting.

5. PUBLIC FINANCIAL ACCOUNTABILITY

    To ensure public accountability on financial matters, an understandable summary of annual accounts of the agency should be available to the media and public on request. Arrangements for the appointment of external auditors should be published.

6. FORMAL COMPLAINTS PROCEDURE

    The agency should adopt, publish and make available to the public a formal complaints procedure. In addition, the agency should publish an annual report on complaints received and dealt with.

7. PUBLIC REGISTER OF PECUNIARY INTERESTS

    The agency should maintain a public register of the direct and indirect pecuniary interests of its board members, in the same way that local authorities maintain a register of interests of their elected members.

8. REPORT ON ANNUAL PERFORMANCE

    The agency should publish an annual report outlining its achievements over the previous year and service targets for the future. This should be widely available to the public and media.

9. ARRANGEMENTS FOR CONSULTATION

    The agency should consult with the relevant local authorities, community groups and other public agencies as appropriate in the discharge of its functions, and should annually publish its consultation arrangements.

10. ENSURING PROBITY

    The agency should nominate a monitoring officer whose duty it should be to ensure that the agency complies with the law. Such an officer shall have an independent right to report to the board of the agency on any possible breaches of law or financial irregularities. The agency should make available to the public such reports and decisions made thereon.

(Source: West Midlands Joint Committee 1994)

Figure 10.1 West Midlands Code of Good Practice

ability and regulation (Etherington 1996), Nolan is indeed looking for generally applicable standards and thus examining 'whether there are ... principles ... which could be [implemented] ... widely across a whole range of bodies delivering public services' (Riddell 1995). Whilst accepting that ministers must retain ultimate responsibility for appointments, Nolan had also concluded that they should only be made after advice from a panel including an independent element. Moreover, it recommended that a public appointments commissioner be established to regulate and oversee departmental procedures, one of a number of proposals subsequently accepted by the Government. In view of mounting concern John Major had, in fact, set up a review to examine the appointments system back in May 1994.

In terms of the reform agenda, however, Stewart (1995) makes an important distinction between changing and tightening the procedures governing NEAs on the one hand and returning to some form of directly elected control on the other. The reforms discussed above clearly fall into the first category. There must be room for doubt about how dramatic a difference even a future Blair Labour government would make in the latter context. Will it succumb to the usual temptation to dispense patronage to its own supporters? There was certainly much evidence of associated network-building as the election approached (White 1996). Of course, this would now be subject to the Nolan reforms on appointments. The Labour Party has also expressed a desire to halt the trend away from elected councils to appointed bodies. But the general rhetoric could not disguise continuing ambiguities in its position (let alone how quickly it would/could proceed with reforms). Thus, the commitment to elected English regional assemblies, one of the components in its constitutional reform package that could have a direct bearing on the scope for increasing the public accountability of non-elected agencies, seemed increasingly lukewarm.

The main effect on the local unelected state of any change in government nationally is likely to be increased local authority membership on agency boards rather than their demise. This is evident from the Labour Party's proposals to make the governing bodies of health commissioning and provider bodies more representative of the community. What is appropriate in any case depends on the type of agency, given the organizational variety that typifies the unelected local state (Stewart, Greer and Hoggett 1995), pointing to the need for a 'menu' of reforms rather than a single blueprint (AMA 1994).

10.8   LOCAL AUTHORITIES AND THE NEW LOCAL GOVERNANCE

10.8.1   Adapting to changing realities

Many of the non-elected local agencies are consequently likely to survive in one form or another for the foreseeable future – if only because the amount of institutional change that has occurred at the local level will take some time to unravel. Local authorities need therefore to come to terms with the realities of the new local governance, thus accepting the fact that:

- The local authority has often moved from a position of power to one of influence.
- Though objecting strongly to the growth of the unelected state, to better promote and protect the interests of the local community they have to work with and influence NEAs.
- Effective service provision now typically depends on constructive relationships with outside agencies.
- These agencies also control significant amounts of resources at the local level. Thus, although it may be difficult to justify the 'infrastructure of support' required to develop relationships with external bodies at a time of acute financial pressures, the local authority does need to avail itself of alternative funding opportunities.
- Local authorities are, in any case, often obliged by statute or regulation to work closely with these outside agencies, as evidenced in the legislation relating to community care and the rules set out in the procedures for single regeneration budget bids (Painter, Rouse, Isaac-Henry and Munk 1995; Painter and Isaac-Henry 1995).

To protect the interests of their communities local authorities have, in fact, found themselves both working with local NEAs (as well as indeed with the private and voluntary sectors) and monitoring the activities of such organizations. In relation to the latter, a number of authorities have produced directories of local public service providers, established scrutiny (or so-called 'quango watch') committees, or launched codes stipulating minimum standards for public accountability (as in the case of the West Midlands example discussed earlier).

As far as the possibilities for co-operation are concerned, obviously much depends on attitudes on either side of the fence. Relationships can be adversarial, especially where agencies are seen as part of a calculated attempt to undermine local government, or where newly-created institutions are eager to assert their independence of the local authority. The educational arena has provided graphic examples of such antagonisms, notably relationships with CTCs and GM schools. But the extent of partnership, collaboration and joint working should not be underestimated, for instance on the urban regeneration and local economic development front, between health and social services (including moves towards joint commissioning of services), or even in order to obtain European funding. If anything, joint working is becoming more common, an indication of the greater pragmatism developing and hence diminishing polarization between the elected and unelected local state.

10.8.2   The variety of responses

There are, however, again particularistic and contingent factors at play, not least the historical evolution of an agency as seen in the earlier Birmingham Heartlands example. Indeed, it is helpful to think of interactions between local authorities and NEAs as a continuum, with very much an arm's length relationship at one extreme and close organic ties at the other (the latter applying particularly where the local authority itself has been instrumental in the creation of an agency). There are, nonetheless, opportunities for the former to exploit, because of the frustration the agencies themselves sometimes feel at the degree of central prescription to which they are subject, especially if this flies in the face of what they know to be local priorities and needs. This can create scope for local alliances and networking to mitigate the worst effects of these central controls.

Moreover, the local authority can carve out for itself an important role when problems are not susceptible to single-agency solutions, given the broader perspective that only it as a multi-purpose body can bring to bear. As Ranson and Stewart emphasize, in this segmented institutional environment there is a high risk of systemic failure:

> The emerging fragmented structure of government increases the need for system management . . . System management becomes more, not less, important in the new patterning.

(1994: 145–6)

Yet, the LGMB research study previously cited found striking differences in the approaches of local authorities to this institutional fragmentation, placing the sample authorities in one of four categories, namely **passive, organic, high profile initiative-taking** and **strategic**:

- The **passive** authorities had failed to respond positively to the growth of the local unelected state, with events either moving too quickly for them or because they had been at a loss to know what to do.
- The authorities adopting an **organic** approach tended to rely on informal processes and networks as a means of exerting influence over outside agencies, with the quality of inter-personal relationships a key determinant of success in this respect.
- The **high profile initiative-taking** authorities were launching discrete formal initiatives – particularly those of a monitoring/scrutiny kind (examples of which were mentioned above). With the attendant publicity, this demonstrated to their local community that they were being proactive in their dealings with NEAs.
- The **strategic** authorities were responding to the new challenges by taking a corporate view of what form the relationships with outside agencies should take and the priorities to be pursued accordingly – in the process thinking fundamentally about the adaptation required in the role of the local authority if it is to function effectively in the changing environment (Painter, Rouse, Isaac-Henry and Munk 1995).

It is the local authorities in the fourth category which particularly are beginning to come to terms with some of the critical **strategic change management** issues now facing local government. Having devoted much of the discussion on management by the unelected state so far to the problematical issues arising from the accountability debate, we are now back on territory dealt with in Chapter 3 on managing change in the public sector. The final section of the chapter therefore focuses upon this theme in the context of the new (fragmented) local governance.

Passive	Organic	High Profile Initiative-Taking	Strategic	RESPONSES
TYPES OF APPROACHES				**RESPONSES**
•				Resigned to loss of responsibilities to NEAs
•	•			In the process of realizing just how important NEAs have become and their increasing impact on local government
•	•			No overall policy on NEAs has been considered
•	•	•		No overall policy on NEAs because thought best to have policies on issues as they arise
		•	•	Lobby and challenge NEAs on important issues
	•	•	•	Informal liaison between officers/members of the authority and NEAs
	•	•	•	Extensive development of informal networks as basis for developing partnership working
		•	•	Setting up quango 'watches' and quango data banks
			•	Focus on changing role of local government to fit the changing environment
			•	Plans for changing structures and practices to implement new strategic policy

(Source: Local Government Management Board 1995)

Figure 10.2 Local Authority approaches to non-elected agencies

10.9   STRATEGIC REPOSITIONING IN LOCAL GOVERNANCE NETWORKS

10.9.1   Managing the 'new world'

The changing realities of local governance means that there is something fundamental at stake for local government.

> What is essentially at issue for local authorities is **organizational (re)positioning** in the light of a changing environment – given that their effectiveness now often depends on influencing and working through others rather than on direct action.

Such (re)positioning is precisely what is at the heart of the strategic as opposed to operational management function. A senior officer in a London borough, interviewed as part of the LGMB research study, confided that the 'local authority ... will just die if they don't, not just respond to it, but manage the new world' (Painter, Rouse, Isaac-Henry and Munk 1995: 55). As this study emphasizes, the required strategic orientation must, however, be underpinned by supporting strategic analysis.

This needs to incorporate an audit of local NEAs; strategic mapping of relationships to identify the key interfaces with the local authority; the authority's resources of influence and how they can be effectively mobilized; the constraints on that influence; and an assessment of the success or otherwise of past partnerships with a view to strategic learning, deriving lessons that can be more widely applied. In the light of this analysis strategic choices can be made, for example, about those agencies which might most profitably be targeted, so that scarce resources are not spread too thinly. It is a lesson taken on board by the London Borough of Lewisham, observing with respect to external liaison that it is:

> not practical for this ... to take place with every appointed organization ... However there are ... bodies ... whose activities impact a great deal more than others, or where the council has the potential to make a larger impact ... it is proposed that the efforts of the council be focused ... and should build on ... links where they exist.
>
> (*Interview by author 1994*)

In this situation it is essential moreover that the local authority is clear about what it wants to achieve, in order to avoid being 'co-opted' by external agencies for their own purposes. Moreover, if policy is to be shaped at the crucial formative stage then the local authority's organizational intelligence and environmental scanning capability is at a premium (Painter, Rouse, Isaac-Henry and Munk 1995).

10.9.2 Mobilizing resources of influence

But the nature of the relationships between local authorities and NEAs – touched on earlier – are affected by 'resource interdependencies' (Rhodes 1988). There are limits to what the agencies can achieve without the local authority as well as vice-versa. Examples were cited to those conducting the LGMB research study of the local authority providing staffing expertise to complement a TEC's possession of financial resources. Hence the significance of resources of influence mentioned in the context of strategic analysis above. On the local authority side these resources can take many forms – legal and regulatory (e.g. planning permission); financial (e.g. council grants); physical (e.g. lease of land and buildings); human (staff skills); informational (technical knowledge, as well as knowledge of local community groups and sensitivities); and most importantly democratic resources (e.g. the legitimacy stemming from the fact of election).

Of course, the structure of local governance and incentives woven into that framework are largely the prerogative of central government. And the terms on which 'resource exchanges' take place are inevitably affected by the distribution of resources:

> It is frequently contended that the ... restructuring associated with the quango state is a calculated change in the 'rules of the game', hence a deliberate mobilization of bias to stack the odds against democratically elected local government. But this makes it even more imperative for local authorities to deploy whatever resources they possess to maximum effect in the relevant networks.
>
> *(Painter and Isaac-Henry 1995: 64)*

The point is, however, that these potential resources of influence have not necessarily been deployed as skillfully as might be the case, not least the resource of democratic legitimacy. There are clear opportunities given the increasing sensitivity of NEAs about their community links and credentials. But the ability to capitalize is partly dependent upon the local authority strengthening its own community roots (Painter, Rouse, Isaac-Henry and Munk 1995). Thus, the challenges facing local government require innovation in democratic practice as well as management practice; yet in comparison with the multitude of management changes in recent years there has been relatively little change of the former kind to build on the resource of democratic legitimacy (Stewart 1995b).

10.9.3 Transcending organizational boundaries

The fourth **strategic** category of local authority identified above is very much at he 'leading edge' of policy developments towards the local unelected state. One example of such an authority mentioned previously is the London Borough of Lewisham.

There are also those local authorities making considerable strides towards revamping political management structures to enhance their effectiveness in the changing local governance. An example of such a council is Coventry City Council.

Lewisham is focusing efforts on those (of the many hundreds of eligible) non-elected agencies where there is a real prospect of making an impact, aware that it is not only a matter of influencing service quality at the point of delivery, but of making sure that the needs and views of the local community are addressed in the overall planning of services.

Lewisham is also assessing opportunities for building on previous links with outside agencies and looking to apply the lessons learnt more widely. There is recognition that in so far as an effective strategy entails partnership working this will not occur of its own volition. The council thus has a major role to play in promoting and maintaining such partnerships where they would benefit the community and fulfil the authority's objectives. It would like in fact to embed this notion in its management style and training.

But Lewisham is also keen to have explicit criteria for determining the suitability of partnership in any given set of circumstances. These criteria include the extent to which an issue is beyond the council's sole capability to handle; whether partnership will attract funding otherwise unavailable, or involves complex transactions with all the attendant costs; and indeed the contribution in enabling the council to promote its democratically legitimated objectives. Chief Officers were accordingly asked to examine partnership opportunities in their own area of responsibility, analysing the issues and reporting back to the Management Team.

(Source: Local Government Management Board 1995)

Figure 10.3   Lewisham Council and the local unelected state

Therefore, to act as effective 'guardians' or 'advocates' for community interests local authorities need increasingly to cross their own organizational boundaries. Hence there are those who see the future role of local authorities in terms of 'community government' or 'community leadership' (albeit recognizing the diversity as well as areas of commonality characteristic of local communities). Yet, even in this era of contracting and purchasing/commissioning of services rather than their direct provision, the essential rationale for local government has remained a service rather than a community one (Stewart 1995b).

What is at issue where the local authority is not able to act exclusively is its capacity to have more rather than less (indirect) influence, thereby maximizing the benefits flowing to the community. It does mean being realistic about the scope for such influence given constraints as well as opportunities, not least the extent to which many NEAs must respond to a centrally-driven rather than locally-determined agenda. Even so the stakes can take a very tangible form, if it is a matter for example of unlocking the often considerable financial resources at the disposal of other agencies. For instance, the Welsh Development Agency has been prepared to finance up to 80% of the costs of jointly agreed schemes. If such benefits are to accrue it:

> involves local authorities assuming a more proactive and strategic role in their relationship with the non-elected agencies that are now part of the local governance network, so that they can shape their activities accordingly. In the past not even the limited opportunities to use membership on these agencies to exert

This West Midlands metropolitan authority has recently undertaken a review in pursuit of a broader community leadership vision for the council. Structures were being established so that members could better influence the policies and work in partnership with other agencies providing public services to the City.

Set out in a Report of the Political Management Working Group entitled *Democracy, Accountability and Leadership* and implemented in October 1994, the reforms in question were centred on the creation of Policy Teams with designated Lead Members. These will develop, promote and champion specific policy issues both inside and outside the council. Where appropriate a single Lead Member will assume responsibility for liaising with external agencies, notably if appointed to such an organization on the council's behalf. These structures will be underpinned by a small number of co-ordinating committees operating in broadly defined areas of public policy, drawing together functions which interface in a way that makes sense both within and outside the City council.

The changes also make provision for policy and performance review, including services not within the direct management of the council. This required a facility for joint investigations with other agencies. It is anticipated that this can be done in such a way as to bring maximum public exposure and so enhancing accountability within the City.

(Source: Local Government Management Board 1995)

Figure 10.4   Coventry City Council and community leadership

influence have necessarily been effectively exploited, councillors often expressing confusion about their purpose in serving on such bodies.

(Painter and Isaac-Henry 1995: 62)

Demanding a reappraisal of the role and rationale for the practices traditionally adopted by local authorities, clearly the **management of strategic change** is therefore very much at the heart of the challenges that they now face.

Because of the complex realities of contemporary local governance, the effectiveness of the local authority's relationships with other agencies that affect the welfare of the local community indeed constitutes one of THE key strategic issues now to be addressed.

10.10 CHAPTER SUMMARY

The following key learning points emerge from this chapter:

- The controversy about the growth of the unelected or quango state is not something just of recent origin. There was indeed a heated debate about the growth of non-departmental public bodies prior to 1979 and the attendant issues of ministerial patronage and democratic accountability.
- What we have seen more recently however is a proliferation of local non-elected agencies and hence particularly the growth of the unelected local state, with the fragmentation of local service delivery this inevitably entails.
- The transfer of responsibilities from local government to these non-elected bodies therefore raises issues of local accountability.
- But this begs the question of accountability for what and to whom? Managerially non-elected agencies would claim to be highly accountable given the development of a performance ethos. But their position is clearly more problematic if we take as a benchmark wider concepts of public accountability.
- Because of the variability of agency practice on open scrutiny of their activities, some local authorities have taken the initiative in promoting codes of good practice, though pressure for greater codification from other quarters has become evident.
- However, local authorities themselves have responded in a variety of ways to the new local governance and associated fragmentation of responsibilities.
- Yet the challenge facing them is nothing less than the strategic management of change and organizational re-positioning in the light of a changing environment. To maximize influence on behalf of the local community they need increasingly to work with and through other agencies.

TEXT-BASED QUESTIONS

1. Identify the similarities and dissimilarities in the controversies surrounding the growth of the unelected state in the 1970s and 1990s respectively.

2. What is meant by **managerial** accountability? Why is it not a sufficient – as opposed to necessary – form of accountability if we are dealing with the delivery of public services?

3. What was the principal purpose of the *Code of Good Practice* launched by the West Midlands Joint Committee?

4. Identify the four categories used in this chapter as a basis for classifying the nature of the responses from local authorities to the growth of the unelected local state.

5. Strategic management is ultimately concerned with organizational (re)positioning in the light of a changing environment. Are there grounds for arguing that the pattern of local service delivery now presents local authorities with a challenge of this magnitude?

6.   Outline the main elements of the 'quango strategy' adopted by the London Borough of Lewisham.

7.   What is the significance with respect to the new local governance of the changes carried out in Coventry City Council's political management structures?

ASSIGNMENT 1

A challenging applied exercise involving a library search and/or some limited field work is to take the current organizational distribution of responsibilities for the delivery of local public services and compare this with the distribution of the same responsibilities 10/20/30 years ago.

In this way it is possible to map in a very concrete way the restructuring of the local state, and significance of the trend towards organizational fragmentation and transfer of functions away from direct local authority responsibility.

ASSIGNMENT 2

Another interesting exercise involving some field work is to select two contrasting local authorities (a county and district authority; a unitary and non-unitary authority; a metropolitan and non-metropolitan authority etc.), then to ascertain what policies they have respectively adopted, or initiatives they have launched, in relation to local non-elected agencies.

Each of the selected authorities can, in the light of this information, be compared with the four categories used in the chapter to differentiate the approaches towards non-elected agencies, establishing whether there is a close correspondence with any one of those categories and if so the implications of such a match.

FURTHER READING

Davis, H. and Stewart, J. (1993) *The Growth of Government By Appointment*, Local Government Management Board, Luton. Considers how the cumulative effect of the encroachment of government by appointment has transformed the way in which local communities are governed.

Painter, C. and Isaac-Henry, K. (1995) Local Government and Non-Elected Agencies: Strategic Positioning in Local Governance Networks, *Strategic Government*, **3** (1), pp. 55–66. Summarizes research carried out in the West Midlands indicating the widely varying practices adopted by non-elected agencies and reflecting on the implications for local authorities of the changing structures of local governance.

Painter, C., Rouse, J., Isaac-Henry, K., and Munk, L. (1995) *Changing Local Governance: Local Authorities and Non-Elected Agencies*, Local Government Management Board, Luton. Major national research report dealing with 'good practice' on the part of local authorities in their dealings with non-elected agencies and identifying examples of 'leading edge' strategies in this connection.

Stewart, J. (1995) Appointed Boards and Local Government, *Parliamentary Affairs*, **40** (2), pp. 226–41. Lucid analysis of the changing governance of local communities and part of a special edition of this Journal devoted to the 'quango debate'.

Stewart, J. and Davis, H. (1994) A New Agenda For Local Governance, *Public Money and Management*, **14** (4), pp. 29–36. Succinct account of the main issues arising from the growth of the local unelected state and how the weaknesses of the developing system of local governance might be overcome.

Weir, S. and Hall, W. (eds) (1994) *Ego-Trip: Extra-Governmental Organizations in the United Kingdom and Their Accountability*, Charter 88 Trust, London. An influential national report charting the magnitude and scale of the contemporary unelected state and the problematical nature of mechanisms for accountability in this context.

MANAGING RELATIONS WITH THE EUROPEAN UNION: THE CASE OF LOCAL GOVERNMENT

11

Francis Terry

11.1   CHAPTER PREVIEW

This chapter examines how Britain's membership of the European Union (EU) has fundamentally affected the functions and powers of public authorities. It presents the changes that have occurred since 1973 (when Britain joined what was then the European Community) in terms of:

- **Obligations** placed on public sector organizations *either* to enforce new standards and procedures affecting our economic and social life *or* to comply with European standards and procedures themselves.
- **Opportunities** to benefit financially from being a member of the EU.
- **Institutional** changes which have made it possible for public sector bodies below the level of national government to interact with central organizations of the EU or with their opposite numbers in other member states.

The analysis of how relations with Europe are managed is illustrated with particular reference to local government, though many of the key points have similarities in the health service, education and central government.

The implications of EU membership have called for **strategic** changes in the way local government manages its activities and **cultural** changes in the outlook and behaviour of both officers and members of local authorities. Staff numbers dealing with the enforcement of obligations have steadily expanded, against a general trend towards reducing staff in local government as a whole; new methods of working and new flows of information have been introduced in order to take advantage of opportunities for securing funds from Europe for local economic development. Institutional changes are most noticeable at the national level, but within local authorities the appointment of staff to manage relationships with the European Commission and to prepare bids for funding is now widespread.

The overall impact of Britain's membership of the EU was initially slight. It is now so much a regular part of local authorities' decision-making that it is no longer the preserve of small, specialized units, but is embedded in the work of most main departments. The chapter concludes by showing how growing confidence and experience in handling European affairs has led local government to seek to influence directly the agenda of the Commission and to play a progressively larger role in its work.

11.2   INTRODUCTION

This chapter examines some impacts on the management of local authorities which have resulted from British membership of the European Union (EU). The emphasis is upon structure, manpower and finance, particularly during the years leading up to the formal completion of the Single European Market in 1992 and subsequently. The theme of this review is that on joining what was then the European Community the predominant focus was on the obligations, which managers in public authorities were required either to enforce or with which they themselves had to comply. This perception, shared also by policy makers, shifted in the 1980s towards maximizing the financial and other advantages of Community membership by accessing the various European funds. Increasingly this strategy has led local authorities to seek to influence the agenda of the EU decision-making organs and to foster forms of organization which facilitate the representation of their interests. The prospect of further reorganization in local government structure (and the possibility of regional government in the UK, if Labour were to take control at Westminster) has tended to divert attention and staff resources elsewhere, making it hard to recognize a consistent picture. But many local authorities appear to have entered a 'mature' phase of relationships with the Union, characterized by the incorporation of policies and procedures into their regular management systems which will deliver their enforcement and regulatory responsibilities, while enabling them to exploit opportunities for exerting influence (or attracting resources) as they arise. This process took another step forward with the signing by member states of the Treaty of Maastricht in 1993 which, among many other provisions, created the Committee of the Regions in an advisory role to the Commission.

In many respects, the changes in rules and responsibilities which have affected local government also impacted on central government departments, the public service utilities (gas, water, etc), and the health service (e.g. in procurement). Central government has usually had to work with these other agencies in negotiating with Brussels over the terms of particular directives and regulations, and it has often had to rely on them in securing implementation, particularly in the regulatory field. Local government has frequently been at the 'sharp end' of these changes in the sense that it has had to move first in adapting its organization, procedures and finances to fulfil European obligations. But is has also been highly instrumental in achieving some important benefits of EU membership.

When the UK acceded to the European Community in 1973, it became party to the 1957 Treaty of Rome which at that time was the principal framework governing relationships between member states. Over a transition period, the UK had to move into line with existing European legislation; indeed it had begun to do this for some time previously, in anticipation of Community membership. It may be thought that the key provisions of the Treaty relating to the promotion of free trade (Articles 30–6 and 59–66) would have few implications for public authorities. To an extent this was true; for many years European legislation had little impact on such local services as education, housing or social services. But the picture has markedly changed in the 1990s (CECSNET 1989; Bongers 1990).

11.3   ENFORCEMENT

Turning first to the enforcement responsibilities which followed from EU membership, the Common Agricultural Policy had considerable implications in the field of trading standards and consumer protection. Here, European legislation enlarged the range of responsibilities, powers and duties and continues to influence the work of those departments in local government more directly than any other (Audit Commission 1991). The composition of foodstuffs and the later setting of general standards of food safety, hygiene and labelling, were typical areas in which local authority officers had first to understand the regulations and then to devise effective means of monitoring and compliance.

The view of central government at the time of the UK's accession and subsequently has been that these responsibilities would largely overlay or supersede existing regulatory functions already exercised by local authorities and government agencies. Certainly this seems to have been true of central government's own role in enforcing European legislation, where an assessment of measures involved showed that 40% of them required only minor amendment to regulations, standards or procedures already obtaining in the UK (National Audit Office 1991). But there were other reasons why central government found it convenient to minimize the burdens of joining the Community. First, it was seen as important for presentational reasons to minimize the costs of compliance with foreign-made rules which the UK's accession actually required. Although the UK referendum on continued membership of the Community in 1975 had produced a clear majority in favour, the government was still wary of any groundswell of anti-European sentiment emerging. Second, it was concerned to avoid new regulatory responsibilities being used as a bargaining counter by local authorities seeking to take on additional staff. In 1975, the Manpower Watch (later the Joint Staffing Watch) had been set up to monitor closely the growth in local government manpower, as part of a political commitment to reduce 'town hall' bureaucracy.

A typical test case was the training of poultry meat inspectors. After joining the Community, the UK was obliged to implement the provisions of a European Commission directive (71/118/EC) governing standards of hygiene in handling poultry meat. The Environmental Health Officers Association (later the Institution of EHOs) appealed to the Department of the Environment to contribute towards the training of additional poultry meat inspectors, which the Department firmly refused. In the end, the Association had to accept the official view that this was a matter to be handled by shifting the priorities for existing expenditure on local government training – something which was already under the control of local authorities (through the then Local Government Training Board).

Interestingly, the reluctance of central government to render additional assistance in such circumstances had the side-effect of stimulating various professional bodies to strengthen their advisory, information and training services to members. The Institute of EHOs and the Institute of Trading Standards Administration both developed valuable information services for their members, and the Chartered Institute of Purchasing and Supply (CIPS) is now a prime source of reference on the obligations imposed by EU directives in its field (CIPS 1989). This trend towards self-help has accelerated among the central organizations of local government (Digings 1991) and the professional bodies, as European integration has progressed.

Staff numbers are less explicitly a focus for policy actions now than previously, mainly because tight central controls over local spending, efficiency measures and the advent of compulsory competitive tendering (CCT) have achieved far more dramatic reductions in manpower (LACSAB/LGMB 1985–94). The total numbers of local government staff have fallen by more than one-third since 1975; but the numbers of non-manual staff engaged on environmental health and consumer protection work has steadily grown (see Table 11.1), in line with a succession of directives and regulations which they are responsible for enforcing. The fall in manual staff is accounted for largely by contracting out of non-inspectorial functions. Though it is harder to

Table 11.1 Trends in local government staff total numbers, environmental health and consumer protection (England and Wales, 000s)

Q1	All staff		Envt. health		Cons. protect.	
	Ftenm(a)	Ftem(b)	Ftnem	Ftem	Ftenm	Ftem
1975	1289.4	767.5	13.2	8.7	3.5	0.1
1980	1360.8	726.9	14.5	7.4	3.6	<0.1
1985	1370.2	643.5	14.2	6.5	3.7	<0.1
1990	1438.2	584.5	15.3	4.9	3.9	<0.1
1992	1469.3	521.1	16.8	3.9	4.2	<0.1
1994	1378.9	462.0	16.9	4.0	4.3	<0.1

(*Source: Local Government Management Board*)

Ftenm(a) = Full Time Equivalents, non-manual employees
Ftem(b) = Full Time Equivalents, manual employees

demonstrate, because figures are not collected centrally, the number of staff engaged on work arising from other aspects of joining the Community has also grown in some key areas, as will be explained below.

11.4   COMPLIANCE

The second important way in which UK membership of the Community affected the management practices of public authorities related to compliance with European legislation. In contrast to the responsibilities for enforcing what might be called 'Euro-regulation', public sector organizations themselves became subject to a number of new obligations imposed upon them directly. An example of this is the procure-ment of works, supplies and services. Purchasing by public bodies was, and remains, one of the most important single categories of economic activity within the EU, accounting for more than 15% of the total GDP of Member States (Cecchini 1988). Promoting competition in public procurement was seen as essential by the Commission in achieving closer economic integration, keener prices for purchasers and business opportunities for suppliers. The obstacles in the way of this policy can be broadly classified into those which are physical (custom posts, frontier controls, etc.), fiscal (rates of VAT for example) or technical (standards) (see Table 11.2).

The original European Directive on Public Works (71/305/EEC) came into force in July 1973 and a public supplies directive (77/62/EEC) which was under negotiation at the time of the UK's accession came into force in 1978. The two directives required that invitations to tender above a given threshold in value should be brought to the attention of companies and suppliers throughout the Member States, chiefly by publication in the *Official Journal of the European Communities* (OJ), and that contract-awarding bodies should not discriminate against organizations from other member states. A list of objective criteria to be used when evaluating tenders is prescribed and it is illegal to split up contracts so that individually they fall below the thresh-olds.

The entry into force of these directives was overseen by the Department of the environment (DoE), because local authorities and central government were the prin-cipal parts of the public sector that were affected. Major exceptions to the directives

Table 11.2 Barriers to trade within Europe

Physical:	Border formalities
	Control over the free movement of goods, equipment and livestock
Technical:	Standards specified for a wide range of products and services traded among member states
	Administrative and other restrictions on the free movement of labour
	Controls in markets such as financial services, transport and communications
	Legal, fiscal and administrative restraints on the operation of business
	Barriers to the free movement of capital
Fiscal:	Differing rates of VAT
	Differing excise duty rates

were also allowed where issues of public health or security (including defence) were involved, or where the product concerned would not meet the technical standards obtaining in the country of the purchaser.

At that time, in the mid-1970s, the approach of 'government by consensus' was favoured among ministers and the DoE played a persuasive and consultative role in seeking to smooth the introduction of the European legislation. The European Joint Group, composed of local authority representatives and Whitehall officials, had been set up in 1971 to examine regularly the implications for local government of European legislation. On purchasing, DoE drew up guidance in the form of two substantial circulars (DoE 59/73 and DoE 158/73) which were produced after discussion with the CIPS and a body known as the Joint Advisory Committee on Local Authority Purchasing (JACLAP), serviced by the local authority associations. A similar circular (DoE 46/78) followed in connection with the supplies directive.

Despite what some managers had feared, research by the author indicates that the directives led to relatively minor changes in organization and procedure and many of these were encompassed by a broader trend towards professionalizing the purchasing function in local government. This was facilitated by the larger scale of local authorities, recently reformed under the Local Government Act 1972. Some appointed Directors of Supplies at senior level; others formed purchasing consortia to exploit the potential for buying in bulk and achieving discounts thereby. It seemed to many purchasing managers that the thrust of the new legislation was unhelpful, however, because buying in bulk also made it more likely that the threshold for advertising in the OJ would be crossed. They were unconvinced that the additional effort in compliance would be compensated by a greater choice of tenders or keener prices. Even the advent of an electronic information system – Tenders Electronic Daily (TED) – in 1982, which made the notification of and response to tendering opportunities much more rapid, seems to have had little impact on choice or price.

There is no doubt that some administrative effort was incurred in placing advertisements in OJ, while the response from firms in other member states was invariably minimal. When a new directive was issued for services and revised directives were issued in 1988 (for works) and 1989 (for supplies) the thresholds were raised and are periodically reviewed to keep pace with inflation. They currently stand at 5 million ECU (about £3.5 million) for public works, 200,000 ECU (about £141,000) for supplies (DTI 1992) and 200,000 ECU (£141,000) for services.

In economic terms, the impact of the procurement legislation was scarcely noticeable. While public bodies in the UK seem to have complied with the requirements of the purchasing directives (at any rate their practices were never challenged), the industrial policies of member states and the reluctance of firms to exploit their opportunities within the EU has tended to maintain the status quo. The choice of tendering procedures allowed under the purchasing directives also left very wide scope for legitimate avoidance by public bodies. By contrast, the use of technical standards which were peculiar to a member state often had the effect, intentionally or otherwise, of excluding foreign firms. The remedies for firms discriminated against proved slow and expensive to operate. Research demonstrated that barely 1% of works or supplies contracts were actually being placed with foreign companies (Commission of European Communities 1988).

Considering these two examples, one relating to enforcement, the other to compliance, the clear impression is one of modification in the rules and procedures, rather than in the managerial roles, which resulted from EU membership. The adjustments were handled in a co-operative spirit by local authorities, professional bodies and central government working together. There is, however, a major contrast between these examples in the manpower and financial implications. Enforcement responsibilities have steadily raised the numbers of staff and costs to local authorities – a trend which has persisted through the 1990s. Compliance on the other hand has, up to now had little effect on manpower or costs.

11.5   OBTAINING THE BENEFITS OF EUROPEAN UNION MEMBERSHIP

During the late 1970s, growing familiarity with the UK's enhanced role in Europe led both local authorities and government departments to pursue the more tangible benefits. These included loans from the European Investment Bank and financial aid from the Community's structural funds, especially:

- The European Social Fund (ESF); and
- The European Regional Development Fund (ERDF).

The guidance section of the European Agricultural Guidance and Guarantee Fund (EAGGF) is a third fund, but is of only minor importance in the UK context, being chiefly applicable to rural areas in southern Europe. The structural funds at that time were not large (less than £3 billion) and a wide range of public bodies could bid, in open competition, up to the limit of the 'quota' allocated to the UK by the Commission. The City of Sheffield (Poulsford 1985) and the then North West Water Authority (NWWA 1981; 1982; 1985) were two examples of public bodies which achieved some success in obtaining capital sums towards infrastructure investment.

The growing awareness among local authorities in the 1980s of the importance of promoting economic development seems to have been a strong incentive to seek European funds. This particular function had been carried out by local government for many years (Young 1990) and was greatly facilitated by the passing of the Land Act 1963. Nevertheless, the Board of Trade had usually taken a critical view of such local initiatives because it was felt that they interfered with the workings of the government's regional policy. This tension evaporated after the demise of a national policy for regional development in 1981 and local authorities became more innovative and more confident in attracting resources for development.

There was even a measure of positive encouragement from central government to apply to the European funds, as a way of ensuring that the UK received its 'fair share' in return for the substantially larger contributions which by now it was having to make. At the political level, these contributions increasingly became a target for criticism from the Prime Minister of the day, Margaret Thatcher, and with some justification. Britain's **net** contributions to Europe (in real terms) amounted to £102 million in 1973, reached £959 million in 1979 and £1.98 billion in 1985 (Burkitt and Baimbridge

1992). The problem in applying to the funds, from a local authority point of view, was that considerable effort in preparation was required, but there was no certain prospect of a successful application bringing in additional resources. The reason is that for structural funds to have real impact, the Commission intends they should increase total spending power in regions that are economically disadvantaged. HM Treasury, however, for a long time viewed the funds as replacing public expenditure which would otherwise have been incurred.

The problem is complicated because the Commission can never establish with certainty what central government, or local authorities, would have spent had European funds not been available. This is particularly difficult when the Commission has itself given an indicative commitment to allocate resources at a certain level over a three to five year period to the UK (along with other member states). Moreover, it could be argued that if projects supported from the structural funds were not already being funded by the UK government, they must also by definition represent poorer value for money. The effect was that a local authority used to receive little or no additional funds if its applications succeeded, and under the system of capital controls, it also required government approval before project funds could be spent.

The dispute over 'additionality' (that is, the extent to which appropriations from the structural funds have a genuine economic impact and result in an equivalent increase in the total volume of structural aid) dogged attempts to maximize income from the funds for a number of years. Eventually, under pressure from the Commission, the UK government moderated its position on additionality in 1991 and accepted that some grants from the funds could count as a real net increase in resources. Despite the disincentive from HM Treasury up to that point, local authorities appear to have been remarkably diligent in bidding to the European funds. There was also, perhaps an element of determination not to be beaten down by the succession of major reforms under Mrs Thatcher which had curtailed local government spending and constrained its freedom in other important ways (Marsh and Rhodes 1992b). At any rate, there was a noticeable rise in the number of authorities which set up committees and units to promote local economic development. Often these units were headed by experienced professionals with senior officer status, who had joined from the private sector. Some also transferred from related departments whose functions were being cut back, such as planning, where the easing of development controls in the 1980s and the much reduced emphasis on structure plans had created surplus capacity.

There was a growth too in companies set up and controlled by local authorities which aimed to foster development. Lancashire Enterprises, founded by Lancashire County Council, was a successful example (Terry 1990a) but there were other ventures, taking rather different approaches, in Leeds and Birmingham for instance (Terry 1990b: 1990c). Sometimes they were set up in partnership with private sector developers; almost always they were able to take over areas of land in local authority ownership and realize its development potential. These companies attracted controversy, however, as a result of the former Greater London Council and the erstwhile metropolitan counties using their economic strategies, it was alleged, as part of wider political programmes. The growth and success of such enterprises was curbed by the passage of the Local Government and Housing Act 1990, when it became unlawful for companies to be majority owned by local authorities.

It is impossible to demonstrate a direct relationship between the growth of economic development units or companies and the availability of EU funds; but the opportunity of tapping these funds was seen by them as an important target for their activities and it is still regarded as such. Certainly these new types of organization became expert in analysing the priorities for award of European structural funds and increasingly successful during the 1980s at winning resources from them. From 1979 to 1988 the UK received over £3 billion in aid from the funds (Terry 1992), much of it through ERDF.

This very brief sketch suggests a rising interest, at any rate among the larger local authorities, in the opportunities for financial help from EU membership – opportunities in which they were prepared to invest considerable effort and expertise, despite the merely nominal benefits which initially resulted.

11.5.1   The single market

Despite the interest in securing funds from Europe, the experience of EU membership through the late 1970s and early 1980s had proved disappointing to UK government and probably to many members of the public as well. Cynicism about excess standardization of products and services across Europe, the time taken to reach unanimous agreement on European legislation and a misunderstanding of the Commission's role were all exploited in the popular press and in parliament. The mood was expressed in forthright style by Mrs Thatcher with her attacks on 'Brussels bureaucracy' and her intransigence over the Community budget.

The opportunity for a fresh approach came with the inauguration of Jacques Delors as President of the Commission in 1985. With hindsight, this marked a turning point in European affairs. Delors had a number of radical proposals in mind, aimed at reviving the ideals of the original 'Common Market', stimulating economic growth and promoting the economic and political role of the Commission. They included the idea of a European defence union and a monetary union; but it was the complete dismantling of barriers to trade which, coinciding broadly with a Conservative party belief in the value of free trade, provided the common ground for European leaders to accept that reform of the Treaty of Rome was due.

Before further progress could be made, a political deal had to be struck, based on acceptance by other member states that the UK's contribution to the budget was unacceptably high and that a rebate should be given. After the Fontainebleau summit of 1984, the net contribution of the UK fell from £1.98 billion in 1985 to £635 million in 1987. The signing of the Single European Act by the Council of Ministers in December 1985 established the legal framework, as well as the necessary political backing, for a programme of measures to complete the single European market. The Act came into force in July 1987.

At the Milan summit (June 1985) the Council of Ministers had already been instructed to:

> Initiate a precise programme of action . . . with a view to achieving completely and effectively, the conditions for a single market in the Community by 1992 at the latest, in accordance with stages fixed in relationship to previously determined priorities and a binding timetable.

The programme of action referred to an inventory, among other things, of 300 measures (later simplified to 282) prepared under the direction of the Internal Market Commissioner, Lord Cockfield, and designed to dismantle remaining barriers to trade between member states. Of the 282 measures, most have now been enacted and have at least some implications for the responsibilities and management of public authorities. Over 70 require enforcement by local authorities, for example, and the following sections highlight some of these.

First, there was a renewal of earlier efforts to open up public procurement to wider competition (directives 88/29/EEC on supplies and 89/665/EEC on works). A directive on compliance procedures (89/665/EEC) was added and one on procurement of services (92/50/EEC) came into effect in 1993. Directive 90/531/EEC brought public utilities within the scope of the procurement directives. Compared to earlier purchasing directives, the more recent ones have led to much greater changes in procedures, on account of the so-called 'framework arrangements'. Local authorities can no longer argue that standing 'offers to treat' or period contracts (also called 'call-off' contracts) are outside the scope of the directives. These types of contract, in which the rate per item, terms, delivery dates, etc., could all be negotiated with a supplier but the price would not be known until an individual order was placed, are now covered. The result has been that over 90% of local authority purchasing is now estimated to be affected by the directives.

On the other hand, interviews with purchasing managers, carried out by the author, suggest that both the staffing and financial implications of the directives continue to be minor. The procedural changes in many larger authorities resulted in improvements in systems and control – necessary to ensure compliance – though without increase in staff. The risk however is that a legalistic emphasis on compliance will divert attention from skilful use of purchasing techniques to achieve best prices, because it is often the threat of competition from overseas that helps to influence price negotiations and tendering behaviour among UK suppliers.

Cases where foreign suppliers clearly undercut the domestic ones are reported to be relatively rare. New entrants to the UK market also tend to work through agents or subsidiaries they have set up in this country, rather than trading across frontiers.

The 1993 Directive on services had wider-reaching implication, because it interacts with domestic legislation on CCT under the Local Government Act 1988. Once a local service such as refuse collection is tendered, the field is open to contractors anywhere in Europe, potentially putting many local authority direct service organizations (DSOs) under strong competitive pressure. Most DSOs responded readily to this challenge, losing work in only a very few places to overseas contractors (chiefly from France and Spain). The threat of foreign, as well as domestic, competition has also receded as a result of decisions handed down by the European Court of Justice in the early 1990s. The background is that in 1981 the UK gave effect to the EU Acquired Rights Directive (77/187/EEC). This introduced into English law, via the Transfer of Undertakings (Protection of Employment) Regulations (TUPE), the principle of automatic transfer of contracts of employment, collective agreements and trade union recognition where employees were transferred to a new undertaking carrying on similar work. The principle applies across the board, in both public and private sectors. The Regulations enacted in the UK were however significantly narrower than the Directive, in that they excluded transfers which were 'not in the nature of a commercial venture' and excluded the provision for con-sultation with workers' representatives on transfers. Following enforcement proceed-ings by the European Commission against the UK government (for failing to implement fully the Directive), several of the main advantages exploited by contractors compet-ing for local authority and NHS service contracts – in terms of cutting staff, lowering rates of pay and increasing hours – have been removed. Contractors who take on public sector staff as part of the contracting out process are therefore no longer able to reduce their pay and conditions (Kerr and Radford 1994), though they may make efficiency savings in other ways.

11.5.2   Economic impacts of '1992'

Second, it was recognized in the Single European Act that the expected prosperity from removing barriers to trade would not be evenly spread through member states; indeed certain geographical areas and sectors of industry could well be adversely affected, leading to marked regional disparities. These disparities could obstruct progress towards full economic, political and social integration. The Act therefore acknowledged that positive intervention was required, which would be achieved through reform of the structural funds. The main aim of these reforms was to target funds at specific problems and areas through a more co-ordinated system of pro-grammes, rather than projected-based assistance. This was implemented through five key changes:

1. Strengthening the role of the Commission in selecting regions and administering funds.
2. Simplifying financial procedures.
3. Improving the process of monitoring funds.
4. Co-ordinating the use of separate funds more effectively.
5. Increasing the total size of these funds from £5 billion in 1988 to £16 billion in 1994, with further increases planned up to the year 2000, by which time they are expected to equal about one-third of the Commission's total budget. A major review of the reformed structural funds is expected in 1999.

The effect of the reforms has been to narrow the field of those who are eligible and to sharpen the competition for a share of resources. The structural funds are now intended primarily to compensate those regions which are below the EU averages in terms of employment, education and training, environmental stan-dards and economic growth. The old system of quotas for member states has been abandoned and instead an informal agreement has been reached under which 'indica-tive' allocations are decided in advance.

Structural funds are geared to specific objectives, and total EU allocations for the two years 1994/95 and 1995/96 are summarized in Table 11.3. The UK's indicative allocation from the funds for the five years up to 1999 is shown in Table 11.4. Northern Ireland was the first and for several years the only 'Objective 1' area within the UK, but early in 1993 some other parts of the UK, including Scotland and declining coal field areas were added.

Table 11.3   EU structural funds: Objectives and allocations 1994–96

Objective	Available funds 1994–96 (ECU billions)
Objective 1: Assistance for undeveloped regions	102.030
Objective 2: Assistance for regions affected by the decline of traditional industries	16.220
Objective 3: combating long term unemployment and integrating young people into the labour market	16.775
Objective 4: Helping workers adapt to technological change	
Objective 5(a) Structural reform of agriculture	6.056
Objective 5(b) Assistance to rural areas	6.667
Objective 6: Assistance for the development of underpopulated regions in Sweden & Finland	Figure unavailable as fund introduced only in 1995

Source: Local Government International Bureau, 1995

Table 11.4   UK structural funds allocation (million ECU)

Objective	ERDF	ESF	EAGGF	Total
Objective 1	1332	747.2	245.9	2325.1
Objective 2*	(Combined allocation)			2142
Objectives 3 & 4	(Combined allocation)			3377
Objective 5	(Combined allocation)			1178

* Allocation for Objective 2 is for 1994/95 and 1995/96 financial years only

Source: European Commission General Report 1994

Under Objectives 2 and 5b, the policy of targeting funds more precisely means there is now only a relatively small number of local authorities which can receive funding. These are in areas designated by the Department of Trade and Industry as Assisted Areas (chiefly in north-west England, plus parts of Scotland and Wales). Britain has been allocated the largest share of Objective 2 funds – 2,142 million ECU out of a total of 16,220 billion ECU available under this heading (see Table 11.5), but a review by the Commission of areas eligible for Objective 2 is expected in 1996. This may well lead to a reduction in funds coming to local authorities, though it will not affect Objective 1 areas, where commitments have been made up to 1999.

In the case of Objectives 3, 4, and 5a potentially all local authorities are eligible to receive funds. However, because Objectives 3 and 4 are mainly concerned with financing vocational training and employment schemes, these are controlled and administered by the Department of Education and Employment (DEE) which receives

Table 11.5 Structural fund assistance for Objective 2 regions, UK compared to other Member States (million ECU 1994–96)

Country	ERDF	ESF	Total
Belgium	130.1	29.9	160
Denmark	44.2	11.8	56
Germany	514.5	218.5	733
Spain	870.1	259.9	1130
France	1452	314	1766
Italy	542.3	141.7	684
Luxembourg	6.1	0.9	7
Netherlands	205.9	94.1	300
United Kingdom	(Combined allocation)		2142

Source: European Commission, General Report 1994

the majority of the allocated funds. A further requirement of the reformed structural funds is that applicants should be included within a 'Regional Operational Programme' addressing some particular economic development need.

Apart from the transition to majority voting which speeded up decision-making on a large range of issues, the Single European Act emphasized a new spirit of partnership; between the Commission and the national, regional and local institutions of the member states. This has enlarged the scope for direct relationships between the Commission and public authorities that are not necessarily organs of central government, an important pointer to the Maastricht Treaty (see below). Nevertheless, central government has retained a strong co-ordinating role in the administration of the structural funds. It retains the right of submission to the Commission and can still effectively veto or amend the content of Operational Programmes, even though they are largely prepared by groups of local authorities and other bodies acting as 'quasi-regions'. The process of preparing Programmes has also become more elaborate, as the responsibilities of both local and central government have been split up and parcelled out to other agencies, including some which are private sector dominated such as the Training and Enterprise Councils (TECs) and development corporations. From the local authority point of view, this has complicated the process of acquiring EU funds, on account of the time spent in co-ordination, lobbying parallel interest groups and research in order to demonstrate that a project is consistent with the Objective as defined by the Commission as well, of course, as with current national policies.

The tensions between local and central government over mainstream regional funds have been partially relieved by the growth of separate Community Initiatives, (i.e. specialist funds), aimed at remedying economic problems common to certain categories of regions. Examples of these Initiatives include KONVER (aimed at helping areas affected by the run-down of defence-related industries), RETEX (promoting diversification in regions that are over-dependent on textile and clothing manufacture) and RECHAR (declining coal mining areas). The operation of these funds makes it difficult for central government to forecast the receipts from EU funds in any particular year and therefore to deduct an equivalent amount from what would otherwise be available from the Exchequer.

Funds are also available for Pilot Initiatives in inter-regional co-operation which, by definition, benefit local and regional authorities. The PACTE programme promotes exchanges of experience (by way of seminars, conferences and exhibitions) between authorities, while the OUVERTURE and ECOS programmes, supporting inter-regional co-operation projects and networks of public authorities, aims at transfer of know-how to less developed areas and improving the effectiveness of economic development programmes (CEU 1995). There is considerable scope for enterprising public bodies to take advantage of the Initiatives, although the financial benefits are small compared to regional funds.

The spin-off from what is now an extensive range of EU funding sources is that many local authorities, especially in metropolitan areas, find themselves drawn into international activities at both elected member and officer level. They have developed policies, patterns of influence and sources of funds to promote these activities. An example is Eurocities, the association of 60 cities across Europe which seeks to increase co-operation between its members at a practical level and to share in the decision processes of the EU, (European Association of Metropolitan Cities 1994).

11.5.3   The Committee of the Regions

The growing confidence of local authorities at European level was formally recognized in the Maastricht Treaty of 1992. The Committee of the Regions (CoR) consisting exclusively of representatives from the regional and local authorities of the EU reflects the Treaty's commitment 'to work for an ever closer union among the peoples in Europe, in which decisions are taken as close as possible to the citizen' (European Union 1995). In other words it exemplifies the principle of **subsidiarity**. The application of subsidiarity in practice has tended to be qualified by the UK government which argues that it is chiefly aimed at returning power from EU institutions to national (but not sub-national) institutions. Accordingly, the negotiations surrounding implementation of the Maastricht Treaty saw the government seeking to control in one way or another the selection of UK representatives on the new Committee. In the Autumn of 1992 and early 1993, local authorities mounted a sustained campaign at Westminster and in Whitehall during the passage of the domestic legislation needed to give effect to the Treaty. A combination of well-reasoned argument and back-bench dissidence eventually won the issue in local government's favour.

The Committee consists of 222 elected representatives, drawn from local and regional authorities across the EU, and the allocation of seats is shown in Table 11.6. the UK's representation is not explicitly organized on party political lines (in contrast to the European Parliament) but reflects a balance of gender, geographical areas, types of authorities, political and specialist interests. The Committee has the right under the Maastricht Treaty to be consulted on the following matters:

- the framework of policy on education;
- EU policy on culture;
- EU policy on public health;
- defining guidelines upon the establishment of trans-European communication networks;

Table 11.6 Local and regional government in Europe: representation on the Committee of the Regions

	State regions	2 Non-state regions	County/ province	Unitary or lower tier	Total
Austria	9*	–	–	3*	12
Belgium	12*	–	–	–	12
Denmark	–	–	4*	5*	9
Germany	21*	–	1*	2*	24
Spain	–	17*	–	3*	20
Greece	–	–	–	12*	12
France	–	12*	6*	6*	24
Ireland	–	–	7*	2*	9
Italy	–	12*	5*	7*	24
Luxembourg	–	–	–	6*	6
Netherlands	–	–	6*	6*	12
Portugal	–	2	–	10*	12
Finland	–	–	–	9*	9
Sweden	–	–	4*	8*	12
UK	–	–	8*	16*	24

Key:
* Represent the existence of a uniform tier of directly elected government in that country. Thus Irish Regions and Spanish Provinces are not shown since these are indirectly elected tiers which co-ordinate activities of the lower tier. Portugal and Finland have regional government only for Madeira, Azores and Alund.

- specific action within the framework of policy on economic and social cohesion;
- specific action within the framework and co-ordination of the structural funds and the regulations concerning the implementation of the European Regional Development Fund.

These are, of course, matters for which local authorities are more often than not responsible for implementation or enforcement. The Committee's chief mode of working is to produce a formal Opinion – essentially a brief critique indicating any recommended modifications – in response to legislative proposals by the Commission. Opinions are usually drafted by one or more of the eight commissions and four sub-commissions (see Table 11.7) which are in effect sub-committees of the CoR.

CoR Opinions are not binding on either the Commission or the Council of Ministers and some important areas of policy, such as economic and social welfare are excluded from its purview unless, say, the Economic and Social Committee (or the Council) decided it was appropriate in a particular case. Although the CoR can expect its Opinions to be given serious consideration, because it acts as the voice of local and regional government at the European level, it remains to be seen how much more influence the Committee will have on EU decision-making, especially as some national governments like the UK are sceptical of its value.

Table 11.7　The Eight Commissions and Four Sub-Commissions of the Committee of Regions

Commission number	Function of Commission
1	Regional development, economic development and local and regional finances
Sub Commission 1	Local and regional finances
2	Spatial planning, agriculture, fisheries, forestry, marine environment and upland areas
Sub Commission 2	Tourism and rural areas
3	Transport and communications networks
Sub Commission 3	Telecommunications
4	Urban policies
5	Land use planning, environment and energy
6	Education and training
7	Citizen's Europe, research, culture, youth and consumers
Sub Commission 7	Youth and sport
8	Economic and social cohesion, social policy and public health

(*Source: European Union: Committee of the Regions 1995*)

11.6　MANAGEMENT CHANGES RESULTING FROM CLOSER EUROPEAN INTEGRATION

International developments affecting local authorities, particularly in the 1990s, have had important implications for their internal organization. In some cases, comprehensive management reviews have been undertaken to assess the impact of greater European involvement. A review for the London Borough of Croydon (1991) for example, demonstrated the importance of not compartmentalizing European issues in one unit or department: the advent of the single market and associated policies now have ramifications across a wide range of services. They require co-ordination and awareness at the highest levels and regular machinery for keeping up to date with developments. They also imply a network of relationships running through the organization, so that more junior staff can be informed of regulations and obligations which affect individual services.

Some authorities, such as Birmingham City Council, Kent, Essex, Devon and Cornwall County Councils, maintain offices in Brussels; this is particularly important for authorities which have taken an active role in economic development or provide information to local business and voluntary groups as part of their 'enabling role' (Ennals and O'Brien 1990). Other authorities share joint office arrangements, like the Federation of East Midlands Local Authorities, which provides an information and communication service based in Brussels for the authorities in its region. One indicator of the growing importance of early access to information is the number of European Liaison Officers (ELOs) who have been appointed to maintain contact with the Commission. By the end of 1995, there were over 300 ELOs in post.

The Local Government International Bureau (LGIB), developed from a unit within the Association of Metropolitan Authorities, was set up as an independent body serving local government in 1989. Apart from channelling information to ELOs, it provides an impressive array of publications and services on a more general basis and is a leading force for education and influencing opinions on UK participation in the EU. It also acts as the secretariat for the local government representation on European bodies, notably the CoR. The LGIB's efforts are backed up by other central organizations of local government such as the Local Government Management Board, the local authority associations and the Audit Commission.

Local authority officers also play an important part in negotiations about the setting of common technical standards for products and equipment in the Community. Standardization issues have been increasingly devolved from the Commission officials to the European standards bodies and access to these is considerably easier for local government representatives. A special fund has been created by the local authority associations in the UK to help meet the costs of travel for their delegates to meetings on standards.

Finally, mention should be made of the upsurge in voluntary activities and partnerships, involving local authorities with their counterparts in other EU countries. The major example is town-twinning, which is undertaken almost always for social and cultural reasons but may often lead to commercial and business co-operation. The educational impact of twinning arrangements is difficult to quantify, but it is widely believed to reinforce a European outlook among managers and decision-makers in local government and this is encouraged by all the international bodies reviewed above (CEC 1991).

11.7   INTERNATIONAL LOCAL GOVERNMENT BODIES

The origins of international representation, other than through the EU, go back to the early 1950s and beyond. The Council of European Municipalities was formed in 1951 by a group of local government leaders who believed that the successful rebuilding of Europe required the involvement of local communities working together across national boundaries. It is in effect a federation of national local government associations. The Council changed its name in 1981 to the Council of European Municipalities and Regions (CEMR) to reflect the institution of regional tiers of government in several European states, but its progress was not helped by a long-running friction with the International Union of Local Authorities (IULA), formed in 1913 to exchange experience and undertake comparative studies between local authority practitioners. In 1971, however, CEMR and IULA agreed to collaborate on European matters and in 1990 settled the arrangements for a merger of their operations at European level.

Another organization dating from the 1950s is the Standing Conference of Local and Regional Authorities of Europe (CLRAE), formed under the aegis of the Council of Europe in 1957. For many years CLRAE, like CEMR, sought to raise its influence by communicating views to the European Commission and later the European Parliament. It was agreed at the European summit in Vienna in October 1993 to give CLRAE a firmer constitutional base and increased status. The new title of Congress of Local and Regional Authorities of Europe was adopted and the internal structure of specialist committees was abolished, to be replaced by *ad hoc* working groups on specific topics. The agenda of CLRAE is designed to foster co-operation between local and regional authorities throughout Europe (rather than the narrower grouping of EU countries) and this has a special significance since the demise of the former Soviet Union and countries previously within its sphere of influence. Bulgaria and Romania became full members of CLRAE in 1994 and observer delegations now attend from Russia, Latvia and the Ukraine.

The rise of these international bodies is symptomatic of the striving by local authorities, not least in the UK, for a stronger voice in European affairs. In part, this pressure has been nurtured by the trend in most states of mainland Europe during the 1970s and 80s towards devolving functions and powers to sub-national levels of government. The most obvious example is the creation of a regional tier of government in France in 1982, but there are parallels in Belgium, Spain and elsewhere. UK official policy has been very much out of line with this trend and the Government continues to refuse to sign the European Charter for Local Self-government. Nevertheless, British local authorities have shown growing determination to make their voices heard at the level above national government and a growing expertise in lobbying international institutions.

Perhaps the clearest demonstration of this is the way in which local government has organized itself to influence the 1996 Intergovernmental Conference (IGC) of EU Member States. The Conference marks the next stage in the development of the Union and has potentially wide-ranging constitutional implications. As such, it is important for local authorities that their position is given due recognition. They have agreed to press for the inclusion in the Maastricht Treaty of a clear definition of the principle of subsidiarity, and the creation of a legal base for the principle of local self-government. For the CoR, they would like to see greater independence and a guarantee of its democratic legitimacy; its role in urban policy and racial equality should be given a legal foundation also. The local government IGC campaign has many other facets, including a demand for stronger commitment to partnership in decision-making by central departments, but it is by no means clear what practical impact it will have. That does not however affect the main point that UK local authorities feel confident and clear in their objectives to play a part in European affairs as well as in their local area.

11.8   CONCLUSION

Despite the cautious and rather bureaucratic approach taken initially to EU membership, local government continues to find ways of exploiting the benefits. These benefits are financial, first and foremost, but have become increasingly diverse. There have been wide-ranging impacts on organization and management. Frequently these impacts have been overlaid or obscured by domestic legislation in such matters of CCT, but the rise of staffing numbers and skills related to enforcement responsibilities is clear, as is the growth of local representation in a variety of international decision-making fora.

Many changes resulting from EU membership have been absorbed as a part of the normal process of management and policy-making in local authorities and the effects on manpower or finance are correspondingly slight. With encouragement from the Audit Commission and the central organizations of local government, there is now much greater interest in planning and managing the opportunities from EU membership, whether these are financial (as in the form of access to structural funds) or political (e.g. through international associations) or cultural (as in town-twinning).

11.9 CHAPTER SUMMARY

The following key learning points emerge from this chapter:

- Public sector bodies did not have much knowledge or experience of operating at a European level prior to 1973; their horizons and functions were limited to strictly local or UK domestic activities. 'Joining Europe' provoked a re-appraisal of roles and ambitions.
- Britain's accession to the EU was conceived initially in terms of bringing the public sector 'into line' with European legislation at minimum cost. Compliance was a pre-requisite for playing an active part as a member state.
- It also required the extension and development of enforcement mechanisms, particularly by local authorities. The growth of these inspectorial functions was balanced by reductions in other types of staff and a re-ordering of priorities.
- The renegotiation of the EU budget by Margaret Thatcher was accompanied by much larger allocations of funds available for regional aid. In other words, political success at a national level was accompanied by increasing flows of resources to regions.
- Public bodies, including local authorities, organized themselves to take advantage of funding opportunities. Thus institutional changes were incentive-led, against a background of tight public expenditure control.
- Constraints imposed by central government on public bodies, and especially local government, increased the attractions of seeking influence at the supra-national level. There is a clear trend of institutional development and resource allocation towards strengthening local authorities' participation in Europe and other international fora.
- Cultural contacts and bi-lateral or multilateral co-operation across national boundaries have accompanied the growing experience and confidence of local government at European level.

TEXT-BASED QUESTIONS

1. What were the most important ways in which Britain's accession to the European Community initially impacted on local government? In what respects were the impacts less than expected?

2. Why have local authorities organized themselves to attract resources from EU structural and other funds? How successful have they been?

3. How have relationships between central and local government been modified in the wake of UK membership of the European Union?

4.   Discuss the proposition that local democratic forces continue to assert them-
     selves in the European context, in spite of constraints imposed by national
     government.

5.   What effect has EU membership had on local government manpower levels?
     What other factors can you identify which may have affected these levels?

ASSIGNMENT

Devise a structure and programme of action for a 'European Relations Unit'
within a local authority. Suggest the terms of reference, staff required, functions
and linkages (both internally and externally) that might be required. What skills
and training do you think the staff of the Unit might need?

FURTHER READING

Audit Commission (1991) *A Rough Guide to Europe: Local Authorities and the EEC*, HMSO,
    London.
Bongers, P.N. (1990) *Local Government and 1992*, Longman, Harlow.
Burkitt, B. and Baimbridge, M. (1992) European Community Developments, in *Public Domain
    1992* (eds F. Terry and P. Jackson), Chapman & Hall, London.
The Cecchini Report (1988) *The European Challenge 1992: The Benefits of a Single Market*, Gower,
    London.
Commission of the European Union (1995), *Sources of European Community Funding* (2nd edition).
Digings, L. (1991) *Competitive Tendering and the European Communities*, AMA, London.
Gallacher, J. (1995), *Committee of the Regions: An Opportunity for Influence*, Local Government
    International Bureau, London.
Kerr, A. and Radford, M. (1994) 'TUPE or not TUPE: Competitive Tendering and the Transfer
    Laws', *Public Money & Management* **14** (4), Blackwell, Oxford.
Terry, F. (1992) The Single Market and Public Services, in *Public Domain*, (eds F. Terry and P.
    Jackson), Chapman & Hall, London

CONCLUSION: THE PROBLEMATICAL NATURE OF PUBLIC MANAGEMENT REFORM

12

Chris Painter and Kester Isaac-Henry

12.1 CHAPTER PREVIEW

This concluding chapter draws together, analyses and adds insights to the findings of the preceding chapters, in the process returning to many of the themes discussed in Chapter 1. Although it argues that the period since the late 1970s suffered from too many ill-conceived policy initiatives, with waves of legislation predicated on ideological convictions – causing undue turbulence and uncertainty – it also suggests that it would be churlish to portray recent public management reforms in entirely negative terms. The shifting balance of power between service providers and service users, the enabling state and separation of strategic from operational considerations are encouraging public service managers to give considerable thought to service delivery modes, with potentially liberating consequences for 'reinvented' government. Many public authorities are nonetheless still struggling to come to terms with the magnitude of the challenges thereby presented.

There are, moreover, many paradoxes. The rhetoric does not always accord with the substance of reform. Those preoccupations associated with traditional public administration such as public accountability and probity are now returning with a vengeance to haunt the new public management paradigm. There are signs that the values underpinning the neo-liberal project, forming the political context for public management reforms in the 1980s and 1990s, are beginning to succumb to 'new wave' ideas – for example, those emanating from the 'communitarian' and 'stakeholder' movements.

This final chapter therefore specifically reflects upon:

- the 'biases' of the Conservative public management reform agenda;
- the significance of the concepts of choice, competition, markets and quality in this context;
- what the nature of the 'stakeholder base' reveals about the characteristics of these reforms;
- the accountability issues posed by the management reforms;
- the implications of the way they have been handled for the effective management of change;
- the values that may inform managing future change in the public services and governmental institutions.

12.2   THE PUBLIC MANAGEMENT REFORM AGENDA AND CITIZEN'S CHARTER

A recurring theme when considering public management reform is the extent to which it should take its cue from business management practices. Given the Thatcherite agenda – as indicated in Chapter 2 with public sector practices made prime targets – too much preoccupation with the unique characteristics of the public domain, other than at the most politically-sensitive levels, could easily be construed as a complacent 'can't do' mentality:

> There had been an undue emphasis on the undoubted constraints of a public sector location ... the impediments to change were ... expressed with greater lucidity than was the need for improved performance.
>
> *(Parry 1992: 20)*

Indeed, one of the hallmarks of Thatcherism became the extent to which the principles of good private sector management were seen as worthy of emulation, with state operations reconstructed along 'business' lines as in the case of the *Next Steps* departmental agencies. As Chapter 8 pointed out, this was to mean challenging even the unique nature of health service administration. Yet, the belief in the distinctiveness of the public services still widely persists. Examining the key differences shaping management behaviour and culture Pollitt and Harrison contend:

> This does not make public service management totally different ... but it does imply that many of the prescriptions of generic management will require considerable adaption before they will fit in this distinctive context.
>
> *(1992:2)*

Thus, against the background of the management competencies movement, Chapter 5 highlighted the case for a new public services managerialism rather than generic commercial managerialism.

Nonetheless, many of the developments explored in '
underlined the extent to which a 'consumerist-marke'
taken hold in the public services.

It was graphically highlighted in Chapter 7 on education and in Chapter 8 on health, where the greater emphasis on consumer needs and satisfaction has had the supporting infrastructure not only of the *Patient's Charter* but of the community health councils (CHCs). This consumerist-orientation has shifted the balance of power away from the hitherto dominant professional service providers. An initiative to which John Major repeatedly reaffirmed his commitment, it was the paradigm that lay at the heart of the *Citizen's Charter* (Prime Minister-Cm 1599 1991) as it spawned innumerable individual public service charters, including the patient's charter referred to above. Indeed, it has been observed that:

> In ... areas such as 'managerialism', where change was relatively incremental under Thatcher, the tempo of change appears in fact to have increased since November 1990, being accentuated by policies, such as the Citizen's Charter, which Major has claimed as his own ... in this area Major may have been more radical than his predecessor, pushing neo-liberal reforms further than she was willing or placed to do.
>
> (*Atkinson and Cope 1994: 51*)

The *Citizen's Charter's* central themes have been touched upon in a number of the chapters, but they are worth reiterating, providing as they do a very clear guide to

---

- raising public service standards, explicitly indicating what can reasonably be expected, and making these services more answerable to users by taking account of their convenience and views, therefore with appropriate channels for consultation;

- the perceived importance in this connection of greater choice and competition (subjecting more local council services to tendering and a radical extension of 'market testing' in Whitehall being notable manifestations);

- independent review of performance and the publication of information so derived, preferably in a form enabling comparisons to be made (as in the case of school national curriculum tests and public examination league tables);

- providing remedies in the event of specified standards not being achieved, including financial compensation (in relation for example to targets for punctuality and reliability on the railways), with improved complaints and disputes procedures for service users

---

Figure 12.1 Key Citizen's Charter principles

the primary directions in which public management reform has increasingly been steered.

However, as this book has demonstrated, the practical application of a number of these principles to the public sector remains problematic. Choice and competition provide two immediate instances of such difficulties, closely intertwined as they are.

12.3 CHOICE, COMPETITION, CONSUMERS AND MARKETS

Choice is central to consumer behaviour in economic markets, yet in the public services it can be more apparent than real and of largely symbolic significance for the desired changes in relationships between service producers and consumers. Thus, Chapters 7 and 8 considered the problems in addressing the needs of the latter in education and health respectively, with expectations often not being fulfilled. Whatever the aspirations regarding parental empowerment, in practice it is often the educational producers who remain in the driving seat, with parental choice at best heavily circumscribed. The more popular schools 'select' pupils rather than the reverse, especially with the easing of the rules applying to selective admissions in the state sector. In the NHS the general practitioner chooses on behalf of the patient. Chapter 8 highlighted the role of the community health councils as formally constituted statutory bodies to represent and articulate consumer views. Yet, even in this connection there were a number of factors undermining their capacity to effectively promote consumer interests.

Moreover, account must be taken of the level at which budgetary and expenditure priorities continue to be determined. Do public service users have any real say on absolute levels of service spending, or whether this service or another will be given greater relative resource priority? Again, in economic markets changing consumer preferences should be reflected in changing patterns of production, with resources reallocated accordingly. But in the case of public services we are ultimately thrown back on the (collective) political process which, if opinion survey data is to be believed, only imperfectly registers public preferences (Common, Flynn and Mellon 1992: 47–9). Indeed, just when service users are emerging as significant micro-level players, so the scope for influencing the larger macro-level issues may actually be diminishing, even the professional service deliverers and local politicians finding themselves increasingly excluded at this level (Richards 1992b). And in the prevailing public expenditure climate, the language of restricted entitlement and selective targeting has become more striking. The reality therefore is one of limited access and resource rationing, not least in the delivery of health care (Chapter 8), rather than promotion of service usage. Consequently, given revenue and resource constraints, one of the distinctive burdens on public service managers remains combating 'excess demand' (Pollitt and Harrison 1992: 7).

Difficulties arise too with the idea of a more competitive environment. On the surface this is an increasing reality for the public services. The publication of performance data – one of many developments underlining the increasing strategic importance of information as a resource (Chapter 6) – is assisting those limited customer choices that are available. Also, Chapter 7 emphasized how marketing skills are assuming growing significance as part of successful public services management. The Education (Schools) Act 1992 even made provision for 'failed' institutions to be put into the equivalent of 'receivership', responsibility for running them to be taken over by special teams. Such schools may ultimately be closed, a power that has indeed now been activated (Chapter 7). Moreover, competitive tendering challenged formerly monopolistic service suppliers, promoting fresh organizational thinking about service outputs and performance.

Even in this connection, however, any evaluation depends on how widely the 'balance sheet' is drawn with respect to potential costs as well as benefits (discussed below). Furthermore, there are criticisms of performance targets and indicators set externally (for example by government departments or the Audit Commission) which may well skew the way services are developed to the detriment of locally expressed needs. In any case, service aspects most likely to be measured are those relating to quantity as opposed to quality because of the often unweighted nature of relevant variables, as in the case of school league tables (or other so-called 'star ratings') (Chapter 4).

Indeed, like choice, competition may be present more in form than substance. Common, Flynn and Mellon (1992: 14) point out that often 'reforms which purport to introduce competition stop short of establishing free, competitive markets' – not least because of the continuing importance of government in determining funding. There are also the statutory restrictions on the competitive repertoires that can be adopted in the new public service markets, including the freedom of managers to diversify, change the organization's portfolio of activities and therefore the nature of its 'business' (Pollitt and Harrison 1992).

Moreover, with the emphasis during the ascendancy of Thatcherism on government and bureaucratic failure, less prominence was accorded to the market imperfections of monopoly power, external effects on third parties and information asymmetries (where one or more parties to a transaction are disadvantaged because of lack of information): 'In the rush to introduce the virtues of the market economy into government operations it often seems that the known limitations of markets are being forgotten' (Bowers 1992: 46). Thus, one or more of the above market failures are likely to apply to the privatized utilities, the contracting out process, or the (internal) markets devised for health care and education and with price signals in any case often rigged or manipulated to produce what – from the Government's point of view – is the desired outcome. In this respect, as in others, the application of competition to education has proved problematic (Chapter 7). The market is often managed. One interesting example of market failure relating to private security provision was cited in Chapter 9. Certainly, the characteristics of actual public service markets and their implications need to be borne in mind, rather than just theoretical abstractions or ideological rhetoric. Where elements of competition are present, which of the many varying characteristics of 'real' market structures prevail can also be crucial when devising appropriate competitive organizational strategies (Common, Flynn and Mellon 1992: Ch 2–3; Flynn 1990: Ch 4).

12.4   STANDARDS, QUALITY, STAKEHOLDERS AND MOTIVATION

12.4.1   Quality and shifting sands

The *Citizen Charter's* concern with public service standards immediately raises the issue of quality. As Ransom (1992: 58, 59) observes, it 'has focused a spotlight on quality of service . . . and the extent to which this can ultimately only be measured by the responses of those using a public service . . .' Yet, as explained in Chapter 4, here is another problematical idea when applied to the public services: 'quality is a slippery concept, which carries a range of meanings and serves a variety of purposes' (Coote and Pfeffer 1991). Those meanings, mostly originating in the commercial sector, include the attainment of luxury standards; differences in identified tangible attributes (e.g. league tables); fitness for purpose and conformance to specification or recognized standards (e.g. education inspectorate reports); and not least the satisfaction of customer requirements (emphasizing user evaluation) (Coote and Pfeffer 1991; Knox and McAlister 1995; Rees 1992; Walsh 1991b). Determining quality raises more difficulties in services than in manufacturing products because of the former's special features and is particularly elusive to pin down in the case of public services (Gaster 1995; Rees 1992; Walsh 1991), not least because of the complexity of the transactions undertaken by these people-processing operations (Pollitt and Harrison 1992).

With elements of coercion, dependency and stigma often present, the interactions between public service providers and users can be very different from conventional commercial transactions. The precise nature of the relationships involved – and indeed judgements about who are the primary 'customers' – is therefore a crucial consideration when designing service delivery systems (Commons, Flynn and Mellon 1992: Ch 6; Flynn 1990: Ch 7).

> But what is particularly at issue is how public services also have to take account of wider reference groups than just the immediate consumers (Pollitt and Harrison 1992; Rees 1992).

It is important for those public managers who are operating in increasingly competitive-like conditions to take on board the significant contribution of marketing. But because of the many 'publics' to whom they must answer – not least their organizational 'sponsors' (ultimately responsible for resourcing given the nature of public sector funding) – its role too is more multi-dimensional than in the normal business model (Alexander 1992). This is not to mention the long-standing tradition of social 'marketing' or public education campaigns. Hence the contention that a distinctive approach to quality is required for a modern welfare system which, in adapting the various techniques derived from the commercial sector, recognizes that public services do have different objectives from private enterprises, including the need to consider a much wider number of stakeholders and interests (Coote and Pfeffer 1991).

But approaches to quality in the public sector have reflected broader shifts of emphasis (Rees 1992). The former public administration paradigm centred on the political and professional domains, with administrators acting in an essentially mediatory role. But this gave way to the efficiency paradigm, transforming the administrative role into a managerial one, so exerting pressure on professional service deliverers to realize central politicians' objectives of lower spending. Then came another paradigm, making consumers increasingly significant actors, presenting challenges to both the political and professional domains (Richards 1992b).

Thus, during the 1980s heyday of the so-called efficiency paradigm quality was very closely associated with value for money (VFM) and the performance indicators movement (Chapter 4), notably the search for measures that could act as surrogates for profitability in the private sector. The controversy thereby generated has already been alluded to, both in terms of what was being measured and whether the most significant service quality dimensions were indeed susceptible to quantifiable or numerical values. The terms 'economicization' and 'accountingization' have been used to encapsulate a proclivity to elevate measurable outputs at the expense of less quantifiable considerations (Hood 1995). It also exemplifies how ideas in fashionable currency can be renovated versions of earlier doctrines (Jordan 1994c). The so-called 'new' public management has been portrayed as a late twentieth-century equivalent of 'Taylorism' (named after a leading light in the much earlier scientific management movement):

> the particular species of managerialism which Reaganite Washington and Thatcherite Whitehall sought to introduce to the public services in the 1980s had a certain 'neo-Taylorian' character ... Taylorism ... proceeded on the basis that previously unmeasured aspects of the work process could and should be measured, by management, and then used as the basis for controlling and rewarding effort ... This is not so far ... from the ... public-service systems of performance indicators, individual performance review and merit pay.
>
> *(Pollitt 1990: 15,16)*

Chapter 9 indicated the limitations of performance measures/comparisons and associated debate about what constitutes useful indicators in the policing context. But it is particularly the school tests and examination league tables that again come to mind. Even heads of independent schools (likely to emerge favourably in the rankings) contended that that which is to be most valued is immeasurable, for example pastoral care, or activities designed to inculcate some notion of wider social responsibility, as opposed to formal examination results (Chapter 7). For the service providers, there was also the paradox of aspirations to higher quality existing alongside the evident 'deprofessionalization' or 'deskilling' of public services – seen in measures to dilute professional training standards, use of ancillary staff or outsourcing – and induced by pressures for less costly delivery systems.

By the 1990s, as can be gleaned from the *Citizen's Charter*, the focus of attention had moved to service recipients, that is towards a customer orientation, thus raising in importance user evaluations of quality. It posed a further challenge to producer power and professional autonomy. Past neglect of consumer wants, taken in conjunction with the shortcomings of professional peer review, in fact provided a rationale for managerial intervention as part of the quality assurance process. But the issues arising from this managerial-professional relationship are just as delicate as those of the user-professional one if insensitively handled. Perceived threats discourage professionals from adopting a frank and open attitude to quality, especially where suspicion lingers that cost-cutting remains the hidden agenda (Pollitt 1990). Indeed, a positive restructuring of relationships was not helped when 'the attempts to increase control and enforce economy in the early and mid-1980s sometimes engraved resentment in the minds of service providers' (Pollitt and Harrison 1992: 133). Despite more recent emphasis on quality improvement and meeting user requirements, the pressure on public budgets – if anything – was becoming even more intense:

> quality and consumer responsiveness sit alongside a fierce and continuing concern with economy and efficiency. It is not clear which group of values will take priority when a trade-off has to be made.
>
> (*Pollitt 1993: 189*)

Pre-electoral pressures on the Major government for tax cuts from within the ranks of the Conservative Party went some way towards answering that question!

12.4.2   Stakeholderism and power relations

From the perspective of a user focus, apart from the problems generated by information asymmetries because of the differential information respectively available to service providers and consumers (Walsh 1991), we are driven back to the wider (social) reference groups for the public services. The 'stakeholder' concept, as noted in Chapter 4, clearly has resonance in this context given the multiple interests that have to be accommodated (Pollitt and Harrison 1992) – not just customers, but also taxpayers and citizens, politicians, professionals, managers and staff, as well as various other organized groups.

The principle of 'stakeholderism' nonetheless has a very tenuous basis in the UK's institutional structures. The model of corporate governance is not one of 'stakeholder capitalism'. The 'winner-take-all' principle characteristic of our political system is itself a symptom of the lack of a 'stakeholder democracy' (Hutton 1996). The 'managerialization' of public institutions has – if anything – the effect of further narrowing the stakeholder base, notably where governing bodies have been reconstituted as streamlined business-style boards (as in the case of health authorities) (Painter 1991). This exclusivity rather than inclusivity is something that has been particularly pronounced in the management of the unelected state dealt with in Chapter 10. It was thus perhaps no accident that Blair's 'New Labour' therefore began to see political mileage in embracing the principle of the 'stakeholder society' (Hutton 1996).

> But what has been going on only makes sense when seen in terms of shifting power relations between potentially conflicting interests.

Certainly, as indicated above, it is about changing alignments involving political, managerial, professional and customer domains (Richards 1992b). As emphasized in Chapter 4, even the concept of quality itself is value-laden in the final analysis. Yet:

> To read some of the gurus it would be easy to suppose that quality is a value free concept, aiming to achieve something as apparently scientific and neutral as statistical control, conformance to specification ...
>
> (*Gaster 1995: 9*)

On the contrary, Walsh (1991) saw it as a contested issue, reflecting the particular perspective from which judgements are formed and a manifestation of changing social values.

12.4.3 Professionals, compliance and empowerment

Despite the ambiguities involved in distinguishing human resource management (HRM) from the more traditional personnel management function, Chapter 5 pointed to the importance of integrating new HRM initiatives into the broader strategic aims of the organization, given that the delivery of quality services is very much bound up with unlocking the potential of people:

> An important aspect of the service relationship is the way the organization treats its own workforce ... A demoralized workforce is unlikely to do more than a barely adequate job. In recent years, there has been a progressive demoralization of the workforce, especially the professional workforce, in many parts of public service.
>
> (*Flynn 1990: 182*)

The reasons for this partly relate back to the earlier discussion of changing power structures, notably the continuing tensions between the professional, managerial and political domains (Painter 1989).

CASE STUDY 12.1: The professional domain in the public services

- Some of the pertinent issues were highlighted by Metcalfe and Richards' case study of the Government Statistical Service, with its underlying theme of how the 'management of professionals is a major issue in public management . . .' (1990: 113).

- The professionals had seen their autonomy eroded by managerial incursions with the object of promoting cost-consciousness and in deference to the principle of customer sovereignty, notwithstanding wider public interest considerations bound up with the availability of government statistics.

- Professional integrity was also compromised by political interests, government tempted to ride roughshod over professional standards.

- Considerations of compliance seemed to be taking precedence over those of motivation when 'the major management problem in the professional field is how to get the best out of them, rather than how to get them to toe the line' (ibid.: 129).

The prominence of professionals therefore continued to raise distinctive management challenges in a public services context (Pollitt and Harrison 1992). This has applied particularly to the NHS with the pivotal importance of the health professionals and delicate issues involved in challenging organizational medical power (Chapter 8).

More generally, Duncan (1992a: 205) observes: 'Effective service delivery . . . depends crucially upon successful methods of managing, rewarding and motivating human resources.' This applies particularly to the employee commitment, so essential to the successful implementation of a consumer-oriented philosophy. It demands a climate very different from the hierarchical ethos of machine bureaucracies, sensitive to how the treatment by managers of their staff in turn affects attitudes towards the public. There is a powerful case for the empowerment of the 'front-line' employees nearest to the customer, as part of a culture based on trust, openness and support (Lovell 1992). Chapter 5 also addressed the need for management development strategies which reflect good practice, so that those concerned can more effectively meet the new challenges and changing demands of their own jobs. Some observers do indeed detect signs of a more positive approach to people management within government and therefore to human resource policy (Ransom 1992).

However, the efficacy of the 'new motivational substructures', put in place as a result of the dismantling of traditional public sector collective negotiating frameworks in favour of devolved bargaining and individual performance-related pay systems, is far from proven. There are many associated problems, not least the extent to which these new frameworks can be reconciled with the job attitudes and aspirations of public service employees (Duncan 1992a). The restructuring and downsizing of public service agencies – as elsewhere in the economy – also produces an environment of considerable insecurity. Moreover, as pointed out in Chapter 5, it would seem that competitive tendering has not only adversely affected employment terms and conditions, but also damaged equal opportunities policies.

Yet, these are increasingly critical matters given the emergence of quality management and related endeavours to institutionalize an ethos of continuous organizational improvement (Chapter 4). It is a notion integral to the *Citizen's Charter* philosophy, with its emphasis on performance standards that are to be progressively raised. In this respect, the quality issue is itself becoming bound up with one of the underlying themes of this book, namely the effective management of organizational change.

12.5   ACCOUNTABILITY: MANAGERIALISM AND DEMOCRATIC DEFICITS

12.5.1   The Balkanization of government

The debate about the accountability issues posed by public sector management reforms shows no signs of abating. This was addressed, for example, in Chapter 9 given the more tenuous links that the new police authorities have with elected local authorities, let alone the implications of the Security Service moving into traditional policing functions and the increasing prominence of a largely unregulated private security industry. It was also very much to the fore in Chapter 10 in the context of the growth of the unelected state.

> However, in common with the other concepts considered in this conclusion, the idea of accountability is an inherently ambiguous one.

Accountability to whom and for what? Different forms of accountability were identified in Chapters 1 and 4. The many forms included in Lawton and Rose's (1991) catalogue include political accountability (to an external public audience); managerial accountability (the internal organizational processes); professional accountability (peer reference groups); client accountability (consumer responsiveness); and legal accountability (judicial review). It is little wonder therefore that they regard accountability as 'a complex phenomenon' with 'a number of dimensions' (ibid: 23). This complexity clearly accords with the notion of multiple stakeholders and competing domains – including associated value conflicts – in the public sector.

It is the impact of recent developments on political or public accountability that has particularly ignited controversy, especially the repercussions of dismantling previously unified institutional structures. This fragmentation has taken various forms, but notably transferring powers and responsibilities from elected to appointed bodies. As highlighted in Chapter 10, the process has taken its toll on the structures of local democracy and accountability, bringing to the fore again the contentious issue of patronage. This trend threatens to compromise policy coherence and co-ordination. Ironically, it also increasingly places a premium on skills that do not necessarily come naturally to the new public managers. Previously adept in securing the compliance of their workforce and challenging countervailing power structures, they now need to be even more skilful in orchestrating agency networks, given the knock-on effects of the above for multi-agency collaboration. The complexity of associated multiple relationships has long been something with which public service organizations have had to grapple (Pollitt and Harrison 1992). But new linkages and partnerships are now having to be developed and cultivated

If anything, this fragmentation – or balkanization – of public service delivery has been accelerating (the dismantling of the railway service for privatization presenting an extreme example of this process!). Hence successive waves of self-governing hospital trusts. There has also been an attempt to accelerate the number of grant maintained schools, albeit with only limited success, notwithstanding the financial inducements to leave LEA control. Although it has always been difficult to discern any ordered pattern, recent developments have thus accentuated the 'organizational mess' of British administration – so that in the case of central administration now not only are there core departments but also executive agencies, non-departmental public bodies and increasing numbers of private contractors delivering services (Jordan 1994c).

There may come a point when this is so counter-productive that the virtues of previous organizational paradigms are re-discovered:

> Bureaucracies ... provide direct, hands-on control of services ... Should any future government rail against the constraints of fragmented service delivery systems and seek to steer, the tool it will turn to will be bureaucracy ...'
>
> *(Rhodes 1994: 151)*

Yet, this may underestimate the strategic capability of the system as a result of 'managerialization'. With public officials subject to explicit policy frameworks and charged with achieving specified performance targets, in fact scope exists for achieving tighter strategic policy control from the 'political centre' (Hood 1995). However, there are the usual ironies. In some respects, the restructured public sector may be fostering even more extreme bureaucratic pathologies, for example, the mounting paper chase that came to light when the tensions between prison management and Home Office ministers boiled over as a result of Derek Lewis's removal from the position of Director-General of the Service. This is not to mention the increasing transaction costs arising from contractual relationships, the purchaser-provider split and the internal market now characteristic of the organization of health care for example (Chapter 8).

> Moreover, apart from the threat posed to the values of local democracy by recent developments, there are also profound implications for the position of national elected institutions.

The experiences of Gerald Kaufman, the former Labour frontbench spokesman, when writing to the 'responsible' minister concerning constituency social security cases – letters promptly passed on to the Chief Executive of the Benefits Agency – make this abundantly clear. He maintained that it is a situation replicated in all the Next Steps agencies, described as 'bits and pieces ... of government departments which were once accountable' (Kaufman 1992). His reflections are therefore worth quoting in some detail. Referring to the position of MPs, Kaufman observes:

> I want all of us, when we raise an individual case concerning our constituents, to have that case considered by a minister. Members of Parliament have ... only two rights. One is the right of privileged speech within Parliament. The other is the right of access to ministers ... If ministers seek to eliminate one of those rights, as they are doing by delegating cases to agencies ... they are diminishing the rights of our constituent ... They are diminishing democracy.

The minister, Kaufman continued, did not seem to understand that whatever the content of a letter:

> if he signed it he would have had to have read it, or at any rate to have pretended to read it ... he would have been accountable to Parliament. Parliamentary accountability is an essential part of ... democracy.

12.5.2 Ministerial responsibility and public ethics

Thus, at the operational, as distinct from strategic, level a form of 'depoliticization' is taking place with – a theme pursued in Chapter 10 – the emphasis increasingly being placed upon internal managerial accountability rather than external public accountability (despite it being the intention of the *Citizen's Charter* that appropriate performance information should be made available to public service users). Those of Kaufman's persuasion see this as a recipe for diminished responsiveness and sensitivity: 'However inconvenient I may be to the unhampered running of the bureaucratic [managerial?] process, I am determined to do whatever I can ...!'

There is a distinct danger of the concept of ministerial responsibility being dismissed as unimportant in the age of 'new management'. With this constitutional convention repeatedly refined it is indeed being qualified to death (Jordan 1994)! Yet, there are still those who believe that ministers should act honourably and that their failure to do so threatens public sector organizations and political institutions with a loss of public confidence. As one observer put it: 'A well run society needs to know that the servants and ministers responsible for bad decisions are prepared to resign' (Porter 1992).

However, to take just one of many possible snapshots, there were a succession of issues in late 1992 pointing to a virtual breakdown of this principle – the spectacular reversal of policy represented by the pound's withdrawal from the European exchange rate mechanism; attempted decimation of the coal industry by enforced pit closures without due process and consultation; dubious and undisclosed use of public money to allay expenses incurred by ministers apparently acting in a private capacity. Dating from the same period, even the publication in February 1996 of the Scott Report on the arms-to-Iraq controversy – documenting the failure to inform Parliament of a change of policy guidelines towards the export of defence-related equipment and criticizing the role of the Attorney General in the handling of the Matrix Churchill prosecution – was not considered by the Government to warrant any ministerial resignations. With a growing question mark over the integrity of politicians, this has been construed as a debasing of the ethic of public service:

> Ministers cling lamentably, embarrassingly . . . to their offices, with private and party political advantage considerations seeming to play an inordinately large . . . part in their deliberations.

> (O'Toole 1993: 3)

In the words of another commentator: 'scarcely anyone ever takes responsibility for anything. Accountability is becoming a fossilized concept' (Phillips 1993). The adoption of a business ethos and pursuit of market testing raised equally disconcerting issues about the tainting of the public service ethic more generally.

Conversely, even when public service status is formally denied, as with the utilities, associated ideas still survive, evident from their regulatory structures (in fact creeping into mainstream services, as with the Office for Standards in Education – OfSted), and from the fact that the *Citizen's Charter* covered gas, electricity, water and telecoms despite now being in the private sector. Nonetheless, the regulators are again appointed not elected. Issues of behavioural propriety have arisen, as in the case of the Director-General of the lottery regulatory agency (OfLot). There has been much outcry about alleged regulatory failure. And the public shock in autumn 1992 over the pit closure programme crystallized how, under the privatized regimes (the electricity generators and distributors in this instance), it had become much more difficult to ensure precedence was given to wider strategic and public interest considerations.

12.5.3　Irreversible changes or swings of the pendulum?

As far as institutional fragmentation and the preference for greater organizational differentiation in contrast to unified structures more generally is concerned, it must be borne in mind that what is regarded as good administrative practice remains deeply contestable. This is the fallacy of the belief in 'one best way' and that there is a 'right' answer to organizational design, when in fact difficult dilemmas exist in reconciling potentially incompatible goals and values (Jordan 1994c). Hence the rapid turnover of doctrines in what Hood and Jackson refer to as the 'administrative fashion trade' (1991: 24). Partly reflecting a hegemonic political project, this applies as much to the shifts of doctrine that the 'new public management' represented as to any other administrative philosophy:

> judgements about the durability of institutional trends, whether developmental or cyclical, do depend on the time frame used as a point of reference . . . it is only a matter of twenty years or so since the prevailing tendency was the opposite one of institutional aggregation, bureaucratic juggernauts at that time believed to provide optimal administrative arrangements.
>
> (*Painter 1995: 27*)

Does the NPM therefore represent a paradigm shift in tune with an environment that has changed out of all recognition – and from which consequently there is no turning back – or is it more a matter of swings of the pendulum?

There are powerful arguments for the latter position as well as the former:

> we might expect that in time the negative aspects of . . . today's trends may come to make the positive aspects of its currently unfashionable alternative seem attractive . . . Most ideas in public administration have an earlier life . . . return and recurrence is a notable feature of its intellectual dynamic.
>
> (*Hood 1995: 180*)

12.5.4   The domestic-European interface

But returning directly to the theme of accountability, the impact of Europe must also be taken on board and not only because the UK Parliament is bound by decisions taken by the European Union and the inadequate domestic scrutiny of draft EU legislation. There is also the fabled weakness of the elected European Parliament relative to other EU institutions (the so-called European 'democratic deficit'). At least the Union has recognized the need to make itself more 'user-friendly'. This was evident in the position taken at the 1992 Edinburgh Summit regarding 'subsidiarity' (the principle that the EU should only act when member states cannot act as effectively themselves), as well as on greater transparency and openness in decision-making (though the implementation of the latter left much to be desired). Particularly fascinating, however, are the changes in how the interface between public authorities and the EU has been managed. As Chapter 11 demonstrated, following UK membership of the then European Community the approach initially was predominantly one of fulfilling obligations, undertaking enforcement responsibilities and compliance with European legislation. Subsequently came more recognition of the new opportunities for securing funds and maximizing the tangible financial benefits of membership, with the European dimension becoming more embedded for example in the work of local authorities.

Chapter 11 indicated that local authorities, moreover, have shown a growing determination to make themselves heard and influence directly the EU agenda, developing greater expertise in lobbying international institutions and also fostering associated representational structures. Indeed, this input has achieved formal recognition in EU institutional development, with the Committee of the Regions established to act in an advisory role to the Commission as the voice of local and regional government at the European level. Such trends hold the prospect of increasing circumvention of national authorities through direct communication with supra-national institutions. In fact, given the threats that have hung over UK local authorities in recent years the principle of subsidiarity, taken to its logical conclusion of decisions made at the lowest practicable level, potentially provides a real window of opportunity. What emerges from Chapter 11 then is how after very tentative beginnings the European arena has increasingly been seen by sub-national public authorities in terms of opportunities rather than threats. Here at least is one instance of an increasingly positive and proactive approach to the management of change.

12.6   CHANGE MANAGEMENT: IMPOSITION, CONSULTATION AND POWER

12.6.1   Management change and ideological turbulence

Striking a rather different tone from the pendulum theory, Chapter 3 highlighted the view that in the face of far-reaching challenges from economic, political, socio-cultural and technological developments change management had become imperative for the public sector. Hence the premium now placed upon the learning organization (Chapter 5). It is indeed worth recalling Clarke and Stewart's (1990) preference for thinking in terms of the **management of changing**, rather than the management of change with its once-and-for-all connotations. But the magnitude of the task is not to be underestimated if it is to be other than surface change, given that what is entailed in the final analysis is attitudinal/behavioural change – and recollecting the many impediments to organizational change. Thus, Chapter 6 emphasized the inhibiting as well as positive forces in the exploitation of IT; Chapter 5 drew attention to the scepticism about cultural change initiatives that can still be pervasive on the part of the workforce. In Chapter 3 the need for coherent strategies in managing this change process was therefore stressed, not least for dealing with the inevitable resistances to change.

This applies to the handling of specific changes as well as more generally. Thus, the management of information and communication technology is indicative of wider change management agendas in the public sector. But specific innovation can also facilitate more general change. There are those who believe that IT is coming into its own because it is an essential key to unlock the potential for reinventing and reinvigorating government, raising the question addressed in Chapter 6 of whether 'informatization' itself is becoming a transformational force by enabling a move away from traditional 'command' bureaucratic structures. Alternatively it may be under-pinning a traditional control ethos and therefore neo-Taylorism by making possible a degree of performance monitoring and measurement hardly conceivable prior to the 'new information age' (Hood 1995). There is also a fear that the impact of this technology on employment patterns and the labour market will result in the creation of a new 'digital proletariat' (Keegan 1996)!

The overview taken of the change management process in Chapter 3 indicated that change is not by definition a positive value; this depends on its appropriateness and on the costs as well as benefits involved. As evident in the case of IT where there have been a number of spectacular failures, high risks can be involved not just high potential (Chapter 6).

Arguably the period since the late 1970s suffered from too many ill-conceived policy initiatives, with successive waves of legislative change often driven forward on ideological grounds.

There is a certain irony in a Party which before the 1970s was renowned for its pragmatism displaying such ideological zeal (Chapter 2), many policy mistakes put down to what by British standards was a highly doctrinaire phase of government. Though the associated public service reforms were construed in some quarters as revitalizing, critics saw more signs of great public institutions being undermined than of positive reconstruction: 'They have had their limbs amputated rather than receiving a life-enhancing blood transfusion' (Painter 1991: 79)! Chapter 2 pointed out that one of the legacies of the Thatcher era was its destabilizing effect on structures of authority generally as well as on social cohesion. Hence another irony, with Michael Portillo – a leading light on the Right of the Conservative Government – suggesting that the public should respect traditional institutions! In the case of the Civil Service the new public management may have heralded the end of an administrative tradition dating from the reform programme of the 1850s directed at rooting out corruption and patronage (Greenaway 1995). In terms of its public service ethos, for some the Government's proposal to privatize Whitehall's Recruitment and Assessment Services Agency (RAS) – responsible for running the competitions for 'fast stream' (graduate) entry – was indeed the final straw (Bancroft 1995).

Lately, there have been signs of a more proactive stance on the part of public authorities towards change, as exemplified above in the European context. Chapter 3 noted important developments in relation to strategic organizational capabilities, although Chapter 10 drew attention to the magnitude of the challenge facing local authorities in strategic 'repositioning' for a changing environment. But the sheer pace of change has also been a classic cocktail for reactive or crisis management. There was simply not sufficient time and opportunity to think things through. This obviously impinged on the effective management of change, as did the tendency for much of the change to be externally imposed. Of course, as noted elsewhere, external pressures for change can facilitate desired internal organizational reforms. The most effective strategy for change will also depend on the particular contingencies being faced and the timescales involved. One change strategy is to deliberately set about destabilizing the established order so as to create opportunities for building anew. The difficulty with this scenario however is that it is easier to destroy than to subsequently reconstruct. And the baby may be thrown out with the bathwater!

12.6.2   Whose interests and values?

Opposition to change in the public sector has often been accentuated by staff commitment to public services, the labour-intensive nature of these people-processing organizations and by professional resistance to line management structures (Pollitt and Harrison 1992). Imposition may therefore prove counter-productive, certainly for inducing changes of organizational culture. An alternative consultative strategy – the importance of which was identified, for example, in Chapter 7 – relying on techniques of persuasion and communication though often slow and painstaking is, other things being equal, ultimately more effective in making change stick. Yet, if anything, formerly collegial or consensual cultures have been the target of public sector management reform in moving towards a top-down ethos, which does indeed place more emphasis on control and compliance. As previously argued, when stripped of the rhetoric, this had much to do with changing power structures. Hence the observation in Chapter 3 that attitudes towards change inevitably depend on the organizational vantage point.

> The fundamental issue is whose interests and values are to prevail. A political perspective on the change process is accordingly essential.

Chapter 3 also drew attention to differential progress in implementing change given the nature of its diffusion. Paradoxically the impact of 'globalization' is that many aspects of public sector management reform now seemingly transcend national boundaries – reflecting the rapidity with which administrative ideas (fashions?) spread internationally (Hood 1995). All the more interesting, then, are the variations that emerge when comparing progress in different public services within the UK. Chapter 9 indicated that the police service became less immune in the 1990s to the changes affecting other public services than it had been in the 1980s, with privatization beginning to leave its mark not least because of the review of 'core' and 'ancillary' policing functions. But even these more recent proposals for reform did not succeed in achieving the radical change initially envisaged. There are many possible explanations, including the existence of a strongly entrenched organizational and professional culture; effective mobilization of a powerful opposing alignment of interests; and the instrumental importance politically of the police during a time of radical social restructuring.

12.7   MANAGING FUTURE CHANGE: REDISCOVERING LOST VALUES

12.7.1   Narrow accounting and creative restructuring

The recurring allusions to political and cultural factors in this concluding assessment is no accident. There is the obvious importance of the political environment for the role assigned to the public sector and the management of public services. This is evident from the ideological ascendancy of the New Right and hence watershed significance of the post-1979 Thatcher governments in dismantling the post-war (social democratic) settlement (Chapter 2). A number of the changes dealt with in this book although ostensibly technical – such as performance management (Chapter 4) and information technology (Chapter 6) – in fact raise much broader behavioural, cultural and political issues and a reason why reforms, not least in the management of resources, can prove more contentious than initially anticipated (Pollitt and Harrison 1992). Moreover, Chapter 6 drew attention to the dangers of technology driving the organization rather than being harnessed to an information strategy. Nor should public sector accounting be seen primarily in narrow technical terms. In discussing the problematical nature of accountability above, the evident difficulty was not just a matter of accountability to whom. Views about what is regarded as important or significant will also be reflected in that which is accounted for; hence the inescapable 'intrusion of interests and values, illustrating the political nature of accounting . . .' (Harte 1992: 202).

Although the public sector has embraced value for money auditing, with yet more changes planned in the form of resource accounting and budgeting (RAB) to further improve the management of resources and assets (Likierman, Heald, Georgiou and Wright 1995), this merely fuels the performance indictors controversy (what is being measured and how). In the context of the so-called '3Es' there continued to be a bias towards economy/efficiency rather than effectiveness measures (Pollitt and Harrison 1992). Given the danger of neglecting valuable dimensions of performance a need arises therefore to extend:

> accountability beyond the . . . efficiency biased performance indicators . . . At the present time, public sector accounting provides a convenient rationale for cost-cutting, and can be used to control discussion of the wider economic and social consequences of public sector policy. A social accounting approach can bring out into the open aspects of performance or impact hidden by the narrowness of . . . accounting.
>
> (*Harte 1992: 201*)

Indeed, under-resourcing and a decaying public infrastructure has been construed in some unlikely quarters as marking the return of 'private affluence and public squalor' (Painter 1991).

Yet, it would be churlish to portray recent public management reforms entirely in negative terms. Greater emphasis on outputs as opposed to inputs must be regarded as a step in the right direction, whatever the associated difficulties. In Chapter 9 we saw how achieving greater value for money was the main motive for latterly reforming the police service. The shift in the balance of power from service producers to the 'customer' domain, in so far as this is reality rather than rhetoric, has also been widely regarded as a positive development. As Chapter 7 on education indicated there is the danger that some public service users will exploit the opportunities presented by any choice more successfully than others. There are also daunting challenges in searching for new ways of delivering services (Common, Flynn and Mellon, 1992). Nonetheless, much creative thinking about how operations are managed is taking place. The 'enabling' concept informing so much of the restructuring process in the public sector and the separation of strategic from operational considerations – enshrined in the commissioner/purchaser-provider principle – too has potentially liberating consequences. Taking the impact on local authorities, there are threats involved but also opportunities since a local government freed from operational service detail can focus more effectively on wider local community concerns – a debate addressed in Chapter 10. The operational managers themselves, given more autonomy, no doubt view this changing framework as less inhibiting.

Yet, Chapter 5 showed there is another side to the picture. Line managers can feel inhibited by the inflexibility of the new contract culture. With the creation of internal markets, new forms of external collaboration have been accompanied by a hardening of internal organizational boundaries. In some respects operational service delivery is moving from problem-solving to more routine management modes. Schools, for instance, are no longer in a position to make certain choices, given the 'nationalization' of the educational curriculum (Chapter 7). This again underlines the significance of the distinction between macro and micro-decisions.

Recalling the demand from some quarters for a much broader accounting approach, is there not a danger moreover of losing sight of the public service mission to manage for social results as distinct from managing for financial results?

Have the new public management class (consciously or unwittingly) allowed themselves to become vehicles for a particular (narrow) set of political objectives? What about seemingly lost or discarded values, notably those of equity, fairness and justice – let alone issues of control, ownership and accountability?

12.7.2 The return of the probity agenda

Are we indeed beginning to pay the price for downgrading the importance of due process and weakening some traditional safeguards under the public management reforms (Hood 1995)? It surely is no accident that honesty and integrity in public life – and hence the proper conduct of public business – has again become a pivotal issue:

The speed and direction of devolved managerial autonomy, together with the promotion of an entrepreneurial culture and of privatization as a goal . . . have raised questions about the vulnerability of public sector organizations . . .

(Doig 1995: 207)

Hence the lapses in expected standards earning rebuke from the Commons Public Accounts Committee. There was one especially notorious example:

The negative aspects of public service reform were crystallized by events at the Wessex regional health authority, centred on the tendering process for an integrated computer system . . . this saga contained . . . failures in basic controls, the breaking of rules, improprieties arising from conflicts of interests and, in the final analysis, with enormous resource wastage at the expense of patient care.

(Painter 1994: 258)

The last point is full of irony given the preoccupations – economizing and service quality – of the 1980s and 1990s. And this is not to mention the impact of outsourcing on the effective organizational management of a core resource such as information (Chapter 6).

The very existence of the Nolan Committee was testimony to the scale of the problem that has led to the re-emergence of the traditional probity agenda and renewed debate about the ethical basis for behaviour on the part of those entrusted with public office.

Yet, there have also been currents in the opposite direction because of the growth in the significance of judicial review of the activities of public officials. This 'juridi-fication' is 'an alternative to "managerialization", in so far as it tends towards formalization, due process and elaborate procedure as against a substantive results-oriented approach' (Hood 1995: 178).

12.7.3 Managerialism, constitutionalism and community values

If public service consumers are now more valued as a consequence of the public management reforms, this also leaves the question of the social duties and responsibilities that rest more easily alongside a broader notion of citizenship.

The significance of the 'new communitarianism' (associated with Amitai Etzioni) is in its concern with strengthening social infrastructure and countering the forces undermining community through building responsible democratic citizenship, balancing the recent stress on individual freedoms with a greater awareness of obligations to others.

Following the post-1979 ascendance of the neo-liberal agenda (as Chapter 2 indicated there was never an unequivocal acceptance of the Thatcher reforms by the British public), this is symptomatic of how 'the community is rising towards the top of the agenda for governments' (Tam 1995: 23). The policy implications are not always clear and there is a concern in some quarters that communitarianism could assume the guise of a new social authoritarianism. Yet, even viewed through a consumerist lens there are many client groups losing their significant stake in society who are far from satisfied – for starters the homeless, the unemployed and claimants who have seen the real value of their benefits reduced. When placed in this wider frame of political and social values, the concepts of consumerism and citizenship therefore begin to converge. The related stakeholderism debate is essentially about forms of economic, political and social inclusivity as opposed to exclusivity.

There is the view nonetheless that we are inexorably moving to some sub-Thatcherite consensus on 'the evolving concept of public management'(Duncan 1992b: xii). Yet, Chapter 2 concluded that a new consensus on the role of the state, and by extension the scope and management of the public sector, has failed to materialize. There was also the disarray in which the Major government often found itself from autumn 1992. Paradoxically, given the equation of the management movement with improved organizational performance, the successive crises even showed symptoms of systemic failure, for example the manner in which the pound's suspension from the European exchange rate mechanism was handled! This renders even more significant the makings of a rather different agenda. What we have seen is 'the increasing dominance of a "business-consumerist" as opposed to a "governmental-citizenship" paradigm, therefore a preoccupation ... with managerialism rather than constitutionalism' (Painter, 1995: 19). Apart from the impact of reforms on traditional public administration values, by exploiting the constitutional structure of a pre-modern state (Chapter 2) the Thatcher-Major years graphically exposed the fragile basis of the safeguards in our system. This era marked the onward march of centralized, executive-dominated government (Painter, 1991). Yet:

> whereas the 1980s were preoccupied with micro issues to do with how public services are managed, there are indications that the 1990s in contrast may eventually move on to the constitutional high ground of how we are governed ...
>
> *(Painter 1995: 36)*

The case for a wide-ranging new constitutional settlement was identified in Chapter 2. This would be 'reinventing' government in a more fundamental sense. Significantly, developments such as the alleged politicization of the civil service have been attributed as much to the longevity of one-party government as to the new managerial culture. But the latter has also taken its toll of public accountability. Chapter 9 concluded that one of the key challenges for a future government is to re-establish a more democratic foundation for policing in England and Wales, given the importance of this to the effectiveness of that service. Thus, one way or another, perhaps the real challenge is no less than that of 'reinventing' democracy!

12.8 CONCLUSION

The above are matters for future resolution and how this works out will obviously affect the climate in which the public sector operates. But enough should by now have been said in this book to indicate just how problematic and perverse the application of some fashionable managerial ideas to the public services remains. Public managers certainly will continue to have to grapple with a number of distinctive, long-standing and difficult dilemmas in a changing environment (Common, Flynn and Mellon 1992; Pollitt and Harrison 1992). Though not taken very seriously on the Left of the political spectrum, the success of any future Labour administration – should there be another swing of the political pendulum – could nevertheless turn on its own awareness of good management practice, particularly the ability to run the government machine more effectively and its skills in strategic policy management (Walker 1995). The further evolution of public management as the twentieth century draws to its close should – for all sorts of reasons – therefore be fascinating to observe!

12.9 CHAPTER SUMMARY

The following key learning points emerge from this chapter:

- The Citizen's Charter indicates the main direction in which public management reform has been steered in the 1990s, with its emphasis on public service users and therefore in fact its 'consumerist' bias (see Figure 12.1).
- Despite a parallel desire to import business management practices, the analogy of customer choice in economic markets continues to present many difficulties notwithstanding the development of public service markets.
- Preoccupation with individual service users also obscures the wider public interest considerations that public service provision must take into account.
- There are in fact multiple stakeholders in this context, yet the public sector managerial reforms have often had the effect of narrowing the 'stakeholder base'.
- In any case, the recent emphasis on quality improvement and meeting user requirements still sits uneasily alongside the continuing pull of an economizing agenda.
- Moreover, the treatment and reactions of public service professionals have been symptomatic of a control rather than motivational ethos (see Case Study 12.1).
- There must be questions about whether such 'disempowering' of front-line staff has been conducive to a customer-orientation and a culture of continuous quality improvement.

- The top-down imposition of change indeed raises issues about the effective management of change.
- Stripped of rhetoric the reforms are about power structures and therefore the changing relative position of different stakeholder groups. It is a matter of whose values and interests prevail in the final analysis.
- Therefore, even seemingly technical reforms can raise wide-ranging behavioural, cultural and political issues.
- Moreover, the toll the management reforms have taken on public accountability may in some respects actually be reducing the responsiveness and sensitivity of the system (not overlooking the increasing significance of the European Union in this connection).
- The sheer extent of the changes since the late 1970s may also have been counter-productive, even raising the spectre of systemic failure.
- But on past experience administrative trends (fashions?) can change quickly. Is it therefore a matter of 'no turning back' or of 'swings of the pendulum'?
- The dysfunctional consequences of recent management reforms in fact are highlighting again some of the virtues of the earlier public administration paradigm – not least the ethic of public service.
- The desire to move the customer domain to centre stage has nonetheless been welcomed in many quarters, inducing some creative thinking about the delivery and management of public services.
- There are benefits moreover to be derived from public sector restructuring looked at from both the strategic and operational vantage points.
- This still leaves legitimate concerns about neglected values, notably those of equity and probity – with a price being paid for the downgrading of due process (though the growth of judicial review is a pressure in the opposite direction), evident from the fact that honesty and integrity in public life is now once again a central issue.
- There is related apprehension about the compromising of the public service mission to manage for social as opposed to financial results, neglected wider community values highlighted by the 'communitarian' movement.
  Furthermore, the fragile basis of the constitutional safeguards in the UK system, exposed during the Thatcher-Major years, underlines the contrast between the dominant 'business-consumerist' paradigm and an alternative 'governmental-citizenship' paradigm.
- Accordingly, there is evidence of an increasing interest in how we are governed as opposed to simply how public services are managed.

TEXT-BASED QUESTIONS

1. What problems arise from the application of
    (a) the principles of choice and competition; and
    (b) the concept of quality to the public services?

2. Why have the UK public management reforms been characterized as 'neo-Taylorian'?

3. What has been the impact of these reforms in relation to the concept of 'stake-holderism'?

4. Is the institutional fragmentation of public service delivery a legitimate cause for concern, not least in relation to public accountability? Illustrate the relevant issues with reference to one or more of the main public services examined in this book.

5. Public management reforms can be regarded as irreversible or merely another swing of the pendulum in terms of fashionable administrative doctrines. What are the arguments both ways?

6. To what extent are successive waves of imposed legislative reform
    (a) a recipe for reactive crisis-ridden management; and
    (b) a counter-productive strategy for inducing changes in organizational culture?

7. However technical public management reforms may appear on the surface broader cultural, behavioural and political considerations are invariably at stake. What is the justification for such a claim? Illustrate with reference to a particular area of reform addressed in this book.

8. What have been the main positive achievements of the public management reforms? Relate the achievements identified to any of the case study materials incorporated in earlier chapters.

9. Indicate which values have been eclipsed as a result of the general thrust of these reforms.

10. Why has the probity agenda moved back to centre stage? Does this suggest there is cause for concern about public service ethics?

11. What are the implications of the 'new communitarianism'?

12. What is the significance of ascribing a 'business-consumerist' label to the Thatcher-Major public management reforms?

ASSIGNMENT

One of the significant issues touched upon in the latter part of this concluding chapter is the extent to which the prevailing values and preoccupations of the Thatcher-Major era are on the wane. It can be used as a catalyst for small group exercises (using brainstorming techniques for example) designed to induce reflections on the prospective public management agenda as the new millenium approaches.

This may then form the basis for an assignment which:

(a) Sets out possible alternative scenarios for the next 5–10 years;
(b) Weighs up the probability of each scenario materializing in the light of available evidence (or informed conjecture).

FURTHER READING

Doig, A. (1995) Mixed Signals? Public Sector Change and the Proper Conduct of Public Business. *Public Administration*, **73**(2), pp. 191–212. Indicates why honesty and integrity in public life has again become an issue of concern, highlighting tensions between the managerial performance ethos and considerations of due process.

Hood, C. (1995) Emerging Issues in Public Administration. *Public Administration*, **73**(1), pp. 165–83. Succinct survey of the issues associated with a number of significant trends alluded to in the chapter – namely those of globalization, economicization, managerialization, informatization and juridification.

Painter, C. (1991) The Public Sector and Current Orthodoxies: Revitalization or Decay? *The Political Quarterly*, **62**(1), pp. 75–89. Examines the preoccupations underlying the managerial reform agenda and implications for democratic values.

Painter, C. (1995) The Next Steps Reforms and Cuurent Orthodoxies, in *Next Steps:Improving Management in Government*? (eds. B.J. O'Toole and G. Jordan), Dartmouth, Aldershot, pp. 17–36. Explores the 'business-consumerist' and 'governmental-citizenship' paradigms specifically with reference to the departmental agency reforms.

Pollitt, C. (1993) *Managerialism and the Public Services*, Blackwell, Oxford. Considers the recent emphasis on public service quality improvement and user responsiveness in the context of the long-standing economizing agenda.

Prime Minister (1991) *The Citizen's Agenda*, Cm 1599, HMSO, London. The initiative that did so much to set the tone of continuing managerial reform during the Major Conservative administrations.

Walsh, K. (1991) Quality and Public Services. *Public Administration*, **69**(4), pp. 503–14. Examines the meaning of the concept of quality and the problems of managing quality in a public service setting.

BIBLIOGRAPHY

Abel-Smith, B. (1992) The benefits of Beveridge, *The New Statesman and Society*, **5.**

Abbott, B. (1986) The problem of IT in the NHS. *Information Technology & Public Policy*, **5** (1), pp.1–5.

Adam Smith Institute (1993) Address To ACPO.

Addison, P. (1977) *The Road to 1945; British Politics and the Second World War*, Quartet Books, London.

Alderman, G. (1984) *Pressure Groups and Government in Britain*, Longman, London.

Alexander, N. (1992) Marketing and public services, in *The Evolution of Public Management* (ed. C. Duncan), Macmillan, London, pp.84–100.

AMA (1994) *Changing The Face of Quangos: A Discussion Document*, Association of Metropolitan Authorities, London.

Anderson, A. and Sims, R. (1990) Managing for quality: getting the right framework for information technology, *Public Money and Management*, Autumn, 1990, pp.33–8.

Argyris, C. and Schon, D. (1974) *Theory and Practice – Increasing Professional Effectiveness*, Jossey Bass, London.

Armstrong, P. (1989) *People in Organizations*, Elm Publications, Cambridge.

Asquith, A.R. (1991) The Harris experiment revisited. *Local Government Policy Making*, December, pp.30–4.

Asquith, A.R. (1994) *Change Management in Local Government: Strategic Change Agents and Organizational Ownership*. PhD Thesis, University of Central England, Birmingham.

Atkinson, R. and Cope, S. (1994) Changing styles of governance since 1979, in *Public Policy in Britain* (eds S.P. Savage, R. Atkinson and L. Robins), Macmillan, London, pp.31–52.

Audit Commission (1986) *Performance Review in Local Government*, HMSO, London.

Audit Commission (1988a) *Competitive Council*, HMSO, London.

Audit Commission (1988b) *Performance Review in Local Government: A Handbook for Auditors and Local Authorities*, HMSO, London.

Audit Commission (1990a) *Preparing an Information Strategy: Making IT Happen*, HMSO, London.

Audit Commission (1990b) *Knowing What IT Costs*, HMSO, London.

Audit Commission (1990c) *Acquiring IT*, HMSO, London.

Audit Commission (1991) *A Rough Guide to Europe: Local Authorities and the EEC*, HMSO, London.

Audit Commission (1994a) *Paper 13, Checks and Balances*, HMSO.

Audit Commission (1994b) *High Risk/High Potential – A management handbook on information technology in local government*, HMSO, London.

Audit Commission (1995) *For Your Information: A study of information management and systems in acute hospital*, HMSO, London.

Bancroft, Lord (1995) An ethos up for sale. *The Guardian*, 20 December

Barker, A. (ed.) (1982) *Quangos in Britain*, Macmillan, London.

Barnes, C. (1993) *Practical Marketing for Schools*, Blackwell, Oxford

Bayley, D. (1995) *Police for Future*, OUP, Milton Keynes

BBC Radio 4 (1992) File on Four, 12 October.

Bellamy, C. and Taylor, J. (1992 Informatisation and Public Administration: Towards a Research Agenda, Paper to the Seminar Information, Communication and New Technology in Public Administration, March, London.

Bellamy, C. and Taylor, J. (1994) Introduction: exploiting IT in public administration: towards the information polity. *Public Administration*, **72**(1) pp.1–12.

Bellamy, C. (1994) Managing strategic resources in a next steps department: information agendas and information systems in the DSS, in *Next Steps: Improving Management in Government?* (eds B. O'Toole and G. Jordan), Dartmouth Publishing Company, Aldershot.

Bellamy, C., Horrocks, I. and Webb, J. (1995) Exchanging Information with the Public: From One Stop Shops to Community Information systems. *Local Government Studies*, **21**(1), pp 11–30.

Benjamin. I. *et al.* (1987) Information technology: a strategic opportunity, in *The Strategic Use of Information Technology* (ed. S. Madnick), Oxford University Press, London, pp.17–28.

Beer, S.H. (1982) *Britain Against Itself: The Political Contradictions of Collectivism*, Faber & Faber, London.

Birch, A. H. (1964) *Representative and Responsible Government*, Allen and Unwin, London.

Birmingham City Council (1986), Finance and Management (Computer and New Technology Sub-Committee), 7 October.

Birmingham City Council (1989) Finance and Management (Purchasing and Computer/New Technology Sub-Committee), 22 February.

Birmingham City Council (1992) *Information/Information Technology Management Strategy*

Blair, T. (1996) Battle for Britain, *The Guardian*, 29 January.

Blaxter, M., (1995) *Consumers and Research in the NHS: consumer issues within the NHS*, Department of Health, London.

Blunkett, B. and Baimbridge, M. (1992) European Community developments, in *Public Domain 1992* (eds F. Terry and P. Jackson) Chapman and Hall, London.

Bongers, P.N. (1990) *Local Government and 1992*, Longman, Harlow.

Borrie, G and Diamond, A.L., (1973) *The Consumer, Society and the Law*, Penguin, London.

Bovaird, T. Gregory, D. and Martin, S. (1988) Performance measurement in urban economic development, *Public Money and Management*, **8**(4) pp.17–22.

Bovaird, T. and Nutley, S. (1989) Financial management in the public sector, in *An Introduction to Public Sector Management* (eds I. Taylor and G. Popham), Unwin Hyman, London, pp.61–87.

Bowers, P. (1992) Regulation and Public Sector Management, in *The Evolution of Public Management* (ed. C. Duncan), Macmillan, London pp.23–48.

Brindle, D. (1995) The consultation cure. *The Guardian*, 10 May.

Brooke, R. (1989) *Managing the Enabling Authority*, Longman, Essex, London.

BTEC (1992) *National Vocational Qualification at Level 5 in Management Part 2: Standards*, BTEC, London.

Buckland, S. (1992), Community Health Councils: An Effective Mechanism for Presenting Consumers in the NHS? Paper presented to the British Association Annual Conference, Southampton University, 27 August

Buckland, Y. and Joshua, H. (1992) Nottingham into the 1990s – managing change in a district council. *Public Money & Management*, July-September, pp.21–5

Bulpitt, J. (1989) Walking back to happiness ? Conservative party, governments and elected local authorities in the 1980s, in *The New Centralism – Britain Out of Step in Europe* (eds C.Crouch and D.Marquand), Basil Blackwell, Oxford, pp.56–73.

Burkitt, B. and Baimbridge, M. (1992) European Comunity development in *Public Domain 1992* (eds F. Terry and P. Jackson), Chapman & Hall, London.

Burningham, D. (1990) Performance Management and the Management of Professionals in Local Government, in *Output and Performance Measurement in Government: the State of the Art* (eds M. Cave, M. Kogan and R Smith), Jessica Kingsley, London, pp.124–42.

Burningham, D. (1992) An overview of the use of performance indicators in local government, in *Handbook of Public Service Management* (eds C. Pollitt and S. Harrison), Blackwell Publishers, Oxford, pp.86–100.

Butler, R. (1994) Reinventing British government. *Public Administration*, **72**(2), pp.263–70.

Butler, J.R. and Vaile, M.S.B. (1984) *Health and Health Services*, Routledge & Kegan Paul, London.

Butt, H. and Palmer, R. (1985) *Value for Money in the Public Sector: The Decision Maker's Guide*, Basil Blackwell, Oxford.

Carnall, C. (1991) *Managing Change*, Routledge, London.

Carter, N., Klein, R. and Day, P. (1992) *How Organizations Measure Success: the Use of Performance Indicators in Government*, Routledge, London.

Caulfield, I. and Schultz, J. (1989) *Planning For Change: Strategic Planning in Local Government*, Longman, London.

Caulkin, S. (1994a) This year's moral. *The Observer*, 16 October.

Caulkin, S. (1994b) Another fine mess. *The Observer*, 2 October.

Caveman, G. (1992) Privatizing the ministers. *The Guardian*, 7 December.

CCTA (1984) Review of the Central Computer and Telecommunications Agency, HMSO, London.

CCTA (1990a) *Managing Facilities Management*, Norwich, HMSO.

CCTA (1990b) *Managing Information as a Resource*, HMSO, London.

CCTA (1990c) *Information Technology in Central Government – Changes and Trends – 1988–89*, HMSO, Norwich.

CCTA (1991a) *Office Automation in Government Departments*, HMSO, London.

CCTA (1991b) *Cost Management for IT Services*, HMSO, London.

CCTA (1991c) *Ministry of Defence: Support Information Technology*, HMSO, London.

CCTA (1992a) *Human Factors in IS Strategy*, HMSO, London.

CCTA (1992b) *UK Civil Service: capital IT budgets 1991/92*, HMSO, London.

CCTA (1995a) *CCTA Services Catalogue*, CCTA offices, London

CCTA (1995b) *Information Superhighways*, CCTA offices, London.

The Cecchini Report (1988) *The European Challenge 1992: The Benefits of a Single Market*, Gower, London.

Cellan-Jones, R. (1992) The business of benefits. *The Guardian*, 23 June.

Central Statistical Office (1991) Employment trends in the public and private sectors. *Economic Trends*, December, pp.98–105.

Centre for Public Services (1994) *Tender Evaluation – A Detailed Handbook*, Centre for Public Services, Sheffield.

Chapman, R.A. (1991) Concepts and issues in public sector reform: the experience of the United Kingdom in the 1980s. *Public Policy and Administration*, 6(2), pp.1–19.

Chapman, R.A. (1994) Change in the civil service. *Public Administration*, 72(4), pp.599–610.

Chartered Institute of Purchasing and Supply (1989) *The European Community Supplies Directive*, CIPS, Stamford.

Checkland, S. (1983) *British Public Policy 1776–1939: An Economic, Social and Political Perspective*, Cambridge University Press, Cambridge.

Cheeseright, P. (1994) Cost liability urged for quango members. *Financial Times*, 29 September.

Chell, E. (1987) *The Psychology of Behaviour in Organisations*, Macmillan, London.

Chief Executive Corporate Support Network (CESNET) (1989) *1992 – the Impact on County Council Services*, Kent County Council, Maidstone.

Clarke, M. and Stewart, J. (1988) *The Enabling Council*, Local Government Training Board, Luton.

Clarke, M. (1993) On reinventing government. *Local Government Management*, 1(4), p.19.

Clarke, M. and Stewart, J. (1990) *General Management in Local Government: Getting the Balance Right*, Longman, London.

Clarke, M. and Stewart, J. (1991) *Choices For Local Government For the 1990s and Beyond*, Longman, London.

Clarke, P.(1992) *A Question of Leadership*, Penguin, Harmondsworth, Cm 555, 1989) *Working for Patients*, (HMSO, London.

Cm 1599 (1991) *The Citizen's Charter*, HMSO, London.

Cm 1520 (1991) Public Expenditure Analyses to 1993–94 (Statistical Supplement to the 1990 Autumn Statement), HMSO, London.

Cm 2626 (1994) *Better Accounting for the Taxpayer's Money: Resource Accounting and Budgeting in Government*, HMSO, London.

Cm 2627 (1994) *The Civil Service: Continuity and Change*, HMSO, London.

Colville, I., Dalton, K. and Tomkins, C. (1993) Developing and understanding cultural change in HM Customs and Excise, *Public Administration*, 71(4), pp.549–66.

Collingridge, J. (1986) The appeal of decentralization, *Local Government Studies*, 12(3), pp.9–16.

Collingridge, D. and Margetts, H (1994) Can government information systems be flexible technology? The operational strategy revisited. *Public Administration*, **72**(1) pp.55–72.

COLPA Committee of Local Police Authorities (1995), Eaton Square, London.

Commission of European Communities (1988) *Research on the 'Cost of Non Europe'*:1, ECSC-EEC-EAEC, Luxemburg.

Commission of European Communities (1988) *European Towns and Cities*, ECSC-EEC-EAEC, Luxemburg

Commission of European Union (1995) *Sources of European Community Funding* (2nd ed).

Common, R., Flynn, N. and Mellon, E. (1992) *Managing Public Services*, Butterworth Heinemann, Oxford.

Cooke, P. (ed) (1989) Localities: *The Changing Face of Urban Britain*, Unwin Hyman, London.

Coote, A. and Pfeffer, N. (1991) Quality and the equality gap. *The Guardian*, 17 July.

County News April (1995a), ACC Publications, pp.22–3.

County News June (1995b) ACC Publications, p.6.

County News July (1995c) ACC Publications.

Cousins, C. (1987) *Controlling Social Welfare*, Wheatsheaf, Brighton.

Cronbie, J. and Edwards, B (1994) Corporate re-engineering: holy grail or empty vessel? *Local Government Management*, **1**(9), pp.18–19.

Crosland, S. (1982) *Tony Crosland*, Jonathan Cape, London.

Danziger, J. and Dutton W. (1977) Technological innovation in local government: the case of computers, *Politics and Policy*, **6**(2), pp.27–49.

Davies, H. (1992) *Fighting the Leviathan: Building Social Markets that Work,* The Social Market Foundation, London.

Davies, J. and Easterby-Smith, M. (1984) Learning and developing from managerial work experiences. *Journal of Management Development*, **21**(20), pp [PAGE NUMBERS MISSING]

Davis, H (1993) *A First Guide to Appointed Local Executive Bodies in the West Midlands*, Institute of Local Government Studies, University of Birmingham.

Davis, H. and Stewart, J. (1993) *The Growth of Government By Appointment*, Local Government Management Board, Luton.

Day, P. and Klein, R. (1987), *Accountabilities: Five Public Services*, Tavistock, London

Deakin, N. (1987) *The Politics of Welfare*, Methuen, London

Delderfield, J., Puffit, R. and Watts, G. (1991) *Business Planning in Local Government*, Longman, London.

Denning, R.W., Hussey, D.E. and Newman, P.G. (1978) *Management Development: What to Look For?*

Department of the Environment, (1991) *Competing for Quality*, HMSO, London.

Department of Health, (1992) *The Patient's Charter – a summary*, The Department of Health, London.

Department of Health, (1995) *Consumers and Research in the NHS: involving consumers in local health care*, Department of Health, London.

Department of Trade and Industry (1992) *The Single Market: A Guide to Public Purchasing*, HMSO, London

Devlin, B. *et al.* (1990) *Medical Care: is it a consumer good?* IEA Health Unit Paper 8, (RA 395.G7), London.

DHSS (Department of Health and Social Security), 1972, *Management Arrangements for the Reorganised National Health Service*, HMSO, London.

DHSS (1979) *Patients First*, HMSO, London.

DHSS (1983) NHS management enquiry (Griffiths Report), HMSO, London.

Dickinson, D. (1995) Managing the margins. *Employment Policy Institute*, **9**(1).

Digings, L. (1991) *Competitive Tendering and the European Communities*, AMA, London.

Doig, A. (1979) The machinery of government and the growth of governmental bodies, *Public Administration*, **57**, pp.309–31.

Doig, A. (1995) Mixed signals? Public sector change and the proper conduct of public business. *Public Administration*, **73**(2), pp.191–212.

Doig, A. and Wilson, J. (1995) Untangling the threads of sleaze: the slide into Nolan, *Parliamentary Affairs*, **48**(4), pp.562–78.

Downes, P. (1989) *Managing Education in the 1990s*, CIPFA, London.

Drucker, P. (1974) *Management: Tasks, Responsibilities and Practices*, Harper & Row, New York.

DSS (1995) *Next Steps: An Evaluation of Information Technology Services Agency – Raising Standards*.

Duncan, C. (1992a) Remuneration and motivation, in *The Evolution of Public Management* (ed. C. Duncan), Macmillan, London, pp.205–38.

Duncan, C. (1992b) Introduction, in *The Evolution of Public Management*, Macmillan, London, pp.xii-xvi.

Dunleavy, P. (1955) Policy disasters: explaining the UK's record, *Public Policy and Administration*, **10**(2) pp. 71–87.

Earl, M. (1989) *Management Strategies for Information Technology*, Prentice-Hall, London.

Efficiency Unit (1991) *Making the Most of Next Steps*, HMSO, London.

Elcock, H. (1990) Implementing management change, in *Implementation in Public Policy* (ed. T. Younis), Dartmouth, Aldershot, pp.65–72.

Elcock, H. (1991) *Change and Decay? Public Administration in the 1990s*, Longman, London.

Elcock, H. (1993) Strategic management, in *Managing the New Public Services* (eds D. Farnham and S. Horton), Macmillan, London, pp.55–77.

Elcock, H., Jordon, G. and Midwinter, A. (1989) *Budgeting in Local Government: Managing the Margins*, London, Harlow.

Ennals, K and O'Brien, J (1990) *The Enabling Role of Local Authorities*, Public Finance Foundation, London.

Equal Opportunities Commission (1995) *Gender Impacts of Compulsory Competitive Tendering*, EOC, Manchester.

Etherington, S. (1996) Switching off the remote control, *The Guardian*, 17 January.

Etzioni, A.(1995) *The Spirit of Community: Rights, Responsibilities and the Communitarian Agenda*, Fontana, London.

European Association of Metropolitan Cities (1994) *Eurocities*, Brussels

Farnham, D. and Horton, S (1993) *Managing the New Public Services*, Macmillan, Basingstoke.

Farrell, C. and Gilbert, H. (1995), Report: Patients Empowerment, Workshop Paper, University of Warwick.

Feintuck, M.(1994) *Accountability and Choice in Schooling*, Open University Press, Buckingham.

Fenwick, J. (1995) *Managing Local Government*, Chapman and Hall, London.

Field, S. (1990) *Trends in Crime and their Interpretation*, HMSO.

FITLOG (1992), *Fit for Business : the management and practice of information technology in local government*, SOCITM.

Flynn, N. (1989) The new right and social policy. *Politics and Policy*, **17**(2), pp.97–109.

Flynn, N. (1990) Stirring up supply, *Insight*, 23 May.

Flynn, N. (1993) *Public Sector Management* (2nd edn), Harvester Wheatsheaf, Hemel Hempstead.

Flynn, N. (1994) Control, commitment and contracts, in *Managing Social Policy* (eds J. Clarke, A. Cochrane and E. McLaughlin), pp.210–25.

Fowler, A. (1980) *Personnel Management In Local Government*, IPM, London.

Fowler, A. (1988) *Human Resource Management in Local Government*, Longman, London.

Frissen, P.(1992) Informatization in Public Administration. Paper presented to PICT seminar, 12 March, London.

Gallacher, J. (1995) *Committee of the Regions: An Opportunity for Influence*, Local Government International Bureau, London.

Gamble, A. (1988) *The Free Economy and the Strong State*, Macmillan, London.

Gamble, A. (1984) Thatcherism and conservative politics, in *The Politics of Thatcherism*, Lawrence & Wishart, London, pp.109–31.

The Guardian (1990) A Town Hall in Chaos, 24 October.

Gaster, L. (1995) *Quality in Public Services*, Open University Press, Buckingham.

Gay, O. (1994) *Quangos and Non-Departmental Public Bodies*, Research Paper 94/67, House of Commons Library, London.

Gewirtz, S., Ball, S. and Bowe, R (1995) *Markets, Choice and Equity in Education*, Open University Press, Buckingham.

Giddens, A. (1994) What's Left for Labour? *New Statesman and Society*, 30 September, pp.37–40.

Gilmour, I. (1992) *Dancing with Dogma: Britain under Thatcherism*, Simon and Schuster, London.

Gowling, W. (1994) *Operational Systems in Information Management in the Health Service* (ed. J. Keen), OUP, pp 31–49.

Gray, A. and Jenkins B. *et al.* (1991) The management of change in Whitehall: the experience of FMI. *Public Administration*, **69**(1), pp.41–59.

Gray, A. and Jenkins, B. (1995) From Public Administration to Public Management: Reassessing a Revolution. *Public Administration*, **73**(1), pp 77–99.

Gray, A. and Jenkins, B. (1991) Administering local government, in *Politics UK* (ed. B. Jones), Philip Allan, Cambridge, pp.440–66.

Gray, J.(1993) *Beyond the New Right: Markets, Government and the Common Environment*, Routledge, London.

Gray, J. (1994) Suicide of the leviathan, *The Guardian*, 7 November.

Gray, J. (1996) Putting Britain together, *The Guardian*, 29 January.

Green, D.G., Neuberger, J., Dartington, Lord Young of., and Burstall, M.L., (1990) *The NHS Reforms: Whatever happened to consumer choice?*, IEA Health & Welfare Unit, London.

Greenaway, J. (1995) Having the bun and the halfpenny: can old public service ethics survive in the new Whitehall? *Public Administration*, **73**(3), pp.357–74

Greenleaf, W H (1983a) *The British Political Tradition, vol. 1, The Rise of Collectivism*, Methuen, London.

Greenleaf, W.H.(1983b) *The British Political Tradition, vol. 2, The Ideological Inheritance*, Methuen, London.

Greenwood, J. and Wilson, D. (1989) *Public Administration in Britain Today*, Unwin Hyman, London.

Greer, P. (1992) The next steps initiative: an examination of the agency framework documents. *Public Administration*, **70**(1), pp.89–98.

Greer, P. (1994) *Transforming Central Government*, Open University Press, Buckingham.

Gretton, J. and Jackson, M. (1976) *William Tyndale: Collapse of a School – or a system?* George Allen & Unwin, London.

The Guardian (1990) A Town Hall in Chaos, 24 October.

Guest, D. (1989) Personnel and HRM. Can you tell the difference? *Personnel Management Studies*, **24**(5).

Gunn, L. (1988) Public management: a third approach. *Public Money and Management*, **8**(1&2), pp.21–6.

Hadley, R. and Young, K. (1990) *Creating a Responsive Public Service*, Harvester Wheatsheaf, Hemel Hempstead.

Hall, S. (1983) The great moving right show, in *The Politics of Thatcherism* (eds S. Hall and M. Jaques), Lawrence & Wishart, London, pp.19–39.

Ham, C. (1992) *Health Policy in Britain: The Politics and Organisation of the National Health Service*, (3rd edn), Macmillan, London.

Hambleton, R. (1990) *Urban Government in the 1990s*, School for Advanced Urban Studies, Bristol.

Hampshire County Council (1992) *Managing Information – A News Letter for County Council Managers.*

Hampshire County Council (1994) *Framework for Information Management.*

Handy, C. (1989) *The Age of Unreason*, Hutchinson, London,

Hansard , H.C. Deb. 15 March 1995, Col. 907–52.

Harris, R. and Seldon, A. (1977) *Not For Benevolence: Twenty Years of Economic Dissent*, Institute of Economic Affairs, London.

Harrison, R. (1993) *Human Resource Management Issues and Strategies*, Addison, London.

Harrison, S. (1986) Management culture and management budgets. *Hospital and Health Service Review*, January, pp.6–9.

Harrison, S. (1988) The workforce and the new managerialism, in *Reshaping the NHS* (ed. R. Maxwell), Policy Journals, London.

Harrison, S. and Pollitt, C. (1994), *Controlling Health Professionals: The Future of Work and Organisation in the NHS*, Open University Press, Buckingham.

Harrow, J. and Shaw, M. (1992) The manager faces the consumer, in *Rediscovering Public Services Management* (eds L. Willcocks and J. Harrow), McGraw Hill, Maidenhead, pp.113–40.

Harrow, J. and Willcocks, L. (1990) Public services management. *Journal of Management Studies* **27**(3) pp.281–304.

Harrow, J. and Willcocks, L. (1992) Management, innovation and organizational learning, in *Rediscovering Public Services Management* (eds L. Willcocks and J. Harrow), McGraw Hill, Maidenhead, pp.50–83.

Harte, G. (1992) *Social Accounting Techniques, in The Evolution of Public Management* (ed. C. Duncan), Macmillan, London, pp.185–204.

Harvey, H. (1992) Health Service Management – Information Strategies Paper to PICT seminar on Information and Communication Technologies in Public Administration, London.

Harvey-Jones, J. (1988) *Making It Happen*, Collins, London

Hay, C. (1994) Labour's Thatcherite revisionism: playing the 'politics of catch-up'. *Political Studies*, **42**(4), pp.700–7.

Hayek, F.A. (1944) *The Road to Serfdom*, Routledge, London.

Health Care 2000 (1995) *UK Health and Health Care Services: Challenges and Policy Options.*

Henkel, M. (1992) *The Audit Commission*, in *Handbook of Public Service Management* (eds C. Pollitt and S Harrison), Blackwell Publishers, Oxford, pp.72–85.

Her Majesty's Inspector of Constabulary (1994) *West Yorkshire Police Report*, Home Office.

Her Majesty's Inspector of Constabulary (1995a) *Lancashire Constabulary Report*, Home Office.

Her Majesty's Inspector of Constabulary (1995b) *Cheshire Constabulary Report*, Home Office.

Hickson, D.J., Butler, R.J., Cray, D., Mallory, G.R., and Wilson, D.C. (1989) Decision and organization – processes of strategic decision making and their explanation. *Public Administration*, **67**(4), pp.373–90.

Hill, P. (1990), Measuring the intangibles, *Local Government Chronicle Supplement*, 21 September.

Hinings, C.R. and Greenwood, R. (1988) *The Dynamics of Strategic Change*, Blackwell, Oxford.

Hinton, P. (1993) Quality in public services and the 1990s, in *Issues in Public Service Finance and Management* (eds J. Wilson and P. Hinton) Tudor, Sevenoaks, pp.62–80.

Hirst, J. (1992) A chill wind whistles down Whitehall. *The Guardian*, 15 July.

Hoggett, P. (1987) A Farewell to Mass Production. Decentralization as an Emergent Private and Public Sector Paradigm in Decentralization and Democracy, (P. Hoggett and R. Hamblett) Occasional Paper No. 28, School For Advance Urban Studies, Bristol University.

Hoggett, P. (1990), Modernisation, political strategy and the welfare state: an organisational perspective. *Studies in Decentralisation and Quasi-Markets*, No 2, Bristol, School for Advanced Urban Studies.

Hoggett, P. (1991) A new management in the public sector? *Policy and Politics*, **19**(4), pp.243–56.

Hogwood, B.W. and Gunn, L.A. (1984) *Policy Analysis for the Real World*, Oxford.

Holliday, I. (1991) The conditions of local change. *Public Administration*, **69**(4), pp.441–57.

Holtham, C. (1992) Key challenges for public service delivery, in *Rediscovering Public Services Management* (eds L. Willcocks and J. Harrow), pp.84–109.

Home Affairs Committee (1995) *First Report (1994/95) The Private Security Industry* (HMSO).

Home Office (1993) *Police Reform: A Police Service for the Twenty-first Century*, HMSO, London.

Home Office (1995) *Circular 27/94, Policing Plans*, HMSO.

Home Office (1995) *Review of Police Core and Ancillary Tasks*, HMSO.

Hood, C. (1979) *The World of Quasi-Government*, Annual Conference of the JUC Public Administration Committee, University of York.

Hood, C. (1990) Beyond the Public Bureaucracy State? Extended text of an inaugural professorial lecture, London School of Economics, 16 January.

Hood, C. (1991) A public management for all seasons? *Public Administration*, **69**(4), pp.3–19.

Hood, C. (1994) Contemporary public management: a new global paradigm? *Public Policy and Administration*, **10**(2), pp.104–17.

Hood, C. (1995) Emerging issues in public administration. *Public Administration*, **73**, Spring, pp.165–83.

Hood, C. and Jackson, M. (1991) *Administrative Argument*, Dartmouth, Aldershot.

Hood, C. and Wright, M. (eds) (1981) *Big Government in Hard Times*, Martin Robertson, Oxford.

House of Lords (1985) Science and Technology in Local Government Volume I (*Report*), Select Committee on Science and Technology, HMSO, London.

Howard, M. (1994), Disraeli Lecture, St Stephens Club, Central Office, London.

Hudson, M. (1995) Charities seek inner resources, *The Observer*, 17 December.

Hughes, O.E. (1994) *Public Management & Administration*, Macmillan, London.

Hunter, D. (1988) The impact of research on restructuring the British National Health Service. *The Journal of Health Administration Education*, **6**(3) pp.537–53.

Hurd, D. (1994) Charting the clear, blue water. *The Guardian*, 12 October.

Hutton, W. (1996a) Stake that claim. *The Guardian*, 9 January.

Hutton, W. (1996b) *The State We're In*, (rev.ed), Vintage, London.

Information Technology Services Agency (1995) Annual Report and Accounts, 94/95, HMSO, London.

Information Technology Services Agency (1995) *Framework Document*, HMSO, London.

IPPR (1992) *Managing effective schools* (pamphlet), IPPR, London.

Isaac-Henry K. (1987) Information technology and the public sector, a case study of a local authority. *Teaching Public Administration* **7**(2), pp.10–26.

Isaac-Henry, K. and Painter, C. (1991) The management challenge in local government-emerging trends, *Local Government Studies*, **17**(3), pp.69–89

Isaac-Henry, K. and Painter C. (1991b) Organizational Response to Environmental Turbulence: The Management of Change in English Local Government. *The International Journal of Public Sector Management*, **4**(4), 5–20.

Isaac-Henry, K. and Painter, C. (1992) The changing face of local government: the reforming impetus continues. *Local Government Policy Making*, **18**(4), pp.29–34.

Jackson, P.M. (1988) The management of performance in the public sector. *Public Money and Management*, **13**(4), pp.11–16.

Jackson, P.M. (1990) Public choice and public sector management. *Public Money and Management*, **10**(4), pp.13–21.

Jackson, P. M. (1993) Public Service Performance Evaluation: A Strategic Perspective. *Public Money and Management* 8(4), pp.9–14.

Jackson, P.M and Palmer, A. (1993), *Developing Performance Monitoring in Public Service Organizations*. Management Centre, University of Leicester.

Jenkins, S. (1995) *Accountable to None. The Tory Nationalisation of Britain*, Hamish Hamilton, London.

Johnson, N. (1979) Quangos and the structure of government, *Public Administration*, **57**, pp.379–95.

Jones T. and Newburn, T. (1995) *ESRC Study, The Private Security Industry*, Policy Studies Institute, London.

Jones, T. and Newburn, T. (1995) How big is the private security industry. *Policing and Society*, **5**(3), pp.233–48.

Jones, R. and Pendlebury, M. (1988) *Public Sector Accounting*, Pitman, London.

Jordan, G. (1994a) From next steps to market testing: administrative reform and improvisation, *Public Policy and Administration*, **9**(2), pp.21–35.

Jordan, G. (1994b) Reinventing government: but will it work? *Public Administration*, **72**(2), pp.271–9.

Jordan, G. (1994c) *The British Administrative System: Principles Versus Practice*, Routledge, London.

Juran, J.M. (1979) *Quality Control Handbook* (3rd edn.) McGraw Hill, New York.

Kanter, R.M. and Summers, D. (1987) Doing well while doing good: dilemmas of performance measurement in non-profit organizations and the need for a multi-constituency approach, in *The non-Profit Sector: A Research Handbook* (ed. W.W. Power), Yale University Press, Yale. pp 98–110.

Kaufman, G. (1992) Privatizing the ministers, *The Guardian*, 7 December.

Kavanagh, D. (1987) *Thatcherism and British Politics – The End of Consensus*, Oxford University, London.

Kavanagh, D. and Seldon, A.A. (1994) *The Major Effect: Educational Policy*, Macmillan, Basingstoke.

Kay, J.A. (1993) *Foundations of Corporate Success*, Oxford University Press, Oxford.

Keegan, V. (1994) Hard work, if you can get it. *The Guardian*, 19 January.

Keen, J. *et al.*, (1991) Complexity and Contradiction in NHS Computing, *Public Money & Management*, **11**(3), pp.23–9.

Keen, J. (ed) (1994a) *Information Management in Health Services*, Open University Press, Buckingham.

Keen, J. (1994b) Information policy in the National Health Service, in *Information Management in Health Services*, Open University Press, Buckingham, pp.16–28.

Keen, J. (1994c) The politics of information, in *Information Management in Health Services*, Open University Press, Buckingham, pp.124–34.

Keen, J. (1994d) Evaluation: informing the future, not living in the past, in *Information Management in Health Services*, Open University Press, Buckingham, pp.173–83.

Kerley, R. (1994) *Managing in Local Government*, Routledge, London.

Kerr, A and Radford, M (1994) TUPE or not TUPE: competitive tendering and the transfer laws. *Public Money & Management*, **14**(4), pp. 36–47.

King, D.S. (1987) *The New Right: Politics, Markets and Citizenship*, Macmillan, London.

Kingdom, J. (1991) *Local Government and Politics in Britain*, Philip Allan, London.

Klein, R. (1991) On the Oregon trail: rationing health care. *British Medical Journal*, **302**(5) pp. [PAGE NO?]

Knox, C. and McAlister, D. (1995) Policy Evaluation: Incorporating Users' Views. *Public Administration*, **73**(3), pp.413–36.

Kotler, P. and Fox, K. (1985) *Strategic Marketing for Educational Institutions*, Prentice-Hall, Englewood Cliffs, NJ.

Kotter and Schlesinger (1979) Choosing strategies for change. *Harvard Business Review*, **57**(10), pp.6–14.

Kraemer, K. and King, J. (1988) The role of information technology in managing cities. *Local Government Studies*, March/April, pp.23–46.

LACSAB/LGMB (1984–92) *Survey of the Employment Effects of Central Government Initiatives*, (annual), LGMB, Luton.

Lawton, A. and Rose, A. (1991) *Organization & Management In The Public Sector*, Pitman, London.

Leach, S. *et al.* (1993) *Challenge and Change*, Local Government Management Board, London.

Leach, S., Stewart, J. and Walsh, K. (1994) *The Changing Organisation and Local Management of Local Government*, Macmillan, Basingstoke.

Legge, K. (1995) *From Personnel Management to Human Resource Management*, Macmillan, London.

Le Grand, J. (1990) Quasi-markets and social policy, *Studies in Decentralisation and Quasi-Markets*, No. 1, Bristol, School for Advanced Urban Studies

Le Grand, J. and Bartlett, W. (eds) (1993) *Quasi-Market and Social Policy*, Macmillan, London.

Letwin, S.R. (1992) *The Anatomy of Thatcherism*, Fontana, London.

Levitt, R. (1980) *The People's Voice in the NHS*, King Edward's Hospital Fund for London, (RA 395.G7), London.

Levitt, R., Wall, A. and Appleby, J. (1995) *The Reorganised National Health Service*, Chapman & Hall, London.

Lewisham, Borough of (1994) *Lewisham Council and the Unelected State*, Borough of Lewisham.

LGIU (1995) *Secret Services?* Local Government Information Unit, London.

Likierman, A. (1993) Performance indicators: 20 early lessons from managerial use, *Public Money and Management* **8**(4), pp.15–22.

Likierman, A., Heald, D., Georgiou, G. and Wright, M. (1995) Resource accounting and budgeting: a symposium. *Public Administration*, **73**(4), pp.561–90.

Lindblom, C. (1959) The science of muddling through. *Public Administration Review*, **9**, pp.70–88.

Lindblom, C. (1979) Still muddling, not yet through. *Public Administration Review*, **29**, pp.517–26.

Local Government Management Board (1988) *IT and Competition*, LGMB, Luton.

Local Government Management Board (1992) *Survey of the Employment Effects of Central Government Initiatives, March 1990–March 1991*, LGMB, Luton.

Local Government Management Board (1993a) *Challenge and Change: Characteristics of Good Management in Local Government*, LGMB, Luton.

Local Government Management Board (1993b) *Survey of the Employment Effects of Central Government Initiatives, March 1991–March 1992*, LGMB, Luton.

London Borough of Croydon (1991) *Implications of the Single Market*.

Loveday, B. (1990) The road to regionalization. *Policing*, **6**(4), pp.639–60.

Loveday, B. (1994) Police reform in strategic government, *ACC Policy Journal*, **2**(1), pp.7–23.

Loveday, B. (1995) Contemporary challenges to police management. *Policing and Society*, **5**, pp.281–302.

Loveday, B. (1996) Business as Usual, Police Authorities and the Police and Magistrates' Courts Act, *Local Government Studies*, (forthcoming).

Lovell, R. (1992) Citizen's charter: the cultural challenge. *Public Administration*, **70**(3), pp.395–404.

Mallabar, N. (1991) *Local Government Administration – in a time of change*, Business Education Publishers Ltd, Newcastle upon Tyne.

Mansfield, B. (1993) Competence-based qualifications: a response, *Journal of European Industrial Training*, **17**(3), pp 19–22.

Margerison, C (1991) *Making Management Development Work*, McGraw-Hill, Basingstoke.

Margetts, H. (1995) The automated state. *Public Policy and Administration*, **10**(2), pp.88–103.

Margetts, H. (1991) The computerization of social security: the way forward or a step backwards. *Public Administration* **69**(3), pp.325–43.

Marsh, D. (1991) Privatization under Mrs Thatcher: a review of the literature. *Public Administration*, **69**(4) pp.459–80.

Marsh, D. and Rhodes, R.A.W. (1992a) Implementing Thatcherism, Policy Changes in the 1980s, *Parliamentary Affairs*, **45**(1), January 1992, pp.33–50.

Marsh, D. and Rhodes R.A.W. (1992b) *Implementing Thatcherite Policies*, Open University Press, Buckingham.

Marshall, G. and Loveday, B. (1994) The police, in *The Changing Constitution*, (eds J. Jewell and D. Oliver, Open University Press, Buckingham.

Massey, A. (1994) Market testing: some preliminary remarks, *Public Policy and Administration*, **9**(2) pp.1–10.

Maud Report (1967) *Committee on Management in Local Government*, Vols 1–5, HMSO, London.

McBride, G. (1990) Rationing health care in Oregon. *British Medical Journal*, Vol. 301, pp.18–25

McKevitt, D. (1992) Strategic management in public services, in *Rediscovering Public Services Management* (eds. L. Willcocks and J. Harrow), McGraw Hill, Maidenhead, pp.33–49.

Metcalfe, L. and Richards, S. (1990) *Improving Public Management*, Sage, London.

Middlemas, K. (1979) *Politics in Industrial Society: The Experience of the British System since 1911*, Andre Deutsch, London.

Morgan, C. and Murgatroyd S. (1994) *Total Quality Management in the Public Sector*, Open University Press, Buckingham.

Morgan, G. (1986) *Images of Organization*, Sage, London.

Morgan, J. (1991) *Safer Communities*, Home Office, HMSO.

Morgan, R. (1986) Police Consultative Groups: The implication for governance of the police. *Political Quarterly*, **57**(1) pp.83–7.

Morley, D. (1993) Strategic Direction in the British Public Service. *Long Range Planning*, **26**(3), pp.77–86.

Muid, C. (1992) ICTs in Central Government: The Transformation Challenge, Paper to the PICT Seminar on Information, Communication and New Technologies, London.

Muid, C. (1994) Information systems and new public management, *Public Administration*, **72**(1), pp.113–25.

Mumford, A. (1988) *Developing Top Managers*, Gower, Aldershot.

Mumford, A. (1989) *Management Development: Strategies for Action*, IPM, London.

Mumford, A. (1994) Effectiveness in Management Development in *Gower Handbook of Training and Development* (ed. J Prior), Gower, Aldershot.

Mumford, A. (1995) *Learning at the Top*, McGraw Hill, London.

National Association of Head Teachers (NAHT) (1990) *The Marketing Of Schools*, (Council Memorandum, September), NAHT, West Sussex.

National Audit Office (1989a) *Management of Administrative Communications*, HMSO, London.

National Audit Office (1989b) *Department of Social Security: Operational Strategy*, HMSO, London.

National Audit Office (1990) *Managing Computer Projects in the National Health Service*, HMSO, London.

National Audit Office (1991a) *Single European Member States Market (HC 135)*, HMSO, London.

National Audit Office (1991b) *Office Automation in Government Departments*, HMSO, London.

National Audit Office(1991c) *Ministry of Defence: Support Technology*, HMSO, London.

National Audit Office (1992) *Annual Report*, London.

National Institute of Justice, *Bootcamp, An Evaluation and Review*, Department of Justice, Washington DC

Nelson, P. (1970) Information and consumer behaviour, *Journal of Political Economy*, **78**, pp.729–54.

Newman, J. and Clarke, J. (1994) Going about our business? the managerialisation of public services, in *Managing Social Policy* (eds J. Clarke, A. Cochrane and E. McLaughlin), pp.13–31.

Newton, K. (1976) *Second City Politics*, Oxford University Press, Oxford.

Nicklen, S. (1995) The Developing Role of Performance Indicators in the Public Sector, Unpublished paper presented at IIR conference on *Meaningful Performance Indicators*, London, 29 March.

Nolan Committee (1995) *First Report on Standards in Public Life*, Cm 2850, HMSO, London.

North West Water Authority (1981, 1982, 1986) Annual Reports.

Nutley, S. and Osborne, S.P. (1994) *The Public Sector Management Handbook*, Longman, Harlow.

Oakland, J.S. (1989) *Total Quality Management*, Butterworth/Heinemann, London.

O'Brien, D.(1989) Using information technology to improve the quality of management. *Information Technology and Public Policy*, **7**(3), pp.194–9.

Operational Policing Review (1990) Joint Committee, Police Federation, Surbiton, Surrey.

Osborne, D. and Gaebler, T. (1992) *Reinventing Government*, Addison Wesley, Reading, Mass.

O'Toole, B.J and Jordan, G. (1994) *Next Steps – Improving Management in Government?* Dartmouth Publishing Company, Aldershot.

O'Toole, B.J. (1993) The loss of purity: the corruption of public service in Britain. *Public Policy and Administration*, **8**(2), pp.1–6.

Oughton, J. (1994) Market testing: the future of the civil service. *Public Policy and Administration*, **9**(2), pp.11–20.

Painter, C. (1989) Leadership in the British civil service revisited. *Teaching Public Administration*, IX(1), pp.1–9.

Painter, C. (1989) Thatcherite radicalism and institutional conservatism. *Parliamentary Affairs*, **42**(4), pp.463–84.

Painter, C. (1991) The public sector and current orthodoxies: revitalization or decay? *The Political Quarterly*, **62**(1), pp.75–89.

Painter, C. (1995) The next steps reforms and current orthodoxies, in *Next Steps: Improving Management in Government?* (eds B.J. O'Toole and G. Jordan), Dartmouth, Aldershot, pp.17–36.

Painter, C. (1994) Public service reform: reinventing or abandoning government? *The Political Quarterly*, **65**(3), pp.242–62.

Painter, C., Isaac-Henry, K. and Chalcroft, T. (1994) *Appointed Agencies and Public Accountability*, Institute of Public Policy and Management, University of Central England, Birmingham.

Painter, C. and Isaac-Henry, K. (1994) A quango charter. *Parliamentary Brief*, **3**(2), pp.98–9.

Painter, C. and Isaac-Henry, K. (1995) Local Government and Non-Elected Agencies: Strategic Positioning in Local Governance Networks. *Strategic Government*, **3**(1), pp.55–66.

Painter, C., Rouse, J., Isaac-Henry, K. and Munk, L. (1995) *Changing Local Governance: Local Authorities and Non-Elected Agencies*, Local Government Management Board, Luton

Parry, R. (1992) Concepts and Assumptions of Public Management, in *The Evolution of Public Management* (ed. C. Duncan), pp.3–22.

Pedler, M., Burgoyne, J. and Boydell, T. (1991) *The Learning Company*, McGraw-Hill, Basingstoke.

Pedler, M., Burgoyne, J. and Boydell, T. (1994) *A Manager's Guide to Self-Development*, McGraw Hill, Basingstoke.

Perkins, H. (1989) *The Rise of Professional Society*, Routledge, London.

Peters, T. (1992) *Liberation Management*, Macmillan, London.

Peters, T. and Waterman, R. (1982) *In Search of Excellence*, Harper and Row, New York.

Pettigrew, A., Ferlie, E. and McKee, L. (1992) *Shaping Strategic Change – Making Change in Large Organizations: The Case of the National Health Service*, Sage, London.

Pfleger, M. (1992) Information Technology and Information Systems in Central Government: Main Developments and Potential, Paper to the PICT Seminar on Information.

Phillips, M. (1993) Another Day, Another Scandal. *The Guardian*, 16 January.

Plant, R. (1987) *Managing Change and Making it Stick*, Fontana, London

Pliatsky, L. (1980) *Report on Non-Departmental Public Bodies*, Cmnd 7797, HMSO, London.

Pollard, S.(1992) *The Development of the British Economy*, (4th edn) Edward Arnold, London.

Police: (1995) *Voice of the Service*, Surbiton, Surrey.

Pollitt, C. (1986) Beyond the managerial model: the case for broadening performance assessment in the government and public services. *Politics and Policy*, **13**, pp.1–15.

Pollitt C.(1989) Performance indicators in the longer term. *Public Money and Management*, **9**(3), pp.51–5.

Pollitt, C. (1990) Doing business in the temple? Managers and quality assurance in the public services. *Public Administration*, **68**(4), pp.435–52.

Pollitt, C. (1993) *Managerialism and the Public Services*, Blackwell, Oxford.

Pollitt, C. and Harrison, S. (1992) *Handbook of Public Services Management*, Blackwell, Oxford.

Pollitt, C. and Harrison, S. (1992) Introduction, in *Handbook of Public Service Management* (eds C. Pollitt and S. Harrison), Blackwell Publishers, Oxford, pp.1–22.

Porter, H. (1992) This sceptic isle. *The Guardian*, 14 December.

Pottor, J (1987) Consumerism and the public sector: how well does the coat fit. *Public Administration*, **66**(2) pp.149–64.

Poulsford, J, 1985 Paper to the Public Finance Foundation Conference (unpublished).

Prachett, L. (1994b) Open systems and closed networks. *Public Administration*, **72**(1), pp.73–93.

Price Waterhouse (1995) *Executive Agencies, Edition 8, Survey Report 1995*.

Pyle, D. (1995), *Cutting The Cost of Crime*, IEA.

Ransom, E. (1992) Central government, in *Public Domain 1992* (eds F. Terry and P. Jackson), Chapman & Hall, London, pp.55–65.

Ranson, S. (1995) From reforming to restructuring in education, in *Local Government in the 1990s*, (eds J. Stewart and G. Stoker), Macmillan, Basingstoke, Chapter 7.

Ranson, S. and Stewart, J. (1988) Management in the public domain. *Public Money & Management*, **8**(1/2), pp.13–19.

Ranson, S. and Stewart, J. (1988) Management in the public domain. *Public Money and Management*, **8**(1/2), pp.13–25.

Ranson, S. and Stewart, J. (1994) *Management for the Public Domain*, Macmillan, London.

Rees, J. (1992) Managing quality in public services, in *The Evolution of Public Management* (ed. C. Duncan), pp.67–83.

Resin, D. (1993) *Market and Health*, St Martin's Press, (RA 410.5), London.

Revans, R.W. (1980) *Action Learning: New Techniques for Management*, Blond & Briggs, London.

Rhodes, R.A.W. (1987) Developing the public service orientation. *Local Government Studies*, May/June, pp.63–73.

Rhodes, R A.W (1988) *Beyond Westminster and Whitehall*, Unwin Hyman, London.

Rhodes, R.A.W. (1991) Now nobody understands the system, in *New Directions in British Politics? Essays on the Evolving Constitution* (ed. P. Norton), Edward Edgar, Aldershot, pp.83–112.

Rhodes, R.A.W. (1994) The hollowing out of the state: the changing nature of the public service in Britain. *The Political Quarterly*, **65**(2), pp.138–51.

Rhodes, R.A.W. (1994) Reinventing excellence: or how best-sellers thwart the search for lessons to transform the public sector. *Public Administration*, **72**(2), pp.281–89.

Richards, S (1992a) The Distinctive Nature of Strategic Management in the Public Service Sector, paper presented to the Local Government Centre, University of Warwick, May.

Richards, S. (1992b) *Who Defines the Public Good? The Consumer Paradigm in Public Management*, The Public Management Foundation, London.

Riddell, A. (1995) Open door, open mind. *The Guardian*, 15 November.

Riddell, P.(1991) *The Thatcher Era and its Legacy*, Blackwell, Oxford.

Ridley, N. (1988) *The Local Right*, Centre for Policy Studies, London.

Robinson, R. and Le Grand, J. (eds) (1994) *Evaluating the NHS Reforms*, Kings Fund Institute, London.

Rogerston, P. (1995) Performance measurement and policing: police service or law enforcement agency. *Public Money and Management*, **14**(4), pp.25–30.

Savage, S. (1984) Political control or community liaison? *Political Quarterly*, **55**(1), pp.48–59.

SCAA, (1994) *Value Added Performance in Schools*.

Schick, A (1973) A death in the bureaucracy. the demise of federal PPB. *Public Administration Review*, **33**(2), pp.146–56.

Scott Morton, M. (1991) The Corporation of the 1990s: *Information Technology and Organisational Transformation*, Oxford University Press, Oxford.

Selim, G. M. and Woodward, S.A. (1992) The manager monitored, in *Rediscovering Public Services Management* (eds L. Willcocks and J. Harrow), McGraw Hill, London, pp.141–69.

Senge, P. (1992) *The Fifth Discipline, The Art and Practice of the Learning Organisation*, Century Business, London.

Sharp, M. and Walker, W.(1994) Thatcherism and technical advance – reform without progress, in *Britain's Economic Performance* (eds. T.Buxton, P. Chapman and P. Temple), Routledge, London, pp.397–429.

Sheehy, P. (1993) *Inquiry into Police Responsibilities and Rewards*, HMSO, London.

Skidelsky, R. (ed.) (1988) *Thatcherism*, Chatto and Windus, London.

Smith, P. (1995) Performance indicators and outcomes in the public sector. *Public Money and Management*, **14**(4), pp.13–16.

Snell, R. (1990) cited in Mumford, A. (1994) Effectiveness in Management Development, in *Gower Handbook of Training and Development*, Gower (ed. J. Prior), Aldershot.

Social Security Committee (1995) *Minutes of Evidence*, 28 June, 1995.

SOCITM (1993) *IT Trends in Local Government*, Society of IT Managers.

SOCITM (1994) *IT Trends in Local Government*, Society of IT Managers.

South West Thames Regional Health Authority (1993) *Report of the Inquiry into the London Ambulance Service*, February.

Spender, J. (1989) Meeting Mintzberg and thinking again about management education. *European Management* Journal, **7**(3).

Stacey, M. (1976) The health service consumer: a sociological misconception, in *The Sociology of the National Health Service* (ed. M. Stacey), Sociological Review monograph, Keele.

Stanyer, J. and Smith, B. (1976) *Administering Britain*, Fontana, Glasgow.

Stewart, J. (1986) *The New Management of Local Government*, Allen & Unwin, London.

Stewart, J. (1988) *Understanding the Management of Local Government*, Longman, London.

Stewart, J. (1993) The limitation of government by contract. *Public Money and Management*, **13**(3), pp.7–12.

Stewart, J. (1993) Advance of the new magistracy. *Local Government Management*, **1**(6), pp.18–19.

Stewart, J. (1995a) Appointed boards and local government. *Parliamentary Affairs*, **48**(2), pp.226–41.

Stewart, J. (1995b) *Local Government Today – An Observer's View*, Local Government Management Board, Luton.

Stewart, J. (1995c) *Local Government Today – An Observer's View, Summary*, Local Government Management Board, Luton.

Stewart, J. and Clarke, M. (1987) The Public Service Orientation: Issues and Dilemmas. *Public Administration*, **65**(2), pp.161–77.

Stewart, J. and Davis, H. (1994) A new agenda for local governance. *Public Money & Management*, **14**(4), 29–36.

Stewart, J., Greer A., and Hoggett, P. (1995) *The Quango State: An Alternative Approach*, Commission For Local Democracy Research Report No 10, London.

Stewart, J., Stoker, G. (eds) (1995) *Local Government in the 1990s*, Macmillan, Basingstoke.

Stewart, J. and Walsh, K. (1992) Change in the management of public services. *Public Administration*, **70**(4), pp.499–518.

Stewart, J. and Walsh, K. (1994) Performance measurement: when performance can never be finally defined. *Public Money and Management*, **14**(2), pp.45–9.

Stewart, J. and Hamlin, B. (1993) Competence-based qualifications: a way forward. *Journal of European Industrial Training* **17**(6).

Stewart, J. and Hamlin, B. (1994) Competence-based qualifications: a reply to Bob Mansfield. *Journal of European Industrial Training* **18**(1).

Stoker, G. (1989a) Creating a local government for a post-fordist society: the Thatcherite project? in *The Future of Local Government* (eds. J. Stewart and G. Stoker), Macmillan, London, pp.141–70.

Stoker, G. (1989b) *New Management Trends*, Local Government Training Board, Luton.

Stoker, G. (1990) Regulation theory, local government and the transition from Fordism, in *Challenges to Local Government*, (eds S. King and J. Pierre), Sage, London, pp.242–64.

Storey, J. (1991) *New Perspectives on Human Resource Management*, Routledge, London.

Storey, J. (1995) *Human Resource Management: A Critical Text*, Routledge, London.

Stratta, E. (1990) A lack of consultation, *Policing*, Vol.6, Autumn, pp.523–38

Talbot, C. (1993) Developing public managers in the UK. *International Journal of Public Sector Management*, **6**(6), pp. 3–19.

Tam, H. (1995) Community Movement. *Local Government Management*, **1**(14), pp.22–3.

Tannenbaum, R. and Schmidt, W. (1958) How to choose a leadership pattern. *Harvard Business Review*, **38** (March/April), pp.95–101.

Taylor, A. and Williams, H. (1991) Public administration and the information polity. *Public Administration*, **69**(2), pp.170–90.

Technology Strategies (1991) *Overcoming the Barriers to IT investments*, February, pp.19–20.

Technology Strategies (1991) *Wanted 'Hybrid' Managers* (March), pp.14–15.

Technology Strategies (1991) *A formal approach for evaluating IT investments*, (August), pp.5–7.

Terry, F. (1990a) The phoenix in Lancashire. *Local Government Chronicle*, 7 December.

Terry, F. (1991b) Redefining partnership. *Local Government Chronicle*, 18 October

Terry, F. (1991c) The heart of recovery, *Local Government Chronicle*, 16 November.

Thatcher, M. (1993) *The Downing Street Years*, Harper Collins, London.

Thomson, P. (1992) Public Management in a Period of Radical Change: 1979–1992, *Public Money and Management*, **12**(3), pp.33–41.

Thompson, G., Frances, J., Levacic, R. and Mitchell, J. (eds) (1991) *Markets, Hierarchies & Networks: The Coordination of Social Life*, Sage, London.

Tomlinson, J. (1989) The schools, in *The Thatcher Effect: A Decade of Change* (eds D. Kavanagh and A. Seidon), Oxford University Press, Oxford pp.187–97.

Tomlinson, S. (1994) *Educational Reform and its Consequences*, Rivers Oram Press.

Torrington, J. and Weightman, J. (1989) The management of secondary schools. *Journal of Management Studies*, **26**(5), pp.519–30.

Train, C.J. and Stewart, C. (1992) Strategic management in the prison service, in *Handbook of Public Services Management* (eds C. Pollitt and S. Harrison), Blackwell, Oxford, pp.258–67.

University of Portsmouth, IPCS (1995) *Survey of Independent Police Authority Members 1994/95*.

Vinten, G. (1992) Reviewing the current managerial ethos, in *Rediscovering Public Services Management* (eds L. Willcocks and J. Harrow), pp.3–32.

Waldegrave, W. (1993) *Public Services and the Future: Reforming Britain's Bureaucracies*, Conservative Political Centre, London.

Walker, P. (1995) New Labour, New Broom. *The Observer*, 15 October.

Walsh, K. (1991a) Citizens and Consumers: Marketing and Public Sector Management. *Public Money and Management*, **11**(2), pp.9–16.

Walsh, K. (1991b) Quality and the Public Services. *Public Administration*, **69**(4), 503–14.

Walsh, K. (1994) Citizens, charters and contracts in *The Authority of the Consumer* (eds R. Keat, N. Whitely and N. Abercrombe), Routledge, London.

Walsh, K. (1995) *Public Services and Market Mechanisms – Competition, Contracting and the New Public Management*, Macmillan, Basingstoke.

Wapshott, N. (1992) Whitehall powers to be stripped in Major 'revolution'. *The Observer*, 10 May.

Wedgewood-Oppenheim, F. (1990) *Information Management in Local Government*, The Local Government Training Board, Luton.

Wedgwood Oppenheim, F.(1994) *Making Information Management Work*, Local Government Management Board, Luton.

Weir, S. and Hall, W. (eds) (1994) *Ego Trip: Extra-Governmental Organizations in the United Kingdom and Their Accountability*, Charter 88 Trust, London.

Wells, J. (1994) Crime and unemployment, *Employment Policy Institute*, London, **9**(1) pp.1–5
Wellesley, J. and Tritter, J. (1995) Evaluation, in *Department of Health*, Department of Health, London.
Westcott, B. (1993) *The Fifth Resource – Information*, Local Government Management Board.
White, M. (1996) Quangos and coronets. *The Guardian*, 5 February.
Whitehead, C. (ed) (1988) *Reshaping the Nationalized Industries*, Policy Journals, Oxford.
Whittington, R. (1993) *In Search of Strategy*, Routledge, London.
Wildavsky, A. (1964) *The Politics of the Budgetary Process*, Little Brown, Boston.
Willcocks, L. (1992) The Manager as a technologist, in *Rediscovering Public Services Management* (eds L. Willcocks and J. Harrow), McGraw-Hill Books Company, London, pp.170–96.
Willcocks, L. (1994) Managing information systems in UK public administration: issues and prospects. *Public Administration*, **72**(1) pp.13–32.
Willcocks, L. and Harrow, J. (1992) *Rediscovering Public Services Management*, McGraw Hill, London.
Willetts, D. (1992) *Modern Conservatism*, Penguin, London.
Wilson, D.C. (1992) *A Strategy of Change*, Routledge, London.
Wolfe, J. (1991) State power and ideology in Britain: Mrs Thatcher's privatization programme. *Political Studies*, **39**(2), pp.237–52.
World Health Organisation (1985) *Health for All by the Year 2000*, WHO, Geneva.
Wright, A. (1989) Ideological politics now, in *Party Ideology in Britain*, (eds L. Tivey and A. Wright), Routledge, London, pp.206–16.
Wright, T. (1995) *Beyond the Patronage State*, Fabian Pamphlet 569, Fabian Society, London.
Wyatt, S. (1990) Understanding IT innovation in public services. *Information Age*, **12**, p.1.
Young, H. (1989) *One of Us, a Biography of Margaret Thatcher*, Macmillan, London.
Young, K. (1990) *The Future Role of Local Government*, Public Finance Foundation, London.
Zifcak, S. (1994) *New Managerialism – Administrative Reform in Whitehall and Canberra*, Open University Press, Buckingham.

INDEX